CPT Jackie J. Bryant

CPT Jackie J. Bryant

Program Design
with Pascal

Program Design with Pascal

Principles, Algorithms, and Data Structures

Thomas L. Naps
Lawrence University

Bhagat Singh
University of Wisconsin Center System

West Publishing Company
St. Paul   New York   San Francisco   Los Angeles

PRODUCTION CREDITS

Copyediting Janet M. Hunter
Design John Edeen
Interior art Pete Thiel
Composition Bi-Comp, Inc.
Cover Pete Thiel

COPYRIGHT © 1988   By WEST PUBLISHING COMPANY
                       50 W. Kellogg Boulevard
                       P.O. Box 64526
                       St. Paul, MN 55164-1003

Printed in the United States of America

Library of Congress Cataloging-in-Publication Data

Naps, Thomas L.
  Program design with Pascal.

  Includes index.
  1. Pascal (Computer program language) I. Singh,
Bhagat, 1940–   . II. Title.
QA76.73.P2N374 1988   005.13′3   87-34508
ISBN 0-314-62540-2

Dedicated to

LaVerne and Jeanette Kosmerchock
and
Harpal Singh Chauhan

Contents

Sections marked with an asterisk may be skipped without affecting understanding of other material.

_____ **Chapter 6**

Stacks and Simple Recursion   182

_____ **Chapter 7**

Binary Trees, General Trees, and Graphs   239

_____ Unit III

The Techniques: Recursion,
Sorting, and Searching   295

_____ Chapter 8

A Closer Look at Recursion   297

_____ Chapter 11

Computer Science: Theory Meeting
Practice   413

_____ Appendix A

Review of Standard Pascal   453

_____ Appendix B

Conformant Array Parameters in
Pascal   459

_____ Appendix C

Random Access Files in Various
Versions of Pascal   462

_____ Appendix D

Hints and Solutions to Selected
Odd-Numbered Exercises   466

Preface

*If the auto industry had done what the computer
industry has done in the last 30 years, a Rolls-Royce
would cost $2.50 and get 2,000,000 miles per gallon.*

Caption for advertisement in
Computerworld

Background and Objectives

Almost everyone is aware that the computer industry has made phenomenal strides in the last 30 years. One of the factors underlying this advance
has been the rapid evolution of the discipline of computer science. As
recently as a decade ago, most teachers and students viewed formal education in computer science as the learning of a variety of computer languages. The problem-solving strategies around which programs in any
language must be built did not necessarily find their way into the computer
science curriculum in a coherent fashion. In many cases, such strategies
were dismissed as "tricks of the trade" that one would see upon entering
industry.

What a difference the 1980s have made in our attitudes toward computer science education! The complexities of designing large software have
made us collectively realize that the focus of computer science education
belongs not on programming languages but rather on understanding algorithms and related problem-solving techniques. Consequently computer
science curricula have been restructured. Now a major portion of students'
formal exposure to learning the syntactical details of a programming language occurs in their first computer science course. Usually the language
students learn is in a first course in Pascal. The second course in computer
science begins to expose students to strategies for developing large, effective programs that solve problems frequently encountered by computer

scientists. Students' knowledge of a language such as Pascal thus becomes a necessary tool that is to be used in the second course, analogous to the way that algebra must be used in a calculus course.

At the forefront of this rapid evolution of computer science education has been the Curriculum Committee of the *Association for Computing Machinery*. Their guidelines for the second course in computer science (as set forth in "Recommended Curriculum for CS2" by Elliot Koffman, David Stemple, and Caroline Wardle, *Communications of the ACM* (August 1985)) have been recognized on a nationwide basis by universities and by the Advanced Placement Program of the College Board as setting the appropriate tone for students' early experiences in computer science.

In writing *Program Design with Pascal: Principles, Algorithms, and Data Structures,* we endeavored to meet the Curriculum Committee's guidelines *and* stimulate student interest in the discipline of computer science. To achieve this, our text is structured around four main objectives.

1. To demonstrate the application of software engineering principles in the design, coding, and testing of large programs.

2. To introduce students to essential data structures such as linked lists, queues, stacks, trees, and (to a lesser extent) graphs. This introduction emphasizes the definition of each structure as an abstract data type before discussing implementations and applications of that structure.

3. To provide a systematic approach to studying algorithms which focuses first on understanding the action of an algorithm and then on analyzing the algorithm from a time/space perspective. In particular, searching, sorting, and recursive algorithms are covered in detail.

4. To present students with an overview of what lies ahead in their study of computer science.

To concentrate on these four objectives, we must assume that the reader has a working knowledge of introductory Pascal which includes familiarity with control structures, procedures and functions, parameter passing, arrays, and records. Advanced features of Pascal, such as file processing and pointer variables, are covered when the need for them arises.

Organization

The text is divided into four units reflecting these objectives. Unit I consists of the first three chapters; collectively, these chapters introduce the software engineering principles which are then reinforced throughout the remainder of the book. Chapter 1 presents the notion of an abstract data type and its implementation. In keeping with the emphasis on providing a rationale for data abstraction, the abstract data type is discussed in terms of the modeling phases which a software engineer goes through in designing a system. A case study, the registrar's system, is introduced in Chapter 1 as an illustrative example of an actual data processing activity which may be modeled by an abstract data type. This data type is the general list, and we take this opportunity to develop criteria which are used to evaluate various implementations of a list in later chapters. Chapter 2 introduces big-O analysis as the essential tool used by the computer scientist in evaluating alternative strategies from a time/space perspective. Simple sorting and searching algorithms are used as examples of the application of big-O analysis. The phases of the software system life cycle (analysis, design, coding, testing/verification, and maintenance) are discussed in Chapter 3 and then illustrated by a complete implementation for the registrar's system case study.

Units II and III cover data structures and more complex programming techniques respectively. They also serve to reinforce and expand upon the software engineering principles to which the student has been exposed in Unit I. Our presentation of software engineering ideas is therefore spiral in nature. We begin with the essentials in Unit I and then weave other software engineering topics into later chapters as appropriate, often through the use of the Designer's Workbenches which appear in Chapters 3 through 10. This spiral approach insures that there is a solid foundation upon which to study data structures and more complex searching/sorting algorithms and that the elements of style and design are not forgotten or ignored as other topics are studied.

The four chapters in Unit II cover essential data structures and introduce recursion as a programming technique. Each data structure is first defined as an abstract type. Then various implementations are discussed and compared using the big-O terminology of Chapter 2. This provides a convincing demonstration of the utility of big-O analysis. Chapter 4, devoted to linked lists, discusses how they might be used as an alternative implementation strategy for the registrar's system case study. Chapter 5 covers queues, providing a simulation case study. Chapter 6 presents stacks and uses them as the vehicle to explain how recursion works. The chapter also includes a discussion of expression parsing and a complete case study in which the parsing algorithm is used as the basis for a program which interactively evaluates integrals. Chapter 7 provides examples of the utility of recursion by using it as the primary technique for processing data in binary trees, general trees, and graphs. The importance of ordered binary trees as an alternative way of representing general lists is also discussed, with comparisons being drawn to the array and linked list implementations covered in Chapters 3 and 4 respectively.

The background in software engineering and data structures found in Units I and II prepares the students for the more complex algorithmic techniques in Unit III (Chapters 8–10). Chapter 8 takes a closer look at recursion, exploring trial-and-error backtracking as a programming technique and examining some of the time and space costs implicit in recursive algorithms. After completing Chapter 8, students should have complete confidence in their ability to use recursion. In Chapter 9, sorting methods which break the $O(n^2)$ barrier are investigated. These include shell sort, quick sort, heap sort, and merge sort. Chapter 10 scrutinizes search techniques such as hashing, indexing, indexed sequential search, B-trees, and tries.

Chapter 11, which constitutes Unit IV, is designed to meet our fourth objective: provide students with an overview of what lies ahead in their study of computer science. To do so, it reviews the Relevant Issues which have appeared in each of the earlier chapters and uses them as lead-ins to more complete discussions of four areas of advanced computer science;

1. Compilers

2. Operating Systems

3. Software Reliability and Formal Verification

4. Artificial Intelligence and the Halting Problem

The manner in which Chapter 11 is employed will no doubt vary greatly from instructor to instructor. The discussions are intended to be independent from each other so that they may be integrated into a course as interesting supplementary topics. For instance, instructors who wish to emphasize formal verification of algorithms may choose to incorporate this topic from Chapter 11 into the discussion of empirical testing and verification found in Chapter 3.

Possible Orderings and Coverages of Topics

The ordering of topics in the first seven chapters (Units I and II) allows for several variations:

1. Sections marked with an asterisk in the table of contents may be skipped without affecting understanding of later chapters.

2. Chapter 6 ("Stacks and Simple Recursion") may be covered before Chapter 5 ("Queues").

3. All of Chapters 1 through 7 (except those sections marked by an asterisk) should be covered before moving on to Unit III.

4. Chapters 8, 9, and 10 are independent of one another; hence they may be used in any order after Unit II has been covered.

5. The material in Chapter 11 may be brought in at almost any point in the course. For example,
   a. The material on language compilers in Section 11.2 may be used to augment the discussion of parsing in Section 6.4.
   b. The material on operating systems and memory management in Section 11.3 may be used to augment the discussion of variations of linked lists in Section 4.5.
   c. The material on formal verification in Section 11.4 may be used to augment the discussion of software testing and empirical verification of programs in Section 3.2.
   d. The material on artificial intelligence and the halting problem in Section 11.5 may be used to augment the discussion of recursion in Sections 8.2 and 8.3.

If time runs short, Chapter 11 could be skipped entirely without destroying the integrity of the course.

Features of the Text

A text which offers only complete topical coverage is not enough. Such coverage must be couched in a style of presentation which both fosters student understanding and stimulates student interest in the material. Toward these ends, we have integrated many unique features into the text. These include:

1. Three case studies fully developed from initial user specifications to complete Pascal code. This development process includes a modular structure chart and module specifications for each case study, making them easy to understand and modify. The registrar's system case study in Chapter 3 is essential to discussions in later chapters. As developed in Chapters 5 and 6 respectively, the case studies on simulation and parsing are not essential to the chapters which follow and hence may be covered in detail at the discretion of the instructor.

2. Extensive use of figures and graphic documentation allows students to visualize the effect of algorithms on data. Algorithms are pictorially traced for students in a way which brings them to life in the students' minds. It is our feeling that this visualization of data structures and algorithms represents true data abstraction, allowing students to understand at the conceptual level while also seeing the implementation of the algorithm in Pascal code.

3. Designer's Workbenches in Chapters 3 through 10. These sections reinforce and expand upon the software engineering principles which are the main topic of Unit I. In later chapters they insure that students do not abandon these essential design principles as more complex data structures and algorithms are studied.

4. Relevant Issues in Chapters 1 through 10. These vignettes provide glimpses of how the topic under discussion in a particular chapter finds application in a more advanced area of computer science and also occasionally discuss potential societal impact of such an application (for instance, military systems and artificial intelligence). The Relevant Issues are tied together and expanded upon in Chapter 11, thus providing students with a solid idea of what lies ahead in their study of computer science.

5. Frequent use of tables in chapter-ending summaries which comparatively evaluate various data structures and algorithms. Such compact, side-by-side comparisons emphasize the importance of knowing the relative advantages and disadvantages of the various techniques studied. There are often many ways to solve a problem; the skilled computer scientist is able to pick the best one based on a careful analysis of alternatives.

6. Numerous exercises and programming problems at the end of each chapter. The exercises tend to be short and thought-provoking. They ask the student to react to an issue brought up in the Designer's Workbench, trace an algorithm studied in the chapter, provide a brief essay answer to a conceptual question, or write a short procedure to accomplish a specific task. The programming problems are more substantial in nature; solutions to them should be implemented in Pascal by students.

7. Appendixes provide:
   a. A quick review of standard Pascal.
   b. A discussion of conformant array parameters in Pascal.
   c. A discussion of file processing in Pascal with particular attention given to nonstandard, system-dependent random access file processing in Turbo Pascal, Macintosh Pascal, Lightspeed Pascal, and VAX Pascal.
   d. Hints and solutions to selected odd-numbered exercises.

Ancillary Materials for Instructors

Adopters of the text receive an instructor's manual which includes:

1. Helpful hints on presenting the material in each chapter.

2. Transparency masters of many key figures and algorithms.

3. Hints and solutions to selected even-numbered exercises for each chapter.

4. Supplementary test questions for each chapter.

5. Complete modular test data for the registrar's system case study.

6. Fourteen completely coded solutions, including test data, for end-of-chapter programming problems throughout the text.

Also available on magnetic media are the three case studies appearing in the text, the fourteen solutions given in the Instructor's Manual, and all accompanying test data. Availability is limited to PC-compatible diskettes, Macintosh diskettes, and VAX/VMS tapes.

Acknowledgments

Of course, no textbook could successfully exist without students. We thank ours for their insight and inspiration. The conscientious efforts of the reviewers are greatly appreciated.

Stephen J. Allan, Utah State University
Richard A. Beebe, Simpson College

Andrew Bernat, University of Texas at El Paso
John Thomas Berry, Foothill College
Douglas Bickerstaff, Eastern Washington University
Daniel A. Canas, University of Kansas
Cecilia Daly, University of Nebraska—Lincoln
Herbert Dershem, Hope College
Richard J. Easton, Pan American University
David A. Eichmann, University of Iowa
Henry A. Etlinger, Rochester Institute of Technology
Michael Hennessy, University of Oregon
John D. Holt, California State University—Fresno
Janice Honeyman, Kansas State University
Ronald Mann, University of Louisville
Timothy S. Margush, University of Akron
Andrea Martin, Louisiana State University
Robert McCoard, California State University—Northridge
William Nico, California State University—Hayward
Kenneth E. Oberhoff, University of Houston—Downtown Campus
Edwin D. Reilly, Union College
John Rezac, Johnson County Community College
Diane Rykken, California State University—Sacramento
Terry Smith, Northeastern University
Theodore Sjoerdsma, Washington & Lee University
Darrell Turnidge, Kent State University
Vicki Walker, Arizona State University

Their suggestions helped make the text immeasurably better. This is the third project we have done with Jerry Westby, our editor at West Publishing Company, and each one has been a more positive experience than the last. Copy editor Janet Hunter and production editor Peggy Adams both did excellent work in insuring the quality of the text and keeping the project on schedule. Perhaps no one suffered more than our typist, Joyce Naps, who survived three different word processors and numerous unreasonable demands from one of the authors. To our families, we owe a still greater debt of gratitude; by merely being there, they make everything a pleasure!

Program Design
with Pascal

The Method: Software Engineering Principles

From Abstract Concept to Implementation

My central focus is not on the machine but on the mind.

Seymour Papert
Mindstorms: Children, Computers, and Powerful Ideas

1.1

Introductory Considerations

This is a text on *advanced* programming methodology. Since opinions of what separates advanced methodology from introductory programming may differ, we will begin by describing our perception of your present background in computer science. You have completed a first course in programming, preferably in Pascal since that is the computer language which we will be using. Hence, you should feel comfortable with Pascal syntax and writing programs which use the following Pascal tools:

- Decision control structures: **IF . . . THEN . . . ELSE** and **CASE**
- Repetition control structures: **WHILE, REPEAT,** and **FOR**
- Procedures, functions, parameter passing by value and reference

□ Declaration and use of structured types including **ARRAY**s, **RECORD**s, **SET**s, and (sequential) **FILE**s

If you are not familiar with some of these topics, now is the time to read the brief treatment of them presented in Appendix A. A more detailed presentation of these topics may be found in numerous introductory books on Pascal programming, such as *Pascal: Understanding Programming and Problem Solving* by Douglas W. Nance (St. Paul, Minn.: West Publishing, 1986).

Your previous experience in computing has no doubt demonstrated that successful programming involves far more than knowing the details of Pascal syntax. Instead, any successful program represents the implementation in software of a conceptual solution to an abstract problem. That is, there are two distinct phases to virtually any computerized problem solution. First, the problem to be solved must be thoroughly understood at an abstract, conceptual level. Descriptions of the problem at this level usually take the form of semiformal English (such as pseudocode), graphic tools (flowcharts, for example), and mathematical symbolism. At this level you are involved in designing a solution to the problem, and the key to that design is the building of an accurate abstract model which enables you to understand the essence of the problem and its solution. Once you have developed such a model, you then implement the model in an actual computer program which represents the tangible solution to the problem.

Given this statement of where you have been, we shall now describe some of the new goals we hope this text will help you to achieve. First, those skills you have already developed in designing and implementing solutions to computerizable problems will be sharpened. We will introduce you to several new aspects of design and the Pascal techniques used to implement them. In short, you will become a more proficient designer and implementor. Second, upon finishing this text, you should have a firm grasp of the "tricks of the trade" with which every computer scientist must be familiar. These include linked lists, stacks, queues, trees, recursion, search algorithms, and sort algorithms. As such, the text presents somewhat of a potpourri of topics. They provide the basis for your proceeding into more specialized areas of computer science such as compiler design, operating systems, and artificial intelligence. Third, you will also develop the skills to evaluate alternative solutions to a problem and decide which is best for the situation at hand. This goal is closely tied to our goal of introducing you to the tools and techniques of the trade. That is, you will see that many problems allow several different solutions which can be selected from the techniques you know. The ability to choose that solution which best utilizes the resources available is an important skill to develop. Among the factors you will have to consider in this regard are the execution speed of the program and the amount of memory needed to store all data involved in the solution. Frequently this evaluation of alternatives is termed a time/space analysis: time referring to execution speed; and space, to data storage resources which are used. As we shall see, these two factors often conflict. That is, to achieve fast execution speeds, we may need to use more space. Conversely, if our primary objective is to minimize space requirements, we may have to pay a price in execution speed. Hence, in this regard you will have to become adept at evaluating trade-offs in time and space considerations.

The final, overriding goal, which actually includes the others we have discussed, is that you develop your abilities to design programs which not only work but are

☑ *Large*. Actually such programs could properly be called systems since they typically involve numerous modules which interact to solve one complex problem.

☑ *Reliable*. In this regard the measure of a system is that it anticipate and be prepared to handle all types of exceptional circumstances.

☑ *Flexible*. The system should be easily modified to handle circumstances which may change in the future.

☑ *Expandable*. If the system is successful, it will frequently spawn new computing needs. Solutions to these new needs should be easily incorporated into the original system.

☑ *Efficient*. The system should make optimal use of time and space resources.

☑ *Structured*. The system should keep related tasks together, so that potentially troublesome areas can be quickly identified and improved.

_____1.2

The Software Engineering Approach

The goals that we have set are clearly nontrivial. How can we have a reasonable chance of attaining them? The evolution of the answer to this question is an indication of how far the young discipline of computer science has progressed. In the late 1950s and early 1960s, there was a widely held belief that designing effective software systems was akin to a black art. That is, those who succeeded in designing such systems did so for a variety of mysterious reasons that could not be discerned. Their success, as opposed to the high percentage of software designers who failed, was somewhat mystical—similar to the spark of unfathomable inspiration that seems to separate a great painter from a doodler.

However, this view of successful software designers began to change in the latter part of the 1960s. As the methodology of such designers was studied, their work seemed to be more typical of an engineer's approach to problem solving. What characterizes this engineering approach? To answer the question, let us consider the various phases involved in the successful development of a complex structure such as a bridge. First, the engineer gets together with the (often nontechnical) people who want the bridge built to learn about the function of the bridge: is it to be part of a heavily traveled urban freeway or a one-lane country road? From such meetings, the engineer develops a conceptual picture of the bridge. This picture exists as an abstract entity in the engineer's mind and perhaps in very rough form as an initial drawing that the engineer may have made. At this stage the engineer is working with ideas and ignoring most physical construction details. What are the next steps? They are essentially steps that will allow the engineer to come successively closer to the tangible implementation of the bridge as a physical structure. A miniature prototype of the bridge will be built, and this model will allow the engineer to come face-to-face with many potential construction problems and also serve as a means of checking whether the bridge will serve the needs specified by those who originally wanted the bridge built. This prototype will be followed by the development of detailed plans in blueprint form. Again this represents a step away from the purely abstract view of the bridge toward its actual implementation. These blueprints provide the essential details to the contractor who will eventually build the bridge. This contractor completes the entire process by implementing the engineer's plans in the physical structure of the bridge.

As we review the process described in the preceding paragraph, two important points should be made. First, note that the entire process which culminates in the building of the bridge is a series of refinements from an abstract view of the bridge to its very tangible implementation. This process parallels very closely the movement from abstraction to implementation which we have previously described as part of the software development process. Second, note that this engineering approach is one which truly places the emphasis on design issues. The design process is a very creative endeavor. Typically, during the design process, engineers will want to try out various combinations of possible options and will frequently change their minds about many significant aspects of the overall design. The time for such experimentation is when the design exists only in abstract form. That is when such creative considerations are possible, indeed, even encouraged by the openness of the conceptual model. As the model draws nearer to actual implementation, a myriad of details specific to the chosen implementation make similar "what-if" reasoning expensive and often impossible for all practical purposes.

As early software developers analyzed frequent programming failures, they looked to the already established field of engineering for a paradigm. The engineering methodology of successively refining abstract models toward an eventual implementation made sense as an approach to developing programs also. A system designer who moves too quickly into the coding phase of a programming project is analogous to an engineer who allows construction of a bridge to begin before adequate planning has been done. Both are heading for final results which are inelegant and riddled with serious flaws. However, because of the more rigorous design methodology embedded for years in their profession, engineers did not find themselves in this predicament as often as programmers. The solution seemed obvious; that is, attempt to embed a similarly rigorous methodology into the discipline of computer science. Hence software engineering has developed into an important area of study within computer science. It represents an attempt to apply the structured methods of engineering to software development. Its goal is to assure that software is produced in a way which is both cost-effective and reliable enough to deserve the increasing trust we are placing in it. We will follow its dictates as we begin our excursion into advanced programming.

——————————————————————————————————— **1.3**

A Case Study: The Registrar's System at the University of Hard Knocks

The best way to illustrate software engineering principles is by example. Let us therefore introduce a case study which we will use again at various points throughout the book. In this chapter, we will approach the case study at the abstract level. In later chapters, we will refine this abstract view into the details associated with several possible implementations.

Imagine yourself in the following situation. You are Director of Data Processing at the prestigious University of Hard Knocks and receive the following communication from the registrar at the school.

MEMORANDUM
University of Hard Knocks

TO: Director of Data Processing

FROM: Head Registrar

DATE: July 29, 1992

RE: Automation of recordkeeping on students

As you know, we presently maintain our student records by manual methods. We believe the time has come to computerize this operation and request that you do so for us.

Here is what we need. Each student's record consists of his or her name, the number of credits that student has taken, the number of credits earned, and the total grade points for that student (based on a scale of 4 for an A, 3 for a B, 2 for a C, 1 for a D, and 0 for an F). We maintain these records in alphabetical order by student's last name. Of course, at numerous times, we must add new students to our records and remove those who have graduated or withdrawn from school. Students often come into our office and request to see their current record, so we must be able to quickly find that information. At the end of each semester we print a grade report for each student. This report consists of the four items cited plus the student's GPA (computed by dividing credits taken by total grade points). At the end of the year, the Dean of Students requests two lists of graduating seniors (a student who has earned at least 120 credits). One of these lists is to be printed in alphabetical order by student name. The other is to be printed in order by student grade point average.

Certainly the situation described in this memo is an oversimplification of any real college registrar's office. However, even this relatively unsophisticated situation can offer us some interesting food for thought as we begin a consideration of the software engineering issues associated with an actual problem.

Recall that the first phase in this process as we have described it is to build an abstract model of the situation posed in the problem. Here we are fortunate enough to have a registrar who has given us a fairly clear statement of the problem. Such a statement greatly facilitates the construction of an abstract model. In many real situations it is much more difficult to transform users' descriptions of the problem into an abstract form suitable for implementation. Doing so is the job of the system analyst, whose role will be considered again when we complete an initial implementation for this problem in Chapter 3.

_____ 1.4

Introduction to Abstract Data Types

To illustrate this abstract perspective, consider the data which must be manipulated to accommodate the system described in the registrar's memo. By "abstract perspective" we mean that we initially want to specify the data types involved apart from considerations of how such types will be implemented in Pascal or other computer languages. It turns out that some abstract data types will have very easy implementations in Pascal. The Pascal implementations for others will be much less direct. The point is, at this stage of our problem analysis, we don't want language considerations to influence our solution to the problem. Such considerations should come later, after we have accurately described the problem.

The specification of an abstract data type involves three factors:

1. A description of the elements which compose the data type

2. A description of the relationships between the individual components in the data type

3. A description of the operations that we wish to perform on the components of the data type

Note that all of these factors are language-independent. An abstract data type is a formal description of data elements and relationships as envisioned by the software engineer; it is thus a conceptual model. Ultimately this model must be implemented in an appropriate computer language via declarations for the elements and relationships and instructions (often in the form of procedures and function calls) for the operations. At an even deeper level, the implementation of the abstract data type in a computer language is translated by the compiler into a physical, electronic representation on a particular computer.

This hierarchy of levels of abstraction is illustrated in Figure 1.1. As much as possible, each level in this hierarchy should be shielded from the details of a level which appears below. Consider, for instance, the separa-

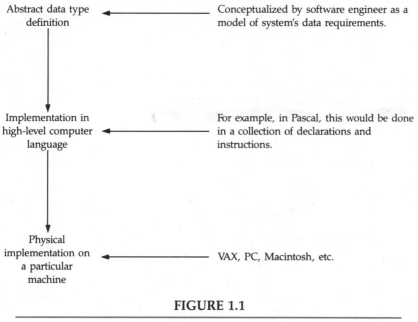

FIGURE 1.1

Levels of abstraction in specifying data

tion between the definition of an abstract data type and its implementation in a computer language. There may be several ways to implement an abstract data type. Each of these implementations will carry with it its own collection of declarations and instructions. This collection should form a cohesive package which meets all the specifications in the definition of the abstract data type. From the perspective of the abstract data type, we are not concerned with the details of how the data relationships and instructions are implemented in this package, only that they meet the specifications of the definition. Indeed, hiding these details as much as possible will make it relatively easy to interchange one package of declarations and instructions which implements an abstract data type with another package implementing the same type. Such interchangeability is very desirable when we want to comparatively evaluate the performance characteristics of several implementation strategies for a given abstract data type. Information hiding is a term often used to describe the ability of a package to meet the specifications of an abstract data type in a self-contained fashion which allows use of the package without having to know how it achieves the implementation.

The Record: An Example of an Abstract Data Type

At this stage we need to look at an example of an abstract data type to illustrate some of the general principles we have just discussed. The registrar's system case study introduced in Section 1.3 provides several such examples. One abstract data type occurring in the specifications for this system is the record. We propose the following definition for the record abstract data type:

Record A record is a grouping under one label of an arbitrary number of elements which may be of potentially different subordinate data types. Each element of a record is called a field. The operations to be performed on a record are

    ☐ Retrieve the contents of an entire record.

    ☐ Modify the contents of an entire record.

    ☐ Retrieve the contents of an individual field within a record.

    ☐ Modify the contents of an individual field within a record.

For example, in the registrar's system, a student record may be viewed as indicated in Figure 1.2. In this figure, the label BestStudent identifies the entire record. The fields within the record are Name, CredTaken, Cred-Earned, and TotalGradePts. Note that the fields within the record are not all the same data type; it is said that the fields within a record are heterogeneous. This is one of the features that distinguishes a record from a list, the next abstract data type we will consider.

Also note that the concept of a record is one abstract data type for which there is a very straightforward implementation in Pascal. This is illustrated in the following Pascal type and variable declarations:

```
CONST   StringLength = 40;
 .
 .
 .

TYPE    String = PACKED ARRAY [1..StringLength] OF char;
        StudentRec = RECORD
                        Name : String;
                        CredTaken : integer;
                        CredEarned : integer;
                        TotalGradePts : integer
                     END;
 .
 .
 .

VAR     BestStudent, SomeStudent: StudentRec;
        MostGradePts: integer;
```

Pascal also makes it very easy to implement the four operations specified in our definition of the abstract data type record. To retrieve the contents of the BestStudent record and at the same time use it to modify the contents of the entire SomeStudent record, we need merely use the Pascal

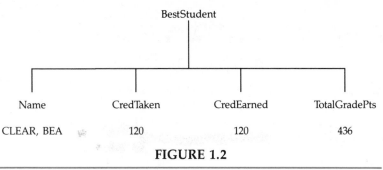

FIGURE 1.2

Student record at University of Hard Knocks

assignment statement:

```
SomeStudent := BestStudent
```

To access the individual field TotalGradePts within the BestStudent record, the statement

```
MostGradePts := BestStudent.TotalGradePts
```

may be used to retrieve the field and assign it to another memory location. Conversely, the statement

```
BestStudent.TotalGradePts := MostGradePts
```

may be used to modify the contents of the field within the record.

Two final comments regarding the abstract data type record are in order. First, relative to the registrar's system, note that this abstract type is the conceptual embodiment of an actual student record in that particular system. Hence we now have a more precise way of specifying how the records in that system are to be manipulated. Second, note the care we have taken to separate the concept of a record from its implementation in Pascal. The reason for this is that, as designers, we want to be able to talk about this concept whether or not we are programming in Pascal. In this situation it happens that the abstract data type record can be almost trivially implemented in Pascal, but that will not always be the case. For instance, languages such as FORTRAN and BASIC have no direct implementation for the record concept. This does not mean that we cannot implement records in these languages. Rather it means that the implementation becomes more involved. We will soon see that Pascal also does not have direct implementations for many of the abstract data types we will be considering. However, it is safe to say that one reason why Pascal has replaced FORTRAN and BASIC in many applications is the ease with which it allows you to implement abstractions. The future, in turn, may well find Pascal replaced on a widespread basis by newer languages such as Modula-2 and Ada. These languages are even more conducive to implementing abstract data types in a fashion which completely hides from calling routines the details of how the implementation is carried out.

Introduction to the List Abstract Data Type and the ACIDS Criteria for Lists

Although the information required for each student at the University of Hard Knocks can be conceptualized as a record, we need another structure to store the data for all students. This new abstract data type is called a general list and is pictured in Table 1.1. A formal description of a list is given by:

General list A general list is a collection of data items, each of which is the same data type. The elements of a list are related to each other by their relative position in the list. That is, there is a first element, a second element, a third, and so on. The operations to be performed on the list include:

- Add an element to the list.

- Change the value of a list element.

- Inspect the value of a given list element.

- Delete an element from the list.

- Sort the list in a specified order.

This definition of a list requires some further discussion, particularly as a means of conceptualizing the registrar's system we are currently considering. Note that the elements of a list are required to be homogeneous, that is, of the same type. This is one aspect in which a list differs from a record, which may have heterogeneous fields. From Table 1.1, we see that each element of the list for the registrar's system is actually one student record.

	Name	CreditTaken	CredEarned	TotalGradePts
1st	AVREG,JOE	96	93	208
2nd	CLEAR, BEA	120	120	436
3rd	SMART,LES	80	60	120
	.		.	
	.		.	
	.		.	
nth	WOOD,HOLLY	123	120	357

TABLE 1.1

Records for the *n* students at University of Hard Knocks

There are several ways in which we might consider an ordering of elements in the list. One would be to consider the ordering imposed by the relative position of the entry in the list, that is, the relative ordering of the list. However, we could also contemplate ordering the list by various other criteria. For instance, we might want to focus on an ordering based on using Name as an alphabetical key. However, recalling the specifications in the registrar's memo, an ordering based on computed grade point average as a key would also be important for the registrar's system. Clearly there can potentially be many such keyed orderings of a list but only one relative ordering. In a situation where several keyed orderings are needed, one of the crucial questions that must be considered by the designer is the following: which keyed ordering (if any) should coincide with the relative ordering of the list? For instance, the four records shown in Table 1.1 indicate that the relative ordering by position in list coincides with an alphabetically keyed ordering based on Name. That is, the Name field in record k precedes the Name field in record $(k + 1)$. Because of this coincidence, it is very easy to proceed through the list alphabetically by Name, but much harder to proceed through the list in order by grade point average. A strategic selection among the alternatives in this regard can greatly enhance the efficiency of the resulting software system.

The notion of keys is important not only in the ordering and sorting of lists but also in the other operations specified in our definition of a list. For instance, when we inspect a given student's record, it is obvious the record must first be found before it can be appropriately examined. However, such a request for a record will likely not take the form of "Inspect the third record" but rather "Inspect the record of SMART, LES." Hence the inspection is based on the key Name rather than on the relative position of the record. Similarly, the change and delete operations for the registrar's system would be based on the key Name. The add operation for the registrar's system would have to take into consideration whether or not the relative ordering of the student records should coincide with the ordering by the key Name. The considerations cited here and in the preceding paragraph are typical of what we shall call the ACIDS criteria for lists. (The acronym ACIDS is taken from the five list operations: Add, Change, Inspect, Delete, and Sort.) The ACIDS criteria provide a convenient checklist which can be used in evaluating the effectiveness of many data processing systems. We will often return to a discussion of these criteria as we discuss different implementations for a list in this and later chapters.

An Array Implementation of a List

The conceptual list of records shown in Table 1.1 may be implemented in Pascal by declaring an array of such records. Such an implementation strategy would necessitate the following additions to our earlier declarations for the student records themselves.

```
CONST    StringLength = 40;
         NumberOfStudents = 800;
```

```
TYPE      String = PACKED ARRAY [1..StringLength] OF char;
          StudentRec = RECORD
                         Name : String;
                         CredTaken : integer;
                         CredEarned : integer;
                         TotalGradePts : integer
                       END;
          StudentList = ARRAY [1..NumberOfStudents] OF StudentRec;
             .
             .
             .

VAR       BestStudent, SomeStudent : StudentRec;
          Students : StudentList;
          MostGradePts : integer;
```

This implementation of a list should not be surprising to those of you who have just completed an introductory Pascal course, since it uses only Pascal tools with which you are already familiar. So, have we really done anything new? The answer is no if your perspective is limited to Pascal syntactical details. However, we hope that you reflect for a moment about what led up to this Pascal implementation; that is, formulating the notion of a list as an abstract data type with a group of specified operations. From this perspective, you should realize that this particular implementation may just be one of several implementations which are possible for this concept. Moreover, some of these other implementations may offer advantages not available with the preceding array implementation. Consider some of the criteria by which an implementation strategy for a list may be evaluated and judged.

□ How efficient is it with respect to handling the five operations in the ACIDS criteria? From what we have discussed earlier in this chapter, it is clear that an answer to this question must carefully address both time and space considerations.

□ Does it allow and/or demand that its relative ordering coincide with a particular ordering by key?

□ Does it allow random access of an entry by its relative position or is sequential access the only possibility? For example, to access the 24th entry in the relative ordering of the list, must we first access the preceding 23 entries (sequential access) or can the 24th entry be accessed directly (random access)?

□ How permanent is the list? That is, when the program that manipulates the list stops running, is the list retained as a disk file or is it strictly in primary memory and hence lost?

As we develop the initial registrar's system in Chapter 3, we shall again refer to these questions as a means of evaluating our efforts. It will turn out that, for most cases, the seemingly obvious array implementation is not a very effective choice for this particular application.

The Two-Dimensional Table Abstract Data Type: Flight/Pilots Data Base for Wing-and-a-Prayer Airlines

We will conclude this chapter with an example which will give some indication of how the designers of a Pascal compiler become involved in the abstraction-to-implementation scenario. A convenient way to introduce the problem is to again allow you to assume a high-level position of great responsibility. This time you are computer operations manager for Wing-and-a-Prayer Airlines and hence receive the following important memorandum:

MEMORANDUM
Wing-and-a-Prayer Airlines

  TO: Computer Operations Manager
FROM: Vice President in Charge of Scheduling
DATE: August 28, 1992
  RE: Matching Flights and Pilots

As you know, we presently have 1,500 flights (with identification numbers 3,000–4,499) and employ 1,400 pilots (with identification numbers 1,000–2,399) to fly them. However, because of factors such as type of airplane, amount of pilot experience, pilot geographic locations, and FAA regulations, each of our pilots qualifies to fly on only a relatively small percentage of flights.

To help our schedulers, we frequently need to answer questions such as the following:

 □ Given a flight, what are identification numbers of the pilots qualified to fly it?

 □ Given a pilot number, what are the flight numbers which that pilot is qualified to fly?

 □ Given a flight number and a pilot number, do we have a match? In other words, is the pilot specified qualified for the particular flight?

Right now our schedulers attempt to answer such questions by time-consuming manual methods. I'm sure that you can easily computerize this task for them. Thanks in advance for your help in this matter.

Faced with this charge, one abstract conceptualization which you might consider is that pictured in Table 1.2.

Flight No.	3000	3001	3002	. . .	4498	4499
Pilot No.						
1000	Yes	No	No	. . .	Yes	No
1001	No	No	No	. . .	Yes	Yes
1002	Yes	Yes	No	. . .	No	No
.	.	.	.	.	.	.
.	.	.	.	.	.	.
.	.	.	.	.	.	.
2398	No	Yes	No	. . .	No	No
2399	No	No	Yes	. . .	No	Yes

TABLE 1.2

Flight/pilot data base for Wing-and-a-Prayer Airlines

We can now formally define the abstract data type two-dimensional table.

Two-dimensional table   A two-dimensional table is a collection of data of the same type arranged as a rectangular grid. Any entry in the grid may be specified by giving its row and column position. The rows and columns themselves are each indexed by a separate contiguous range of some ordinal data type, such as the integers. The operations performed on a table are

☐ Retrieve the entry in the Ith row and Jth column.

☐ Assign a value to the Ith row and Jth column.

Your previous experience should make it clear that Pascal has made it extraordinarily easy to implement such a two-dimensional table. In particular, the following declarations would be suitable for Table 1.2.

```
CONST    LowFlight = 3000;
         HighFlight = 4499;
         LowPilot = 1000;
         HighPilot = 2399;



TYPE     FlightRange = LowFlight..HighFlight;
         PilotRange = LowPilot..HighPilot;
         FPTable = ARRAY [PilotRange,FlightRange] of boolean;



VAR      FP = FPTable;
```

We wish to discuss two issues with respect to this implementation of Wing-and-a-Prayer's table. First, in a situation such as this where Pascal provides an obvious and direct implementation of the abstract data type, how does Pascal itself implement your declarations? That is, the designers of your Pascal compiler must translate the declarations and instructions in your Pascal programs into a suitable representation in the internal machine code of your computer. Recall that this deeper level implementation issue was alluded to in Figure 1.1 though not discussed in detail when that figure was introduced. We now more fully realize that the designers of a compiler are concerned with implementing abstractions from a perspective which is different than that of the users of the compiler. In the case of a two-dimensional table, the implementation issue facing designers of a compiler is how to represent a two-dimensional structure on a machine in which units of computer memory are invariably arranged as a one-dimensional sequence of cells. Second, after discussing the compiler's implementation of your declaration for a two-dimensional table, we will want to evaluate that implementation. How efficient is the compiler's implementation of your structure with respect to time and space considerations? This is a particularly important question for exceedingly large tables such as the one we need in our current Wing-and-a-Prayer application. We will see that the compiler's implementation of a two-dimensional table may be, at best, inefficient and, at worst, totally impractical for our application.

Row-Major Implementation of Two-Dimensional Arrays

To simplify the discussion that follows, let us momentarily leave Table 1.2 and work instead with the following more manageable declaration:

```
VAR Numbers : ARRAY [1..6,1..5] OF integer
```

A sample assignment of values to the table Numbers is pictured in Figure 1.3.

From the perspective of the compiler writer, a two-dimensional array declaration represents a level of abstraction because internally computer

Row \ Column	1	2	3	4	5
1	10	18	42	6	14
2	13	19	8	1	44
3	63	80	12	90	51
4	16	13	9	8	4
5	12	11	12	14*	83
6	1	4	18	99	90

FIGURE 1.3

Values in the ARRAY Numbers

memory is not arranged as a rectangular grid. Instead, computer memory locations are arranged in a linear sequence beginning with location 1, and then 2, 3, 4, and so on. Because of this, there must be manipulations behind the scenes when a program requests the entry in the fifth row and fourth column of a two-dimensional array (as indicated by the * in Figure 1.3). Essentially, the coordinates of fifth row and fourth column must be transformed into an address within this linear sequence of memory locations. The nature of the transformation is dependent upon how the designers of the compiler have chosen to implement the application programmer's mental image of rows and columns within the linear sequence of memory locations. Suppose that our compiler has chosen to store the 30 entries in the two-dimensional array Numbers as indicated in Figure 1.4.

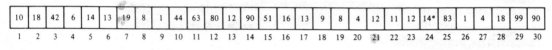

| 10 | 18 | 42 | 6 | 14 | 13 | 19 | 8 | 1 | 44 | 63 | 80 | 12 | 90 | 51 | 16 | 13 | 9 | 8 | 4 | 12 | 11 | 12 | 14* | 83 | 1 | 4 | 18 | 99 | 90 |
| 1 | 2 | 3 | 4 | 5 | 6 | 7 | 8 | 9 | 10 | 11 | 12 | 13 | 14 | 15 | 16 | 17 | 18 | 19 | 20 | 21 | 22 | 23 | 24 | 25 | 26 | 27 | 28 | 29 | 30 |

FIGURE 1.4

Linear storage of data from Figure 1.3

According to this arrangement, the first row would take up the first five locations in the list allocated for the array, the second row, the second five locations, and so on. The entry in the fifth row and fourth column would in fact be located in the 24th position within the list. In this array the Ith row and the Jth column must be transformed into the

$$(5 * (I - 1) + J)\text{th}$$

position in the list. In even more general terms, if NCol is the number of columns in the array, then the entry in the Ith row and Jth column is given as the

$$(NCol * (I - 1) + J)\text{th}$$

entry in the linear list corresponding to the two-dimensional array. Most high-level computer languages implement two-dimensional arrays (and higher) in such a row-major fashion and do so in a way which is largely transparent to the applications programmer. However, all programmers should be aware that multidimensional arrays are inherently less efficient than one-dimensional arrays because of the computations required by the transformation from row/column to linear address each time an entry in the array is accessed. Such a transformation is often called a mapping function.

Those readers who have programmed in FORTRAN will recall that, when initializing a two-dimensional array via a DATA statement, the entries for the array must be listed by column; that is, first column, second column, and so on. This is because FORTRAN is one of the few high-level languages which chooses to store a multidimensional array in column-major order, as indicated in Figure 1.5.

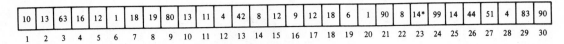

10	13	63	16	12	1	18	19	80	13	11	4	42	8	12	9	12	18	6	1	90	8	14*	99	14	44	51	4	83	90
1	2	3	4	5	6	7	8	9	10	11	12	13	14	15	16	17	18	19	20	21	22	23	24	25	26	27	28	29	30

FIGURE 1.5

Data from Figure 1.3 in column-major form

To access the entry in the Ith row and the Jth column of a two-dimensional array stored in column-major order, the transformation

$$NRow * (J - 1) + I$$

is required, where NRow represents the number of rows in the array. The fact that this transformation requires the number of rows but not the number of columns also explains why many FORTRAN compilers insist that a subroutine be informed of the number of rows in an array passed down from a calling program but not the number of columns.

Introduction to the Sparse Table Problem

From what has been said about the compiler's possible implementation strategy for a two-dimensional array, it should be clear that we might be paying a very high price in memory for the flight/pilot table of Wing-and-a-Prayer Airlines. In particular, we would be charged for 2,100,000 (1,500 × 1,400) Boolean memory locations if our Pascal compiler implemented the array in row-major fashion. Since many Pascal compilers allocate one byte of storage for each Boolean location, your seemingly simple declaration of a two-dimensional table may require over two megabytes (two million bytes) of memory. Depending on your computer, this is quite likely to exceed the amount of memory which a program is allowed to consume. Thus, we have a real problem from the perspective of a space efficiency analysis. Our Pascal declarations for the Wing-and-a-Prayer table may be nothing more than a wishful pipe dream which is not remotely realizable on the particular machine on which we are working.

Does this mean that you cannot implement the conceptual flight/pilot table of Table 1.2 for the Vice President in Charge of Scheduling? For the sake of your job, we hope not! Rather, this illustrates that designers must be acutely aware of how the compiler may automatically implement certain concepts for them and be prepared to implement them in a different fashion when the compiler's strategy will fail. In this instance, we propose to take advantage of an additional fact given to us in the Vice President's specifications. That is, any given pilot qualifies to fly on only a relatively small percentage of flights. This means that relatively few entries in the conceptual table of Table 1.2 will be **true**. A table such as this, in which a high percentage of the data storage locations will be one uniform value (**false** in this case), is called a sparse table. It will turn out in later chapters that we can utilize the sparseness of true values in the table to implement it by strategies other than row-major or column-major form (and hence save your job). However, note that, regardless of the implementation we choose, we are still working with a table at the abstract level.

A Relevant Issue . . .

Sparse Tables and Language Compilers

Two-dimensional tables play a crucial role in many language compilers. To see why, consider a problem substantially easier than writing a compiler. Suppose that you are reading a stream of characters which is intended to identify one of the 12 months. You are to read these characters until you have read enough to uniquely identify a month or until you can conclude that the stream of characters will not identify any month. Thus, upon reading 'D', you could declare the month to be DECEMBER. However, you would have to read the three characters 'JUL' before you could declare the month to be JULY. Moreover, if you read the three characters 'JUK', you could declare that the input stream cannot possibly identify any month. (Note that the problem we are describing does not demand that the input stream be a completely correct spelling of some month, only that the input stream begin with characters which uniquely define a month. Thus, both 'DECEMBER' and 'DIZZY' would be viewed as input streams which uniquely identify the month DECEMBER because you could quit processing characters as soon as the leading 'D' is read.)

The driving force behind an algorithm which would allow you to process an input stream in the fashion just described is a two-dimensional table such as that pictured here. The columns of this table are indexed by the letters of the alphabet, and the rows are indexed by the various "frames of mind" (officially called states) in which you may find yourself after having read a portion of the input stream. For instance, this table indicates that, if

you begin processing characters in the start state and read the character 'J', then you switch to the j state. Once in the j state, you are expecting to encounter either 'A' or 'U' as the next character, which will cause you to switch to the ja state or the ju state, respectively. In addition to the states which index the rows of this table, we also have the states

jan, feb, mar, apr, may, jun,
jul, aug, sep, oct, nov, dec

which correspond to your having recognized a uniquely defined month and the state error which is indicated by the vacant entries in the table.

Given this table, the algorithm to recognize a month is extremely compact. It follows in pseudocode form:

```
state := start
REPEAT
    read(c)
    state := table [state,c]
UNTIL eoln
    OR state = error
    OR state is one of months jan . . . dec
```

Why is our month-recognition algorithm a relevant issue with respect to the topics we have discussed in this beginning chapter? First note that the two-dimensional table for this algorithm clearly embodies the sparse table concept we have discussed in this chapter. In this particular sparse table, the vast majority of entries are the error state. Hence, our algorithm to recognize a month from an incoming stream of

Summary

Chapter 1 has been a stage-setting chapter. More than anything else we have attempted to present the flavor of the software engineering approach to computer problem solving. This is an approach which emphasizes that a solution is best obtained by first approaching your problem at an abstract, conceptual level. Once the problem is thoroughly understood at this level,

STATE / LETTER

STATE \ LETTER	A	B	C	D	E	F	G	H	I	J	K	L	M	N	O	P	Q	R	S	T	U	V	W	X	Y	Z
start	a			dec		feb				j			m	nov	oct				sep							
j	jan																				ju					
m	ma																									
a																apr					aug					
ju												jul		jun												
ma																		mar							may	

characters is dependent on our ability to implement a sparse table. (See the Programming Problems at the end of the chapter for a suggestion as to how this may be done.)

Second, this particular example is representative, on a small scale, of an entire class of algorithms which concern themselves with recognizing a valid sequence of symbols arriving on an input stream. In fact, this is precisely what must be done by a compiler for a high-level language such as Pascal. That is, it must successively read the symbols in the source program which serves as its input stream and declare the sequence of symbols valid or invalid according to the rules of the language. Many compilers are actually driven by a table similar to the one we used for our month-recognition algorithm. One of the major differences in such a compiler table is the increased size of the table due to the complexity of the language vis-à-vis our simple month-recognition example. Hence, an efficient representation of a sparse matrix can be crucial to determining whether or not a compiler can process source programs at a reasonable rate of speed.

Algorithms which are driven by a table such as the one we have discussed here are known as finite state machines, or finite state automata. Although we will not be exploring finite state automata in depth in this book, if our discussion here has spurred your curiosity, we encourage you to consult Chapter 7, "Automata, Grammars, and Languages," of *Discrete Mathematics* by Richard Johnsonbaugh (New York: Macmillan, 1984) for a very readable introduction to this fascinating topic.

it is then successively refined into a more specific, detailed implementation. It is crucial to realize that the development of successful software is intimately tied to your abilities to think abstractly about the problem first and then implement those abstractions.

Two extensive examples were presented to highlight the difference and the relationship between abstraction and implementation. The registrar's system for the University of Hard Knocks introduced the notion of an abstract data type. In particular, the record and list abstract data types were discussed in the example. Each was formally defined in terms of its elements, the existing relationships between those elements, and the operations to be performed on the elements. This is typical of an appropriate specification for any abstract data type. Additionally, the array implementation for a list was introduced and will be expanded upon in Chapter 3. This implementation of a list and other implementations we will study in later chapters can be systematically evaluated using the ACIDS criteria—Add, Change, Inspect, Delete, and Sort.

The second example, the flight/pilot matching problem for Wing-and-a-Prayer Airlines, introduced the notion of a table as an abstract data type. Even more importantly, it illustrated that the implementation of abstractions is an issue in the writing of compilers as well as in writing Pascal application programs. The importance of this for the person who uses Pascal is to realize that the implementation automatically used by the compiler may not always be appropriate or even possible. The sparse table problem is an example of this, and we will resume our discussion of it in later chapters.

Key Terms

abstract data type
abstraction
ACIDS criteria for lists
array implementation of list
column-major
element
error state
field
finite state automata
finite state machines
general list
heterogeneous
homogeneous
implementation
information hiding
inspect
keyed orderings
keys

mapping function
operations
ordering
package
random access
record
relationships
relative ordering
row-major
sequential access
software engineering
sparse table
start state
state
systems
time/space analysis
two-dimensional table

Exercises

1. What are the characteristics of the software engineering approach to system development?
2. What factors are involved in a time/space analysis?
3. Whose responsibility is it to translate the needs of the user into specifi-

cations which then guide the programmers in developing a software system?

4. What does the acronym ACIDS stand for? How does it relate to the notion of a general list?

5. Show by an example how the row-major and column-major implementations for a two-dimensional array would differ.

6. What would the mapping function be for a three-dimensional table implemented in row-major form? Can you generalize this to tables of even higher dimensions?

7. Give some examples besides the registrar's system of applications which, at the abstract level, call for a general list.

8. Give some examples besides the flight/pilot data base of applications which, at the abstract level, call for a sparse table.

9. Is a two-dimensional M by M array more or less efficient than a one-dimensional array of extent M^2? Explain your answer.

10. Many languages such as Pascal, allow subscripts for an arbitrary range of ordinal values, not necessarily always integers starting at one. Specify how this would affect the mapping functions discussed in this chapter to translate two-dimensional table coordinates into linear-list positions.

11. Consider from an abstract perspective the records which a library might keep on its books. For instance, take into account such information as title, author, identification number, whether or not the book is checked out, and so on. Then write a record description to implement such a book record in Pascal. Finally, write a Pascal **TYPE** declaration which uses an array to implement a list of such book records.

12. Consider from an abstract perspective the records which a bank might keep on its customers. For instance, take into account such information as customer name, customer identification number, the type of accounts the customer holds with the bank, balance in each account, transactions (withdrawals and deposits), and so on. Then write a record description to implement such a bank customer record in Pascal. Finally, write a Pascal **TYPE** declaration which uses an array to implement a list of such records.

Problems

1. If your university has a cooperative registrar, invite him or her to your class to discuss the type of data processing operations in which the registrar's office is typically engaged. After this discussion (which should no doubt include time for questions which arise), describe the data involved in the operation of your registrar's office in terms of abstract data types.

2. If you are familiar with the notion of a set from your previous work in mathematics and computer science, formalize a definition of a set as an abstract data type. Since Pascal offers its users a predefined set type, do some browsing in the reference manuals for your computer and its

software (often referred to as local reference manuals) to find out how your version of Pascal implements sets. What are the limitations of this particular implementation? Give some examples of applications where this compiler-provided implementation would be insufficient. Finally, develop your own implementation for such an application.

3. After reading A Relevant Issue in this chapter, write a program which will appropriately recognize a month from an input stream of characters. Implement the sparse two-dimensional table pictured in that section as a Pascal function which uses **CASE** and/or **IF . . . THEN . . . ELSE** statements. This function should receive a current state and a character and return the next state which is given by that table.

4. (This problem is especially appropriate for a class of 15 or more students.) After reading A Relevant Issue in this chapter, write a program which appropriately recognizes a first name of a member of your computer science class. Use the following strategy. Obtain a list of first names of all class members; discard any duplicates from this list. Then develop a two-dimensional table analogous to the table developed for month names given in A Relevant Issue. The same algorithm described to recognize month names may now be used to recognize names from members of your class. Implement the sparse two-dimensional table needed for this algorithm as a Pascal function which uses **CASE** and/or **IF . . . THEN . . . ELSE** statements. This function should receive a current state and a character and return the next state which is given by the table.

Space and Time Considerations for Algorithms

A good workman is known by his tools.

Proverb

Introductory Considerations

Our discussion in Chapter 1 focused more on the description of data than on the algorithms which manipulate that data. That is, we specified operations to be performed on an abstract data type (such as sorting a list) without specifying the methods by which such operations were to be carried out. Indeed, the essence of abstraction requires that we first carefully specify *what* is to be done before we worry about *how* it will be done. But clearly, considerations about "how" can only be postponed so long, if the system is ever to be actually implemented. Moreover, as we indicated in the first chapter, many conceptual problems will allow several different algorithmic solutions. These solutions will vary in the amount of memory they consume (space considerations) and the speed with which they execute (time considerations). As a designer and implementor of programs, you must be able to select that solution which is most appropriate for the situation at hand.

In this chapter we shall begin to present some of the standard algorithms which computer scientists often call upon as they encounter certain types of problems. In particular, we will consider as problems two of the operations we specified as part of the ACIDS criteria for lists: sorting the list in a specified order and inspecting the value of a given list element. The inspection operation will require that the list be searched for an entry whose key field matches the key being sought. The sorting and searching algorithms we will present in this chapter are relatively simple and straightforward; you may well have encountered some of them in an introductory programming course. However, our purpose here is not to give isolated examples but rather to begin stocking your algorithmic toolbox. Just as the woodworker selects from a range of tools for a given job, so you should begin to think in terms of frequently encountered problems and the algorithmic solutions which have already been developed for them. This initial stocking of your toolbox with simple tools will provide the basis for an initial implementation (in Chapter 3) of the registrar's system at the University of Hard Knocks as described in Section 1.3.

We shall also use this chapter to begin our discussion of how algorithms may be systematically analyzed from a time and space efficiency perspective. Conducting such analyses is critical to the software engineering approach described in Chapter 1. The results of such analyses guide the software systems designer in selecting the best implementation alternative for a particular conceptual model. It will turn out that, using a technique known as Big-O notation, we can often conveniently categorize the efficiency of an algorithm, particularly with respect to time. The simple sort and search algorithms of this chapter will provide convenient examples for introducing this technique. The same analysis technique will be applied to more complex algorithms throughout the rest of the book. Moreover, by subjecting these simple algorithms to this type of analysis, we will see why they are frequently inadequate for the tremendously complex situations that occur in the real world. In fact they will prove only minimally adequate for the implementation of the registrar's system we will develop in Chapter 3. Should this be a cause for despair? Indeed not! It merely means that, as you would expect, artificially simple algorithms provide solutions only to artificially simple problems. The fact that more sophisticated methods are usually needed is the reason your study of computer science must go beyond Unit I of this text.

_____ 2.2

Simple Sorting Algorithms

Our discussion in this section will assume an array implementation of a list as described in Section 1.3. For the sake of simplicity we will also assume that

1. The list is to be sorted in ascending (that is, smallest to largest) order.

2. The list is merely a list of keys, not of records containing fields and other associated data.

As you will find out in the exercises for this chapter, these assumptions are not conceptually restrictive. Rather they just simplify the Pascal code that we will use to implement our algorithms. Hence the following Pascal declarations provide a suitable setting for our sorting problem:

```
CONST MaxIndex = 100; {Easily Adjusted}
      StringLength = 40;
TYPE  String = PACKED ARRAY [1..StringLength] OF CHAR;
      SortType = String; {Easily Adjusted}
      SortArray = ARRAY [1..MaxIndex] OF SortType;
```

In general, we wish to write a procedure which meets the following specifications:

```
PROCEDURE Sort (n : integer; VAR KeyList : SortArray);

    {Given array KeyList containing entries in locations 1 through n,
     return KeyList with these n entries arranged in
     ascending order.}
```

Note that the fashion in which we have made our **CONST** and **TYPE** declarations will allow this procedure to eventually sort an array of any size and base type provided that the definitions of MaxIndex and SortType are altered. This method of declaration represents an attempt to make the Pascal procedure abstract in the sense that it will embody an algorithm which can sort a variety of data types. The fact that the user has to alter some code outside of the procedure to take advantage of this abstraction is an unfortunate necessity due to the way in which declarations must be made in Pascal. This awkwardness is being addressed in more recent versions of Pascal which allow conformant array parameters. In particular, conformant array parameters are part of the new ISO (International Standards Organization) standard for Pascal; their use is discussed in Appendix B. In the main text itself, we will adhere to the original standard for Pascal and, therefore, not use conformant arrays. You should check local documentation to determine if the version of Pascal which you use supports this more powerful parameter-passing scheme. Now, however, since we have completely specified *what* our sorting algorithm is to do, let us turn our attention to a consideration of *how* it can be done.

Bubble Sort

The general idea of the bubble sort may be described as follows. Given a list of names (or other data) stored in an array, pass through the array and compare adjacent pairs of names. Whenever two names are out of order with respect to each other, interchange them. The effect of such a pass through a list of names is traced in Figure 2.1, where a "snapshot" of the array after each comparison is given. Notice that after such a pass, we are

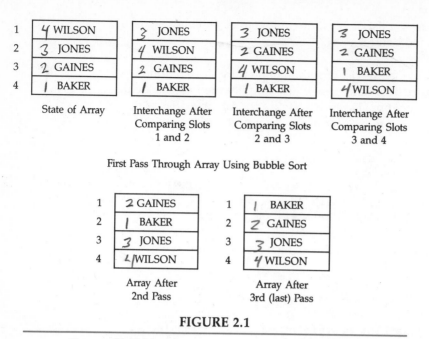

First Pass Through Array Using Bubble Sort

FIGURE 2.1

Trace of bubble sort on an array with four names

assured that the list will have the name which comes last in alphabetical order in the final array position.

If one pass through an array of n names can guarantee that the name which comes last in alphabetical order is in the appropriate position, then slicing off the last element and passing through the remaining $n - 1$ entries using the same logic will guarantee that the name which comes second to last in alphabetical order is in its appropriate position. Repeating the process for a total of $n - 1$ passes will eventually insure that all names are in their appropriate alphabetical positions, as indicated in Figure 2.1. In general, on the ith pass through the array, $n - i$ comparisons of pairs must be made.

Thus, the bubble sort algorithm will involve two nested loops. The outer loop will control the number of (successively smaller) passes through the array. The inner loop will control the pairs of adjacent entries being compared. The complete Pascal procedure to implement this algorithm follows. The procedure assumes the existence of appropriate **CONST** and **TYPE** declarations as discussed earlier in this section. We also use this procedure to illustrate the graphic documentation that will be used to enhance the clarity of Pascal algorithms throughout the book. This graphic documentation will be used to supplement normal Pascal documentation. Based on the proverb that "one picture is worth one thousand words," it will pictorially trace how a given segment of Pascal code affects the data it is acting upon.

```
PROCEDURE BubbleSort (n:integer; VAR KeyList:SortArray);
    {Given array KeyList containing entries in locations 1 through n,
    use bubble sort algorithm to return KeyList with these n
    entries arranged in ascending order.}
```

```
VAR i,j : integer;
    Temp : SortType;

BEGIN
   FOR i := 1 TO n-1 DO {Number of passes}
     FOR j := 1 TO n-i DO {Number of comparisons on ith pass}
       IF KeyList[j] > KeyList[j+1] THEN {Must interchange}
          BEGIN
          Temp := KeyList[j];
          KeyList[j] := KeyList[j+1];
          KeyList[j+1] := Temp
          END
END; {BubbleSort}
```

In the next section we will analyze in detail the run-time efficiency of the bubble sort. You may already have some ideas about how to make it more efficient. But, before conducting that analysis, we should consider two other sorting algorithms to which the efficiency of bubble sort may be compared: insertion sort and selection sort.

Insertion Sort

Like the bubble sort, the insertion sort compares adjacent entries in the array being sorted. However, the motivation for doing so is slightly different in insertion sort. Here the goal is that on the ith pass through, the ith element among

```
KeyList[1], KeyList[2], . . . KeyList[i]
```

should be inserted into its rightful place among the first i entries in the array. Thus, after the ith pass (i starting at 2), the first i elements of the array should be in sorted order. The following steps will achieve this:

1. Start a pass counter i at 2.

2. Start an index j at i.

3. Check if KeyList[j] < KeyList[$j - 1$]. If so, interchange them, set j to $j - 1$, and repeat the check unless j has reached 1.

4. For each of $i = 3, 4, \ldots , n$, repeat steps 2 and 3.

In effect, for each pass, the index j begins at the ith element and interchanges that entry with the preceding one until it has been inserted in its appropriate place in the first i positions. This is analogous to the fashion in which many people pick up playing cards and arrange them in order in their hands. That is, holding the first $(i - 1)$ cards in order, a person will pick up the ith card and compare it with cards already held until its appropriate spot is found. Insertion sort is traced for each value of i in Figure 2.2. In each row of this diagram the data items are sorted in alphabetical order relative to each other above the item with the asterisk; below this item the data are not affected.

KeyList	i=2	i=3	i=4	i=5	i=6
PAM .	PAM .	DAVE .	ARON .	ARON .	ARON
SINGH :	SINGH*:	PAM :	DAVE :	DAVE :	BEV
DAVE :	DAVE :	SINGH*:	PAM :	PAM :	DAVE
ARON :	ARON :	ARON :	SINGH*:	SINGH:	PAM
TOM :	TOM :	TOM :	TOM :	TOM* :	SINGH
BEV :	BEV :	BEV :	BEV :	BEV :	TOM*

FIGURE 2.2

Trace of repeated passes from insertion sort

To implement the insertion sort algorithm in Pascal we have the following code:

```
PROCEDURE InsertionSort (n:integer; VAR KeyList : SortArray);

{Given array KeyList containing entries in locations 1 through n, use
  insertion sort algorithm to return KeyList with these n entries
  arranged in ascending order. }

VAR   i,j : integer;
      Done : boolean;
      Temp : SortType;
BEGIN
  FOR i := 2 TO n DO {On pass i, the ith element must be positioned.}
    BEGIN
      j := i;
      Done := false;   {As soon as jth element > (j-1)th element,
                        we know it is appropriately positioned.}
```

```
WHILE (j >= 2) AND NOT Done DO
      IF KeyList[j] < KeyList[j-1] THEN ─────────────────────┐
               {Move jth entry to position j-1}              │
         BEGIN                                               │
         Temp := KeyList[j];                                 │
         KeyList[j] := KeyList[j-1];                         │
         KeyList[j-1] := Temp;                               │
         j := j-1                                            │
         END                                                 │
      ELSE    {We know array is now sorted in first i positions.}
         Done := true {So shut off the inner loop}           │
      END {FOR loop}                                         │
END; {InsertionSort}                                         │
```

Insertion sort

Array at the ith stage

ith

1   2   3   ···   i − 1

Sorted   Unsorted

ith element inserted in its
rightful place among
"first i entries
on ith pass"

Selection Sort

Recall that the motivation of the bubble sort was to place the (current) largest array value in the (current) last array slot, then seal off that slot from future consideration, and repeat the process. The selection sort algorithm is somewhat similarly motivated, but it attempts to avoid the multitude of interchanges of adjacent entries to which the bubble sort is prone. To do this, on the ith pass through the array, it will determine the position of the largest entry among

```
KeyList [1], KeyList[2], . . . , KeyList[Last]
```

where Last is $n - i + 1$. Then this largest entry will be swapped with the Last entry, Last reduced by 1, and the process repeated. Figure 2.3 illustrates how this algorithm will work on repeated passes through an array with six entries. The asterisks in this figure are used to indicate the successive largest (alphabetically) entries as they are being correctly located in the array.

The Pascal procedure for selection sort uses, as its inner loop, a simple algorithm to find the maximum entry and store its position in a variable MaxPosition. It is important to note that this inner loop avoids the poten-

KeyList	i=1	i=2	i=3	i=4	i=5
DAVE .	DAVE .	DAVE .	DAVE .	ARON .	ARON*
SINGH:	SINGH:	BEV :	BEV :	BEV :	BEV*
PAM :	PAM :	PAM :	ARON :	DAVE* :	DAVE*
ARON :	ARON :	ARON :	PAM* :	PAM* :	PAM*
TOM :	BEV :	SINGH*:	SINGH*:	SINGH*:	SINGH*
BEV :	TOM* :	TOM* :	TOM* :	TOM* :	TOM*

FIGURE 2.3

Trace of selection sort

tially frequent interchange of array values that is necessary in the inner loop of BubbleSort.

```
PROCEDURE SelectionSort (n : integer; VAR KeyList : SortArray);

    {Given array KeyList containing entries in locations 1 through n,
    use selection sort algorithm to return KeyList with those n
    entries arranged in ascending order.}

VAR  i, j, MaxPosition, Last : integer;
     Temp, MaxValue : SortType;

BEGIN
    FOR i := 1 TO n-1 DO {number of passes}
      BEGIN
      Last := n-i+1;
      MaxPosition := 1; {Initially assume 1st is largest}
      FOR j := 2 TO Last DO  {Test previous largest}
        IF KeyList[j] > KeyList[MaxPosition]
            THEN MaxPosition := j;
                {Must change our view of largest}
      Temp := KeyList[Last];   {Now swap largest outside the inner loop}
      KeyList[Last] := KeyList[MaxPosition];
      KeyList[MaxPosition] := Temp

      END
END;  {SelectionSort}
```

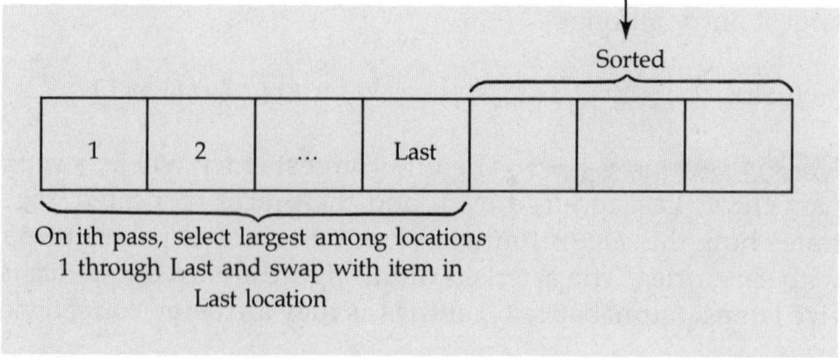

On ith pass, select largest among locations
1 through Last and swap with item in
Last location

Certainly the selection sort algorithm has achieved an intuitive improvement in run-time efficiency over bubble sort by locating the interchange of array entries in the outer loop instead of the inner loop, but is this improvement a significant improvement? Or, have other subtle inefficiencies been introduced to offset this apparent gain? These are difficult questions to answer unless we have a better grasp of how to measure program efficiency. Toward that end, the next section will introduce a notation for categorizing the run-time efficiency of algorithms and apply that notation to the three sorts we have discussed here.

_____ 2.3

Which Sort Is Best? A Big-O Analysis

Computers do their work in terms of certain fundamental operations: comparing two numbers, moving the contents of one memory word to another, and so on. It should come as no surprise to you that a simple instruction in a high-level language such as Pascal may be translated (via a compiler) into many of these fundamental machine-level instructions. On most modern computers the speeds of these fundamental operations are measured in microseconds—that is, millionths of a second—although some larger supercomputers are beginning to break the nanosecond (billionth of a second) barrier. Let us assume, for the sake of argument, that we are working with a hypothetical computer that requires one microsecond to perform one of its fundamental operations.

With execution speeds of this kind, it makes little sense to analyze the efficiency of those portions of a program which perform only initializations and final reporting of summary results. The key to analyzing a procedure's efficiency is to scrutinize the loops and, even more importantly, the nested loops within that procedure. Consider the following two examples of nested loops intended to sum each of the rows of an $n \times n$ two-dimensional array a, storing the row sums in a one-dimensional array Sum and the overall total in GrandTotal.

Version 1.

```
GrandTotal := 0;
FOR i := 1 TO n DO
    BEGIN
    Sum[i] := 0;
    FOR j := 1 TO n DO
        BEGIN
        Sum[i] := Sum[i]+a[i,j];
        GrandTotal := GrandTotal+a[i,j]
        END
    END
```

Version 2.

```
GrandTotal := 0;
FOR i := 1 TO n DO
    BEGIN
    Sum[i] := 0;
    FOR j := 1 TO n DO
        Sum[i] := Sum[i]+a[i,j];
    GrandTotal := GrandTotal+Sum[i]
    END
```

If we analyze the number of addition operations required by these two versions, it should be immediately obvious that Version 2 is apparently better in this respect. Because Version 1 incorporates the accumulating of GrandTotal into its inner loop, it requires $2n^2$ additions. That is, the additions Sum[i] + $a[i, j,]$ and GrandTotal + $a[i, j]$ are each executed n^2 times, for a total of $2n^2$. Version 2, on the other hand, accumulates GrandTotal after the inner loop, hence only requiring $n^2 + n$, which is less than $2n^2$ for any n after 1. Version 2 is seemingly guaranteed to execute faster than Version 1 for any nontrivial value of n. But note that "faster" here may not have much significance in the real world of computing. Assuming that our hypothetical computer will allow us to declare a 1,000 by 1,000 array, Version 1 would require two seconds to perform its additions while Version 2 would require just over one second. On a larger 100,000 by 100,000 array, Version 1 would crunch numbers for slightly under six hours whereas Version 2 would take about three hours. The point here is that, although Version 2 is certainly better from an aesthetic perspective, it is not good enough to be appreciably different from a user's perspective. That is, in situations where one version will respond within seconds, so will the other. Conversely, when one is annoyingly slow for users, the other will be also. In terms of the order of magnitude of run-time involved, these versions should not be considered significantly different. For the 1,000 by 1,000 array, both versions would be fast enough to allow their use in an interactive environment. For the 100,000 by 100,000 array, both versions would dictate an overnight run in batch mode since an interactive user will be no more willing to wait three hours than six hours for a response.

Thus, because of the phenomenal execution speeds and very large amounts of available memory on modern computers, proportionately small differences between algorithms usually have little practical impact. Such considerations have led computer scientists toward devising a method of algorithm classification which makes more precise the notion of order of magnitude as it applies to time and space considerations. This method of classification, typically referred to as big-O notation, hinges on the following definition:

Big-O notation Suppose there exists a function $f(n)$ defined on the nonnegative integers such that the number of operations required by an algorithm for an input of size n is less than some constant k times $f(n)$ for all but finitely many n. That is, the number of operations is proportional to $f(n)$ for all large values of n. Such an algorithm is said to be an $O(f(n))$ algorithm relative to the number of operations it requires to execute. Similarly, we could classify an algorithm as $O(f(n))$ relative to the number of memory locations it requires to execute.

If we consider the two-dimensional array of size n from our earlier example, we see now that both Version 1 and Version 2 of our nested loop fall into the $O(n^2)$ category of algorithms.

Two questions merit further discussion at this stage. First: How well does the big-O notation provide a way of classifying algorithms from a real-world perspective? To answer this question, consider Table 2.1. This table considers some typical $f(n)$ functions we will be using to classify algorithms and their order of magnitude run-time for an input of size 10^5 on our hypothetical computer.

f(n)	Order of magnitude run time for input of size 10^5 (Assuming proportionality constant k = 1)
$\log_2 n$	2×10^{-5} second
n	0.1 second
$n \log_2 n$	2 seconds
n^2	3 hours
n^3	32 years
2^n	centuries

TABLE 2.1

Comparison of some typical $f(n)$ functions

From this table, we can see that an $O(n^2)$ algorithm will take hours to execute for an input of size 10^5. How many hours is dependent upon the constant of proportionality in the definition of the big-O notation. Regardless of the value of this constant of proportionality, a categorization of an algorithm as an $O(n^2)$ algorithm has thus achieved a very practical goal. That is, we now know that, for an input of size 10^5, we cannot expect an immediate response from such an algorithm. Moreover, we also know that, for a reasonably small constant of proportionality, we have an algorithm for which submission as an overnight job would not be impractical. That is, unlike an $O(n^3)$ algorithm, we could expect the computer to finish executing our algorithm in a time frame which would be acceptable if it could be scheduled at a time which would not interfere with other uses of the machine. On the other hand, an $O(n^3)$ algorithm applied to a data set of this size would be completely impractical.

The second question which must be answered relative to big-O analysis is how one determines the function $f(n)$ which categorizes a particular algorithm. We will give an overview of that process here and then illustrate it by doing actual analyses for our three sorting algorithms. It is generally the case that, by analyzing the loop structure of an algorithm, we can estimate the number of run-time operations (or amount of memory units) required by the algorithm as a sum of several terms, each dependent on n, the number of items being processed by the algorithm. That is, typically we are able to express the number of run-time operations (or amount of memory) as a sum of the form

$$f_1(n) + f_2(n) + \ldots f_k(n)$$

Moreover, it is also typical that we identify one of the terms in this expression as the dominant term. A dominant term is one which, for bigger values of n, becomes so large that it will allow us to ignore all the other terms from a big-O perspective. For instance, suppose that we had an expression involving two terms such as

$$n^2 + 6n$$

Here, the n^2 term dominates the $6n$ term since, for $n \geq 6$, we have

$$n^2 + 6n \leq n^2 + n^2 = 2n^2$$

Thus, $n^2 + 6n$ is an expression which would lead to an $O(n^2)$ categorization because of the dominance of the n^2 term. In general, the problem of big-O categorization reduces to finding the dominant term in an expression representing the number of operations or amount of memory required by an algorithm.

To assist in our future big-O analyses of algorithms, the list of frequently occurring dominant terms given in Table 2.2 will prove helpful.

n dominates $\log_a n$, a is often 2

n $\log_a n$ dominates n, a is often 2

n^m dominates n^k when m > k

a^n dominates n^m for any a and m

TABLE 2.2

Common dominant terms in expressions for algorithmic efficiency

It is worthwhile to briefly characterize some of the classes of algorithms that arise due to the dominant terms listed in Table 2.2. Algorithms whose efficiency is dominated by a $\log_a n$ term (and hence are categorized as $O(\log_a n)$) are often called logarithmic algorithms. Since $\log_a n$ will increase much more slowly than n itself, logarithmic algorithms are generally very efficient. Algorithms whose efficiency can be expressed in terms of a polynomial of the form

$$a_m n^m + a_{m-1} n^{m-1} + \cdots + a_2 n^2 + a_1 n + a_0$$

are called polynomial algorithms. Since the highest power of n will dominate such a polynomial, such algorithms are $O(n^m)$. The only polynomial algorithms we will be concerned with in this book will have $m = 1, 2,$ or 3 and are called linear, quadratic, or cubic respectively.

Algorithms with efficiency dominated by a term of the form a^n are called exponential algorithms. Exponential algorithms are one of a class of algorithms known as NP algorithms (for Not Polynomial). It could be said that NP might also stand for "Not Practical" because generally such algorithms cannot reasonably be run on typical computers for moderate values of n. (However, to see why this last statement may have to change in the future, be sure to read A Relevant Issue in this chapter.)

Big-O Analysis of Bubble Sort

We are now ready to carry out some real comparisons between the three sorting methods we have discussed so far: bubble, insertion, and selection. To do so, we must determine functions $f(n)$ which allow us to make statements like "Sorting algorithm X requires $O(f(n))$ comparisons." If it turns out that all three sorts share the same $f(n)$ function, then we can conclude that the differences between them are not approaching an order of magnitude scale. Rather, they would be more subtle distinctions which would not appear so dramatically in run-time differences.

We also realize that the key to doing a big-O analysis is to focus our attention on the loops in the algorithm. We will do that first for the bubble sort. Recall the loop structure of the bubble sort.

```
For i:=1 TO n−1 DO
   FOR j:=1 TO n−i DO                             
      IF KeyList[j] > KeyList[j+1] THEN    } Inner  } Outer
      .                                      Loop     Loop
      . (Swap)
      .
```

If we consider the comparison at the top of the inner loop, we note that it will be executed first $n - 1$ times, then $n - 2$ times, and so on down to one time for the final execution of the inner loop. Hence, the number of comparisons will be the sum of the sequence of numbers

$$
\begin{array}{c}
n - 1 \\
n - 2 \\
. \\
. \\
. \\
1
\end{array}
$$

A formula from algebra will show this sum to be $n(n - 1)/2$. Therefore, we conclude that the bubble sort is an $O(n^2)$ algorithm.

You may have already surmised that the version of the bubble sort we have discussed is not the most efficient version possible. By introducing a Boolean variable to short-circuit the outer loop, we can avoid potentially many unnecessary comparisons should the procedure receive an array which is already in order or which is put in order during an early pass through the array. You will do this in the exercises at the end of the chapter. This will reduce the number of comparisons required by bubble sort to $O(n)$ magnitude but only in the best case when it gets data nearly ordered to start with. In the worst case situation, this technique will in fact make the algorithm less efficient since the outer loop will not be short-circuited, and now the Boolean variable must be tested in addition to the other comparisons that are being made. Thus, regardless of tricks that we may introduce, we cannot claim with any certainty that bubble sort is better than an $O(n^2)$ algorithm for random data.

Big-O Analysis of Insertion Sort

Recall that the loop structure of the insertion sort is given by

```
FOR i:=2 TO n DO
  BEGIN
  j:=i;
  Done:=False;

  WHILE (j > = 2) AND NOT Done DO
    IF KeyList[j] > KeyList[j−1] THEN
       .
       . (swap)
       .
       j := j−1
    ELSE
       Done:=True
       .
       .
       .
```

Inner Loop

Outer Loop

Here, if the inner loop is never short-circuited by Done, the comparison appearing as its first statement will be executed once for the first execution of the outer loop, then twice, and so on, reaching $n - 1$ executions on the final pass. Hence we have a situation virtually identical to our preliminary analysis of the bubble sort. That is, the number of comparisons can be bounded by $n^2/2$ and the algorithm is therefore $O(n^2)$. Of course, with the insertion sort, the hope is that the setting of the Boolean variable Done in the **ELSE** clause can frequently reduce the number of comparisons made by the inner loop. However, it is clear that we can concoct many data sets for which this will have little or no effect. Hence, as with bubble sort, we are forced into concluding that insertion sort cannot guarantee better than $O(n^2)$ comparisons.

Big-O Analysis of Selection Sort

The loop structure of this algorithm was given by

```
FOR  i:= 1 TO  n−1 DO
  BEGIN
  Last:=n−i+1;
  MaxPosition:=1;
  FOR j:=2 TO Last DO
    IF KeyList[j] > KeyList[MaxPosition] THEN
          MaxPosition:=j
       .
       .
       .
```

Inner Loop

Outer Loop

A little investigation will uncover a familiar pattern to the nested loops of the selection sort. Observe that the first time the inner loop is executed, the comparison in the **IF** statement will be made $n - 1$ times. Then it will be made $n - 2$ times, $n - 3$ times, . . . , and finally just 1 time. This is precisely the way the **IF** statement in the bubble sort was executed in repeated passes. Thus, like the bubble and insertion sorts, the selection sort is an $O(n^2)$ algorithm in terms of number of comparisons. The area in which the selection sort potentially offers better efficiency is that the number of interchanges of data in array locations is guaranteed to be $O(n)$ because the swap in selection sort occurs in the outer loop. In both of the other sorts, the swap occurs in the inner loop but is subject to a conditional test. This means that, in their worst cases, both of the other algorithms require $O(n^2)$ swaps as well as $O(n^2)$ comparisons.

Despite the fact that selection sort will usually fare better in the number of data interchanges required to sort an array, it has a drawback not found in the other two. It is apparently impossible to short-circuit either of the nested loops in selection sort when it is given a list in nearly sorted order. So, for such data sets, the selection sort may be an order of magnitude worse than the other two. This is initially rather disheartening news. It seems as if it is impossible to declare any sort a decisive winner. Indeed, our big-O analyses indicate that there is little to choose from the bubble, insertion, and selection algorithms. But the fact that we were able to systematically reach such a conclusion is significant in itself. It portends of how informative the results of a big-O analysis can be. After all, even knowledge of such a negative variety can be valuable in choosing appropriate algorithms under certain circumstances. For instance, if a particular application usually involved adding a small amount of data at the end of an already sorted list and then re-sorting, we now know to avoid selection sort. Moreover, when we study more powerful sorting techniques (in Chapter 9), we will see that it is indeed possible to break the $O(n^2)$ barrier limiting each of our three methods.

_____ **2.4**

The Space/Time Trade-off: Pointer Sort

Early in our discussion of efficiency considerations, we noted that true run-time efficiency was best measured in fundamental machine operations and that one instruction in a high-level language may actually translate into many such primitive operations. To illustrate this, suppose that the data being sorted by one of our algorithms are strings, each of length-80 characters. Then, depending on your computer, it is entirely conceivable that one comparison or assignment statement in a high-level language could generate a loop with 80 repetitions of such fundamental byte-level operations—one for each of the characters that must be swapped. Those seemingly innocent portions of code which swap two strings using a temporary storage location actually lead to the movement of 240 characters inside the machine. The first question we address in this section is whether, in such a situation, we can replace this large-scale internal character transfer with the much swifter operation of swapping two integers. Although the solution we discuss will not achieve an order of magnitude speed increase in the big-O sense, it will nonetheless cut the number of actual machine-level swaps by a factor of the string length involved, a factor which could produce a noticeable improvement in the procedure's run-time.

Bubble Sort Implemented with Pointers

So far our algorithms to sort data have implicitly assumed that the data are to be physically sorted; that is, the data are to be arranged alphabetically in computer memory. Hence, the data in the first subscript of our KeyList array are the data which come first in alphabetical order, the data in the second subscript are second in order, and so on. However, if we are interested only in processing the data of KeyList in alphabetical order, is it really necessary that the data be arranged in physically alphabetical fashion in computer memory? The answer is no. It is possible to step logically through the data in alphabetical order without physically arranging it that way in memory. To do so we must use another array of pointers. These pointers keep track of the logical order of the data without requiring it to be physically moved. At the end of our sorting routine, Pointer[1] tells us the location of the data that should come first in our alphabetical listing; Pointer[2] contains the location of the data that should come second, and so on. The sorting algorithm itself uses the logic of the bubble sort to interchange pointers instead of interchanging actual data. The actual data never move, remaining precisely where they were stored upon initial input. Instead of the expensive, time-consuming swapping of strings, we are able to quickly swap integer pointers.

A Pascal procedure to implement this pointer sort technique is given at the end of this subsection. In addition to the declarations we have already been using in Chapter 2, this procedure assumes an external declaration of the form

```
TYPE
   .
   .
   .
PointerArray = ARRAY [1..MaxIndex] OF integer;
```

Besides the Keylist array, the procedure receives an array Pointer of type PointerArray. The procedure initializes the Pointer array to the state pictured in the "Before" snapshot of Figure 2.4. Then, via repeated swaps of integer pointers, the array is returned as shown in the "After" snapshot of this same figure. As the figure indicates, the KeyList array itself is never altered. Upon return from **PROCEDURE** PointerBubbleSort, a higher-level

	KeyList	Pointer		KeyList	Pointer
1	MAXWELL	1		MAXWELL	4
2	BUCKNER	2		BUCKNER	2
3	LANIER	3		LANIER	3
4	AARON	4		AARON	1

Snapshot of *Keylist* and *Pointer* immediately after initialization

Snapshot of *KeyList* and *Pointer* returned by *PointerBubbleSort*

FIGURE 2.4

"Before" and "After" snapshots of pointer sort

procedure could process its key items in alphabetical order via the loop

```
FOR i := 1 TO n DO
    Process (KeyList[Pointer[i]]);
```

Here we are assuming that this higher-level procedure would also be using the identifiers KeyList, Pointer, and n in the same sense that **PROCEDURE** PointerBubbleSort did and that an appropriate **PROCEDURE** Process exists.

```
PROCEDURE  PointerBubbleSort (n : integer;
                             KeyList : SortArray;
                             VAR Pointer : PointerArray);
VAR  i,j,Temp : integer;
BEGIN
   {Begin by initializing Pointer array}
   FOR := 1 TO n DO
       Pointer[i] := i;
   {Now begin n-1 passes}
   FOR i := 1 TO n-1 DO
       FOR j := 1 TO n-i DO
           {Compared values referenced by Pointer}
           IF KeyList[Pointer[j]] > KeyList[Pointer[j+1]] THEN
             {If necessary, swap pointers but not data.}
             BEGIN
             Temp := Pointer[j];
             Pointer[j] := Pointer[j+1];
             Pointer[j+1] := Temp p;
             END
       END; {PointerBubbleSort}
```

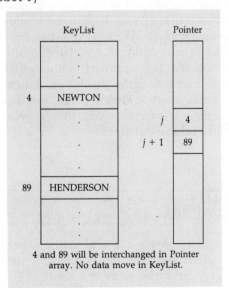

4 and 89 will be interchanged in Pointer
array. No data move in KeyList.

Efficiency Analysis Pointer Sort

We note that the pointer technique illustrated here for the bubble sort may also be used with the insertion and selection algorithms. In any of these cases, the mere introduction of the pointer strategy will not reduce the big-O categorization of the sort. However, in cases where the data items being sorted use enough internal storage to substantially slow down swapping times, the pointer sort can attain a considerable savings in run-time.

Is this run-time savings achieved without any sacrifice? A saying that has been passed down by computer people since the days of the early vacuum tube machines is "You get nothing for nothing." We have not escaped the consequences of that adage by using pointers to increase run-time efficiency. The pointers store data about data; this requires additional memory. If your application is not approaching the limits of memory, this cost may not be crucial; but in certain situations, it could be the last straw for a program that is running short of memory. Thus, the pointer sort is essentially a trade-off; by using more memory, we get a program which runs faster. This time/space trade-off is one that continually recurs in the analysis of computer algorithms. Many sophisticated techniques to increase speed will need to store substantial data about data to do so. Those algorithms that solve a problem in a fashion which both saves space and decreases run-time are indeed worthy of special praise. We will be sure to make note of them when we encounter them.

A final observation on the pointer sort strategy is that, from a data abstraction perspective as discussed in Chapter 1, the implementation of a pointer sort in Pascal is somewhat awkward. This is because, as we have written the pointer sort, the higher-level procedure which calls it must be aware that a pointer array is being used to logically order the KeyList. Without this knowledge, the calling procedure would have no way of utilizing the results of the pointer sort. That is, the calling procedure cannot be completely shielded from the details of how the sort is being accomplished. In this regard, Pascal has some distinct drawbacks as a language to facilitate information hiding as discussed in Chapter 1: the ability of a low-level procedure to hide the details of its implementation from calling procedures. One alternative which you are asked to explore in the Programming Problems is to declare the pointer array as a variable local to the pointer sort procedure. As you will see, this approach, although better from an information hiding perspective, forces the sorting procedure itself to process the data which is being sorted. Hence it has the disadvantage of incorporating other processing considerations into a procedure which should be concerned with nothing but sorting.

_____ 2.5

Simple Search Algorithms

Most software systems make extensive use of algorithms that find a particular data item in a large collection of such items. Such algorithms, typically called search algorithms, are given the value of a key field which identifies the item being sought and then return either all the data associated with that particular key or a flag indicating that it could not be found. For instance, the registrar's system at the University of Hard Knocks (from Section 1.3), which we will implement in its initial form in Chapter 3, will

require a search algorithm as a subordinate procedure to each of the Inspect, Delete, and Change operations in the ACIDS criteria.

Assuming that we use an array implementation of a list as discussed in
Chapter 1, the general setup for the search algorithms we will discuss in
this chapter is given by the following skeletal declarations:

```
CONST    MaxIndex = 100; {Easily Adjusted}
           .
           .

TYPE     KeyType = {Appropriate data type for key field in record};
         DataRec = RECORD
                       Key : KeyType;
                       OtherData : {Appropriate Type}
                   END;
         DataArray = ARRAY [1..MaxIndex] OF DataRec;
           .
           .

PROCEDURE   Search(Target:KeyType;
                   SearchList:DataArray;
                   VAR InfoWanted:DataRec;
                   VAR Found:boolean);

{Given:  A collection of records in SearchList and Target storing key value
         of record being sought.
 Return: All data associated with Target in InfoWanted and Found set to true
         or false indicating whether or not the search was successful. }
```

Figure 2.5 graphically portrays this setup. Specific search algorithms may
require some additional information for their implementation; for example,

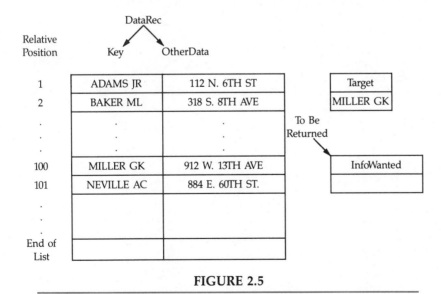

FIGURE 2.5

_____

General Setup for Search Algorithm

a particular sentinel value which marks the end of the list or knowledge of the number of entries in the list. These particulars will be treated when we discuss the individual algorithms themselves.

Sequential Search Algorithm

The task of a computer scientist working with search algorithms may be compared to that of a librarian. Just as the librarian must devise a method of storing books on shelves in a fashion that allows patrons to easily find the books they want, so must a computer scientist devise methods of organizing large collections of electronic data so that records within that data can always be quickly found. Imagine the plight of the librarian who just throws books upon shelves as they are unpacked from shipping boxes, without any consideration toward organizing the chaos. Unless the library had an artifically small collection, it would take patrons an impractical length of time to find their reading material. Because of the lack of any organizational order imposed on the books, the only search strategy available would be to pull books from the shelves in some arbitrary sequence until the desired book was found. As a programmer given a completely

© 1982 by Sidney Harris—"What's So Funny About Computers?" William Kaufmann, Inc., Los Altos, CA

"This used to take hours."

unordered set of data, this is the same strategy you would have to follow. The logic of such a sequential search strategy is extremely simple and appears in the following **PROCEDURE** SequentialSearch. This procedure assumes that the final record in the list is flagged by a special Sentinel value in its Key field.

```
PROCEDURE SequentialSearch  (Target : KeyType;
                             Sentinel : KeyType;
                             SearchList : DataArray;
                             VAR InfoWanted : DataRec;
                             VAR Found : boolean);

  {Given:   List of records in SearchList,
            Target storing key value being sought, and
            Sentinel value marking end of list.
   Task:    Sequentially pass through SearchList seeking Target.
   Return:  DataRec associated with Target in InfoWanted.
            If not found, return false in boolean variable Found.}

  VAR i : integer;
  BEGIN
     Found := false; {Initially set to false and not changed unless find
                      Target.}
     i := 1;
     WHILE (SearchList[i].Key <> Sentinel) AND NOT Found DO
     BEGIN
       IF SearchList[i].Key = Target THEN
         BEGIN
         Found := true;
         InfoWanted := SearchList[i]
         END
       ELSE
         i := i+1
     END {WHILE}
  END; {SequentialSearch}
```

Efficiency of the Sequential Search. Unfortunately, the simplicity of the sequential search is offset by its inefficiency as a search strategy. The average number of probes into the list before the target key is found will be $n/2$, where n is the number of records in the list. For unsuccessful invocations of the procedure, all n records must be checked before we can conclude failure. Thus, in terms of a big-O classification, the method is clearly $O(n)$. This may not seem bad when compared to the $O(n^2)$ efficiency of our sorting methods, but searching is conceptually a much simpler operation than sorting; so it should be significantly faster. Moreover, though $O(n)$ may seem fast enough at microsecond speeds, there are many applications where an $O(n)$ time factor can be unacceptably slow. For instance, when a compiler processes your source program in Pascal, it must continually search a list of identifiers that have been previously declared. (This list is typically called a symbol table.) Hence, in such an application, the search operation merely represents the inner loop within a much more complex outer loop that is repeating until it reaches the end of your source file: an inner loop which, repeated at $O(n)$ speeds, would make your compiler intolerably slow. Another situation in which $O(n)$ is not good enough for searching occurs when the list being searched is stored in a disk file instead of a main memory array. Now, because accessing data on disk is a much slower operation than accessing data in main memory, each probe into the list might conceivably require approximately one millisecond (one-thousandth of a second) instead of a microsecond. Searching such a list of one million records at $O(n)$ speed would hence require one thousand seconds instead of just one second; such a wait for one record is certain to generate angry users. We conclude that, although the sequential search may be fast enough for small and infrequently accessed lists stored in main memory, we need something which is better by an order of magnitude for many practical applications.

Binary Search Algorithm

By paying what may initially seem like a small price, we can dramatically increase the efficiency of our search effort using a simple technique called the binary search. The price we must pay is threefold.

1. The list of records with keys must be maintained in physically sorted order unless we are willing to use an additional list of pointers similar to that used in the PointerBubbleSort algorithm. (See the Exercises at the end of this chapter.)

A Relevant Issue . . .

Artificial Intelligence, the Complexity of Algorithms, and Parallel Processing

Perhaps no area of computer science demands as much in terms of efficient algorithms as does artificial intelligence (AI). Those engaged in research in this field are concerned with writing programs that have the computer mimic intelligent human behavior in limited domains such as natural language understanding, theorem proving, and game playing. Why is efficiency so important in such programs? Typically the strategy behind such a system is to have the computer search an enormous number of possibilities for the solution to the problem it is given. These possibilities comprise what is typically called the state space for the problem. For instance, for a computer program that plays a game like checkers or chess, the state space would be a suitable representation of all game board configurations that could eventually be generated from the current state of the game. The computer's goal in such a situation is to search through the state space, looking for a

state in which it would win the game. The state space determined by the initial configuration of a chess game has been computed to be about 10^{120} different possible moves. The time required for a computer to examine each of these different moves, assuming it could examine one every microsecond, would be 10^{95} years. Even for a simpler game such as checkers, the time required for a computer to search all states in the game would require 10^{23} years.

The reason for these extraordinarily large and impractical time frames is that a "brute force" strategy of searching all states in such AI applications leads to NP algorithms. To avoid such NP algorithms, researchers in artificial intelligence have attempted to follow the lead of human reasoning. That is, the human mind seems able to eliminate many of the possibilities in a search space without ever examining them. Similarly AI programmers attempt to weed out large sections of the state space to be

2. The number of records in the list must be maintained in a separate variable.

3. We must be able to randomly access, by relative position, records in the list.

For instance, suppose that the list of integer keys appearing in Figure 2.6 has the access facility of the third point just cited and that we wish to locate the random data associated with the Target key 1649. The strategy of the binary search is to begin the search in the middle of the list. In the case of Figure 2.6, this would mean beginning the search with the key found at position 5. Since the Target we are seeking is greater than the key found at position 5, we are able to conclude that the key we want will be found among positions 6 through 10 if it is to be found at all. We will split those positions that remain viable candidates for finding the Target by accessing position

$$(6 + 10)/2 = 8$$

Since the key at position 8 is greater than Target, we are able to conclude that the key being sought will be found in position 6 or 7 if it is to be found at all. Notice that after only two accesses into the list, our list of remaining viable candidates for a match has shrunk to 2. (Compare this figure to a sequential search after two accesses into the same list.) We now split the

searched using what are known as heuristics. Heuristics are rules of thumb which enable one to rule out a vast number of possible states by doing some relatively simple computations. For instance, in a game such as checkers or chess, a heuristic might involve a mathematical formula which attached a positive or negative weight to a particular state of the game. Those states for which the heuristic value indicates a probable lack of success in future searching are simply eliminated from the state space. Since a heuristic is the computational equivalent of an educated guess, it runs the risk of making an error. However, it is often viewed as a risk which is worthwhile if it can enhance the efficiency of the search algorithm to a category which is no longer NP.

In addition to the use of heuristics to increase algorithmic efficiency, there is another ray of hope on the horizon for those presently working in AI research and other fields where NP algorithms are often encountered. That ray of hope is parallel processing. A parallel processing computer has a network of processors which allow many operations (such as those involved in searching a state space) to be performed simultaneously; that is, in parallel. From a theoretical perspective, if a sufficient number of processors can be linked into such a parallel processing network and if the logic of a particular algorithm is such that many operations may be performed in parallel, then it is conceivable in the future that some NP algorithms may actually run in reasonable time frames. The success or failure of parallel processing computers will definitely play an instrumental role in the future of artificial intelligence and other areas of computer science in which NP algorithms are frequently encountered. If parallel processing succeeds, we may find ourselves in the exciting position of having to completely redefine what makes an algorithm practical or impractical.

Location	Key
1	1119
2	1203
3	1212
4	1519
5	1604
6	1649
7	1821
8	2312
9	2409
10	3612

Number of Records N=10
Target=1649

FIGURE 2.6

Physically ordered random access list of keys for
binary search

distance between positions 6 and 7, arriving (by integer arithmetic) at
position 6. Here we find the key being sought after a mere three probes
into the list.

Crucial to the entire binary search algorithm are two pointers, Low and
High, to the bottom and top respectively of the current list of viable candidates. We must repeatedly compute the Middle index of that portion of the
list between Low and High and compare the data at that Middle index to
the Target using the following logic:

```
IF Target < SearchList[Middle].Key   THEN
   High must be reduced to Middle-1

ELSE IF Target > SearchList[Middle].Key   THEN
   Low must be increased to Middle+1

ELSE
   Search is done
   Target has been found in SearchList
```

Should these pointers ever cross, that is, if High were to become less than
Low, we would conclude that the Target does not appear in the list. The
entire algorithm is formalized in the Pascal procedure which follows:

```
PROCEDURE  BinarySearch (Target : KeyType;
                         n : integer;
                         SearchList : DataArray;
                         VAR InfoWanted : DataRec;
                         VAR Found : boolean);

{Given:  List of records in SearchList,
         Target storing key value being sought, and
         n storing number of records in the list.
```

```
    Task:    Apply binary search algorithm.
    Return: DataRec associated with Target in InfoWanted.
            If not found, return false in boolean variable Found.)

VAR  High,Low,Middle : integer;
```

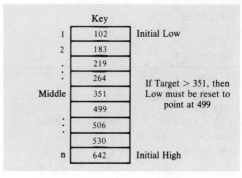

```
BEGIN
    Found := false;
    Low := 1;
    High := n;
    REPEAT
        Middle := (Low+High) DIV 2;
        IF Target < SearchList[Middle].Key THEN {Work with low end}
            High := Middle-1
        ELSE IF Target > SearchList[Middle].Key THEN {Work with high end}
            Low := Middle+1
        ELSE  {Success!} found It
            BEGIN
```

	Key	
1	102	Initial Low
2	183	
.	219	
.	264	
Middle	351	If Target > 351, then Low must be reset to point at 499
	499	
.	506	
.	530	
n	642	Initial High

```
            Found := true;
            InfoWanted := SearchList[Middle]
            END
    UNTIL Found OR (High < Low)
END; {Binary Search}
```

Efficiency of the Binary Search. The effectiveness of the binary search algorithm lies in its continual halving of the list to be searched. When applied to the list of keys in Figure 2.6, the method in the worst case would require four accesses. For an ordered list of 50,000 keys, the worst case efficiency is a mere sixteen accesses. (In case you do not believe this dramatic increase in efficiency as the list get larger, try plugging 50,000 into a handheld calculator and count how many times you must halve the displayed number to reduce it to 1.) The same list of 1,000,000 records stored on disk that would require approximately 1,000 seconds to search sequentially will result in a virtually instantaneous response for the user when the binary search strategy is employed. More formally, for a list of n items, the maximum number of times we would cut the list in half before finding the target item or declaring the search unsuccessful is

$$(\log_2 n) + 1$$

Thus, the binary search is the first $O(\log_2 n)$ algorithm we have studied. In terms of the categorizations discussed in Section 2.3, it is a logarithmic algorithm. Expressions involving a $\log_2 n$ factor will arise frequently as we analyze other algorithms and are extremely fast when compared to $O(n)$ algorithms, particularly for large values of n.

The drawback of the binary search lies not in any consideration of its processing speed but rather in a reexamination of the threefold price that must be paid for being able to use it. What appears on the surface to be a relatively small price is in fact quite steep. We must, for instance, maintain a count of the number of records in the search list. For a volatile list (that is, one undergoing frequent insertions and deletions), that consideration can be a nuisance. Much more than a mere nuisance is the need to keep the list physically ordered. As we shall see in Chapter 3, this requirement makes the binary search awkward for small lists, and, for large lists, makes the operations of adding and deleting records so inefficient that the very fast search speed is all but negated. Thus, relative to the ACIDS criteria for evaluating a list implementation strategy, we conclude that an array implementation which relies on the binary search algorithm would perform very well on the Inspect operation but very poorly on the Add and Delete operations.

Summary

In this chapter, we have studied a collection of fairly simple algorithms from which we will choose when doing our initial implementation of the registrar's system in Chapter 3. For sorting, we discussed bubble sort, insertion sort, selection sort, and pointer sort as alternatives. For searching, the sequential search and the binary search were offered as choices. One of the important points to stress regarding this chapter is that it begins to present you with those techniques which, as a computer scientist, you should have at your fingertips, available to apply when the appropriate situation arises. Much of the rest of the book will just enlarge upon the collection started here.

As choices are made from such a collection, it is important to have formal criteria upon which to base your selections. Toward that end, we introduced the big-O notation as a means of classifying algorithms with respect to their time and space efficiency. The results of our applying such a big-O analysis to the sort and search algorithms of this chapter are summarized in the following table:

Algorithm	Time Efficiency	Additional Comments
Bubble sort	$O(n^2)$ comparisons and interchanges in worst case	Can be faster if input data are already almost sorted.
Insertion sort	$O(n^2)$ comparisons and interchanges in worst case	Also can be faster if input data already almost sorted.
Selection sort	$O(n^2)$ comparisons, $O(n)$ interchanges in worst case	Not significantly faster if input data already almost sorted.
Pointer sort	Reflects number of comparison of method upon which it is layered	Though number of interchanges not reduced, amount of data swapped for each interchange is potentially less. Drawback is the additional memory required for pointers.
Sequential search	$O(n)$ probes into list in worst case	Most inefficient of search algorithms we will study, but nonetheless appropriate for small lists stored in main memory.
Binary search	$O(\log_2 n)$ probes in worst case	Drawbacks are that we must continually maintain a count of number of records in list and that the list must be maintained in physically sorted order.

Key Terms

algorithmic toolbox
artificial intelligence
best case
big-O notation
binary search
bubble sort
compiler symbol table

conformant array parameters
cubic algorithm
data about data
disk file
dominant term
exponential algorithm
graphic documentation

heuristics	pointer sort
insertion sort	polynomial algorithm
linear algorithm	proportional
logarithmic algorithm	quadratic algorithm
logically sorted	search algorithm
$\log_2 n$ search algorithm	selection sort
NP algorithm	sequential search
order of magnitude	state space
parallel processing	time/space trade-off
physically sorted	worst case
pointers	

Exercises

1. Perform a big-O analysis for those statements inside each of the following nested loop constructs:

   a.
```
FOR i := 1 TO n DO
        FOR j := 6 TO m DO

              .

              .

              .
```

   b.
```
FOR i := 1 TO n DO
         BEGIN
         j := n;
         WHILE j > 0 DO
                  BEGIN

                  .

                  .

                  .

                  j := j DIV 2
                  END
         END;
```

   c.
```
i := 1;
   REPEAT
           j := 1;
           REPEAT

                  .

                  .

                  .

                  j := 2 * j
           UNTIL j >= n;
           i := i + 1
   UNTIL i >= n;
```

2. An algorithm has an efficiency $O(n^2 \operatorname{Sin}(n))$. Is it any better than $O(n^2)$ for large integer n?

3. Suppose that each of the following expressions represents the number

of logical operations in an algorithm as a function of n, the size of the list being manipulated. For each expression, determine the dominant term and then classify the algorithm in big-O terms.

    a. $n^3 + n^2\log_2 n + n^3\log_2 n$
    b. $n + 4n^2 + 4^n$
    c. $48n^4 + 16n^2 + \log_8 n + 2^n$

4. Suppose that, initially, an array contains seven integer entries arranged in the following order:

1	43
2	40
3	18
4	24
5	39
6	60
7	12

Trace the order of the array entries after each successive pass of the bubble sort.

5. Repeat Exercise 4 for the selection sort.
6. Repeat Exercise 4 for the insertion sort.
7. Suppose that an array contains key values

$$18 \quad 40 \quad 46 \quad 50 \quad 52 \quad 58 \quad 63 \quad 70 \quad 77 \quad 90$$

in index locations 1 through 10. Trace the index values for the Low, High, and Middle pointers in the binary search algorithm if the Target 43 is being sought.

8. Devise sample data sets to demonstrate the best case and worst case behavior of each of the following algorithms: bubble sort, selection sort, insertion sort, and binary search.
9. Explain the difference between physical and logical ordering.
10. Cite an application in which the mere logical ordering of data, as achieved by the pointer sort technique, would not be sufficient; that is, an application in which physical ordering of the data is required.
11. What is the time/space trade-off?
12. What is a compiler symbol table? Explain why a sequential search applied to such a table is not a practical strategy.
13. Explain the difference in run-time efficiency considerations for a program which manipulates data in a main memory array versus one which accesses data stored in a disk file.
14. When the bubble sort was modified with an array of pointers, did it in a real sense improve its $O(n^2)$ run-time efficiency? Why or why not?
15. Suppose you have 1,000 records to be sorted. Would the run-time efficiency of the pointer sort increase significantly if the 1,000 records were broken into four groups, each group sorted and then appended together as one large sorted array as compared to sorting the initial unsegmented array? Why or why not?

16. How many times would the **REPEAT** loop in the **PROCEDURE** BinarySearch (see Section 2.5) be executed if $n = 1,000,000$?
17. Make the bubble sort more efficient by using a Boolean variable to terminate the inner loop upon making a pass through the array in which no interchanges of data are made. Can your technique also be applied to the pointer sort? If so, implement it.
18. Modify the sorting algorithms of this chapter so that they will sort records based on a key field and so that they receive an additional argument indicating whether the sort should be in ascending or descending order.
19. Incorporate the pointer sort technique into the selection sort algorithm.
20. Incorporate the pointer sort technique into the insertion sort algorithm.
21. The requirement for the binary search that the data in an array be physically ordered can actually be circumvented by keeping track of the logical order of the data via a pointer array analogous to that used in the pointer sort. Rewrite the binary search algorithm under such an assumption. Explain why it might be advantageous to use this technique.
22. Implement the following modification to the sequential search algorithm. Temporarily insert the key for which you are searching at the end of the list. Search sequentially until you find this key; then examine the position where you found it to determine whether or not the search was successful. Note that this strategy requires your knowing the number of items in the list rather than a sentinel value stored at the end of the list. Comment on the run-time efficiency of this new strategy in relation to the sequential search algorithm discussed in this chapter.

Programming Problems

1. Suppose that you know the keys in a list are arranged in increasing order. How could the sequential search algorithm presented in this chapter be improved with this knowledge? Rewrite the Pascal procedure to incorporate this improvement and then test your new procedure in a complete program.
2. Rewrite the binary search algorithm presented in this chapter with a splitting strategy other than halving. One possibility here would be to use an interpolation strategy which would examine the target's distance from the current low and high pointers. This is more analogous to the way in which we look up names in a phone book. That is, for a name which begins with an S, we do not open the phone book to the middle page but rather to a point approximately two-thirds of the way from the beginning of the book. Test run your program against a pure binary search and, through tracing the performance of each algorithm, determine whether there is any significant difference between the two techniques.

3. Repeat Problem 2, but change your algorithm so that, after the initial interpolative guess as to the location of the target, data locations are then examined sequentially in an appropriate direction until the key is found or until it can be determined that the key is not in the list.

4. Consider a list of records for students at the University of Hard Knocks which consists of fields for student name, credits taken, credits earned, and total grade points. Write a program which, based upon a user's request, will sort such a list of records in ascending or descending order keying on one of the four fields within the record. For instance, the user might specify that the sort should proceed in descending order according to credits earned. As much as possible, try to refrain from having to write a separate sort procedure for each particular ordering and field.

5. Consider the same list of records as in Problem 4. Now write a procedure which will sort the records in descending order by credits earned. Records having the same number of credits earned should be arranged in descending order by total grade points. Those which have the same number of credits earned and total grade points should be arranged alphabetically by name. Incorporate this procedure into the complete program that you wrote for Problem 4.

6. Rewrite the pointer sort with the pointer array as a local variable instead of a global variable. How would this affect a higher-level procedure which calls upon the pointer sort? Illustrate by calling it from a sample main program which you write for testing purposes.

7. Merge the segmenting strategy described in Exercise 15 with the insertion sort, bubble sort, and selection sort algorithms. Empirically test how this affects the run-time of the sort on a file of 1,000 records. Does altering the number of segments affect the run-time?

8. Implement the binary search algorithm for a disk file containing approximately 1,000 records of the structure used by registrar at the University of Hard Knocks (as discussed in Chapter 1). Refer to Chapter 1 for a description of this record structure.

Software Engineering and the System Life Cycle

We take a handful of sand from the endless landscape of awareness around us and call that handful of sand the world.

Once we have the handful of sand, the world of which we are conscious, a process of discrimination goes to work on it. This is the knife. We divide the sand into parts. This and that. Here and there. Black and white. Now and then. . . .

Classical understanding is concerned with the piles and the basis for sorting and interrelating them. Romantic understanding is directed toward the handful of sand before the sorting begins.

Robert M. Pirsig
Zen and the Art of Motorcycle Maintenance

3.1

Introductory Considerations

In Chapter 1 we discussed a philosophy of software design called software engineering. This philosophy emphasized an evolutionary progression from the building of a conceptual model of the system to the eventual implementation of that model in a programming language such as Pascal. At the heart of this progression lies the abstract data type as a means of conceptualizing the data needs of the system before considering how those needs are to be implemented.

In Chapter 2, we described some relatively simple algorithms to help understand operations on lists and illustrated how to evaluate such algorithms using big-O notation. The purpose of this description was twofold. First, as software designers, we need to be aware of the variety of algorithms available to perform a particular task such as sorting or searching. Chapter 2 began to equip us with this knowledge in a systematic, organized fashion. Second, along with an understanding of various algorithms, we must be able to evaluate and select the best of all possible algorithms for a particular application. Big-O analysis provides us with a guide for such evaluation and selection.

It is now time to apply the methods of Chapter 2 to a real-world problem and show that the software engineering approach actually works in practice. In particular, we will develop a system to meet the needs of the registrar at the University of Hard Knocks. In so doing, we will be proceeding through a series of phases that have come to be known as the software system life cycle. In developing this system, we will come to realize the inadequacies of the simple tools introduced in Chapter 2. Evaluated in terms of the ACIDS criteria for lists, they cannot provide an efficient implementation for all of our needs. In later chapters, we shall explore new tools that offer significantly better overall performance with respect to the ACIDS criteria.

_____ **3.2**

The Software System Life Cycle

The case studies discussed in this book will be introduced, as they were in Chapter 1, by a memorandum from a user who wants a computer solution of a particular problem. We have chosen to introduce case studies in this fashion to emphasize that programs are written not for computer scientists but rather for computer users—users who often may know virtually nothing about the computer other than a vague (and often inaccurate) notion that it can magically take care of all of their recordkeeping and computational needs. Bridging the gap between potentially naive users and the computer-oriented people who eventually are responsible for implementing the software system constitutes the first phase of the system life cycle.

Phase I: Analysis

Though many people are aware that systems analysts work with computers in some way, few know specifically what a systems analyst does. More than anything else, the systems analyst is responsible for the analysis phase of the system life cycle. A systems analyst talks to the users who initially request the system to learn exactly what these users need. This is done not only by talking to users, but also by studying in detail what these users do. For instance, a systems analyst working for a bank on an automated teller system would have to become an expert on the various duties and responsibilities of a teller. Having learned what the automated system is supposed to do, the systems analyst must then develop formal specifications describing the system and its requirements. The technical people who design and code the software will work from these specifications. In this sense, the systems analyst serves as a liaison and translator between the users and the implementors of the system. Depending on the size and structure of the organization, the systems analyst may or may not become involved in the design and coding of the system. Typically, such involvement will occur in smaller organizations where the analyst may wear many hats, but not in larger organizations where staff size allows a greater degree of specialization.

Since an exact assessment of the end user's needs is vital for the most satisfactory design of the system, the systems analyst must have excellent interpersonal communications skills as well as a strong computer background. It is beyond the scope of this text to present any detailed treatment of systems analysis strategies. Instead, we will continue to present specifications for programs in the form of memoranda from hypothetical users. These memoranda will serve as realistic reminders of the role of the user in the software development process. Yet, at the same time, they will be simplistic enough to allow us to avoid the massive headaches often connected with the analysis phase of a project. Instead, we will concentrate on the next phase of the software systems life cycle.

Phase II: Top-Down Design

Given specifications for the user's requirements, the next phase in the system's development is the construction of a relatively detailed design plan. This will guide future work on the implementation of the system. The key feature of such a design plan is that it must effectively divide the overall problem being addressed by the system into a collection of smaller, more manageable problems. Each of these smaller units will be handled by a separate program module in the implementation phase which follows. These modules are tested, verified, and debugged individually before being integrated into the entire system.

We can draw certain analogies between this modular structuring of a program and the boss-worker relationships that typically exist in any large corporation. Just as any effective boss must be able to delegate responsibilities, program modules which control the major logical decisions in a software system must be able to rely on lower-level modules to reliably perform subordinate tasks. A graphic tool known as a modular structure chart is often used by software designers to reflect the relationships between the modules which comprise the entire software system. An example of such a structure chart for a hypothetical three-module system is shown in Figure 3.1. An analogous chart for the more complex registrar's system will be developed in Section 3.3.

What does such a structure chart tell us about the system's design? It briefly expresses what ultimately will become calling protocol between procedures when the system is finally implemented. For instance, the modular structure chart of Figure 3.1 tells us that BOSS-MODULE must call on WORKER1-MODULE for one subordinate task and WORKER2-MODULE for another. The chart says nothing about the logical sequencing or repetition of these calls. Rather, we are merely informed that, for BOSS-MODULE to do its job, it relies upon WORKER1 and WORKER2. Of

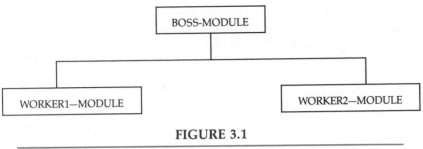

FIGURE 3.1

Module structure chart for three-module system

course, in a system larger than this three-module example, the boss may supervise many more than two workers. Moreover, the workers just below the top-level boss may in fact be mini-bosses themselves, with subordinate workers who are responsible to them instead of to the top-level boss.

What distinguishes a good modular structure from a poor one? To answer this question we may again draw some apt comparisons between software structuring and corporate boss-worker relationships. First, we note that such a structure should be developed in a top-down fashion. The overriding principle of top-down design is that we make decisions about the responsibilities of top-level bosses before deciding what the lower-level workers are to do. If such decisions are made in a way which progresses downward on a level-by-level basis in the structure chart, we find that boss modules truly will control the major logic of a program, just as corporate bosses should be in control of the most important aspects of their corporate policy. To proceed in an opposite (bottom-up) fashion is to court organizational disaster. That is, if we decide what worker modules are to do before considering the responsibilities of boss modules, we frequently run into situations in which a boss module is forced into some very clumsy program logic. If proceeding bottom-up, we are not able to see the full range of subordinate tasks which a boss may require. The end result is that the boss itself will have to take care of minor details: a situation comparable to a corporate executive's having to momentarily leave his or her desk to go out on the assembly line and fasten a bolt that everyone else had forgotten. Such distraction can only result in the boss's doing a poorer job in more important areas of responsibility.

A second criterion to be used in judging the modular structure of a system is the degree to which individual modules are functionally cohesive. That is, each module should focus on achieving one particular predefined task without having unexpected side effects on the performance of other modules in the same system. For instance, a module responsible for formatting an output line in a report should not also be updating a field within a customer's record. This could potentially cause great confusion for the module whose assigned task was to guarantee updating of the entire customer record. Thus, as a system designer, you must insure that your breakdown of the system into its component modules follows the natural lines of decomposition. Acquiring a feel for what such natural lines are is one of the talents which the case studies presented in this book will help you to develop.

Having generated a suitable modular structure for the system, the designer must then describe the general data structures to be manipulated by the system and the logic to be followed by each module. The former can be done by a combination of written and graphic means. The latter is best achieved by using structured English to specify a module's logic. The use of these techniques will be illustrated as we design the registrar's system in the next section.

In summary, the design phase of the systems life cycle includes developing specifications for

- ☐ The modular structure of the program.

- ☐ The layout of major data structures to be used by the program.

- ☐ The logic needed by individual modules.

The system designer thus produces a set of documents which are then used by programmers who will begin the actual coding of the system in an appropriate computer language. As we shall see, an effective design will not only facilitate this coding effort but will also lead to a rather natural way of testing and verifying the correctness of the software that is written.

Phase III: Coding

In this phase, you must churn out the Pascal (or other appropriate language) necessary to put into effect the blueprint which emerged from the design phase. Although the terminology "churn out" may seem a bit degrading considering the amount of effort which must go into the writing of a program, we use it to stress the importance of the design phase. Given an appropriate set of formal specifications from the design phase, coding the programs really can be an easy task. The completeness of the design phase is the key to determining how easy coding is. Time spent in the design phase will be more than repaid by time gained in the coding phase. This point cannot be overemphasized. The most common mistake made by most beginning programmers is jumping almost immediately into the coding phase, thereby digging themselves into holes which could have been avoided by a more thorough consideration of design issues.

A side issue of the coding phase is documentation; that is, the insertion of explanatory remarks into your program so that it makes sense when read by someone else (or by yourself at some time in the distant future). Let us be honest and admit that very few computer scientists like to write documentation. However, that does not eliminate the absolute necessity of writing it. In the real world, programs are worked on by teams of programmers, not just one individual. In such an environment, you must explain what your code is doing to the other people who will have to work with it. Minimally, each module you write should include documentation stating its general purpose, identifying all parameters and major local variables, and clarifying any obscure code segments. We will be following these conventions in all of the Pascal code that appears in this text.

Phase IV: Testing and Debugging

Another common mistake made by beginning programmers is to assume the correctness of their program after one or two successful test runs. Though you should feel confident that your software will be error-free if it has been carefully designed, even such well-designed systems must be thoroughly tested and verified before being released to users. This testing and verification phase is critical. As an example, consider the following statistics, which summarize the percentages of total project time devoted to testing in several computerized systems developed for Air Force space missions.

SAGE	47%
NAVAL TACTICAL DATA SYSTEM	50%
GEMINI	47%
SATURN V	49%

(See R. W. Jensen and C. C. Tonies, *Software Engineering* (Englewood Cliffs, N.J.: Prentice-Hall, 1979), 330.) The general rule of thumb that emerges from these statistics is that the testing phase of a large project can (and should) consume roughly half of the time scheduled for the project. Of course, assignments in a programming course may not be of the same magnitude as an Air Force space mission, but the message is clear. If you fail to schedule a considerable amount of time to verify the correctness of your program, your users (or instructor) will inevitably find bugs in it.

How exactly does one verify the correctness of a large program? One way is to construct formal mathematical proofs of your algorithm's correctness. Though progress is being made in applying this type of formal mathematical approach (see Chapter 11, Section 11.4), the complex problems of most real-world systems do not allow this method to be used efficiently. Consequently, the most-often employed method of verifying a program's correctness is to test it thoroughly.

If testing is important enough to take 50 percent of your time, it must clearly require more than a haphazard approach. Hence, we counsel against strategies such as creating your test data "on the fly" or creating test data by random techniques. Testing must be planned to be convincing. The plan that we shall briefly describe here is called modular testing. Modular testing is the natural outgrowth of the principles of modular design which we have discussed earlier in this section.

The key to modular testing is to test each individual module as it is developed. Do not wait until the entire system has been coded to begin your testing. Thus, testing on the modular level involves

1. Developing short driver procedures which artificially call the modules you have written.

2. Developing short stub routines which (again artificially) report the values computed by the routine being tested.

A Relevant Issue . . .

Software Reliability and Defense Systems

The issue of software testing takes on great importance as we begin increasingly to rely on the computer as an aid in the decision-making process. Consider, for instance, the area of defense systems. In *Computer Power and Human Reason*, Joseph Weizenbaum cites the following portion of a planning paper from the director of a major university's computer laboratory:

> The Department of Defense, as well as other agencies of our government, is engaged in the development and operation of complex systems that have a very great destructive potential and that, increasingly, are com-

manded and controlled through digital computers. These systems are responsible, in large part, for the maintenance of what peace and stability there is in the world, and at the same time they are capable of unleashing destruction of a scale that is almost impossible for man to comprehend. (Joseph Weizenbaum, *Computer Power and Human Reason* (San Francisco: W. H. Freeman, 1976), 241.)

Such systems are somewhat unique in that (we hope) many of them will never actually be used. If they ever are used, it may be too late to engage in the repair of minor flaws that normally

3. Designing test cases which exercise all the logical possibilities the module may encounter. Be aware that such test cases consist of more than just strategically chosen input data. Each set of input data must also include its expected result (sometimes called the test oracle) if it is truly to convince anyone of the module's correctness.

It is in the area of designing test cases that the programmers begin to mix methods of science and art. Every mathematician knows that we can never actually prove anything by testing examples (that is, input data). So, how can we verify a module's correctness by merely concocting examples? One proposed answer is to classify input data according to possible testing conditions. Hence, a finite set of well-chosen equivalence classes of test cases can be sufficient to cover an infinite number of possible inputs. Deciding what such equivalence classes should be is the point at which the process becomes more of an art than a science.

To illustrate these principles with a simple example, suppose that we are working on a module called ParkingFee which is to compute a parking fee for vehicles based on the following rules:

> The module is given two data items: a character which may be 'C' or 'T' indicating whether the vehicle is a car or truck and an integer indicating the number of hours the vehicle spent in the parking lot. Cars are charged $1.00 for each of the first three hours they are in the lot and $0.50 for each hour after that. Trucks are charged $2.00 for each of the first four hours they are in the lot and $0.75 per hour thereafter.

After computing the appropriate charge, the module ParkingFee is to call on a module PrettyPrintTicket which appropriately formats a parking fee

arise in the maintenance phase of the systems life cycle. It is not an understatement to say that the future of the human race may be riding on the thoroughness with which the systems have been tested. Is there any testing strategy that can be convincing enough under these circumstances?

At least one prominent computer scientist, David Lorge Parnas, is very pessimistic in his answer to the preceding question. In June of 1985, Parnas resigned from the Panel of Computing in Support of Battle Management, convened by the Strategic Defense Initiative (SDI) Organization. Among the reasons he cited for his resignation were the following:

> The military software that we depend on everyday is not likely to be correct. The methods that are in use in the industry today are not adequate for building large real-time software systems that must be reliable when first used. . . . It is inconceivable to me that one could provide a convincing proof of correctness of even a small portion of the SDI software. (David Lorge Parnas, "Software Aspects of Strategic Defense Systems." *Communications of the ACM* 28, no. 12 (December 1985): 1326–1335.)

ticket showing the vehicle type, hours parked, and resulting fee. A Pascal candidate for the ParkingFee module follows:

```
PROCEDURE ParkingFee (Category : CHAR;
                      Hours : integer);

   {Given:   Vehicle type in Category and time spent in lot in Hours.
    Compute: Charge for parking and call on PrettyPrintTicket to output
             ticket.}

VAR Charge : real;

BEGIN
  CASE Category OF
    'C': IF Hours <= 3 THEN
            Charge := Hours
         ELSE
            Charge := 3 + (Hours-3) * 0.5;
    'T': IF Hours <= 4 THEN
            Charge := Hours * 2
         ELSE
            Charge := 8 + (Hours-4) * 0.75

  END;
  PrettyPrintTicket (Category, Hours, Charge)
END; {Parking Fee}
```

An appropriate driver main program would simply allow us to repeatedly send data to the ParkingFee module to check its behavior in a variety of situations. An appropriate stub for the call to PrettyPrintTicket would merely inform us that we reached this subordinate module and print the values received so that we could be sure they had been transmitted correctly. At this stage, the stub need not actually concern itself with detailed, formatted output because we are at the moment interested only in testing ParkingFee.

In testing this module, we can minimally identify the following six equivalence classes:

1. A car in the lot less than three hours.

2. A car in the lot exactly three hours.

3. A car in the lot more than three hours.

4. A truck in the lot less than four hours.

5. A truck in the lot exactly four hours.

6. A truck in the lot more than four hours.

Choosing one test case for each equivalence class, we arrive at the following set of test cases:

Category	Hours	Expected Results
'C'	2	Charge = 2.00
'C'	3	Charge = 3.00
'C'	5	Charge = 4.00
'T'	3	Charge = 6.00
'T'	4	Charge = 8.00
'T'	8	Charge = 11.00

The test cases for exactly three hours in the case of a car and exactly four hours in the case of a truck are particularly important since they represent boundary conditions at which a carelessly constructed conditional check could easily produce a wrong result.

This parking lot example, though illustrative of the method we wish to employ, is artificially simple. For a more complex testing situation, consider developing a strategy to test the sorting algorithms we discussed in Chapter 2. Recall that each of these algorithms—bubble sort, insertion sort, and selection sort—received an array of physical size MaxIndex and an integer n to indicate the logical size of the array; that is, the number of items currently stored in the array. Our criterion for choosing equivalence classes of test data for such a sorting algorithm is based on two factors:

1. The size of n: the number of items to be sorted.

2. The ordering of the original data.

The following table presents a partitioning of test data into equivalence classes for this example:

SIZE OF n	ORDER OF ORIGINAL DATA	EXPECTED RESULTS
$n = 1$	Not applicable	Array to be
$n = 2$	Ascending	arranged in
$n = 2$	Descending	ascending
n midsize and even	Descending	order for
n midsize and even	Ascending	all cases
n midsize and even	Randomized	
n midsize and odd	Ascending	
n midsize and odd	Descending	
n midsize and odd	Randomized	
n = physical array size	Ascending	
n = physical array size	Descending	
n = physical array size	Randomized	

Hence the module should be run for a minimum of 12 cases, one for each of the classes dictated by our table. Ideally, a few subcases should be run for each of the randomized cases. We cannot overemphasize the importance of testing seemingly trivial cases such as $n = 1$ and $n = 2$. These lower boundary conditions are typical examples of data which may cause an otherwise perfectly functioning loop to be incorrectly skipped. Similarly, it is important to test the upper boundary condition in which n reaches the physical array size.

Yet another issue in modular testing is the question of how a module will react when it receives invalid data. For instance, in our current version of the ParkingFee module, there is a potentially disastrous side effect that occurs when the module receives a vehicle type other than 'C' or 'T'. (What is it?) A robust module is one that guards against harmful side effects when it receives invalid data. It is probably safe to say that no module of reasonable complexity can be guaranteed to be 100 percent robust. For each safeguard against invalid data which is installed in the module, a user will no doubt find some way of inadvertently bypassing that safeguard in the future. How robust an individual module must be is a reflection of how it fits into the overall modular structure of the system. It is not reasonable to expect every module in a system to guard itself against every potential kind of invalid data. Such a strategy would have the vast majority of modules more preoccupied with this issue than with their assigned responsibility within the system. A better strategy is to have a few modules whose only responsibility is to screen incoming data against invalid values. In this way we can assure that other modules will be called only when we have valid data to give them. The degree to which an individual module should be robust is thus intimately tied to the overall system design and should be stated as part of the specifications for that module.

The main goal of all testing we have discussed is to find errors. Though at first glance this statement may seem counterproductive, we note that it is better for errors to be detected at the testing stage than when the software product is actually in use (or when your instructor is assigning a grade). Given this negative premise of testing, you must also know how to debug your programs when testing achieves its goal of finding errors. If testing can be categorized as an art, debugging could facetiously be described as bordering on black magic. However, you should be reminded of some general guidelines which apply to the debugging of all programs:

1. Typing is no substitute for thinking. Don't be too quick to make changes in your source program. Instead, when an error occurs, take your test cases and trace them by hand through the logic currently present in your module. Here the advantage of modular testing becomes apparent. Such hand tracing is nearly impossible if you are dealing with an entire system; with merely one module it is quite manageable.

2. Make use of various debugging tools which are provided with most compilers. These tools allow you to interactively halt the execution of your program at selected instructions and then examine the contents of crucial variables. This ability to trace a program's execution in an on-line fashion is much more convenient than the process of adding **write** statements for debugging purposes, then recompiling your program, and finally removing the added **write** statements once the program is working correctly. The time you spend in learning how to use such debugging aids will be repaid many times over.

3. Don't assume that, once you've repaired your program for the test case which generated the error, all previous test cases will still work correctly. You now have a new program, and all of your carefully designed test cases need to be applied again.

4. Of course, leave time to debug. This avoids "Band-Aid" patches and encourages alternatives which may actually improve the design of your program. There is nothing wrong with completely scrapping an approach which testing has proved to be ill-conceived. Indeed, to try to make such an approach work by installing repeated and intricate fixes can only lead to a system which is doomed to a very short life.

Phase V: Program Maintenance

Once your program has been thoroughly tested, it is ready to be released to the users who originally requested it. In theory, you are done; these users will live happily every after using the program which you so painstakingly developed. In practice, unfortunately, it rarely works out this way. Instead, users begin to find flaws with your program. (After all, nobody is perfect!) These flaws typically are due to such factors as

☐ Your misunderstanding the users' exact needs during the analysis phase.

☐ Your system's slow performance when it encounters large volumes of user data.

☐ User needs which have changed since you initially did your analysis.

☐ Changes in computer hardware and operating system software.

When such flaws arise, you must maintain your system. That is, you must make the necessary changes to correct the flaws. Here is where good program design and documentation pay off again. It is absolutely essential that you (or someone else assigned to maintenance) be able to understand your code after months or perhaps years away from it. Moreover, if your modules are functionally cohesive, then you should be able to make the appropriate changes in them without causing problems in other modules of the system. That a program must be maintained is not an indication of poor design; it is rather a fact of the software life cycle. That a program can be easily maintained is actually an indication that it was soundly designed from its conception.

Dynamic Nature of the Software Life Cycle

Let us recap the five phases of the system life cycle: analysis, design, coding, testing, and maintenance. Though we have discussed each as a separate entity, we must stress that they are all interwoven into a dynamic, iterative process. The process is dynamic because the dividing lines between the phases are always changing. That is, as you are performing analysis, you are probably already beginning to consider many design and coding issues. The process is iterative in that, from one phase, you may frequently have to return to an earlier phase. For instance, though you may be designing your system, if a question arises about what the user wants, you will have to temporarily return to analysis before completing the design. Similarly, during coding, you may find it necessary to alter certain design considerations. The fact that many people—users, analysts, designers, and programmers—are usually involved in the system life cycle also contributes to the volatile nature of systems development.

Perhaps one of the worst misconceptions about those of us who work in the computer field is that we deal with problems that have very rigid, well-defined solutions. We hope our discussion of the system life cycle has convinced you that nothing could be further from the truth. To truly contribute over the span of the entire life cycle, you must be skilled at communicating with people, thinking abstractly, and then following through on the details of a plan. We hope at this point you find yourself thinking that the effective computer scientist must truly be a person for all seasons. With this perspective in mind, let us turn our attention toward developing a complete solution for the problem cited in our earlier memorandum (Section 1.3) from the registrar at the University of Hard Knocks.

_____ **3.3**

An Initial Implementation of the Registrar's System

Our discussion of the system life cycle in the previous section would indicate that our first step in responding to the registrar's memo from Chapter 1 would be to conduct a thorough analysis of the system being requested. One way of specifying the results of such an analysis is to graphically portray the way in which information flows through the registrar's office.

This is done in Figure 3.2, using a tool known to systems analysts as a data flow diagram. Though we will not be explaining all the intricacies of using data flow diagrams, their utility in graphically summarizing the results of an analysis should be evident. The circles (or "bubbles" as analysts often call them) represent processes which transform data as they move through the system. Hence the process PrintGradeReport in Figure 3.2 will transform a student academic record into an appropriately formatted report card

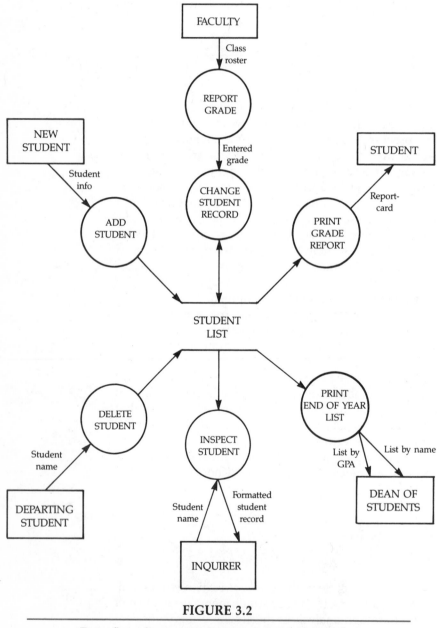

FIGURE 3.2

Data flow diagram indicating information to be
processed in registrar's system

for each student. Similarly, the process ChangeStudent will transform newly reported grades for a student into an appropriately updated student record in the StudentList. (For a more detailed discussion of data flow diagrams, see *Structured Analysis* by Victor Weinberg (New York: Yourdon Press, 1980).)

Designing the System

The data flow diagram of Figure 3.2 is typical of the specification that would be passed from the analysis phase to the design phase in the development of a software system. The processes in the diagram suggest to us, as designers, the modular structure chart of Figure 3.3 as a guide for dividing the registrar's system into smaller modules.

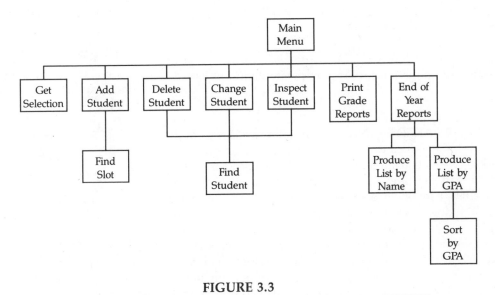

FIGURE 3.3

Modular structure chart for registrar's system

Recall from our discussion of the system life cycle that, in addition to the modular structure chart, a layout of the pertinent data structures and logical specifications for each module should also be produced during the design phase. Let us first turn our attention to the only major data structure involved in the registrar's system: the list of student records. In this particular implementation of the system, we will use an array implementation of the list. We will maintain the array in physical order using student name as a key, hence allowing a binary search of the list when we wish to inspect a student by name. The price we will pay for being able to employ the binary search algorithm in the InspectStudent module will be a potentially excessive amount of data movement in the AddStudent and DeleteStudent modules. To see why this excessive data movement will occur, consider the add situation pictured in Figure 3.4.

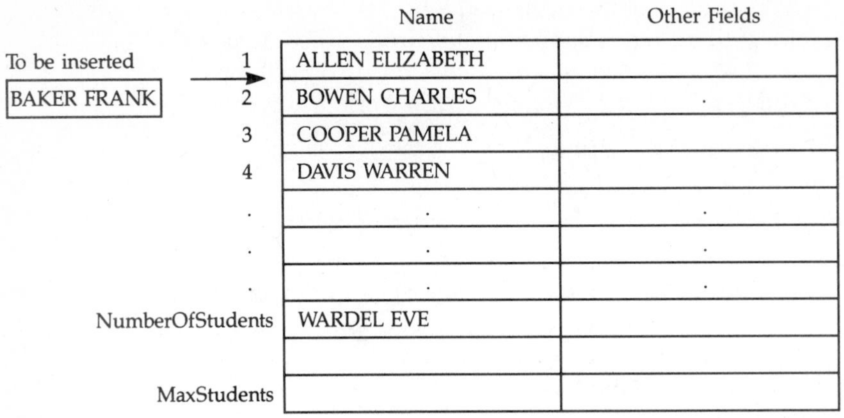

		Name	Other Fields
To be inserted	1	ALLEN ELIZABETH	
BAKER FRANK	2	BOWEN CHARLES	.
	3	COOPER PAMELA	
	4	DAVIS WARREN	
.		.	.
.			
.		.	.
NumberOfStudents		WARDEL EVE	
MaxStudents			

NumberOfStudents=current number of students
MaxStudents=maximum students possible

FIGURE 3.4

Possible add situation for array implementation of list

Here the addition of BAKER FRANK will force all records beginning at the second subscript to be moved down one slot. In a realistic situation where the school may have 10,000 students, each with a record consisting of 500 bytes, this will mean shuffling 5,000,000 bytes of data around in computer storage. If the storage involved is a magnetic disk instead of primary memory, this "pushing down" of all records starting with the second one could well leave the system in a loop that would require several minutes to execute. An analogous problem occurs when a record near the top of the list is deleted. All the records below it must rise one slot to maintain the list in physical order. Thus, the implementation we are proposing here will not fare particularly well with respect to all of the ACIDS criteria. Nonetheless, in this chapter, we will live with these add/delete inefficiencies so that we may illustrate an actual implementation with the techniques we presently know. As more powerful methods are developed later in the text, we shall consider implementation strategies which are able to circumvent these problems and provide better overall ACIDS performance.

Given this implementation decision for the list of student records, it remains for the design phase to produce a set of logical specifications for each module. In rough terms, for each module in the structure chart of Figure 3.3, we must specify the data it will receive as input, the information it returns as output, and the logical steps that transform the input to the output. These logical steps will be specified in what can best be described as structured English. This structured English has very few rules. We firmly believe that introducing a large number of formal rules for module specifications merely results in the design phase getting bogged down in the details of a quasi-programming language. We feel it is more appropriate in the design phase to tackle actual issues and leave formal language considerations to the coding phase. Hence, our structured English style of module specification is perhaps best described by actually doing it for the registrar's system.

Module Specifications for the Registrar's System

The specifications for this system follow:

```
MainMenu Module
   Data Received: None
   Information Returned: None
   Logic:
     Perform necessary initializations.
     Repeatedly call on GetSelection to obtain user choice of
       operation and dispatch to appropriate subordinate module.
```
Module 1

```
GetSelection Module
   Data Received: None
   Information Returned: User choice of operation in form of
     character
   Logic:
     Print menu of possible operations.
     Read user choice from terminal.
```
Module 2

```
AddStudent Module
   Data Received: List of students
                  Number of students
   Information Returned: Transformed list with appropriate addition
                         Updated number of students

   Logic:
     Obtain data for new student.
     Call on FindSlot module to find array location to insert
       student.
     Roll down all entries in array below this location.
     Insert new student at vacated location.
     Update total number of students.
```
Module 3

```
FindSlot Module
   Data Received: List of students
                  Number of students
                  Name of student to add
   Information Returned: Array location to insert student
   Logic:
     Repeatedly examine array location beginning with first
       until we encounter a student whose name alphabetically
       follows that of new student.
```
Module 4

```
DeleteStudent Module
   Data Received: List of students
                  Number of students
   Information Returned: Transformed list with appropriate deletion
                         Updated number of students

   Logic:
     Obtain name of student to be deleted.
     Call on FindStudent module to get the array location of
       this student.
```
Module 5

Provided that the student was found in the array, move
all students following the one to be deleted up one
slot in the array, hence destroying data for deleted
student.
Update total number of students.

ChangeStudent Module
  Data Received: List of students
                 Number of students
  Information Returned: Transformed list with appropriate record
  changed
  Logic:
    Obtain name of student whose record is to be altered.
    Call on FindStudent module to get array location of
      this student.
    Provided that the student was found in the list, determine
      field to be changed and assign the appropriate new value
      to that field in the located record.

> *Module 6*

InspectStudent Module
  Data Received: List of students
                 Number of students
  Information Returned: None
  Logic:
    Obtain name of student to inspect.
    Call on FindStudent module to return that student's
      complete record.
    Provided the student was found, display the record in an
      appropriate format.

> *Module 7*

FindStudent Module
  Data Received: List of students
                 Number of students
                 Target name
  Information Returned: Record containing data associated with
                         target name
                       Array location of that record
                       Boolean flag indicating whether record found
  Logic:
    Binary search algorithm.

> *Module 8*

PrintGradeReports Module
  Data Received: List of students
                 Number of students
  Information Returned: None
  Logic:
    For each student, access record in list and print out
      appropriately formatted report card including grade
      point average.

> *Module 9*

EndOfYearReports Module
  Data Received: List of students
                 Number of students
  Information Returned: None
  Logic:
    Print appropriate headings for report in alphabetical order by
      name.

> *Module 10*

```
        Call on PrintListByName module to print detail lines in
            appropriate order.
        Print appropriate headings for report in order by GPA.
        Call on PrintListByGPA module to print detail lines in
            appropriate order.
```

```
PrintListByName Module
    Data Received: List of students
                   Number of students
    Information Returned: None
    Logic:
        Proceed through list in the physical order in which it has been
            maintained, printing out each student's record in appropriate
            format.
```
Module 11

```
PrintListByGPA Module
    Data Received: List of students
                   Number of students
    Information Returned: None
    Logic:
        Call on SortByGPA to establish pointers which will lead
            through list in descending GPA order.
        Use these pointers to proceed through list in logical order,
            printing each record in appropriate format.
```
Module 12

```
SortByGPA Module
    Data Received: List of students
                   Number of students
    Information Returned: Array of pointers to lead through list
                          in descending GPA order
    Logic:
        Pointer bubble sort algorithm.
```
Module 13

You should notice that we are already taking advantage of the collection of algorithms that we began to develop in Chapter 2. That is, for our FindStudent and SortByGPA modules, we have just cited the binary search and pointer bubble sort algorithms respectively, knowing that their coding is now a relatively trivial matter. Indeed, the most interesting questions are not ones of how to code an algorithm but rather design issues such as how to implement the list, whether to use a binary or sequential search, whether to use a pointer sort technique or an actual physical sort, and so on. These are the issues upon which computer scientists continually reflect.

Coding the Registrar's System

The modular structure chart, data structure layout, and modular logic specifications that we have just formulated are typical of what project designers would pass on to a programming team and say "Go to it." Obviously, for a more realistic and complicated system, the preparation of those design documents can be a very lengthy process. But it does pay off in time saved during coding and in the number of bugs which are later detected. The coding which follows for the registrar's system is a straightforward reflection of the careful design plans that have been laid out. The in-line and graphic documentation which are included in the listing should make evident how closely the code is tied to the design specifications. As an additional indication of how the Pascal code flows from the module specifications, we have matched each Pascal procedure/function with reference to its specifications as a module. Finally, we have included sample runs for a few of the menu options so that you get a feel for the functioning of the system once all the pieces have been tied together. However, these sample runs should by no means be considered complete in terms of testing the system. We will discuss a testing strategy for this system in our first "Designer's Workbench" section, later in this chapter.

```pascal
Program RegistrarSystem(input, output);

  { Array implementation of registrar's system at University of Hard Knocks.
    Allows all ACIDS operations, including grade reports and end of year
    reports sorted by name and end of year reports sorted by grade point
    average. }

  CONST
    StringLength = 40;   {Maximum name size}
    MaxStudents = 800;   {Maximum number of students}
    CredToGrad = 120;    {Credits to graduate}

  TYPE
    String = PACKED ARRAY [1..StringLength] OF char;
    StudentRec =
      RECORD
        Name : String;
        CredTaken : integer;
        CredEarned : integer;
        TotalGradePts : integer
      END;
    StudentList = ARRAY [1..MaxStudents] OF StudentRec;

  VAR
    Choice : char;   {User's choice of menu option}
    NumberOfStudents : integer; {Current enrollment}
    Students : StudentList;  {Array implementation of list}

PROCEDURE GetSelection(VAR Choice : char);

  {Print selection menu and return user's response to it in Choice.}

  BEGIN
    writeln;
    writeln('A)dd Student');
    writeln('C)hange Student Record');
    writeln('I)nspect Student Record');
    writeln('D)elete Student Record');
    writeln('G)rade Reports');
    writeln('E)nd of Year Reports');
    writeln('Q)uit');
    write('Choose by entering first letter of selection-->');
    readln(Choice)
  END;  {GetSelection}
```

See Module 2

```
PROCEDURE AddStudent(VAR Students : StudentList;
                     VAR NumberOfStudents : integer);

  {Receives list of students in Students and current number of
   students in NumberOfStudents. Then prompts user for student to
   add, finds appropriate slot for that student, and returns
   Students and NumberOfStudents in updated form.}

  VAR
    NewStudent : StudentRec;
    i, LocationOfAdd : integer;
```

⎫ *See*
⎬ *Module 3*
⎭

```
  PROCEDURE FindSlot(VAR Students : StudentList;
                     NumberOfStudents : integer;
                     NewName : String;
                     VAR LocationOfAdd : integer);

  {Receives student list in Students, current number of students
   in NumberOfStudents, name of student to add in NewName.  Students
   is sequentially searched for slot to locate NewName.  This index
   is then returned in LocationOfAdd.}

  VAR Found : boolean;

    BEGIN
      LocationOfAdd := 1;
      Found := false;
      WHILE (LocationOfAdd <= NumberOfStudents) AND NOT Found DO
        IF Students[LocationOfAdd].Name > NewName THEN
          Found := true
        ELSE
          LocationOfAdd := LocationOfAdd + 1
      END; {FindSlot}
```

⎫ *See*
⎬ *Module 4*
⎭

```
  BEGIN {AddStudent}
    WITH NewStudent DO
      BEGIN
      write('Enter new student name-->');
      Readln(Name);
      write('Enter credits taken, earned, and total grade
        points-->');
      readln(CredTaken, CredEarned, TotalGradePts);
      {Find slot where new student belongs.}
      FindSlot(Students, NumberOfStudents, Name, LocationOfAdd)
      END;
    {From that slot on, move down rest of records.}
    FOR i := NumberOfStudents DOWNTO LocationOfAdd DO
      Students[i + 1] := Students[i];
    NumberOfStudents := NumberOfStudents + 1;
    Students[LocationOfAdd] := NewStudent
  END;   {AddStudent}
```

⎫ *See*
⎬ *Module 3*
⎭

Roll each record
down one slot,
starting at
bottom

```
PROCEDURE FindStudent(Target : String;
                      NumberOfStudents : integer;
                      Students : StudentList;
                      VAR InfoWanted : StudentRec;
                      VAR Mid : integer;
                      VAR Found : boolean);

  {Receives list of student records in Students, current number
   of students in NumberOfStudents, name to search for in Target.
   Binary search algorithm used to find Target.  If search
   successful, Found returned as true; otherwise returned as false.
   If Target is found, associated record returned in InfoWanted and
   associated position returned in Mid.}

  VAR
    High, Low : integer;


  BEGIN
    Found := false;
    Low := 1;
    High := NumberOfStudents;
    REPEAT
      Mid := (Low + High) DIV 2;
      IF Target < Students[Mid].Name THEN
        High := Mid − 1
      ELSE IF Target > Student[Mid].Name THEN
        Low := Mid + 1
      ELSE
        BEGIN
        Found := true;
        InfoWanted := Students[Mid]
        END
    UNTIL Found OR (High < Low)
  END; {FindStudent}




PROCEDURE DeleteStudent (VAR Students : StudentList;
                         VAR NumberOfStudents : integer);

  {Receives list of student records in Students and current number
   of students in NumberOfStudents.  Prompts user for name of
   student to delete.  Searches for the record to be deleted.  If
   found, removes it and updates NumberOfStudents.  Otherwise,
   error message printed.}

  VAR
    DeleteName : String;
    i, LocationOfDelete : integer;
    Found : boolean;
    DeleteRec : StudentRec;


  BEGIN
    write('Student to delete-->');
    readln(DeleteName);
```

*See
Module 8*

*See
Module 5*

```
    {Call on binary search to locate student.}
    FindStudent(DeleteName, NumberOfStudents, Students, DeleteRec,
              LocationOfDelete, Found);
    IF NOT Found THEN
      writeln('Error in delete.')
    ELSE
      BEGIN
      {Move up all records below delete location.}
      FOR i := LocationOfDelete TO NumberOfStudents - 1 DO
        Students[i] := Students[i + 1];
      NumberOfStudents := NumberOfStudents - 1
      END
  END;   {DeleteStudent}
```

Now Available
Move all these records up one slot, starting at LocationOfDelete

```
PROCEDURE ChangeStudent (VAR Students : StudentList;
                         NumberOfStudents : integer);

  {Receives list of student records in Students
   and current number of students in
   NumberOfStudents. Prompts user for change
   desired.  If change requested is appropriate,
   updated Students is returned.  Otherwise,
   error message is printed.}

  VAR
    ChangeName : String;
    ChangeField : integer;
    Found : boolean;
    ChangeRec : StudentRec;
    ChangeLoc : integer;

  BEGIN
    writeln('Enter name of student to change-->');
    readln(ChangeName);
    {Call on binary search to find record wanted.}
    FindStudent(ChangeName, NumberOfStudents, Students, ChangeRec,
                ChangeLoc, Found);
    IF NOT Found THEN
      writeln(ChangeName, ' not found.')
    ELSE
      BEGIN
      write('Field to change--> 1-Taken,2-Earned,3-Points');
      readln(ChangeField);
      {Obtain new value for appropriate field}
      WITH Students[ChangeLoc] DO
        case ChangeField OF
          1:
            BEGIN
            write('New value for credits taken-->');
            readln(CredTaken)
            END;
```

See Module 6

```
      2:
        BEGIN
        write('New value for credits earned-->');
        readln(CredEarned)
        END;
      3:
        BEGIN
        write('New value for total grade points-->');
        readln(TotalGradePts)
        END
    END    {CASE}
  END
END;   {ChangeStudent}


PROCEDURE InspectStudent(Students : StudentList;
                         NumberOfStudents : integer);

  {Receives list of student records in Students and current number
   of students in NumberOfStudents.  Prompts user for name to
   inspect and calls on binary search to locate that record.}

  VAR
    InspectName : String;
    InspectLoc : integer;
    InspectRec : StudentRec;
    Found : boolean;


  BEGIN
    write('Name of student to inspect-->');
    readln(InspectName);
    {Call on binary search to obtain desired record.}
    FindStudent(InspectName, NumberOfStudents, Students,
                InspectRec, InspectLoc, Found);
    IF NOT Found THEN
      writeln(InspectName, ' not found.')
    ELSE
      WITH InspectRec DO
        writeln(Name, CredTaken, CredEarned, TotalGradePts)
  END;   {InspectStudent}


PROCEDURE PrintGradeReports(Students : StudentList;
                            NumberOfStudents : integer);

  {Receives list of student records in Students and current number
   of Students in NumberOfStudents.  Proceeds sequentially through
   list, computing and printing report card for each student.}

  VAR
    i : integer;
    gpa : real;

  BEGIN
    FOR i := 1 TO NumberOfStudents DO
      WITH Students[i] DO
```

See
Module 7

See
Module 9

```
        BEGIN
        gpa := TotalGradePts / CredTaken;
        writeln('Student .', Name);
        writeln('Taken ', CredTaken);
        writeln('Earned ', CredEarned);
        writeln('GPA', gpa: 6: 2);
        writeln
        END
  END;   {PrintGradeReports}
```

```
PROCEDURE EndOfYearReports (Students : StudentList;
                            NumberOfStudents : integer);


  {Receives list of student records in Students and current
   number of students in NumberOfStudents.  Oversees printing
   of end of year reports for graduating seniors.}
```

See Module 10

```
  PROCEDURE PrintListByName(Students : StudentList;
                            NumberOfStudents : integer);

    {Receives list of student records in Students and current
     number of students in NumberOfStudents.  Sequentially prints
     detail lines in alphabetical order by name, which is also
     the physical order of the list.}

    VAR
      i : integer;

    BEGIN
      FOR i := 1 TO NumberOfStudents DO
        WITH Students[i] DO
          IF CredEarned >= CredToGrad THEN
            writeln(Name: 40, CredTaken: 10, CredEarned: 10,
                    TotalGradePts: 10)
    END;   {PrintListByName}
```

See Module 11

```
  PROCEDURE PrintListByGpa(Students : StudentList;
                           NumberOfStudents : integer);

    {Receives list of student records in Students and current number
     of students in NumberOfStudents.  Establishes GPA order in
     Pointer array. Then prints detail lines in this GPA order.}

    TYPE
      PointerArray = ARRAY [1..MaxStudents] OF integer;

    VAR
      i : integer;
      gpa : real;
      Pointer : PointerArray;
```

See Module 12

```
PROCEDURE SortByGpa(Students : StudentList;
                    VAR Pointer : PointerArray;
                    NumberOfStudents : integer);

  {Receives list of student records in Students and current
   number of students in NumberOfStudents.  Returns in Pointer
   the logical ordering of students by descending GPA.}

  VAR
    i, j, Temp : integer;


  BEGIN
    FOR i := 1 TO NumberOfStudents DO
      Pointer[i] := i;
    FOR i := 1 TO NumberOfStudents - 1 DO
      FOR j := 1 TO NumberOfStudents - i DO
        {Sort algorithm keys on grade point average.}
        IF Students[Pointer[j]].TotalGradePts /
           Students[Pointer[j]].CredTaken <
           Students[Pointer[j + 1]].TotalGradePts /
           Students[Pointer[j + 1]].CredTaken THEN
          BEGIN
          Temp := Pointer[j];
          Pointer[j] := Pointer[j + 1];
          Pointer[j + 1] := Temp
          END
    END;   {SortByGpa}
```

*See
Module 13*

```
BEGIN   {PrintListByGpa}
  SortByGpa(Students, Pointer, NumberOfStudents);
  FOR i := 1 TO NumberOfStudents DO
    WITH Students[Pointer[i]] DO
      IF CredEarned >= CredToGrad THEN
        BEGIN
        gpa := TotalGradePts / CredTaken;
        writeln(Name: 40, CredTaken: 10, CredEarned: 10, gpa:
          7: 2)
        END
  END;   {PrintListByGpa}
```

*See
Module 12*

```
BEGIN   {EndOfYearReports}
  writeln('                    REPORT BY NAME                  ');
  writeln('NAME': 40, 'TAKEN': 10, 'EARNED': 10, 'POINTS': 10);
  PrintListByName(Students, NumberOfStudents);
  writeln;
  writeln('                    REPORT BY GPA                   ');
  writeln('NAME': 40, 'TAKEN': 10, 'EARNED': 10, 'GPA': 10);
  PrintListByGpa(Students, NumberOfStudents);
END;   {EndOfYearReports}
```

*See
Module 10*

```
BEGIN   {Main}
  writeln('Welcome to registrar's system at University of Hard
          Knocks');
  NumberOfStudents := 0;
  REPEAT
    GetSelection(Choice);
    CASE Choice OF
      'A':
        AddStudent(Students, NumberOfStudents);
      'C':
        ChangeStudent(Students, NumberOfStudents);
      'I':
        InspectStudent(Students, NumberOfStudents);
      'D':
        DeleteStudent(Students, NumberOfStudents);
      'G':
        PrintGradeReports(Students, NumberOfStudents);
      'E':
        EndOfYearReports(Students, NumberOfStudents)
      END
  UNTIL Choice = 'Q'   {Q is quit option.}
END.
```

*See
Module 1*

Sample Run.

```
Welcome to registrar's system at University of Hard Knocks

A)dd Student
C)hange Student Record
I)nspect Student Record
D)elete Student Record
G)rade Reports
E)nd of Year Reports
Q)uit
Choose by entering first letter of selection-->A
Enter new student name-->SMART LES
Enter credits taken, earned, and total grade points-->80 60 120

A)dd Student
C)hange Student Record
I)nspect Student Record
D)elete Student Record
G)rade Reports
E)nd of Year Reports
Q)uit
Choose by entering first letter of selection-->A
Enter new student name-->WOOD HOLLY
Enter credits taken, earned, and total grade points-->123 120 357

A)dd Student
C)hange Student Record
I)nspect Student Record
D)elete Student Record
G)rade Reports
```

```
E)nd of Year Reports
Q)uit
Choose by entering first letter of selection-->A
Enter new student name-->AVREG JOE
Enter credits taken, earned, and total grade points-->96 93 208


A)dd Student
C)hange Student Record
I)nspect Student Record
D)elete Student Record
G)rade Reports
E)nd of Year Reports
Q)uit
Choose by entering first letter of selection-->A
Enter new student name-->CLEAR BEA
Enter credits taken, earned, and total grade points-->120 120 436


A)dd Student
C)hange Student Record
I)nspect Student Record
D)elete Student Record
G)rade Reports
E)nd of Year Reports
Q)uit
Choose by entering first letter of selection-->G
Student AVREG JOE
Taken          96
Earned         93
GPA    2.17


Student CLEAR BEA
Taken          120
Earned         120
GPA    3.63


Student SMART LES
Taken          80
Earned         60
GPA    1.50


Student WOOD HOLLY
Taken          123
Earned         120
GPA    2.90


A)dd Student
C)hange Student Record
I)nspect Student Record
D)elete Student Record
G)rade Reports
E)nd of Year Reports
Q)uit
```

```
Choose by entering first letter of selection-->E
            REPORT BY NAME
                          NAME    TAKEN    EARNED    POINTS
CLEAR BEA                          120      120       436
WOOD HOLLY                         123      120       357


            REPORT BY GPA
                          NAME    TAKEN    EARNED     GPA
CLEAR BEA                          120      120      3.63
WOOD HOLLY                         123      120      2.90


A)dd Student
C)hange Student Record
I)nspect Student Record
D)elete Student Record
G)rade Reports
E)nd of Year Reports
Q)uit
Choose by entering first letter of selection-->Q
```

We should point out one weakness of this coding for the registrar's system which is inherent in the way Pascal forces you to declare constants and types. In Chapter 1, we spoke of data abstraction: for example, a list as an abstract data type as opposed to an array implementation of a list. We also commented that implementation considerations for an abstract data type in a particular application should be deferred so that we may think in abstract terms as long as possible. Ideally this separation of the abstract data type from its implementation should be reflected in your modular coding. That is, only those modules that actually manipulate the implementation should be aware of how the implementation is done. For instance, in our current example of the registrar's system, the main menu module has no real concern about how the list is to be implemented. Rather its only concern is that it be able to call lower-level modules to perform appropriate operations on the list. The lower-level modules are then the ones that deal with the details of implementation. However, although the main module has no concern with how the list is implemented from a design perspective, in our Pascal coding we are forced to globally declare the implementation via an array. Hence, in Pascal coding, the implementation details cannot be hidden from modules that should be using the list strictly as an abstract data type.

Some newer languages, such as Modula-2 and Ada, are beginning to address this problem by allowing programmers to write code in separate packages which facilitate the hiding of implementation-related declarations from higher-level modules that are correctly concerned only with the abstract data type. However, you should also realize that, although Pascal may not offer such information hiding tools, this in no way detracts from the value of approaching data types abstractly during the design phase of a software system. Indeed, it is during this phase that abstraction is most important, offering the flexibility that allows you to conveniently weigh and evaluate many alternatives. Nonetheless, more modern languages that offer this ability to separate abstraction from implementation in their coding do offer certain practical advantages. This is particularly true when you are forced into making changes in implementation strategies after coding for a different strategy has been completed. The next section will offer some evidence of the complexities of making these types of changes in Pascal.

_____ 3.4

Maintenance Considerations for the Registrar's System

When our current version of the registrar's system is released to users, several flaws may well be detected. As we have indicated, part of the maintenance phase of the system life cycle is being able to gracefully handle such problems when they arise. The first flaw is the lack of permanency of the student list and is quite serious if the system is ever to be of truly practical use. In the present version of the program, with the student list implemented via an array in main memory, the data in the list will be lost upon selecting the Quit menu option. Hence the program would have to be continuously running to be useful in any practical sense.

The second potential flaw concerns the fashion in which we have chosen to implement strings of characters: in particular, those strings representing student names. Our present implementation for strings is known as the fixed length method and involves merely declaring a **PACKED ARRAY OF char** of length sufficient to store what we foresee as the longest possible string; that is, name. Currently, this maximum possible string length is established as 40 by a global constant declaration for StringLength. Though the fixed length method is very easy to implement, it leads to two potential problems. First, what about the student with the

"Sure you can become a systems analyst if you want to—but tell Daddy, what is a systems analyst?"

exceptionally long name which extends over 40 characters? The fixed length method simply cannot accommodate such a name. We would be forced into an abbreviation that would fit into the 40-character space and thereby run the risk of offending that student. Second, since most student names will be considerably shorter than 40 characters, the fixed length method will waste a sizable amount of memory, storing unnecessary blanks which Pascal typically uses to pad that portion of the array between the logical end of the character string and the physical end of the array. An illustration of this memory waste follows:

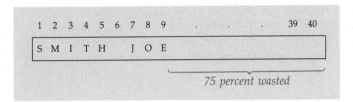

In the remainder of this section, we will consider alternative implementations for the student list and character strings which will address the issues of permanency and wasted space which we have cited here. In the Programming Problems at the end of the chapter, you will be asked to incorporate these changes into the registrar's system as part of the maintenance phase of the system's life cycle.

Implementation of a List as a Random Access File

Your previous study of Pascal should have introduced you to the notion of a Pascal file variable. (If this is not the case, consult Appendix C for a more detailed treatment of file processing in various versions of Pascal.) For instance, the declaration

```
TYPE
  .
  .
  .
  StudentList = FILE OF StudentRec;
  .
  .
  .
VAR
  .
  .
  .
  NextStudent : StudentRec;
  Students : StudentList;
```

will allow you to process records in the disk file Students via Pascal's up-arrow notation, Students^, which accesses the contents of the file's buffer. Essentially, the buffer for the file Students is an area in main memory capable of storing precisely one record from the file (which may have arbitrarily many records stored on a permanent basis). The standard Pascal statement

```
NextStudent := Students^;
```

will assign the contents of the buffer to the record variable NextStudent.
Similarly

```
Students^ := NextStudent;
```

will copy the contents of NextStudent into the buffer. The standard Pascal
statement **put**(Students) will transfer the contents of the buffer to the currently accessed record in the file Students, whereas **get**(Students) will
move data in the opposite direction, that is, from the currently accessed
file record to the buffer. These Pascal file concepts are highlighted in
Figure 3.5.

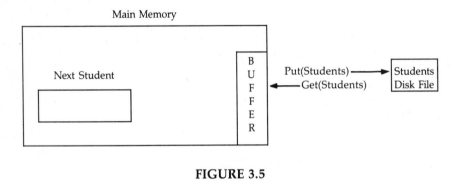

FIGURE 3.5

File operations in standard Pascal

The typical loop to process every record in an already existing Students
file is

```
reset (Students);
WHILE NOT eof (Students) DO
  BEGIN
  NextStudent := Students^;
  ProcessRecord(NextStudent);   {Assume procedure exists}
  get (Students)
  END;
```

Note that **reset** fetches the first record into the buffer; hence the **get** appears at the end of the loop. To create a file, the following loop is used:

```
rewrite(Students);
CreateRecord (NextStudent); {Assume procedure exists}
WHILE  (NextStudent to be added to file)  DO
  BEGIN
  Students^ := NextStudent;
  put(Students);
  CreateRecord(NextStudent)
  END;
```

As a side note, you should know that in standard Pascal, **get** and **put** are used for files which are not of type **text,** and **read** and **write** apply only to files of type **text.** In practice, most Pascal implementations allow **read** and **write** to access non-**text** files also. In such implementations, the single statement

```
read(Students,NextStudent);
```

is equivalent to the two statements

```
NextStudent := Students^;
get(Students);
```

Similarly, the single statement

```
write(Students,NextStudent);
```

is equivalent to

```
Students^ := NextStudent;
put (Students);
```

The popular Turbo dialect of Pascal has gone so far as to only support **read** and **write** in this fashion, hence eliminating the standard **get** and **put** from its repertoire.

The problem with the Pascal file processing statements which we have reviewed is that they only do sequential file processing; that is, processing in which the records in a file are accessed in the order first record, second record, third record, and so on. Hence, to access the 40th record, you would have to previously access the first 39 records. This type of processing is simply not suitable if we are to use a permanent disk file to implement a list. List operations and algorithms such as the binary search require that we be able to randomly access any record by specifying its relative position in the list.

Although random file processing is not part of standard Pascal, it is so essential to file processing algorithms that most Pascal compilers include nonstandard extensions which allow you to perform direct access file operations. For instance, using the Turbo Pascal compiler, the statements

```
seek(Students,i);
read(Students,NewStudent);
```

will directly fetch the ith file record into the record variable NewStudent, with the first file record referenced by $i = 0$. Similarly, the statements

```
seek(Students,i);
write(Students,NewStudent);
```

will directly send the contents of the record variable NewStudent to the ith record position in the file Students. If you are not using Turbo Pascal, you should consult your local system documentation to find out what nonstandard statements will perform similar random access file operations for your compiler. (Appendix C provides a summary of such statements for many popular Pascal compilers.) The point here is that, as long as your version of Pascal supports random file access, our array implementation of a list can be easily converted to a random access file implementation. For instance, again using Turbo Pascal for illustration purposes, the array-based statement

```
Students[i] := NewStudent;
```

would become

```
seek(Students,i);
write(Students,NewStudent);
```

in a file-based implementation. You will be asked to convert the registrar's system to such a random access file implementation in the Programming Problems at the end of the chapter.

The practical importance of file-oriented implementations of abstract data types versus array implementations cannot be overstated. The permanent nature of data stored in files makes such implementations essential in many data processing applications. Files have the additional advantage of being almost limitless in size while arrays are bounded by the restraints of main memory. Of course, what we already have learned about the trade-off often faced by computer scientists should warn you that these advantages do not come without paying a price. With random access files, that price is slower access. Whereas array entries can be accessed at microsecond speeds, random file access is at millisecond speed—slower by a factor of 1,000. This will become a crucial factor as we discuss more powerful search algorithms in later chapters.

Despite the importance of random access files, the case studies we present in this text will typically be written using arrays. There are two main reasons for our doing this. First, the code for arrays tends to be cleaner, usually involving fewer statements to get the same conceptual operation done. Second, the system-dependent aspect of random access file processing in Pascal would tend to make such presentations less worthwhile for those of you who are using different versions of Pascal than we are. However, given what we have already said about the conceptual similarities between arrays and random access files, conversion from the former to the latter should always be a relatively easy matter.

A Different Implementation for Strings: The Workspace-Index Method

The second maintenance consideration we cited was that of a string storage technique that would be both more memory-efficient and less restraining in terms of maximum string length than the fixed length method. The implementation method we propose here is known as the workspace-index method. We shall look at another possible implementation for strings in the next chapter on linked lists.

The idea behind the workspace-index method is that one large memory workspace is allocated to storing all strings. Additionally, an index table of records with two fields for each string is maintained. One field in the record for a string contains the address in the workspace at which that particular string starts, and the other contains the length of each string. This principle is illustrated in Figure 3.6.

Suppose now that we were to add a third string to the collection in Figure 3.6. All that we need to know is where the free portion of the workspace begins (in this case it begins at location 10). We place the string starting at that location, add appropriate entries to our index table, and adjust the pointer to the beginning of the free memory. This threefold process is illustrated in Figure 3.7 for the addition of the string 'CREAM'.

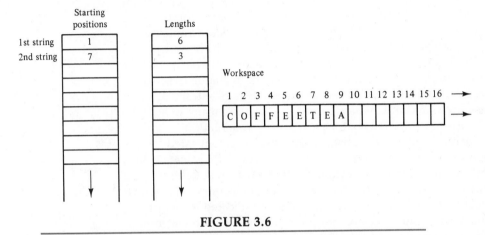

FIGURE 3.6

The workspace-index method of handling strings

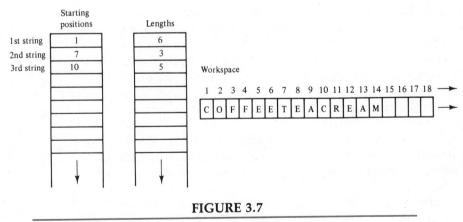

FIGURE 3.7

Addition of the string 'CREAM' to Figure 3.6

The storage advantages of the workspace-index method should be evident. By associating two indexing integers with each string, we are trading off the storage required for two integers against the potentially large number of wasted blanks which pad strings in the fixed length method. Moreover, the only restraint on maximum string length is the amount of storage left in the workspace. In the Programming Problems at the end of the chapter, you will be asked to explore the workspace-index method as an implementation technique for the requirements of the registrar's system.

The Sparse Table Problem Revisited

The discussion of various techniques in the previous section has again brought into focus the abstraction-to-implementation progression underlying all well-designed systems. Let us now consider a possible implementation strategy for the sparse table problem associated with the pilot/flight data base for Wing-and-a-Prayer Airlines, originally presented in a Chapter 1 (Section 1.6) memorandum from the vice president in charge of scheduling flights for this world-renowned airline. As with the registrar's system, the algorithms presented in Chapter 2 now give us the means to actually begin evaluating some alternatives for such an implementation.

Recall from Table 1.2 that the abstract data structure suggested by this memo was an extremely large two-dimensional array of Boolean values with rows indexed by pilot identification number, columns by flight number, and a **true** Boolean value associated with those table entries for which a pilot was qualified to fly a particular flight. As we indicated in Chapter 1, this conceptual table is much too consumptive of memory for most compilers to implement in the usual row-major form. Hence, to succeed in solving this problem, we need to devise an alternate implementation for such a sparse table. In particular, we are seeking an implementation which will conserve memory by not actually storing the high percentage of **false** entries that appear in the conceptual table. One possibility along these lines is simply to store a list of ordered pairs of integers: the first entry in the pair being a pilot number and the second being a flight number. One of those pairs is on the list for each **true** entry in the conceptual table. Conversely, a **false** entry in the conceptual table does not get a (pilot, flight) pair on the ordered list. Hence, a probe into the ith row and the jth column of the conceptual table returns **true** if an appropriate search algorithm can find the pair (i, j) on the list implementation of the table and **false** otherwise. What have we gained? For each **true** value in the conceptual table, we now must store two integers, so there is actually a loss in this regard. However, for the much higher percentage of **false** values, we now store absolutely nothing on the list.

The exercises and problems at the end of this chapter will have you explore this suggested implementation for a sparse table. In designing a system based on this implementation, you will discover certain run-time inefficiencies which have been exchanged for the memory saved by not storing **false** values, inefficiencies which can be at least partially overcome by using the linked list data structure that will be introduced in the next chapter.

DESIGNER'S WORKBENCH

Testing the Registrar's System

The software engineering principles we have introduced in this chapter will permeate the rest of the text. To emphasize the importance of these underlying principles, each chapter will include a "Designer's Workbench" section. In these sections, we will explore in depth how the software engineering principles presented in Unit I relate to the particular topic of that chapter.

This chapter's Designer's Workbench focuses on the testing phase of the software system life cycle. Our presentation of the registrar's system in Section 3.3 did not include the testing which must inevitably accompany a system's development. To put such a system into use without thoroughly testing each module is asking for disaster. Recall from our discussion of testing in Section 3.2 that this testing may occur on two separate fronts.

1. Does the module perform its task correctly for all data which represent valid input to the module?

2. How does the module react when it receives invalid data? Is it robust in the sense that it handles such data gracefully without having harmful side effects?

We will thoroughly develop test cases for the FindStudent procedure of the registrar's system; in the following exercises, it will be up to you to design similar test cases for the other modules. Recall that the FindStudent procedure receives three data items: Target, NumberOfStudents, and Students. It returns three data items: InfoWanted, Mid, and Found. For the sake of holding our presentation to a reasonable length, we will assume that the maximum number of student records allowed in the array (as determined by the **CONST** MaxStudents) is 10 instead of 800. The table on the following page presents our test data for FindStudent.

The complexities of program testing should be more apparent than ever. To convincingly verify a module as simple as FindStudent has required a fair amount of test data. But the situation is not hopeless. By keeping the tasks performed by our modules small and focused, we can make the design of test data an organized and systematic phase of the system's life cycle. We will again explore the role of testing in system development in the "Designer's Workbench" sections of Chapters 7 and 10.

Designer's Workbench Exercises

1. Consider the robustness check in test case VII on the following page. How will the FindStudent module of the present registrar's system react to this test case? Correct the problem so that the expected result occurs.
2. Carry out the modular testing phase for the registrar's system. That is, design equivalence classes of test cases for each module in the system.

	NumberOfStudents	Students	Target	Expected Results	Rationale
Test case I	10	ALLEN BAKER DAVIS GREEN HUFF MILLER NOLAN PAYTON SMITH TAYLOR	Try each name in the Students list	Found **true**. InfoWanted contains associated record Mid contains associated position.	Can we find everything in the full list?
Test case II	10	Same as test case I	Try AARON, NATHAN, ZEBRA	*Found* **false**.	Is Found correctly returned as **false** for Target data items which precede all list elements, follow all list elements, and are interspersed in the middle of the list? This case tests the full list
Test case III	5	ALLEN DAVIS HUFF NOLAN SMITH	Same as test case I	Same as test case I	Can we find everything in a mid-sized list?
Test case IV	5	Same as test case III	Same as test case II	Same as test case II	Same as test case II but for mid-sized list.
Test case V	1	HUFF	HUFF	Same as test case I	Can we handle successful search in a one-element list?
Test case VI	1	HUFF	Same as test case II	Sams as test case II	Can we handle unsuccessful searches in a one-element list?
Test case VII	0		HUFF	Same as test case II	Robustness check. What if we call on FindStudent with the empty list?

Provide a rationale for your choice of classes along with the expected results (test oracle) for each individual test case.

3. Include in your test data for AddStudent a robustness check that will make the present version of the module fail. Then alter the module to correct this problem.

4. Include in your test data for DeleteStudent a robustness check that will make the present version of the module fail. Then alter the module to correct this problem.

5. Include in your test data for PrintGradeReports a robustness check that will make the present version of the module fail. Then alter the module to correct this problem. ■

Summary

In this chapter we have attempted to give you a real-world perspective on software development by presenting an overview of the system life cycle. This life cycle consists of five phases: analysis, design, coding, testing, and maintenance. Though this text will concentrate most heavily on design and Pascal coding techniques, the relationship of what we do to the other three phases should not be ignored. To demonstrate the system life cycle in practice, we have discussed a complete design and the resulting code for an implementation of the registrar's system introduced in Chapter 1. We also pointed out several possible modifications that could be made in our implementation: use of the workspace-index technique to conserve string storage and use of system-dependent random file commands to store the list on a permanent basis. Perhaps the major flaw of the system as implemented in this chapter is the run-time inefficiency caused by excessive data movement in the add and delete operations for the list. This data movement problem, as well as a more effective implementation for a sparse table, will be addressed in the next chapter on linked lists.

Key Terms

Ada
analysis
boundary conditions
coding phase
data flow diagram
documentation
driver module
equivalence classes
file buffer
fixed length method
functionally cohesive
maintenance
Modula-2
modular specification
modular structure chart
modular testing

packages
Pascal file variable
permanency of data
random access file
robust
sequential access file
software system life cycle
strings
structured English
stub module
systems analyst
test cases
testing phase
test oracle
top-down design
workspace-index method

Exercises

1. You have just coded the binary search algorithm. Design appropriate test cases along with a driver and/or stub module to test your coding.
2. Discuss the advantages and disadvantages of an array implementation of a list vis-à-vis an implementation using a random access file.
3. Discuss the advantages and disadvantages of the fixed length implementation for strings as opposed to the workspace-index implementation.
4. What are the boundary conditions for an algorithm?
5. Discuss the inefficiencies involved with the sparse table implementation suggested in the final section of this chapter. For what type of queries would this implementation provide an efficient response? An inefficient response? Why?
6. How would the sparse table implementation scheme described in Section 3.5 have to be adjusted to accommodate non-Boolean data?
7. How would the use of the sequential search algorithm in the registrar's system enhance add/delete efficiency? What would you be sacrificing in doing this?
8. Summarize what is involved in the five phases of the system life cycle.
9. What is meant by the term *functionally cohesive* in reference to modular structure charts?
10. The workspace-index string storage technique described in this chapter requires a list of starting positions and string lengths for each string stored in the workspace and a free space pointer indicating where a new string may be stored. Trace the contents of the list of starting positions and string lengths and the free space pointer as the following strings are added to the workspace:

    YANKEES
    BREWERS
    INDIANS
    ORIOLES
    TIGERS
    BLUEJAYS
    ANGELS

11. Suppose that the total available workspace for the strings of Exercise 10 was 50 characters. Suppose also that it was no longer necessary to store YANKEES and TIGERS (we were done processing them) but that we now wanted to store the string 'PHILLIES'. Is there space available to store this string? Justify your answer. Show what the contents of the workspace, the list of starting positions and lengths, and the free space pointer would be after the string 'PHILLIES' was stored.
12. What is a robust module? Should every module in a system be completely robust? Why or why not?
13. Consider the ParkingFee procedure discussed in Section 3.2. Is it robust? What does it do if it does not receive a 'C' or 'T' for its Category parameter? Rewrite this module to make it more robust.

Exercises 14–18 relate to the implementation of the registrar's system developed in Section 3.3

14. Evaluate the list implementation according to the ACIDS criteria established in Chapter 1. Express this evaluation in terms of a big-O representation of the time efficiency for each operation on the list.
15. Modify the FindSlot procedure so that it employs logic similar to that of the binary search.
16. Make the registrar's system more robust by modifying the GetSelection module to insure that it returns only a valid value in its parameter Choice.
17. What will happen in the ChangeStudent module if the user enters a value other than 1, 2, or 3 for the local variable ChangeField? Modify this procedure to make it robust.
18. Modify the ChangeStudent module to allow students to change names. (After all, students have been known to fall in love, get married, *and* change their names.)

Programming Problems

1. Employees at the University of Hard Knocks are paid by the following rules. Those employees who sign a contract for a total annual wage are paid 1/52 of that amount each week. Hourly employees, on the other hand, receive paychecks based on the number of hours they work in a given week and their hourly rate. They are paid this hourly rate for each of the first 40 hours they work. After 40 hours, they are paid time-and-a-half for each additional hour of work. Moreover, work on holidays is a special case for hourly employees. They get paid double time for all holiday work.

   Write a procedure to compute the pay for an employee of the University of Hard Knocks and then dispatch the appropriate information to a check printing module. Completely test the procedure you write by integrating it with appropriate driver and stub modules and by designing a complete set of test data for the module.
2. Maintain the registrar's system by implementing its string storage via the workspace-index method.
3. Maintain the registrar's system by implementing the general list of student records with a random access file.
4. Design and code a solution for Wing-and-a-Prayer's pilot/flight data base problem (Section 1.6) using the sparse table implementation described in the final section of this chapter.
5. In Programming Problem 2 of Chapter 1 you were asked to provide a definition of a set as an abstract data type. Now consider the following implementation strategy for a set. Each possible element of the set corresponds to an index for a Boolean array. That array index is set to **true** if the element is actually a member of the set and **false** if it is not a member. Let us assume that Pascal did not provide a set type for you. Carry out this implementation for all of the set operations you specified in your answer to Programming Problem 2 of Chapter 1.

6. Define a string as an abstract data type. Be complete in your definition. Include the three necessary components of an abstract data type definition: descriptions of the individual elements, their relationship to each other, and the operations to be performed on them. As a guide to developing this definition, consider the operations a text editor provides for its users.

7. Once you have defined the string abstract data type in Programming Problem 6, implement each of the string operations as a separate program module using the workspace-index technique described in this chapter.

8. Use the modules you developed for Programming Problem 7 to develop a full-fledged text-editing system.

Unit II

The Tools:
Data Structures

4

Linked Lists

A chain is only as strong as its weakest link.

Proverb

Introductory Considerations

In the last chapter we discovered that an array implementation (with binary search) of a general list requires $O(n)$ data record shifts to process the add and delete components of the ACIDS criteria. Attempting to maintain such an array-implemented list in order leads to a situation which parallels the dynamics of waiting in a long line. When someone cuts into the middle of the line, there is a domino-like effect that forces everyone behind that person to move back. When someone in the middle of the line decides to leave the line, the reverse effect occurs; everyone behind the departed person is able to move ahead one slot. It is possible to draw an analogy between people waiting in a line and data items stored next to each other in computer memory. If the data items are arranged in some type of order and it becomes necessary to insert into or delete from the middle of the line, a considerable amount of data movement is involved. This data movement requires computer time and decreases program efficiency. The central motivation behind the linked list data structure is to eliminate the data movement associated with insertions into and deletions from the middle of the list. Of course, by now we might suspect that efficiency in eliminating such data movement can only come by trading off other efficiency factors. One of the crucial questions to ask yourself as we study linked lists is "What price are we paying to handle additions and deletions effectively?"

One way of conceptually picturing a linked list is to think of a game which some parents use to make the opening of holiday gifts particularly exciting for their children. One feature of the game which helps to build children's anticipation is that it insures that minor gifts are opened first, gradually building up to the most substantial gift. (Recall from your own childhood experience the partial letdown that occurred when you opened a gift package containing a mere pair of socks after having already unwrapped something significantly more exciting such as a baseball glove or new doll.) Thus, the premises of this gift-giving game are that gifts may be ranked according to their desirability and that the game is more fun when the most desirable gifts are opened last.

To achieve this end, parents will hide their child's wrapped gifts at various locations throughout the home. For instance, let us suppose a scenario in which parents have the following four gifts for their child, ranked and hidden as indicated.

Ranking	Gift	Hiding Place
Least desirable	Pair of socks	Under bed
↓	Box of candy	Kitchen drawer
	Video game	Basement cabinet
Most desirable	Bicycle	Garage

The parents will then tell the child *only* the location of the least desirable gift; here, for instance, they would give instructions to look under a bed for the first gift. Upon opening that gift, the child will find the uninspiring pair of socks *plus* a more intriguing note with the information that the child's next gift will be in a kitchen drawer. The pattern should now be obvious. From the box of candy, the child follows an informational pointer to a basement cabinet, where the video game is discovered along with a similar informational link to the garage as a location where something bigger and better may be found. Here the now-eager child will uncover a bike along with a final (and no doubt disappointing) note indicating that the end of the chain of gifts has been reached.

A conceptual picture of this chain of gifts is presented in Figure 4.1. Interestingly, this same conceptual picture applies to the linked list abstract data structure we are about to study. In this figure, the arrows connecting packages represent the informational note in each package which tells us the location of the next package. Conceptually, the form taken by this informational pointer is not important. However, it is crucial that we have a reliable pointer to the leading gift (often called a head pointer) and, thereafter, a reliable pointer in each package (often called a node) to the

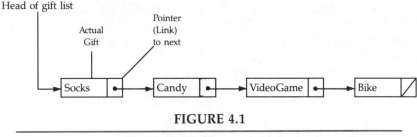

FIGURE 4.1

Conceptual picture of gift list

next package. Should any pointer be flawed, the remaining gifts on the chain become essentially inaccessible (much to the dismay of the child who wanted that bike so desperately).

In addition to introducing us to much of the vernacular that comes with linked lists, this review of a simple childhood game can also give us a hint of the ease with which such a linked chain of nodes can handle additions and deletions. For instance, suppose that a sudden windfall allows the parents of the child in our example to buy a baseball glove in addition to the four gifts they had already purchased. Assuming that this new gift is ranked between the video game and the bicycle in desirability, consider what must be done to link it into the gift chain. We must

1. Find a place to hide it; for example, the attic.

2. Take the informational linking note from the video game package and put it in the baseball glove package. (Why?)

3. Insert a new informational pointer in the video game package, indicating the attic as the location of the next node. (Why?)

The important aspect to note in this series of moves is that no gift which was already in place had to be moved to accommodate adding the new gift. From a conceptual perspective, this is why linked lists will be able to avoid the movement of data that was associated with an insertion into an array-implemented list.

Along the same lines, let us now suppose that our shameless parents devour all of their child's candy before the holiday arrives. Clearly they must remove this package from the chain to hide this disgusting behavior from their child. Convince yourself that the following steps will accomplish this deletion:

1. Remove the now-empty candy package from the kitchen drawer.

2. Before throwing away the empty package, remove the linking note from it and put this note in the package containing the socks.

3. Dispose of the incriminating candy container and the linking note that originally was in the package with the socks.

It is important to note again that no package remaining on the chain had to be physically moved to a new location: a situation much different from what happened when we removed a name from an array-implemented list in the last chapter.

Have we strayed too far from computer science in using such a non-technical, elementary example to introduce our chapter on linked lists? Not at all! In fact, we've achieved two very important goals. First, we note that if you understand all the details of the gift-giving game, then you essentially understand the important concepts involved in the linked list data structure. Second, this is just another illustration of the fact that computer techniques are often just formalizations in a logic machine of the way we, as human beings, have been doing things for many years. Consequently, you should never feel intimidated by such a computer technique; merely try to relate it to an analogous manual method with which you have been familiar for a long time. Doing this will help give substance to the more formal computer science method.

_____ 4.2

The Linked List as an Abstract Data Structure

Recall from Chapter 1 that to formally specify an abstract data structure, we must describe the individual elements of the structure, the relationship(s) between these elements, and the logical operations to be performed on the structure. Such a formalization for the intuitive notion of a linked list which we have already discussed is now given.

> **Linked List**   A linked list is a collection of elements called nodes. Each node contains a data portion and a pointer. The data portions in all nodes are of the same type. The pointer in a given node contains the location of the node which follows the given node in the linear ordering of the list. The entire list is referenced by a separate head pointer to the first element in the linear ordering.

The operations we wish to perform on linked lists are shown in Table 4.1. Notice that embedded in the operations to be performed upon a linked list are the ACIDS criteria for general list manipulation which we introduced in Chapter 1. This should not be surprising since a linked list is another way of implementing a general list. Consequently, we will want to keep the ACIDS criteria in mind as we evaluate a linked list implementation (versus an array implementation) of a general list.

According to our definition of a linked list, an alphabetically ordered linked list with four nodes could be logically viewed as shown in Figure 4.2. The operations of adding a node and deleting a node from such a list may also be conveniently represented in such a schematic form. In fact, you will soon discover that the best way to conceive algorithms which manipulate linked lists is to draw what you want to happen via such logical pictures. Notice that such a picture of a linked list is completely at the

Operation	Explanation
InsertNode(L, P, Prev)	Insert into linked list L, the node referenced by pointer P immediately after the node referenced by pointer Prev.
DeleteNode(L, P)	Delete from linked list L the node referenced by pointer P.
FindNode(L, Target)	Search linked list L for a node whose data field matches a specified Target value.
ChangeNode(L, P)	Change the data field of the node referenced by pointer P in linked list L.
Traverse(L)	Traverse linked list L in order by some specified key in the data portion. Usually this will not involve sorting; it is likely that the list has been maintained in order by that key.
Create(L)	Initialize an empty linked list L.
Empty(L)	Check whether linked list L is empty: does it contain any active nodes?
Full(L)	Check whether linked list L is full: is there space available to add a node?

TABLE 4.1

Operations on linked lists

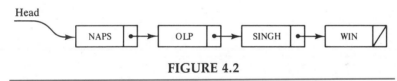

FIGURE 4.2

Alphabetically ordered linked list with four nodes

abstract level, implying nothing about how the linked list will finally be implemented. Once you understand the concept from such a graphic representation, it is usually a straightforward matter to actually implement it.

For instance, we now wish to add a node containing PRIM to the list shown in Figure 4.2, then all we need to do is to store PRIM in an available memory location outside of the list, such as the one pointed to by P in Figure 4.3. We then reset the pointer link of the node containing OLP to point to the node containing PRIM, and the pointer link of the node containing PRIM to point to the node containing SINGH. This logically maintains the alphabetical order of the data in the nodes without physically moving any of the existing nodes.

Similarly, should you then wish to delete an existing node from the linked list, a graphic representation of the list can again indicate how the pointers should be altered to reflect such a change. For example, given the list of Figure 4.3, the diagram of Figure 4.4 pictorially outlines what must be done if we want to delete the node containing OLP. Notice in this figure that, as was the case for insertion, only pointers must be changed to delete a node. Again, no movement of data occurs.

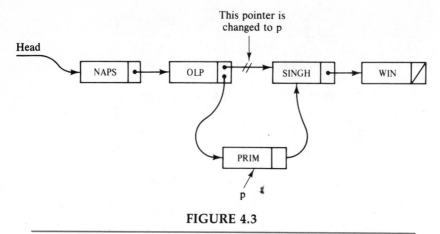

FIGURE 4.3

Insertion of node containing PRIM into linked list of
Figure 4.2

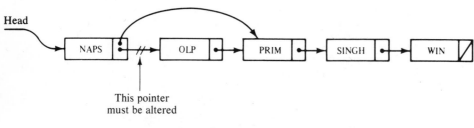

FIGURE 4.4

Deletion of node containing OLP from linked list of
Figure 4.3

Efficiency Considerations for Linked Lists:
The ACIDS Criteria

These addition/deletion considerations may make a linked list an attractive
alternative to an array implementation of a list such as the student record
system that we developed for the registrar in the last chapter. The diagrams of Figures 4.3 and 4.4 indicate that adds and deletes merely require
the exchange of two pointers. Since pointers are merely locations of other
nodes, this means that we are usually manipulating mere integers or similarly simple data in doing such pointer operations. Hence, both additions
and deletions would appear to be O(1) operations in terms of data movement for linked lists. This compares very favorably to the massive movement of entire records which was forced by an addition or deletion on an
array implementation of a list. In general, such insertion and removal
operations will be O(n) in terms of data movement in an array implementation of a list.

Despite this substantive advantage, you should proceed cautiously
and not be too quick to adopt the linked list as a cure for all the ills involved
with list-oriented systems. The experience you have already gained should

make you suspicious that there has to be a trade-off involved to get this superior efficiency for add and delete operations. Here the price we pay is to give up random access on the nodes in the list. For example, to access the fourth node, we must follow the head pointer to the first node, the first node's pointer to the second, and so on, until we reach the fourth node. Hence, any operation that requires finding a particular node on the list will essentially have to invoke a sequential search algorithm. The superb $O(\log_2 n)$ search efficiency that was possible with an array implementation of a list cannot be approached with a linked implementation of the same list because the binary search algorithm we used to achieve this efficiency requires random access into the list. Instead we must settle for the $O(n)$ efficiency of the sequential search. Note that this is even a deterring factor in add and delete operations because, typically, an appropriate spot in the list must be found before the add or delete can occur. Hence, although the add or delete itself may require only $O(1)$ data movement, an $O(n)$ search must usually precede it.

Despite this search inefficiency, linked lists can be used to tremendous advantage when implementing lists that are highly volatile; that is, frequently undergoing insertions and deletions. If the percentage of these operations is sufficiently high in relation to requests for finding and inspecting nodes, then the linked implementation will probably pay off.

Before proceeding, we should clarify one point regarding linked lists as an abstract data structure. That is, although a linked list may be viewed from this abstract perspective, it also represents an implementation strategy for the more general type of abstract list which we defined in the first chapter. In that sense, we can compare it to the array implementation of a general list, which we have already studied, and to several other list implementation schemes which we will present in future chapters. Thus, a linked list is, from one perspective, an implementation strategy and, from another, an abstract structure. This is entirely consistent with what we have said regarding the progression from abstraction to implementation that you go through as a designer of software. The linked list provides another implementation option for the representation of a more general list. But it remains itself an abstraction because we have not yet described how we shall implement a linked list. It is to these implementation considerations that we shall now turn our attention.

_____ **4.3**

Array Implementation of a Linked List

Our previous remarks on the layers between pure abstraction and pure implementation should be heeded here so that you do not confuse the previously presented array implementation of a (general) list with the array implementation of a linked list which we are about to describe. Figure 4.5 makes this distinction more apparent. By using an array to now implement a linked list, we will be providing a different implementation of a general list than via the straightforward array scheme presented earlier. This different implementation will carry with it all of the advantages and disadvantages that come with using linked lists; that is, efficient additions and deletions but slow sequential searching.

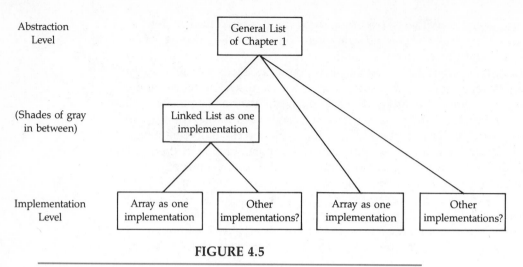

FIGURE 4.5

Levels of abstraction in implementing lists

The technique for implementing a linked list using an array should already be evident from our earlier discussion of the chain of gifts. We merely need to declare an array of records—each with an appropriate Data field and a Link field—to serve as a pointer to the next record on the list. Since the location of this next record can be specified as an array position, it is clear that this Link field need only be an ordinary integer. Figure 4.6 portrays such an array implementation of a simple linked list of five alphabetically ordered names.

In order to implement a procedure for inserting a node into such a linked list, we must first consider where such nodes are to come from. That is, we need a procedure which supplies an unused node from the pool of available unused locations. We call this procedure GetNode. Similarly,

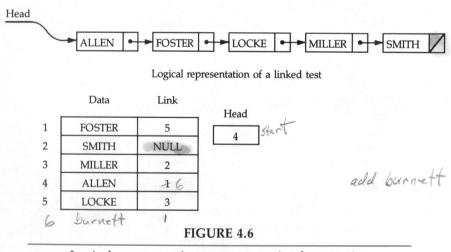

FIGURE 4.6

Logical representation versus array implementation

when a node in the linked list is deleted, we should be able to return it to the pool of available nodes. ReturnNode will be our procedure to do this.

The most convenient way of viewing this available pool of nodes is as a separate linked list with its own head pointer, Avail, which is woven into the same array used by the active nodes on the list. Because the order of nodes is not important in this available space list, all insertions and deletions can occur at its head. The Pascal procedures Initialize, GetNode, and ReturnNode that follow provide a package of procedures which may be used to appropriately manage this available space list. Initialize activates the available space list by initially linking all array locations into the available chain. The graphic documentation that accompanies the procedures highlights how this available node list is then manipulated by GetNode and ReturnNode.

```
{Global declarations}

CONST
  TotalSpace = {Appropriate number};
  Null = 0;    {to flag end of list}

TYPE
  SpaceRec =
    RECORD
    Data :     {Appropriate type};
    Link :  integer
    END;

  SpaceArray :   ARRAY [1..TotalSpace] OF SpaceRec;

PROCEDURE Initialize (VAR Avail : integer;
                      VAR Space : SpaceArray);

  {Initialize an available space list to be used by procedures
   GetNode and ReturnNode.  The head of the list is location 1.
   This value is hence returned in Avail.
   Thereafter location i is linked to location i+1.}

VAR
  i : integer;

BEGIN
  FOR i := 1 TO Total Space - 1 DO
    Space[i].Link := i+1;
  Space[TotalSpace].Link := Null;
  Avail := 1
END; {Initialize}

PROCEDURE GetNode(VAR Avail, p : integer;
              Space : SpaceList);
```

record	Avail = 1 Link
1	2
2	3
3	4
TotalSpace−2	TotalSpace−1
TotalSpace−1	TotalSpace
TotalSpace	NULL

```
  {Returns pointer p to node taken from unused space.
   Avail points to the head node on unused space list.
   Avail = Null means no space is available.}
```

```
BEGIN
  IF Avail = Null THEN
    writeln('NO SPACE AVAILABLE')
  ELSE
    BEGIN
    p := Avail;
    Avail := Space[Avail].Link
    END
END; {GetNode}
```

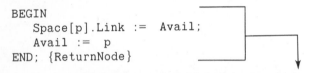

This pointer
altered

p

```
PROCEDURE ReturnNode(VAR Avail,p : integer;
                     VAR Space : SpaceList);
```

{Returns a node, pointed to by p, to the available
 space.}

```
BEGIN
    Space[p].Link :=  Avail;
    Avail :=  p
END; {ReturnNode}
```

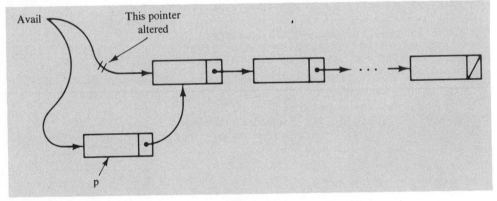

Avail

This pointer
altered

p

Now consider a procedure InsertNode to implement the abstract insertion operation pictured in Figure 4.3. This procedure will act upon a list
pointed to by Head. That is, Head will contain the index of the first node
on the list or Null if the list is empty. InsertNode is to take the node
pointed to by P and link it into the list after the node pointed to by Prev.
Three important aspects of InsertNode should be emphasized. First, InsertNode assumes that the pointer P, which references the node to be
inserted, has already been obtained via a call to GetNode and filled with
appropriate data. Thus, InsertNode is concerned only with the pointer
manipulations that link the node into the list, not with finding the insertion
point. Second, InsertNode assumes that the location in the list where the

insertion is to occur has already been found and stored in Prev. As we will see in the discussion following InsertNode, the actual determination of this location must be done by a separate procedure which is, in effect, a special implementation of the FindNode operation on the abstract data type linked list (see Table 4.1). This procedure will be dependent on the logical order of the data nodes in the list. Third, we will follow the convention that Prev is set to Null when the insertion is to occur at the head of the list.

```
{Assume same global declarations used for GetNode and ReturnNode.}

PROCEDURE InsertNode (VAR Head : integer;
                          p, Prev : Integer;
                          VAR Space : SpaceList);

        {Insert, into a linked list headed by Head, a node
         pointed to by p just after the node pointed to by
         Prev.}
        {Assume p has been obtained by GetNode and filled with
         data.}
BEGIN
   IF Prev = Null THEN {Insert at front}
      BEGIN
      Space[p].Link := Head;
      Head := p
      END
   ELSE
      BEGIN
      Space[p].Link := Space[Prev].Link;
      Space[Prev].Link := p
      END {IF}
   END;  {InsertNode}
```

You should convince yourself that the present version of InsertNode is sufficient to handle all possible cases: insertion in an empty list and insertion at the front, middle, and end of a nonempty list. The best way to do this is to draw an abstract picture of the list for each of these conditions and trace the action of the procedure's statements on that picture. (See Figure 4.7).

Given the InsertNode procedure, we now consider how to find the pointer Prev which it requires. For this discussion, we will assume that the list is to be maintained in ascending order. To determine Prev, we must therefore compare the data in the node referenced by p (the node to be

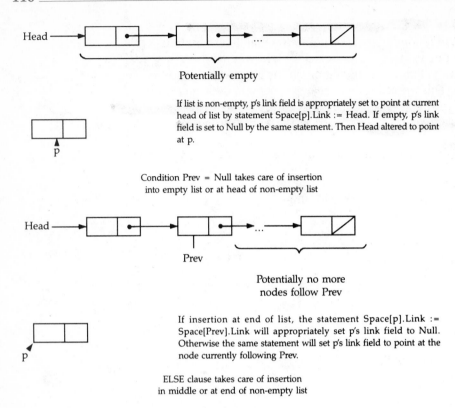

FIGURE 4.7

Tracing of four possibilities in InsertNode procedure

inserted) to the data in successive nodes along the list. We know that we have found the spot to insert the node referenced by p when we come to the first node on the list which contains data greater than (or equal to) that in p. That is, a loop to find the node which should follow p may be roughly given as

```
Start pointer q at head of list
WHILE (data referenced by p > data referenced by q)
     AND not at end of list DO
         Advance q to next node
```

Unfortunately this loop will not find the node after which p belongs but rather the node before which it belongs. This can be easily remedied by adding Prev as a "tag-along" pointer in the loop.

```
Start Prev at Null
Start q at head of list
WHILE (data referenced by p > data referenced by q)
     AND not at end of list DO
         Set Prev to q {Prev tagging along}
         Advance q to next node
```

A Pascal implementation of this logic is given in the following FindInsertionSlot procedure:

```
{Assume same global declarations used for GetNode and ReturnNode.}

PROCEDURE  FindInsertionSlot (Head, p : integer;
                             VAR Prev : integer;
                             Space : SpaceList);

  {Given data node referenced by p and linked list
   referenced by Head,  return in Prev a pointer to the
   node after which p should be inserted.}

    VAR    q : integer;  {Pointer used to advance through loop.}
           SlotFound : boolean;
    BEGIN
    Prev := Null;
    q := Head;
    SlotFound := false;
    WHILE (q <> Null) AND NOT SlotFound DO
      IF Space[p].Data > Space[q].Data THEN
        BEGIN
          Prev := q; {Prev tags along behind q}
          q := Space[q].Link {q advances}
        END
      ELSE
        SlotFound := true
    END; {FindInsertionSlot}
```

(handwritten annotation: = Find)

The Boolean variable SlotFound is required in FindInsertionSlot because of the way in which Pascal may determine the Boolean result of an **AND** conditional. It is tempting to try to avoid using this Boolean and instead rewrite the **WHILE** condition as

```
WHILE (q <> Null) AND (Space[p].Data > Space[q].Data) DO
  BEGIN
    Prev := q;
    q := Space[q].Link
  END;
```

This will work fine as long as the node referenced by p does not belong at the end of the list. However, when p does belong at the end of the list, the conditional test

```
Space[p].Data > Space[q].Data
```

will result in a run-time "Index out of range" error because q is Null. Thus, the SlotFound Boolean variable is necessary to avoid q's becoming an invalid index reference for the Space array.

With the procedures InsertNode and FindInsertionSlot that we have developed, it is now clear how we could build up a linked list. Assuming appropriate variable declarations, the following sequence will create a

linked list referenced by Head and then successively add nodes to it until a
SentinelValue is entered.

```
Create(Head); {Initialize linked list referenced by Head.}
REPEAT
  GetNode(Avail,p,Space);
  ReadInData(Space[p].Data); {Call procedure which fills data portion of
                                 node.}
  IF Space[p].Data <> SentinelValue THEN
    BEGIN
       FindInsertionSlot (Head, p, Prev, Space);
       InsertNode (Head, p, Prev, Space)
    END
UNTIL Space[p].Data = SentinelValue;
ReturnNode (Avail, p, Space); {Return last node entered since not linked
                                 into list.}
```

   The procedure to delete a node can be implemented in a fashion similar
to InsertNode. Using the logic outlined in Figure 4.4, the node is first
unchained from the list. Then a call to ReturnNode restores this node to
the pool of available nodes. In the following procedure DeleteNode, a list
node pointed to by p and preceded by a node pointed to by Prev is deleted
and returned to the list of available nodes. As in the InsertNode procedure,
DeleteNode presupposes that p and Prev have been determined. This
determination could be done in a FindNodeToDelete procedure similar to
(though slightly different from) the FindInsertionSlot procedure we developed. Also, consistent with our InsertNode conventions, DeleteNode will
assume that Prev = Null signals deletion of the first node on the list.

```
{Assume same global declarations used for InsertNode.}

PROCEDURE DeleteNode(VAR Head, Avail : integer;
                         p, Prev : integer);
                         VAR Space : SpaceArray);

  {Delete node pointed to by p and preceded by
   a node pointed to by Prev.}
  {The condition Prev = Null signals deletion of first node.}

  BEGIN
    IF Prev = Null THEN {Delete first node.}
       Head := Space[Head].Link
    ELSE
       Space[Prev].Link := Space[P].Link;
    ReturnNode(Avail, p,Space) {Return the deleted node.}
  END {DeleteNode};
```

   What we have begun to develop in this section is a package of procedures that may be used to process linked lists implemented by arrays.
These procedures are low-level in the sense that they would appear deep
in the modular structure chart of a software system which used linked lists.
They represent essential linked list operations. Note that more such primitive procedures would need to be developed to complete a linked list
package; for example, finding a particular node and traversing the list in a
specified order. Some of these are left for you to write in the exercises at the
end of the chapter.

The particular package we have started upon here represents only one of two possible implementation strategies we will discuss for linked lists. In the next section we shall describe a similar package of procedures for an alternate strategy using a special feature of Pascal called a pointer variable. These two implementation strategies will prove to be interchangeable to a degree. However, each also has inherent advantages and disadvantages which will be contrasted as we present the pointer variable scheme.

4.4

Pascal Pointer Variable Implementation of a Linked List: Dynamic Memory Management in Pascal

Perhaps the biggest drawback of the array method of implementing a linked list is the static nature of the memory storage associated with an array. Suppose, for example, we declare an array Space of size 100. Then the storage for Space is static in the sense that it is allocated at the time the program is compiled, not when it actually runs. Because of this, we are charged for 100 locations whether or not they are all used. When we have only 50 records to process in the array, 50 percent of the memory allocation is being wasted. Even more serious is the limitation that, if we have over 100 records to process, we must edit and recompile the program using a larger array size.

Pascal pointer variables, on the other hand, are an example of a technique known as dynamic memory management. As a feature which is not available in many older languages such as FORTRAN, COBOL, and BASIC, dynamic memory management is used by Pascal to allow the programmer to claim only that amount of memory which is actually needed at run-time.

To understand dynamic memory management, we must first understand the configuration of memory when your program is loaded into it from an external file. As indicated in Figure 4-8, there are memory costs

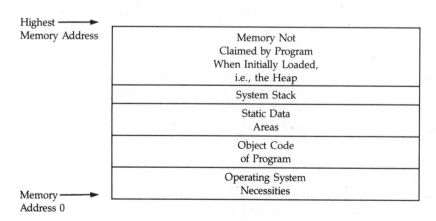

FIGURE 4.8

Computer memory configuration for typical program

that must be paid in addition to the storage space required for the object code of your program. In particular, memory must have room to accommodate:

- □ Various operating system requirements.

- □ A stack used by the operating system for subroutine processing (to be explained in Chapter 6).

- □ The object code of your program; that is, the machine-language version of your program's instructions.

- □ Static data areas; that is, the globally declared arrays and other variables used by your program.

Notice that the four memory components listed generally will not consume all of the available computer memory. What is left over is called the heap. Unless you have already used the dynamic memory allocation scheme of a language like Pascal, your programs until now have never been able to get at the heap and take advantage of it. With Pascal's pointer variables, all this changes. Suppose we have a record declaration, such as that for SpaceRec in our previous procedures and a declaration for a pointer variable to that type of record via Pascal's up-arrow notation:

```
TYPE PtrToSpaceRec : ^SpaceRec;
                 .
                 .
                 .
VAR p : PtrToSpaceRec;
```

We can request that Pascal's heap manager allocate segments of memory in the heap for records of this type as our program runs. The key is a supplied procedure **new**, which takes as its only argument a pointer variable such as p and returns in p a pointer; that is, a memory address indicating the location within the heap where the heap manager has allocated space for the currently requested record. Thus, **new** is essentially a Pascal-supplied dynamic version of the GetNode procedure which we developed ourselves for the array implementation of a linked list. Several facts about the **new** procedure should be emphasized at this point.

- □ It is a run-time request for memory. Unlike an array, you are not charged for the memory requested until you actually have something to store in it. Moreover, unlike static array declarations, you are not charged for an excess of memory that you may not even need for this particular run of the program.

- □ After a call to **new**(p) for a suitably declared pointer variable p, p is a memory address. As such, its actual value is of little concern to you. Suffice it to say that it is an address somewhere in the heap. How the heap manager was able to arrive at such an address involves a system-dependent, more sophisticated version of our own GetNode algorithm. The important point to note here is that, as a memory address, p's actual value is not important. In fact, Pascal won't even let you see what it is since a statement like **write**(p) will result in a syntax error.

☐ However, Pascal will allow you to manipulate pointer variables in the ways which are necessary to implement a variety of data structures, including linked lists. For instance, the contents of one pointer variable may be assigned to another.

☐ Pascal also lets you get at the contents of records which are stored at an address "pointed to" by a pointer variable such as p. To access the contents of such a dynamically allocated record, the up-arrow notation is again used. Hence pˆ refers to the contents of the record at the address pointed to by p. That is, pˆ is the actual data while p is where the data are stored. Figure 4.9 illustrates this crucial difference between the address stored in a pointer variable p and the contents of the record stored at that address. Given p, fields within such a record may be examined by the usual dot qualification, for example, pˆ.Name or pˆ.Address.

☐ Should you request space from the heap manager when none is available, a run-time error will result.

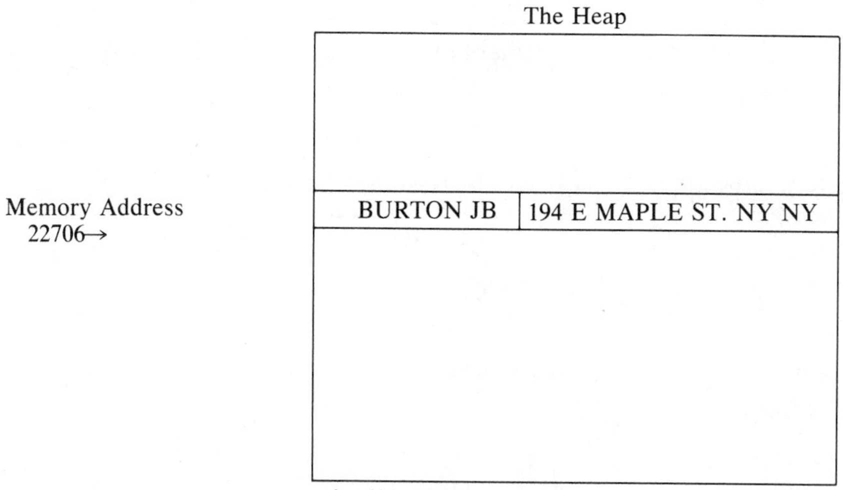

The Heap

BURTON JB	194 E MAPLE ST. NY NY

Memory Address
22706→

p itself is 22706, a memory address. pˆ is the contents of the record at address 22706. Hence pˆ.Name is BURTON JB and pˆ.Address is 194 E MAPLE ST. NY NY

FIGURE 4.9

The difference between p and pˆ

Just as **new** provides an alternative to the GetNode procedure from our earlier array implementation, Pascal also provides a **dispose** procedure as a dynamic alternative to our ReturnNode procedure. If p is appropriately declared as a pointer variable, then the statement

```
dispose(p)
```

will return the memory space being referenced by p to the Pascal memory management system for later use. The amount of space obtained by **new**(p) or returned by **dispose**(p) is always equal to the size of the record associated with p. That is, if p is a pointer generated by the following declaration:

```
TYPE RecPointer = ^SpaceRec; {Note: Allowable in this case to refer to
                                     SpaceRec before it is defined.}
     SpaceRec =     RECORD
                      Data : {Appropriate Type};
                      Link : RecPointer
                    END;
VAR p : RecPointer;
```

then the statement **new**(p) returns a pointer p to a node as follows:

Data	Link →	Pointer to next node

p →

Thus p is simply a pointer returned by Pascal's memory manager referencing an available chunk of memory with enough space to accommodate the declared Data and Link fields. Analogously, the statement **dispose**(p) would restore this chunk of memory to available space in the heap.

To assign a value to the Data field, a statement of the form

```
p^.Data := x
```

would suffice where x is of the appropriate type. The Link field in the node referenced by p could be "aimed at" another node referenced by a pointer q via the statement

```
p^.Link := q
```

Finally, if the node referenced by p has been appropriately chained into an existing linked list, then p can be advanced to the next node on the list by the statement

```
p := p^.Link
```

Adaptation of Linked List Procedures to Dynamic Memory Methods

With these Pascal considerations out of the way, it is now clear that we can write the linked list procedures InsertNode and DeleteNode in the language of pointer variables. The following procedures use the Pascal reserved word **NIL** in the sense that the user-defined constant Null was employed in our array-based procedures. When a pointer variable in Pascal has the value **NIL**, it is well-defined, but it is not pointing to any node in memory. Thus, it is valid to check whether p = **NIL**, but it is not valid to refer to p^ when p is **NIL**. The latter type of reference will usually cause a run-time error. Typically the **NIL** value is assigned to the Head pointer before any nodes are added to the list and to the Link field pointer in the last node on the list. Procedures InsertNode and DeleteNode also make assumptions about the parameter Prev being **NIL**. These assumptions are explained in our documentation for the procedures.

```
{Global declarations}

TYPE
  RecPointer = ^SpaceRec;
  SpaceRec =
    RECORD
      Data : {Appropriate Type};
      Link : RecPointer
    END;

PROCEDURE InsertNode (VAR Head : RecPointer;
                          p,Prev : RecPointer);

    {Insert the node pointed to by p after the node pointed
     to by Prev. This procedure assumes that the insertion
     point on the list has already been found and recorded in
     Prev. If Prev = NIL, insertion is at the Head of the list.
     We also assume that p has been obtained by a prior call
     to new and that its Data field has been assigned an
     appropriate value.}

  BEGIN
    IF Prev = NIL THEN {Insert at front.}
      BEGIN
      p^.Link := Head;
      Head := p
      END
    ELSE
      BEGIN
      p^.Link := Prev^:Link;
      Prev^.Link := p
      END
  END; {InsertNode}

PROCEDURE DeleteNode (VAR Head : RecPointer;
                          p, Prev : RecPointer);

   {Delete a node pointed to by p and
    preceded by a node pointed to by Prev
    on the list referenced by Head.}

  BEGIN
    IF Prev = NIL THEN {Deleting Head node}
      Head := Head^.Link
    ELSE
      Prev^.Link := p^.Link;
    dispose (p)
  END; {DeleteNode}
```

You should verify that these pointer versions of the procedures also work for all possible cases.

Since both the InsertNode and DeleteNode procedures assume that the pointers p and Prev have been appropriately set prior to calling, we should describe how this would be done for a pointer variable implementation just as we did earlier for our array implementation. Hence the following procedure, FindNodeToDelete, is based on a pointer variable implementation. You should carefully compare it to the FindInsertionSlot procedure we developed for an array implementation. Note the similarities in the way the procedures' loops are controlled. Just as we had to use a Boolean variable to avoid a potential Null index reference in the array procedure, so must we use a Boolean variable to avoid a potential reference through a **NIL**-valued pointer in the pointer variable version.

```
{Assume same global declarations as for InsertNode and DeleteNode.}

PROCEDURE  FindNodeToDelete (Head : RecPointer;
                             VAR Prev, p : RecPointer;
                             Target : {Same type as Data field in SpaceRec};
                             VAR Found : boolean);

  {Given linked list referenced by Head, locate node whose data field
   matches Target.  Return p as pointer to this node and Found as true if
   such a match can be made.  Also return Prev as pointer to the preceding
   node or as NIL if Target matches the Head node.  Return Found as false if
   no match can be made.}

BEGIN
Prev := NIL;
p := Head;
Found := false;
WHILE (p <> NIL) AND NOT Found DO
  IF p^.Data = Target THEN
    Found := true
  ELSE {Still looking}
    BEGIN
    Prev := p; {Prev tags along.}
    p := p^.Link {p advances.}
    END
END; {FindNodeToDelete}
```

It is appropriate at this time to compare the two linked list implementations we have discussed. From an efficiency perspective, there is little difference because the algorithms behind Pascal's **new** and **dispose** procedures mirror very closely the logic of their counterparts GetNode and ReturnNode in the array implementation. The array implementation has the advantage of not being specifically tied to Pascal or a similar language that directly supports dynamic memory management. Moreover, the array implementation can be directly converted to a random access file implementation using the strategy for such a conversion that we discussed in Chapter 3. The array implementation also allows for easier program tracing when debugging is needed since the values of the links may be directly printed via **write** statements. However, this advantage is somewhat tempered by the fact that most Pascal compilers come with debugging tools that allow you to actually see the values of pointer variables even though Pascal itself will not let you **write** them. From a convenience perspective, pointer variables emerge a clear winner—totally eliminating your worries about managing available nodes. Pascal's dynamic memory management also allows your linked list (or other data structure) to expand into all of the memory available at run-time. Array implementations, on the other hand, are bounded by the size of an array declared at compile time. In this book, we will tend to use pointer variable implementations for data structures where possible because of the convenience. However, in certain situations where a concept can be more clearly illustrated by giving ourselves some tangible numbers for pointer values, we will occasionally resort to array implementations.

4.5

Variations on Linked List Structures

Linked lists provide a tremendously useful tool in situations where a highly volatile general list must be maintained in some prescribed logical order. Their widespread use has led to the development of several "tricks of the trade" particularly suitable in certain applications. These are ways of fine-tuning the basic linked list structure to tailor it to the needs of particular situations. Four such variations on the linked list are presented in this section: dummy headers, circular lists, doubly linked lists, and multilinked lists.

Dummy Headers

A dummy header node in the list before the first actual data node can often contain useful information about the structure (for example, the number of nodes). A query algorithm can then determine the status of the list by examining the contents of the dummy header node without having to traverse the entire list. This amounts to adding one more node to the list. Figure 4.10 illustrates this concept. Additions to and deletions from the list

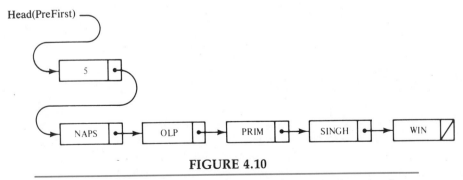

FIGURE 4.10

Linked list with dummy header indicating the length of the list

require changing this information-keeping field in the dummy header node of the list.

There is another distinct advantage of the dummy header node. If the list becomes empty and a dummy header node is not used, then the Head pointer for the list must be made **NIL**. But if the dummy header node is present, then the Head pointer never needs to be changed to **NIL** because it always points to this dummy header. That is, the empty list is only empty in a logical sense. Physically, it still contains the dummy header. This convention can serve to simplify the coding involved in procedures InsertNode and DeleteNode by removing the special handling previously required for inserts and deletes at the beginning of the list. (You will write these simplified procedures as an exercise at the end of the chapter.) This convenience factor alone provides substantial practical motivation for always using dummy headers. Moreover, in real-world applications, you will find that you can almost always use the extra data space in the dummy header to store some valuable items of information.

Circular Linked Lists

Although linked lists are satisfactory in many instances, the presence of a null pointer at the end of the list makes this structure most efficient only if the entire list is to be processed. The efficiency of such list processing algorithms decreases when the linked list is to be processed beginning at an arbitrary point in the list. In such situations, it would be desirable to be able to enter the list anywhere and process it efficiently independent of the entry point. In other words, we need a linked list that has no beginning or end.

Circular linked lists are precisely such data structures. A singly linked circular list is a linked list in which the last node of the list points to the first node in the list. Notice that in circular list structures, there are no **NIL** links. Figure 4.11 depicts a singly linked circular list.

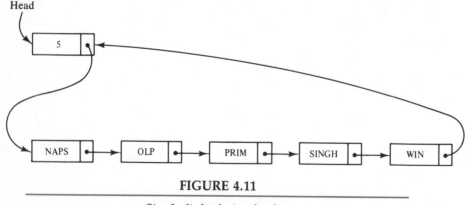

FIGURE 4.11

Singly linked circular list

As an example of the utility of such a circular list in the area of operating systems, suppose the nodes in Figure 4.11 represent current users on a time-sharing computer. In such an environment, the operating system schedules each user for a small time slice on the central processing unit (CPU) and then proceeds to devote its momentary attention to the next user. When the final user has completed his or her time slice, ownership of the CPU must again revert to the first user, and the scheduling cycle starts again. Because of the speed of the CPU, this cyclic scheduling creates the illusion for each user that the computer is dedicated to his or her particular process. Clearly, a circular linked list is made to order for this type of scheduling. The circularity insures no unnecessary interruptions in restarting the scheduling cycle when the end of the user list is reached. The linked nature of the structure enables the operating system to quickly process new users who log on and users who then complete their work and log off.

Doubly Linked Circular List

In the previously developed procedures InsertNode and DeleteNode, we had prior knowledge about where in the list insertions and deletions were to be performed. In general, this information may have to be determined through a routine that searches the entire list. Because search algorithms require time proportional to half the length of the list, run-time can be substantial if the list is very long. As an example, suppose we have a singly linked list in which we wish to insert a node A pointed to by Point1 just before a node B pointed to by Point2. We can change the link field of A to point to B, but we do not know the address of (that is, a pointer to) the node preceding B. If we are to depend upon the current structure of the list, then we must search the list for B: an inefficient procedure we wish to avoid. In other words, even in situations where we may be able to locate B by other means (such as a hashing strategy to be studied in Chapter 10), we must traverse the list up to B to find the previous node.

Inserting node A before node B is shown in Figure 4.12. In a singly

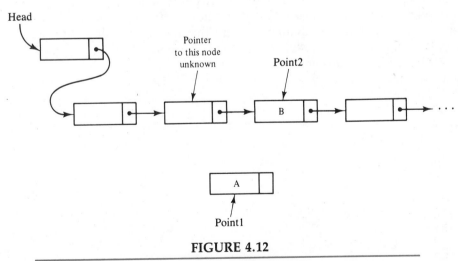

FIGURE 4.12

Inserting node A before node B

linked structure, time-consuming sequential searching is required to determine the address of the node preceding B.

   A satisfactory way of getting around the difficulty presented in Figure
4.12 is a doubly linked circular list in which each node has two pointers: a
forward link and a backward link. The forward link is a pointer to the next
node in the list; the backward link points to the preceding node. The
circular nature of the list, along with a special dummy header node, can be
used to conveniently avoid special conditional checking when adding to or
deleting from the beginning or end of the list. Figure 4.13 illustrates a
doubly linked circular list. This list has five nodes (plus a dummy header),
each having a forward link (Flink) and a backward link (Blink). Flink points
to the successor node, whereas Blink points to the predecessor node. Because the list is circular, Blink of the first node must point to the last node,
and Flink of the last node must point to the first node.

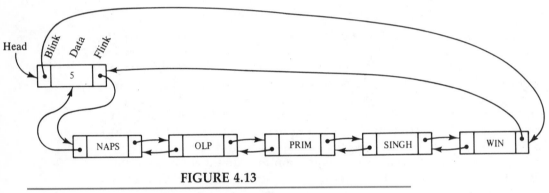

FIGURE 4.13

Doubly linked circular list

   Inserting a node into a doubly linked list, or deleting one from it, is
potentially a much easier task because we do not need a separate pointer to
a preceding node. Hence we may be able to avoid the time inefficiency
inherent in finding such a pointer in situations where the insertion or
deletion point can be found by means faster than traversing the list. The
following procedure InsertNodeDouble inserts a node pointed to by Point1
(already obtained via **new**) into a doubly linked list just before a node
pointed to by Point2.

```
{Global declarations}

TYPE
   RecPointer = ^SpaceRec;
   SpaceRec =
      RECORD
         Data : {Appropriate type};
         Flink : RecPointer;
         Blink : RecPointer
      END; {RECORD}
```

```
PROCEDURE InsertNodeDouble (Pointl, Point2 : RecPointer);

    {Insert a node pointed to by Pointl into a doubly linked
     list just before the node pointed to by Point2.}

  VAR
    Prev : RecPointer;

  BEGIN
    Prev := Point2^.Blink
    Pointl^.Flink := Point2;
    Pointl^.Blink := Prev;
    Prev^.Flink := Pointl;
    Point2^.Blink := Pointl
  END;   {InsertNodeDouble}
```

As indicated in Figure 4.14, the InsertNodeDouble procedure avoids a time-consuming sequential search.

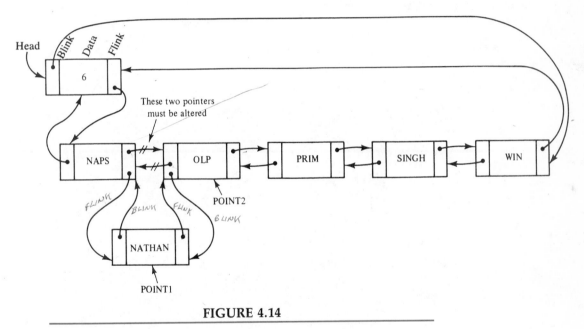

FIGURE 4.14

Insertion using a doubly linked circular list

Note that the procedure InsertNodeDouble illustrates how streamlined insert and delete procedures become when a dummy header is used. In particular, because the empty list appears as

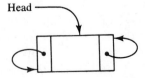

the procedure works without any awkward checking of whether the list is empty or whether the insertion is being made at the front of the list. Clearly a dummy header simplifies procedures in this situation.

The following procedure DeleteNodeDouble deletes a node pointed to by Point1 from a doubly linked list and returns the node to the storage pool of available nodes.

```
PROCEDURE DeleteNodeDouble(Point1 : RecPointer);

  {Delete a node pointed to by Point1
   from doubly linked list.}

  VAR
    Save : RecPointer;

  BEGIN
    Save := Point1^.Blink;
    Save^.Flink := Point1^.Flink;
    Save := Point1^.Flink;
    Save^.Blink := Point1^.Blink;
    dispose(Point1)
  END; {DeleteNodeDouble}
```

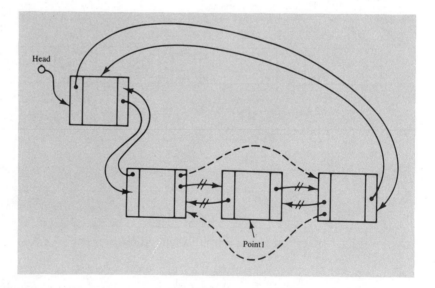

Multilinked Lists

We shall end this discussion of variations on the linked list theme by noting that a doubly linked list is a special case of a structure known as a multilinked list. Because each link field determines an order in which the nodes of a list are to be processed, we can in fact establish a different link field for every different order in which we wish to process the nodes in a

list. Figure 4.15 illustrates such a multilinked list. By following the IdLink
fields, we traverse the list in IdNumber order; by following the NameLink
fields, we traverse the list in alphabetical order by Name.

	IdHead		NameHead	
	4		3	

	Name	IdNumber	NameLink	IdLink
1	SINGH	8316	4	Nil
2	OLP	4212	5	5
3	NAPS	6490	2	1
4	WIN	1330	Nil	2
5	PRIM	5560	1	3

Multilink List

FIGURE 4.15

Link fields for processing nodes

_____ **4.6**

Revising the Registrar's System with the Linked List

Although we will not be developing a new case study from scratch in this
chapter, we can engage ourselves in the maintenance phase of the system
life cycle by examining how some of the work we have done in Chapter 3
may be revised in light of this new tool, the linked list. The actual implementation of these revisions will be left for you to do in the problems at the
end of this chapter.

The revisions possible in the registrar's system using a linked list
should be evident. If the University of Hard Knocks has a volatile student
body, then such an implementation will greatly cut down on the processing time involved with adding and deleting students. Of course this benefit
will only come at the expense of search efficiency when an individual
student record is to be inspected. One way to determine whether this
trade-off will result in a better system for the registrar would be to develop
both implementations and empirically test their performance. Although
the thought of developing two parallel systems merely for comparison
purposes may initially seem to be a tremendous waste of effort, there is a
sound rationale for doing just this upon occasion. First, developing the
alternative implementation will not involve nearly as much work as the
initial one. In fact, if the initial implementation is well-designed, most
changes required for the alternative version can be concentrated in the low-
level modules of the original system structure chart. This is because a
program design emphasizing data abstraction hides such implementation
details in as few modules as possible. This allows high-level modules to

exist in a relatively independent fashion from whatever implementation strategy is chosen. Second, a mathematical approach to algorithm analysis, such as that exemplified by big-O notation, often may not be completely adequate to describe how the system will really perform for the users. In other words, big-O analyses can give us extremely useful guidelines, but sometimes empirical comparisons are required to actually decide between the complex trade-offs posed by two separate implementations. (As a preview of coming attractions, we note that the trade-off of add/delete efficiency versus search efficiency will eventually be eliminated completely when we study a tree implementation of a general list in Chapter 7.)

A final consideration in a linked list version of the registrar's system is that of data permanency; that is, implementing the list via a random access disk file. In this regard we note that, given our discussion of the parallels between arrays and random access files in Chapter 3, an array implementation of a linked list fits directly into a random file implementation. This is not true of a Pascal pointer implementation since the **new** and **dispose** procedures by which Pascal manipulates the heap are designed to work only in main memory.

_____ **4.7**

An Implementation of Strings Using Linked Lists

In Chapter 3 you were informally introduced to some of the problems inherent in string storage and to the workspace-index implementation method as a possible solution to some of those problems. However, the workspace-index method is not necessarily the best answer to all the problems connected with string storage. To see why, we must more formally state exactly what we expect of strings. That is, we must view strings themselves as an abstract data type.

> **String**   A string is a list of characters. Inherent in this statement is the conclusion that the characters in a string are related in linear fashion with an identifiable first element, second element, and so on.

The operations we wish to perform on strings are shown in Table 4.2.

Although the workspace-index table method gracefully solves the problem of having to declare a maximum possible string length and then wasting memory when strings are shorter than that length, it does not adequately solve the problem of having to move a tremendous amount of data when insertions and deletions occur on a larger scale. On the other hand, the linked implementation of strings we are about to describe handles both of these problems. Of course, as we have now come to expect in this world of trade-offs, we shall see that it is not without its own set of problems.

Operation	Explanation
Assignment	The copying of one string variable to another. For example, if Str1 and Str2 are two string variables, then the statement `Strl := Str2` should copy the contents of Str2 to Str1 without destroying the contents of Str2.
Concatenation	The joining together of two character strings. The concatenation of the strings 'BIRD' and 'DOG' is the string 'BIRDDOG'.
Substring Operations	It may be desirable to examine characters I through J of a given string. For example, the substring consisting of the 4th through 7th characters in the string 'TALE OF TWO CITIES' is the substring 'E OF'.
Pattern Matching	The searching of one string for an occurrence of another string. For instance, the string 'BASEBALL' occurs in the string 'MODERN BASEBALL HISTORY' beginning at position 8.
Insertion	In text editing applications, one frequently wishes to insert a given string in the middle of another string. The insertion of ' AND' at position 5 of the string 'SALT PEPPER' results in the string 'SALT AND PEPPER'.
Deletion	The opposite of insertion. To delete the substring occupying positions 5 through 13 of 'SALT AND PEPPER' results in the string 'SALTER'.

TABLE 4.2

Operations on strings

We shall view each string as a circular doubly linked list as described in Section 4.5. Each node in the list contains a backward pointer, a forward pointer, and a data portion consisting of (for the moment) a single character. Clearly, for each such string, we need a pointer to the dummy header node for the list, and, for later use, we want also to keep track of the length of each string. The following conventions will be assumed throughout this section:

- ☐ The array String is an array of records, each of which contains a Head pointer to the dummy header of a string.

- ☐ Each record in String also contains a Len field which stores the length of the string referenced by the Head pointer in the record.

- ☐ The backward pointer for each node will be referred to as Blink, the forward pointer as Flink, and the data portion as Data.

Figure 4.16, which pictures the three strings 'COFFEE', 'TEA', and 'CREAM', with indexes for the length and dummy header location of each string, should help to clarify these conventions.

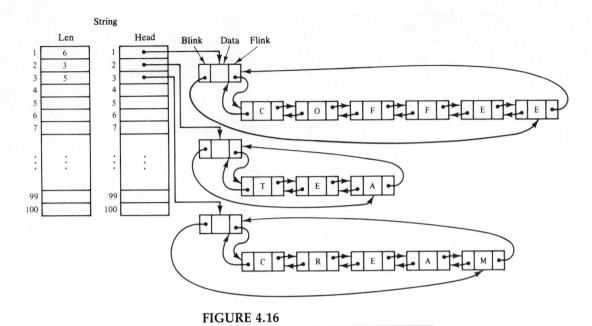

FIGURE 4.16

'COFFEE', 'TEA', and 'CREAM' in a circular doubly
linked list

Let us consider how the string operations we have specified would be
performed in such an implementation. The assignment of one string to
another could be achieved in very slick and efficient (though perhaps
somewhat deceptive) fashion. That is, instead of physically creating two
identical strings, we will simply have two entries in Head point to the same
string. This particular strategy does have some potential repercussions
which might have to be avoided in certain applications (as we'll see in the
Exercises). Pattern matching, as defined in Table 4.2, presents no real
problem and is examined in an exercise at the end of the chapter. Substring
operations do present a problem and will be discussed in greater detail
later in this section. Insertion, deletion, and concatenation (which may be
viewed as a special case of insertion) can be handled elegantly and efficiently using the linked list method.

The following is a procedure, InsertLL, to insert the string pointed to
by Head[j] into the string pointed to by Head[i] beginning at position Pos:

```
{Global variables}

CONST
  NumberStrings = {Appropriate number};

TYPE
  StringPtr = ^StringNode;
  StringNode =
    RECORD
      Blink : StringPtr;
      Data : Char;
      Flink : StringPtr
    END;
```

```
  StringInfo =
     RECORD
        Head : StringPtr;
        Len : integer
     END;

VAR
  String : ARRAY[1..NumberStrings] OF StringInfo;

PROCEDURE InsertLL(i, j, Pos: integer);

  {Insert the jth string in the ith string beginning at
   position Pos. Assume ith string has at least Pos characters.}

  VAR
    k : integer;
    FirstInj, LastInj, p : StringPtr;

  BEGIN
    p := String[i].Head;

    {First find position by traversing list.}
    FOR k := 1 TO Pos DO
      p := p^.Flink;

      {Now link it in.}

      FirstInj := String[j].Head^.Flink;
      LastInj := String[j].Head^.Blink;
      FirstInj^.Blink := p^.Blink;
      LastInj^.Flink := p;
      p^.Blink^.Flink := FirstInj;
      p^.Blink := LastInj;
      {Finally update length.}
      String[i].Len := String[i].Len + String[j].Len
  END;
{END InsertLL}
```

Note that this procedure is doing a task slightly more complicated than our previous insertion algorithm for a linked list. Earlier, we were concerned only with inserting one node. Here we are inserting an entire collection of nodes; we are inserting one linked list within another (see Figure 4.17). This is done with relative ease because our implementation of a doubly linked list gives us convenient pointers to both the first and last nodes in the list. Hence, our linked list implementation of strings has provided a rather neat illustration of the utility of double linking.

Efficiency Considerations for the Linked List Method

In this string-handling application we have seen that the linked list method allows both dynamic string allocation with no practical limit on string length and extremely efficient insertion and deletion operations. However, that does not mean that the linked list method is a universal cure-all that should be used in all applications.

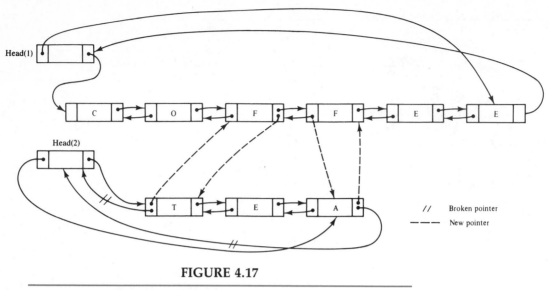

FIGURE 4.17

Two strings from Figure 4.16 after InsertLL(1, 2, 4)

Three general problem areas exist. First, the perceptive reader will already have noticed that, although the procedure InsertLL achieves a very efficient insertion, it renders the *j*th string thereafter inaccessible as a separate entity. This is because the pointers within the *j*th string had to be altered to chain it into the *i*th string. (See Figure 4.17.)

Second, consider an application in which operating with substrings is of more importance than insertion and deletion. With both the fixed length and the workspace-index table methods, the substring consisting of the *i*th through the *j*th characters could be directly accessed because the characters within any given string are physically next to each other. Accessing the same substring via the linked list implementation requires beginning at the initial character in the string and traversing the entire string until the *i*th character is reached. Our implementation of a string as a doubly linked list allows this process to be made somewhat more efficient. In particular, the length of the string from which we want to extract a substring could be checked to determine if the substring occurs in the front or back half. If it is in the back half, the pointer to the last character in the string could be used to begin a traversal from the rear of the list until we reach the desired substring. However, this would still require a sequential processing of the list until the desired substring is found. Hence, for substring operations, the linked list method does not stack up to either of the other two methods.

A third problem arises in the efficiency of memory utilization for the linked list method as we have described it here. If the data portion of a node in the linked list contains only one character, then the two pointers associated with that node could require four to eight times more memory than the data. That is, only 11 to 20 percent of memory is being utilized to store the data in which we are really interested; the rest of the memory is storing data about data.

This memory utilization problem may be somewhat alleviated by making the data portion of a node a cluster of characters. Suppose, for instance, we choose a cluster size of four characters. Then the same strings given in

Figure 4.16 would appear as shown in Figure 4.18. Here we have used the symbol (~) to represent a null character, that is, a character that is always ignored when the string is processed.

Notice that, although this technique has enabled us to devote a greater percentage of memory for storage of data, a significant complication has

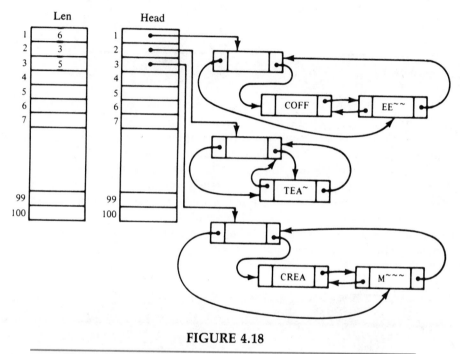

FIGURE 4.18

The strings from Figure 4.16 with a cluster size of four

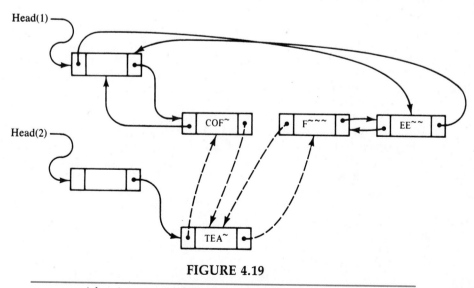

FIGURE 4.19

After insertion of the second string into the first
beginning at position 4

been added in that our code must always account for null characters. For example, if we wish to insert the second string from Figure 4.17 in the first string beginning at position 4, the scheme pictured in Figure 4.19 emerges.

Here the node containing 'COFF' had to be split into the two nodes 'COF~' and 'F~~~' to achieve an effective insertion. As you might expect, we have had to trade-off one feature for another. To gain more effective memory utilization, we have had to make our program code more cumbersome and less efficient in its execution time.

_____ 4.8

A Linked List Implementation of a Sparse Table

In previous sections we have seen how a linked list or variation thereof may be used to efficiently implement general lists and strings. To further emphasize the utility of linked lists, we shall close this chapter with a description of how linked lists may be used to implement a sparse table (as defined in Chapter 1). Consider, for example, the sparse table of integers pictured in Table 4.3. In Section 3.5, we described a strategy for implementing such a table which would have us store a list of those row and column coordinates that do not resolve to zero. Along with each such coordinate pair we would store its associated nontrivial value. The drawback of this approach stems from the implementation of the list of nonzero

A Relevant Issue . . .
Storage of Disk Files and Computer Security

Operating systems typically grant their users disk storage in units called blocks. On the magnetic disk itself, a block is a contiguous area capable of storing a fixed amount of data. For example, a block in DEC's well-known VAX/ VMS time-sharing system is 512 bytes. As a user enters data into a disk file, the system must grant additional blocks of storage as they are needed. In such a time-sharing environment, although each block represents a physically contiguous storage area on the disk, it may not be possible for the operating system to give a user blocks that are physically next to each other. Instead, when a user needs an additional storage block, the operating system may put information into the current block about where the next block is located. In effect, a link is established from the current block to the next block. By the time a naive user has completed entering a four-block file, it may be scattered over the entire disk surface, as indicated in the following diagram:

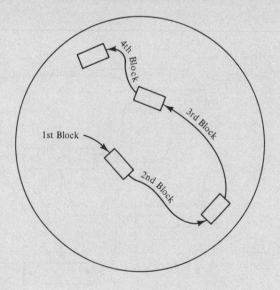

Although this may seem like an ingenious way of extending files indefinitely, one pays

	1	2	3	4	5	6	7	8	9	10	11	12	13	14
1	0	83	19	40	0	0	0	0	0	0	0	0	0	0
2	0	0	0	91	0	42	12	0	0	0	0	0	0	0
3	0	0	0	0	0	18	4	0	0	0	0	0	0	0
4	0	0	0	0	0	0	0	0	71	64	0	13	0	0
5	0	0	0	0	0	0	0	0	0	0	0	0	21	40

TABLE 4.3

Sparse table of integer data

coordinates via an array. The array implementation will result in a solution which is extremely inefficient for any volatile table of data. The reasons for this inefficiency parallel those which made an array implementation of the registrar's system inadequate. That is, if we somehow order the data to enable use of the binary search, adds and deletes (in this case assigning a nonzero value to a location which was previously zero or vice versa) will involve the shifting of large amounts of data. Conversely, if we neglect to order the data, adding new nonzero values can be done efficiently but search efficiency will deteriorate.

The implementation method we now propose uses linked lists to insure no data shifting occurs when a zero value is changed to nonzero (or

in several ways for such scattered blocks. Namely, the read-write head that seeks and puts data on the disk surface is forced to move greater distances, thereby slowing system performance. To combat such inefficiencies, shrewd users can often take advantage of options that allow them to preallocate the contiguous disk storage that will be required for a file. Moreover, system managers may occasionally shut down the entire system to rebuild disks, a process that entails copying all files that are presently scattered over the disk onto a new disk in physically contiguous form.

Yet another more serious price which may be paid for storing disk files in this fashion revolves around the issue of data security and what the operating system does with blocks that are no longer needed by a user. From what we have discussed in this chapter, it is clear that the disk blocks used to store a file are returned to some type of available block list when a user deletes that file from his or her directory. When these blocks are returned to that available space list, the data in them may remain intact until another user's request to extend a file results in the blocks' being reallocated to that new user. This means that, if clever users ("hackers") know how to access the available space list, they may be able to scavenge through data that other users once owned and then released (assuming it was destroyed upon being released). One of the authors was actually involved in an incident in which such a clever student was able to "find" old versions of a test that a professor had typed in on the computer and then discarded into this available block list. Needless to say, the professor whose tests were being explored by the student was somewhat alarmed upon discovering what had happened. As a protection against this type of scavenging, many operating systems will, by default or as an option, actually destroy data that is returned to the available block list.

vice versa). Moreover, by employing many linked lists (one for each row), it reduces the length of sequential searches to the number of nonzero column coordinates in a particular targeted row instead of all nonzero row-column coordinates for the entire table. The method is completely dynamic and requires an array of pointers, each leading to a linked list storing the nonzero data in a given row of the sparse table. Each node in one of these linked lists would need to contain not only an entry from the table but also an indication of which column within that particular row is occupied by the data in this node. We further stipulate that, for efficiency in processing, each linked list be arranged in ascending order of column numbers within that row. Given these conventions, the 5×14 table from Table 4.3 would be represented by Figure 4.20.

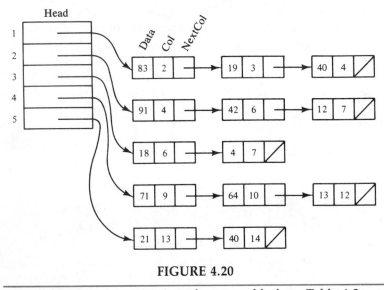

FIGURE 4.20

Linked list representation of sparse table from Table 4.3

By employing procedures analogous to InsertNode and DeleteNode (developed earlier in this chapter), we may now write a function Sparse to implement the retrieval of the value from the *i*th row and *j*th column of such a table and a procedure Assign to implement the assignment of a particular value to the *i*th row and *j*th column.

```
{Global declarations for Sparse and Assign}

CONST
  NumberRows = 100; {Or other appropriate value}

TYPE
  NodePointer = ^RecordPointer;
  RecordPointer =
    RECORD
      Data : integer;
      Col : integer;
      NextCol : NodePointer
    END;
```

```
VAR
  Head : ARRAY [1..NumberRows] OF NodePointer;

FUNCTION Sparse(i,j : integer) : integer;

{This function accesses the (i,j)th entry in a sparse table.}

  VAR
    p : NodePointer;
    Exit : boolean;

  BEGIN
    Exit := false;
    p := Head[i];
    WHILE (p <> NIL) AND NOT Exit DO
      IF p^.Col < j THEN
        p := p^.NextCol
      ELSE
        Exit := true;
    IF p = NIL THEN
        Sparse := 0
    ELSE IF p^.Col > j THEN
        Sparse := 0
    ELSE
        Sparse := p^.Data
  END; (Sparse)
```

Example of p = NIL case, suppose j = 8

Example of p^.Col > j case, suppose j = 6

WHILE loop left p pointing at this node

```
PROCEDURE Assign (i, j, v : integer);

{This procedure inserts a value v in
 the (i,j)th position of a sparse table.}

  VAR
    p, q, Prev : NodePointer;
    Exit : boolean;

  BEGIN
  Exit := false;
  p := Head[i];
  Prev := NIL;
  WHILE (p <> NIL) AND NOT Exit DO
    BEGIN
    IF p^.Col < j THEN
        BEGIN
        Prev := p;
        p := p^.NextCol
        END
    ELSE
      Exit := true
    END;

  IF (p^.Col = j) AND (v = 0) THEN
```

Example of ELSE case, j = 5

WHILE loop left p pointing at this node, 12 to be returned

Example of p^.Col = j case, suppose j = 5

p

If v = 0, delete this node; otherwise, new value needed in data portion

```
          {Assign 0 where nonzero entry had been.
           Call procedure to delete appropriate node
           from ith linked list.}
      DeleteNode(Head[i], Prev)
  ELSE IF p^.Col = j THEN {Assigning nonzero where nonzero has been}
      p^.Data := v

  ELSE IF v <> 0 THEN {Assign new nonzero entry.}
      BEGIN
      New (q);
      q^.Data := v;
      q^.Col := j;
      InsertNode(Head[i], Prev, q)
          {Assume procedure DeleteNode and
           InsertNode similar to those
           developed earlier.}
      END
  END; {Assign}
```

Example of v <> 0 case, j = 6

Data *Col* *NextCol*

Head(i) → [6 | 3 | •] → [12 | 5 | •] → // → [2 | 7 |]

New node to be
inserted here

Efficiency Considerations

Our earlier comments indicated that, with respect to run-time, the efficiency of this implementation of a sparse table will require no wholesale data movement when values are assigned to the array. Moreover, since accessing a particular value in the table requires a sequential search along one of the many linked lists which contain a row, we essentially have a retrieval time of O(NumberOfColumns).

Since the main motivation for an implementation of a sparse table is to save memory space, a more important efficiency consideration is exactly how much space we have saved. To determine this, we define the efficiency ratio of a sparse table implementation by the fraction

$$\frac{\text{Number of storage locations used by particular sparse table implementation method}}{\text{Number of storage locations used by standard row-major form}}$$

Clearly, the smaller we can make this ratio, the better our implementation is with respect to memory utilization. Moreover, this ratio must drop below 1 before a particular method can even begin to surpass standard row-major form. In the case of Table 4.3, if we assume that a pointer takes as much memory as one integer, the efficiency ratio of our linked list method is given by

5 locations for head-of-list pointers
3 locations for each of 13 nonzero values

This yields a total of 44 storage locations compared to 70 for a row-major implementation, hence giving a desirable efficiency ratio of 44/70.

However, our simple example of a 5×14 table is so small that it is hardly worth considering. A more interesting question is attempting to determine, in general, when a linked list implementation as described here achieves a savings in memory over the standard row-major method. We claim that, assuming that the data in a sparse table are of integer type, the efficiency ratio for this linked list implementation of a sparse matrix drops below 1 only when the number of nonzero locations in the table is less than

$$NRow * (NCol - 1)/3$$

where NRow is the number of rows in the original table and NCol is the number of columns. To see this, note that each nonzero matrix entry requires three integers to represent it in the linked list implementation. Moreover, each row requires an integer head pointer. Thus the total number of integers required to store N nonzero entries via the linked list method is

$$NRow + N * 3$$

Since we want to force the efficiency ratio

$$\frac{NRow + N * 3}{NRow * NCol}$$

to be less than 1, we conclude that

$$NRow + N * 3 < NRow * NCol$$
$$N * 3 < NRow * NCol - NRow$$
$$N < NRow * (NCol - 1)/3$$

Similar types of efficiency analyses can be carried out for different base data types and implementation schemes.

Implementation Considerations for Wing-and-a-Prayer's Flight/Pilot Data Base

The linked list implementation for a sparse table now gives us a better strategy for solving the Wing-and-a-Prayer flight/pilot program as presented in Chapter 1. However, there is still a difficulty with one of the queries described in the original memorandum we received from Wing-and-a-Prayer's Vice President in charge of scheduling (Section 1.6). In particular, if we view a flight number as an index for a column of the table (see Table 1.1), then a request to print the numbers of all pilots qualified for a particular flight will prove very awkward to handle. This is because the linked list implementation which we have described is oriented toward conveniently traversing a row instead of a column. In order to allow convenient traversals of both rows and columns (as Wing-and-a-Prayer requires), we must employ a multilinked implementation. That is, not only must we link the nodes representing the nontrivial data along a given row, but also along each column. The picture of such a structure that emerges from Table 4.3 is given in Figure 4.21.

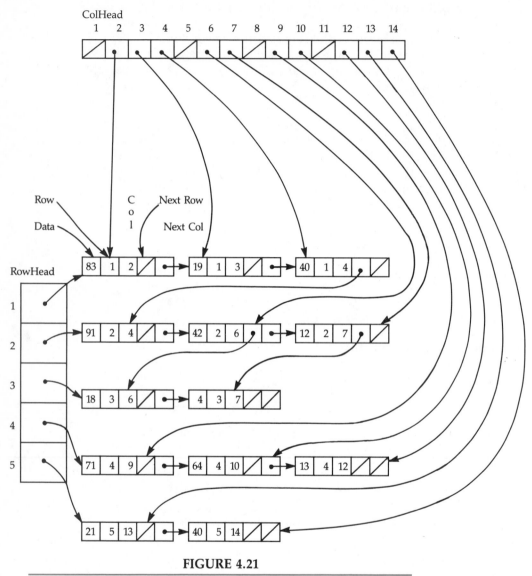

FIGURE 4.21

A multilinked implementation allowing row or
column access

DESIGNER'S WORKBENCH

Bundling Implementation of Abstract Data Types in Records

In this "Designer's Workbench" section, we will consider a Pascal coding technique which can often help bridge the gap between the operations specified for an abstract data type and the eventual implementation of that type in Pascal. Consider for instance our specifications for the operations to be performed on the linked list abstract data type as presented in Section 4.2. In general, we specified these operations as procedures or functions of the form

Operation (L, possibly other parameters)

where L is a linked list. When actually implementing such abstract operations, there is the question of how to conveniently bundle everything involved in the particular implementation strategy for the linked list (or other abstract data type) into one parameter. For example, we encountered this problem in the array implementation of a linked list discussed in Section 4.3. The array implementation of the linked list actually consists of two data items: the array of records in which the data and link fields are stored and the integer pointer to the head of the list. One approach which could be taken is to declare the array globally and then have the procedures which implement the conceptual linked list operations just receive a head pointer into the global array. Although this approach succeeds in identifying the linked list to be processed with just one formal parameter (the head pointer), it has the limitation of being able to affect only a linked list stored in the global array. That is, we cannot pass into the procedure a linked list which happens to be stored in a different array even though the logic of what we would want to do with that linked list is the same logic being performed on the global array.

One way out of this dilemma is to merely specify that the array which stores the linked list be passed as a parameter to our procedures as well as the head pointer. This will certainly work in the sense that it will allow the procedures to affect linked lists stored in a variety of arrays instead of just one global array. However, this new method has the drawback of requiring two parameters to represent one conceptual abstract data type. Hence, our procedures' parameter lists will not mirror as closely the conceptual parameters which appeared in the definition of the operations specified for the abstract data type. Moreover, we will also have a difference in the number of parameters used for a linked list procedure depending upon whether an array implementation is used (now requiring two parameters to represent the linked list) or a pointer variable implementation is used (which still requires only the head pointer to specify the list).

A convenient solution is to bundle the various parameters needed to specify a particular implementation of an abstract data type into one record. Thus, our array implementation of a linked list could be viewed as one parameter of the following type LinkedList.

```
CONST
    TotalSpace = {Appropriate number};
    Null = 0; {To flag end of list}

TYPE
    SpaceRec = RECORD
                  Data : {Appropriate type};
                  Link : integer
               END;
    SpaceArray = ARRAY [1..TotalSpace] OF SpaceRec;
```

```
LinkedList = RECORD
                 Head : integer; {Head Pointer}
                 Space : SpaceArray {DataNodes}
             END;
```

When calling a procedure to process a linked list, we could now specify that the linked list L be of type LinkedList. Within the procedure, we could get at the head pointer via L.Head or access a particular data node via L.Space[i]. The drawback of this bundling technique is that the additional record description slightly complicates the way in which the structure is accessed within the procedure. The advantage of paying this price of increased complexity within the procedure is that the implementation details of the procedure can be more successfully hidden from other routines which call on it. Recall from our discussion in Unit I that the hiding of such implementation details is one of the primary goals of the data abstraction component of the software engineering approach. We have purposely avoided using this bundling technique in the example procedures of this chapter in order to avoid introducing another complication as you begin your study of linked lists. However, the following exercises will ask you to begin exploring the technique, and we will begin to employ it as we discuss implementations of some of the data structures presented in future chapters.

Designer's Workbench Exercises

1. Incorporate the available space pointer for an array implementation of a linked list into the bundled record type LinkedList just described.
2. Rewrite the GetNode and ReturnNode procedures (Section 4.3) for an array implementation of a linked list using the bundled record type you developed for the previous exercise.
3. Using the bundled record type LinkedList, write procedures for an array implementation of each of the eight operations that can be performed on linked lists (see Table 4.1).
4. Write a bundled record type definition for a Pascal pointer variable implementation of a linked list. Use this type definition to write a procedure for each of the eight abstract linked list operations. To as great a degree as possible, the procedures you write for this exercise should be interchangeable with those you wrote for the previous exercise. That is, a program which needs these procedures should see as little difference as possible in the protocol it uses to invoke them.
5. Write a bundled record type definition for an array implementation of a multilinked list.
6. Write a bundled record type definition for a Pascal pointer variable definition of a multilinked list.
7. Write a bundled record type definition for a linked list implementation of a sparse table. ∎

Summary

The linked list structure presented in this chapter is especially convenient for implementing general lists in situations where add and delete operations dominate inspection (and resulting search) operations. This is because the linked list allows adds and deletes to occur by mere pointer manipulation instead of large-scale data movement. The price paid for this gain is the inefficiency of a sequential search strategy. An overview of the advantages and disadvantages of a linked list versus an array implementation of a general list is given in the following table:

	Implementation of general list using array maintained in physical order so that binary search may be used	Implementation of general list using linked list
Add	$O(\log_2 n)$ comparisons to find location where addition should occur. $O(n)$ data interchanges to rearrange list.	$O(n)$ comparisons to find location where addition should occur. $O(1)$ pointer interchanges to rearrange list.
Change	$O(\log_2 n)$ comparisons to find data item to change.	$O(n)$ comparisons to find data item to change.
Inspect	$O(\log_2 n)$ comparisons to find data item.	$O(n)$ comparisons to find data item.
Delete	$O(\log_2 n)$ comparisons to find data item to delete. $O(n)$ data interchanges to rearrange list.	$O(n)$ comparisons to find data item to delete. $O(1)$ pointer interchanges to rearrange list.
Sort	Immediate if the logical order of the sort matches the physical order of the list. Otherwise a pointer sort algorithm must be used.	If more than one logical ordering desired, a multilinked list must be used. That is, a series of links for each ordering must be maintained.
Other considerations	Number of items in list must be maintained. Size of list is bounded by physical size of array.	If Pascal pointers are used to implement, size of list is bounded only by available space.

A linked list can be implemented by an array or by Pascal pointer variables. The latter implementation is more convenient in a Pascal environment because of the supplied **new** and **dispose** procedures and does not limit the size of your list to a compile-time declaration. However, the former implementation may be used in older languages such as FORTRAN, COBOL, and BASIC. Moreover, it also parallels more closely the recordkeeping that you would have to do to implement a permanent linked list using a random access file.

To emphasize the utility of linked lists, we have examined their use in three different applications: the registrar's system, character strings, and sparse tables. Certain of these applications lend themselves to basic variations on the linked list theme such as a dummy header node, circular linking, double linking, and multilinking.

Key Terms

array implementation
assignment
blocks
circular list
cluster
concatenation
data movement
dispose
doubly linked list
dummy header
dynamic memory management
efficiency ratio
head pointer
heap
heap manager

link
linked list
linked list implementation of
    sparse table
linked list implementation of
    strings
list traversal
multilinked list
new
node
Pascal pointer variable
pattern matching
pointer
substring operations
volatile list

Exercises

1. Discuss some of the potential unsuspected results that might occur if
   the string assignment strategy discussed in Section 4.7 were actually
   used. In particular, consider what might happen in the following situation:

   ```
   Str1 := 'COFFEE';
   Str2 := Str1;
   Str1 := 'TEA';
   Output (Str2);
   ```

2. Suppose that you are given the following initial state of an array implementation of a linked list:

	Data	Link
1	47	3
2	89	5
3	66	7
4	100	2
5	13	10
6	55	2
7	112	4
8	178	0
9	79	6
10	19	8

a. Indicate the nodes on the list if the head pointer is 9 and 0 is used to indicate the **NIL** pointer.

b. Indicate the final state of the Data and Link fields after the following program segment is executed:

```
        .
        .
        .

j := 4;
Data[j] := 883;
j := Link[j];
While Link[j] <> 0 DO
    BEGIN
        j := Link[j];
        Data[j] := 912
    END;
```

3. Consider the array implementation of a linked list of names which appears in Figure 4.6. Suppose that the physical order of the five names in that list was given by

Data	Link
LOCKE	?
MILLER	?
SMITH	?
FOSTER	?
ALLEN	?

Head

?

Fill in the Head and Link fields so that the list could be traversed in logical alphabetical order.

4. Indicate the changes in the Link and Head fields from Exercise 3 if MILLER is deleted from the list.

5. Indicate the changes in the Link and Head fields from Exercise 3 if ALLEN is deleted from the list.

6. Consider an array implementation of a linked list of names which is to be maintained in alphabetical order. Trace the status of the Data and Link fields and the Head and Avail pointers as the following operations are performed on the list:

    Insert JAMES
    Insert CHILTON
    Insert SEFTON
    Insert LEE
    Delete CHILTON
    Insert WAGNER
    Delete JAMES
    Insert AARON

7. Repeat Exercise 6 for a linked list in which a dummy header is used.

8. Repeat Exercise 6 for a circular linked list with a dummy header.

9. Repeat Exercise 6 for a circular doubly linked list with a dummy header.

10. Suppose that we also wish to be able to go through the list of Exercise 6 in zip code order where

> JAMES has zip code 54952
> CHILTON has zip code 48649
> SEFTON has zip code 22111
> LEE has zip code 84682
> WAGNER has zip code 11843
> AARON has zip code 99218

Trace the status of all fields (including headers and available space pointer) in an array-based, multilinked implementation of this list of names and zip codes.

11. In what way is the data structure involved with the PointerSort in Chapter 2 not a linked list?

12. What are some advantages of storing information about a list in a dummy header node?

13. What coding advantage does a dummy header node provide in a linked list?

14. What are the advantages and the disadvantages of a linked list structure over an array structure?

15. What main convenience does a doubly linked list offer in comparison to a singly linked list when searching the list?

16. Using a multilist structure, devise a method to implement a sparse table which will make column access as efficient as row access. (Note that the method described in Section 4.8 makes row access much more efficient than column access.)

17. Suppose that you have a program which manipulates a dynamic data structure using Pascal pointer variables. At the end of this program you wish to save this data structure to a file so that it may be reloaded upon the next run of the program. One strategy for doing this is to simply traverse the data structure, writing each node (including its pointer values) to a disk file. Although this approach is legal in Pascal, it will not work. Explain why. Then describe an alternative strategy which will allow saving a data structure from one run of the program to the next.

18. Provide answers to the following two questions:

a. Two techniques of storing strings are the workspace-index method and a doubly linked list (with dummy header) of character clusters. For each method, develop a formula which expresses the percentage of memory devoted to storing "overhead" data (as opposed to actual character data). Each of these formulas should be expressed as a function of the following general parameters:

> P—the number of bytes to store a pointer/integer
> S—the number of bytes to store one character (usually $S = 1$)
> C—the cluster size
> A—the average string length in your application

For each formula you develop, explain how you derive it.

b. Your answer to part a should indicate that the workspace-index method is generally more space efficient than the doubly linked list. However, suppose your application calls for frequently inserting one string in another. For this, the doubly linked list method is more time efficient. Explain why. If it will help, include diagrams in your explanation. Your explanation should also make it evident why a doubly linked list with a dummy header is a more effective structure for this type of application than a singly linked list.

19. The statement

```
p := p + 1
```

advances a pointer to the next node for an array implementation of a general list. What corresponding statement will advance a pointer to the next node for an array implementation of a linked list? For a pointer variable implementation of a linked list? Qualify your answers to these questions by providing the record description from which you are working.

20. In the linked list implementation of a sparse table described in Section 4.8, the array of head pointers is space efficient only if most rows contain a nonzero value. Discuss a strategy for storing head pointers which would be more space efficient in a situation where only a few rows contained nonzero values.

21. Modify the PointerSort procedure of Chapter 2 using a linked list, and then run your program.

22. Incorporate the procedure GetNode into a complete Pascal program.

23. Write a procedure that deletes the last node in a linked list.

24. Initialize a one-dimensional array of size 50 with alphabetic data. Sort the array without physically disturbing the data in the array.

25. Rewrite the procedures InsertNode and DeleteNode using linked lists with dummy headers.

26. Write a program that employs the procedure InsertNodeDouble.

27. Write a program that employs the procedure DeleteNodeDouble.

28. Write a procedure for deleting a node from a doubly linked circular list.

29. Write a procedure for inserting a node in a singly linked circular list.

30. Write a procedure for deleting a node from a singly linked circular list.

31. Write a procedure to traverse a linked list.

32. Write a procedure to find a node in a linked list as specified by a target value for a particular key field.

33. Write a procedure to reverse a linked list.

34. Write a pattern-matching procedure for a linked list implementation of strings. Be sure that you carefully specify the parameters for your procedure.

Programming Problems

1. Wing-and-a-Prayer Airlines maintains four scheduled flights per day which they identify by the numbers 1, 2, 3, and 4. For each of these flights, they keep an alphabetized list of passengers. The data base for the entire airline could hence be viewed as four linked lists. Your task is

to write a problem that sets up and maintains this data base by handling commands of the following form:

    Command→Add
    Flight number→3
    Passenger name→BROWN

    Command→Delete
    From flight number→1
    Passenger name→JONES

    Command→List
    Flight number→2
    (List alphabetically all passengers for the
    specified flight)

Use an appropriate string storage strategy for the passenger names.

2. In order to take care of their growing business, the Fly-by-Night credit card company would like to update their customer data file. Write a program in a high-level language that sets up a doubly linked list into which a record is
    a. Inserted into the list in the correct place, sorted according to the social security number of the customer.
    b. Updated if the customer record exists.
    c. Deleted if the customer no longer wishes to patronize the company.

   In the preceding data manipulation activities, the list should always remain in order sorted by the social security number.

3. As a struggling professional football team, the Bay Area Brawlers have a highly volatile player roster. Write a program which will allow the team to maintain its roster as a linked list in alphabetical order by player last name. Other data items stored for each player are

   □ Height

   □ Weight

   □ Age

   □ University affiliation

   As an added option, allow your program to access players in descending order of weight and age.

4. Develop a line-oriented text editor that assigns a number to each line of text and then maintains the lines in a linked list by line number order (similar to the fashion in which BASIC programs are maintained on many systems). Your program should be able to process the following commands:

    I–line number 'text'

    L–line1–line2
        (instruction to list line1 through line2)

D–line1–line2
(instruction to delete line1 through line2)

If you feel really ambitious, incorporate into your program a string storage strategy which will allow the user to perform editing operations such as inserting and deleting characters within a given line.

5. Write a program that, given a file of text, will add to an index those words in the text that are marked by special delimiting brackets []. The words in the index will be printed after the text itself has been formatted and printed. Words in this index should be listed in alphabetical order with a page number reference for each page of text on which they are delimited by the special brackets. Note that this program would be part of a word processing system an author could use when developing a book with an index of terms.

6. Write a program that allows input of an arbitrary number of polynomials as coefficient and exponent pairs. Store each polynomial as a linked list of coefficient-exponent pairs ordered in descending order by exponent. Note that the coefficient-exponent pairs need not be input in descending order; it is the responsibility of your program to put them in that order. Your program should then be able to evaluate each of the polynomials for an arbitrary argument X and be able to output each of the polynomials in the appropriate descending exponent order. Be sure that your program works for all "unusual" polynomials such as the zero polynomial, polynomials of degree one, and constant polynomials.

7. Implement the registrar's system using a linked list structure.

8. Develop a sparse table solution for Wing-and-a-Prayer's pilot/flight data base using a multilinked list to implement the sparse table.

Queues

The other line always moves faster.

Barbara Ettore
Harper's Magazine

Introductory Considerations

In Chapter 4 we introduced the linked list as a data structure specifically designed to handle conveniently the insertion and deletion of entries in an ordered list. In this chapter, we shall discuss another data structure called a queue which, like the linked list, is a special type of general list as defined in Chapter 1. In particular, the queue is a list with restrictions imposed upon the way in which entries may be inserted and removed. Another name for a queue is a first-in, first-out (FIFO) list. This latter name comes close to completely characterizing the restricted types of adds and deletes which can be performed on a queue. Insertions are limited to one end of the list, whereas deletions may occur only at the other end. The conceptual picture that emerges from the notion of a queue is that of a waiting line; for example, jobs waiting to be serviced by a computer, or cars forming a long line at a busy toll booth. As a highlight of this chapter, we shall use the queue structure to simulate an airport traffic problem.

_____ **5.2**

The Abstract Data Type Queue

The following definition specifies the queue as an abstract data type:

> **Queue**   A queue is merely a restricted form of a list. In particular, the restrictions upon a queue are that all additions to the queue occur at one end, the rear; and all removals from the queue occur at the other end, the front. The effect of these restrictions is to insure that the earlier an item enters a queue, the earlier it will leave the queue. That is, items are processed on a first-in, first-out basis.

The five basic operations which are performed on a queue are shown in Table 5.1.

Operation	Explanation
Create(Queue)	Initialize an empty queue.
Add(Item,Queue)	Insert Item into the Queue. This insertion must occur at the rear of Queue.
Remove(Queue, Item)	Remove the entry at the front of Queue and deposit it in Item.
Empty(Queue)	A Boolean-valued function to determine whether or not Queue is empty.
Full(Queue)	A Boolean-valued function to determine whether or not Queue is full; that is, whether or not it is possible to add a new entry to Queue.

TABLE 5.1

Operations on queues

The conceptual picture that emerges from this definition is given in Figure 5.1.

From this definition of a queue, it is evident that two pointers will suffice to keep track of the data in a queue: one pointer to the front of the queue and one to the rear. This premise underlies all of the queue implementations which we will discuss in the next section.

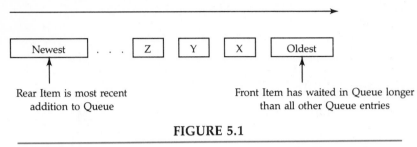

Items Enter at Rear, Leave at Front

Rear Item is most recent
addition to Queue

Front Item has waited in Queue longer
than all other Queue entries

FIGURE 5.1

Abstract data type queue as computer embodiment of
waiting line

_____ 5.3

Implementations of the Queue

We will discuss three implementations of a queue here: array, circular, and
linked list. Additionally, we will discuss a slight variation of a queue,
known as a priority queue, and suggest a possible implementation for it.

Array Implementation of the Queue

Let us consider computer jobs being scheduled in a batch processing environment, a good example of a queue in use. We will further suppose that
all job names are six characters or fewer and that jobs are scheduled strictly
in the order in which they arrive. Then an array and two pointers can be
used to implement the scheduling queue, We will bundle the array and
pointers into a single record type as described in the ''Designer's Workbench'' section of the previous chapter.

```
TYPE   DataString = PACKED ARRAY[1..6] OF Char;
       QueueArray = ARRAY [1..ArraySize] OF DataString;
       QueueType = RECORD
                      List : QueueArray;
                      Front, Rear : integer
                   END;

VAR    Queue : QueueType;
```

Here ArraySize would be set by a **CONST** declaration to the maximum
number of entries which the field List may contain. We shall see that this is
different from the actual number of entries that the queue may contain at a
given time in processing.

   If the Front and Rear pointers are initially set to 1 and 0 respectively,
the state of the queue before any insertions or deletions appears as shown
in Figure 5.2.

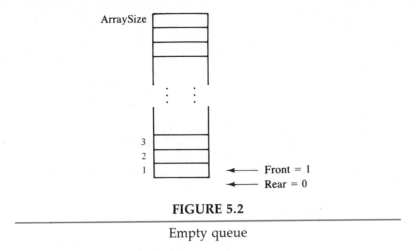

FIGURE 5.2

Empty queue

Recalling that insertions may be made only at the rear of the queue, suppose that job NEWTON now arrives to be processed. The queue then changes to the state pictured in Figure 5.3.

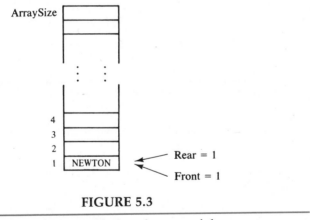

FIGURE 5.3

The job NEWTON added to the rear of the queue

If job NEWTON is followed by PAYROL, the queue's status must change to that of Figure 5.4, which shows that the addition of any Item to the queue requires two steps:

```
Queue.Rear := Queue.Rear + 1;
Queue.List[Queue.Rear] := Item;
```

If the system is now ready to process NEWTON, the front entry must be removed from the queue to an appropriate location designated by Item in Figure 5.5.

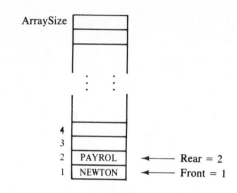

FIGURE 5.4

PAYROL added after NEWTON

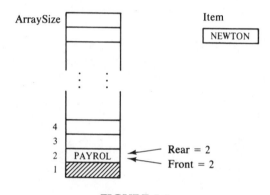

FIGURE 5.5

NEWTON removed from the queue

Here the instructions

```
Item := Queue.List[Queue.Front];
Queue.Front := Queue.Front + 1;
```

achieve the desired effect.

It should be clear from the preceding discussion that the conditions in Table 5.2 signal the associated boundary conditions for an array implementation of a queue.

Condition	Special situation
Rear < Front	Empty queue
Front = Rear	One-entry queue
Rear = ArraySize	No more entries may be added to queue

TABLE 5.2

Boundary condition checks for array implementation of queue

The conditions allow us to develop our brief two-line sequences for adding to and removing from a queue into full-fledged procedures, which in turn assume the existence of the Boolean-valued functions Empty and Full to check whether or not the Remove and Add operations are possible. The actual writing of the Empty and Full functions is left for the Exercises.

```
{ Global declarations }

CONST
  ArraySize = 100;    {Or other appropriate value}
TYPE
  DataString = PACKED ARRAY [1..6] OF Char;
  QueueArray = ARRAY [1..ArraySize] OF DataString;
  QueueType = RECORD
                List : QueueArray;
                Front, Rear : integer
              END;

PROCEDURE Remove (VAR Item : DataString;
                  VAR Queue : QueueType);

{General procedure to remove Front entry from Queue and
 return it in Item. A warning is printed if the Queue
 is empty.}

  BEGIN
    With Queue DO
      IF Empty(Queue) THEN
        writeln ('Attempted removal from empty queue.')
      ELSE
        BEGIN
          Item := List[Front];
          Front := Front + 1
        END
  END; {End Remove}
```

Empty Queue

Rear < Front

Remove

Before Remove   After Remove

Front ≤ Rear

```
PROCEDURE Add(Item : DataString;
             VAR Queue : QueueType);
```

{General procedure to add Item to the Rear of Queue.
A warning message is printed if the operation is unsuccessful
because the queue is full.}

```
BEGIN
   WITH Queue DO
      IF Full(Queue) THEN
         writeln ('Attempted add to full queue.')
      ELSE
         BEGIN
         Rear := Rear + 1;
         List[Rear] := Item
         END
   END;
{End Add}
```

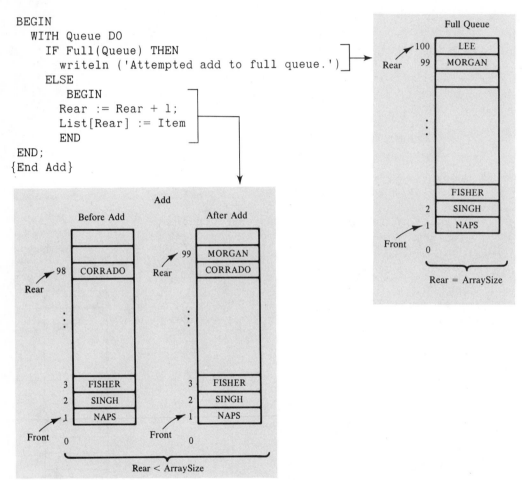

As it now stands, our implementation of a queue as a scheduling structure for jobs in a batch environment functions effectively until Rear matches ArraySize. Then a call to Add fails even though only a small percentage of slots in the array may actually contain data items currently in the queue structure. In fact, given the queue pictured in Figure 5.6, we should be able to use slots 1–997 again.

This is not necessarily undesirable. For example, it may be that the mode of operation in a given batch environment is to process 1,000 jobs, then print a statistical report on these 1,000 jobs, and finally clear the queue to start another group of 1,000 jobs. In this case, the queue in Figure 5.6 is the ideal structure because data about jobs are not lost even after they have left the queue.

However, if the goal of a computer installation were to provide continuous scheduling of batch jobs, without interruption after 1,000 jobs, then

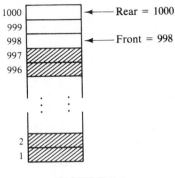

FIGURE 5.6

A full queue

the queue of Figure 5.6 would not be effective. One strategy that could be employed to correct this situation is to move the active queue down the array upon reaching the condition Rear = ArraySize, as illustrated in Figure 5.7.

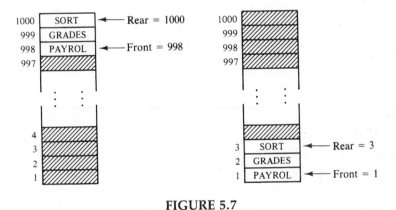

FIGURE 5.7

Active queue moved down

Should the queue contain a large number of items, however, this strategy would not be satisfactory because it would require moving all of the individual data items. We will discuss two other strategies that allow the queue to operate in a continuous and efficient fashion: a circular implementation and a linked list implementation.

Circular Implementation of the Queue

This technique essentially allows the queue to wrap around upon reaching the end of the array. This transformation is illustrated by the addition of the Item, UPDATE, to the queue in Figure 5.8.

To handle the pointer arithmetic necessary for this implementation of a queue, we must make the Front and Rear pointers behave in a fashion

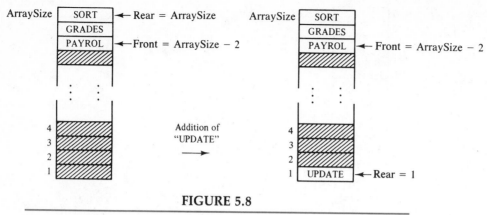

FIGURE 5.8

The queue wraps around when UPDATE is added

analogous to an odometer in a car that has exceeded its mileage capacity. A convenient way of doing this is to use Pascal's **MOD** operator where:

M **MOD** N = remainder of dividing integer M by integer N

(For example, 5 **MOD** 3 = 2 and 10 **MOD** 7 = 3.) It is then immediately clear from Figure 5.8 that Rear < Front will no longer suffice as a condition to signal an empty queue. To derive this condition, consider what remains after we remove an item from a queue that has only a single item in it. There are two possible situations, as illustrated in Figure 5.9.

An inspection of both cases reveals that after the lone entry has been removed, the relationship

(Rear **MOD** ArraySize) + 1 = Front

holds between the pointers. There is a problem, however, with immediately adopting this as a check for an empty queue. This same relationship between pointers also exists when the queue is full—if we allow all slots in the array to be occupied at any one time.

This apparent contradiction can be avoided easily if one memory slot is sacrificed; that is, we view a queue with ArraySize − 1 entries as a full queue. Then the test for fullness is met when the Rear pointer lags two behind Front (including consideration for wrapping around). The results are summarized in Table 5.3.

Front = Rear	One entry queue
(Rear MOD ArraySize) + 1 = Front	Empty queue
((Rear+1) MOD ArraySize) + 1 = Front	Full queue

TABLE 5.3

Boundary condition checks for a circular queue, at most
ArraySize − 1 entries

Case 1: Front = Rear < ArraySize

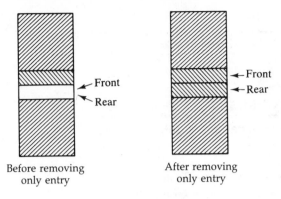

Before removing   After removing
only entry   only entry

Case 2: Front = Rear = ArraySize

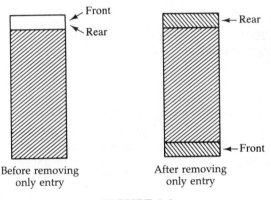

Before removing   After removing
only entry   only entry

FIGURE 5.9

Removing from one-entry queue

Linked List Implementation of the Queue

The linked list method allows the queue to be completely dynamic with size restrictions imposed only by the pool of available nodes. Essentially, the queue is represented as a linked list with an additional rear pointer to the last node in the list so that the list need not be traversed to find this node. To reduce the necessity of handling special cases, we follow the strategy established in Chapter 4 of having a dummy header, which carries no actual data, as the first node in the list. Hence the linked list implementation of the queue containing PAYROL, GRADES, and SORT would appear as in Figure 5.10.

We will follow the convention that the front pointer for the queue points at the dummy header. Hence we access the first actual item in the queue through the dummy header. Table 5.4 summarizes the conditional checks that signal an empty, one-entry, or full queue.

Appropriate procedures for handling additions to and removals from the queue follow. Notice that from a calling module's perspective, it would

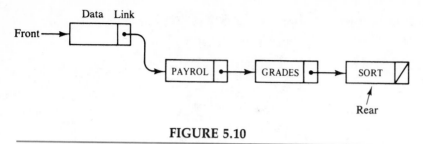

FIGURE 5.10

A queue with three data nodes and a dummy header

Empty Queue ⟶	Rear = Front
One-Entry Queue ⟶	Rear = Front^.Link
Full Queue ⟶	Handled by GetNode or New procedures of Chapter 4

TABLE 5.4

Conditional checks for special situations in the linked list implementation

make little difference whether these low-level procedures used an array or a linked list to implement the queue. For each implementation, we have bundled all the information involved with the queue into a single record of type Queue. Hence the calling protocol for these modules is the same regardless of the implementation being used. That is the essence of data

"The line moves perceptibly faster with computerization."

abstraction. That is, the details of how a data structure is actually implemented are to be hidden as deeply as possible in the overall program structure.

```
{ Global declarations }

TYPE
  DataString = PACKED ARRAY [1..6] OF Char;
  QueuePointer = ^QueueNode;
  QueueNode =
    RECORD
      Data : DataString;
      Link : QueuePointer
    END;

  {Declare QueueType as a bundled record.}
  QueueType =
    RECORD
      Front, Rear : QueuePointer
    END;

PROCEDURE Add (Item : DataString;
               VAR Queue : QueueType);

{Add Item to Queue pointed to by Rear and Front.
 Queue is maintained via a linked list with a dummy header.}
  VAR
    p : QueuePointer;

  BEGIN
    new(p);
    p^.Data := Item;
    p^.Link := NIL;
    Queue.Rear^.Link := p;
    Queue.Rear := p
  END;
  {End Add}
```

Queue before Add

p node obtained via NEW

Inserted

Queue after Adding SORT

```
PROCEDURE Remove(VAR Item : DataString;
                 VAR Queue : QueueType);
```

{Remove Item from Queue pointed to by Rear and Front.
Queue is maintained via a linked list with a dummy header.
Issue warning if Queue is empty and, hence, operation is
unsuccessful.}

```
VAR
   p : QueuePointer;

BEGIN
   IF Empty(Queue) THEN
     writeln ('Attempted removal from empty queue.')
   ELSE
     BEGIN
     p := Queue.Front^.Link;
     Item := p^.Data;
     Queue.Front^.Link := p^.Link;
     IF Queue.Rear = p THEN { Removed from one-entry queue.}
        Queue.Rear := Queue.Front;
     dispose(p)
     END
END;
{End Remove}
```

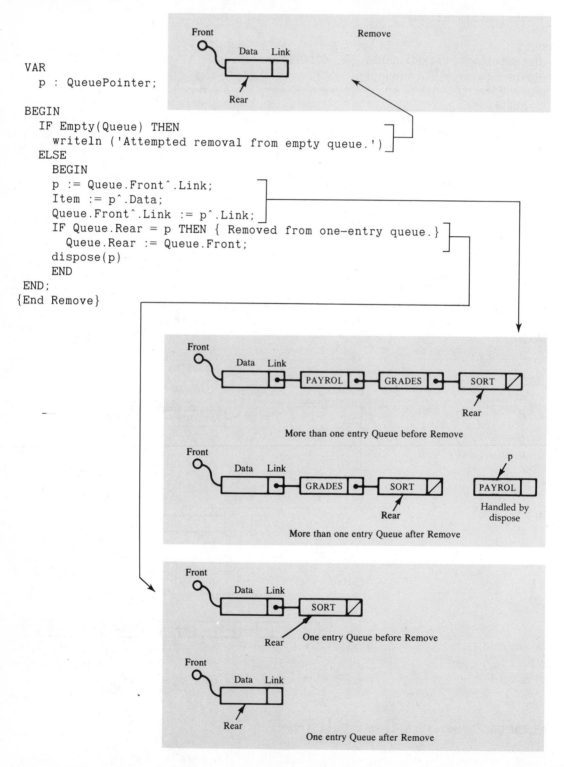

More than one entry Queue before Remove

More than one entry Queue after Remove

Handled by dispose

One entry Queue before Remove

One entry Queue after Remove

Priority Queues

So far we have used a batch scheduling application as an example of how a queue might be used in an operating system. Typically, such batch scheduling might also give higher priorities to certain types of jobs. For instance, at a university computer center, students in introductory computer science courses may receive the highest priority for their jobs to encourage a quick turnaround. Students in upper-division courses may have the next highest priority, whereas jobs related to faculty research, which require a great deal of computation, get the lowest possible priority. These jobs could be classified as types A, B, and C respectively. Any A job is serviced before any B or C job, regardless of the time it enters the service queue. Similarly, any B job is serviced before any C job. A data structure capable of representing such a queue would require just one front pointer but three rear pointers, one for each of the A, B, and C priorities.

A queue with eight jobs waiting to be serviced might appear as shown in Figure 5.11, which tells us that STATS, PRINT, and BANK are the A jobs awaiting service; COPY and CHECK, the B jobs; and UPDATE, AVERAG, and TEST, the C jobs. If a new A job, PROB1, were to arrive for service, it would be inserted at the end of the A queue, between BANK and COPY. Because jobs can be serviced only by leaving the front of the queue, PROB1 would be processed before any of the B or C jobs.

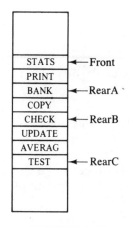

FIGURE 5.11

A priority queue with eight jobs at three priority levels

Because insertions in such a priority queue need not occur at the absolute rear of the queue, it is clear that an array implementation may require moving a substantial amount of data when an item is inserted at the rear of one of the higher priority queues. To avoid this, you can use a linked list to great advantage when implementing a priority queue. Whenever an item arrives to be inserted into a given priority level, the rear pointer for that priority gives us an immediately accessible pointer to the node after which the item is to be inserted. This avoids a costly sequential search for the insertion point. If a dummy header is included at the beginning of the list, the empty conditions for any given priority are as shown in Table 5.5.

Condition	Priority
Front = Rear1	For priority 1, the highest priority
Rear1 = Rear2 Rear(n − 1) = Rear$n$	For priority 2 For priority n

TABLE 5.5

Empty conditions for a priority queue

The specifics of writing procedures to add to or remove from a priority queue are included as exercises at the end of the chapter. In Chapter 7, we will see that priority queues may also be implemented using the special type of tree structure known as a heap (not to be confused with the heap maintained by Pascal's heap manager as described in Chapter 4). Unlike the implementation we have just discussed, using the heap will conveniently allow an unrestricted number of different priorities.

_____ **5.4**

Case Study: Simulation for Wing-and-a-Prayer Airlines

In order to further illustrate the applicability of ideas discussed in this chapter, we shall simulate the solution of the following air traffic problem. The specific problem relating to Wing-and-a-Prayer Airlines was brought to the world-renowned consultant Professor Hardtoget at the University of Hard Knocks. The memo on the next page from the president of the company to Professor Hardtoget describes the problem:

To solve this problem, we will use the design strategy outlined in the solution of the registrar's problem in Chapter 3. It is assumed that the simulation is for a period of four hours. The major iteration in the program will thus be a loop cycling for 240 minutes. Each minute we must check whether or not there is a Wing-and-a-Prayer arrival or departure and whether there is an arrival or departure by some other airline. A key function employed in any type of simulation is a random number generator. Such a function will return a real number between 0 and 1 each time it is called. The fashion in which such numbers are returned obeys statistical properties of randomness. That is, if we were to generate a long sequence of random numbers by repeated calls to the random number generator, we would find that the numbers returned are evenly distributed and yet completely unpredictable. Some versions of Pascal include a random generator as a built-in library function. If yours does not, the function Random in the

---

MEMORANDUM
Wing-and-a-Prayer Airlines

TO: Professor Hardtoget, University of Hard Knocks

FROM: President, Wing-and-a-Prayer Airlines

DATE: September 30, 1992

RE: Wasted Fuel and Time

Dear Professor Hardtoget:

Wing-and-a-Prayer Airlines is becoming increasingly concerned about the amount of fuel being wasted as its planes wait to land at and take off from world-famous O'Hair Airport. Could you please help us write a program to simulate the operation of one day's activity at O'Hair and report on the times spent waiting to land and take off for each Wing-and-a-Prayer flight? Input data to the program should include:

☐ Average number of Wing-and-a-Prayer arrivals each hour

☐ Average number of other airline arrivals each hour

☐ Average number of Wing-and-a-Prayer departures each hour

☐ Average number of other airline departures each hour

☐ Number of available runways

☐ Average time runway in use for an arrival

☐ Average time runway in use for a departure

By appropriately adjusting these parameters, we hope to do some valuable "what-if" analyses regarding the time spent waiting for a runway by our arrivals and departures.

---

case study provides an acceptable one which continually modifies a global "seed" to generate successive random values.

In the case study, we shall make use of a random number to simulate the random fashion in which planes often arrive or depart. For instance, just because we know that, on average, 15 planes are ready for takeoff each hour, we cannot conclude that a plane is ready for takeoff every four minutes. Rather, we say that, in any given minute, there is a 25 percent chance that a plane will be ready to depart. Then we generate a random number. If the number returned is less than 0.25, our program will add a plane to the departure queue.

Departure and arrival queues are the major data structures underlying this simulation. If the random number dictates a new arrival or departure, we add a record to the queue consisting of the time the plane entered the queue and an indicator as to whether or not it is a Wing-and-a-Prayer flight. As a runway becomes available, we remove an entry from the queue, giving it the runway for the appropriate amount of time. The difference between the current time and the time the plane entered the queue can then be added to the proper accumulated total of waiting times. Runways are represented by a simple list structure containing one integer for each runway. At any given time in the simulation, this integer represents the number of minutes remaining until the runway will again become available.

The modular design is shown in Figure 5.12; module specifications and complete code of the solution follow the figure.

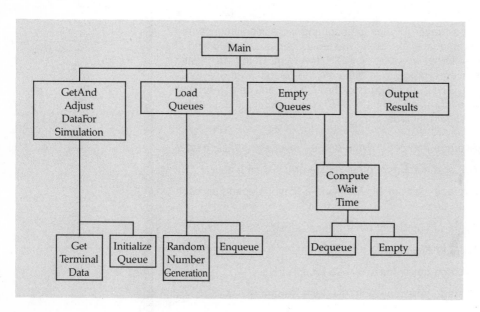

FIGURE 5.12

Modular structure chart for simulation

Module Specifications for O'Hair Simulation

The specifications for this simulation follow:

```
Main Module

Data Received: None
Information Returned: None
Logic:
    Call GetAndAdjustDataForSimulation.
    During the simulation period,
        repeatedly call on LoadQueues and ComputeWaitTime.
    Call EmptyQueues.
    Call OutputResults.
```

Module 1

Random Module

Data Received: None, although a global seed variable is continually
                        altered
Information Returned: Random number between 0 and 1
Logic:
        A simple mathematical routine based on pi and the exp,
        log, and trunc functions found in all versions of Pascal.
        These act to alter the seed in a random fashion each time
        the function is called.

Module 2

GetTerminalData Module

Data Received: None
Information Returned: The values of the seven input parameters

Logic:
        For each parameter
                Prompt for terminal input.
                Get the value of the corresponding parameter.

Module 3

Enqueue Module

Data Received: Front and rear pointers for queue
                        An integer representing current time to be added
                                to queue
                        A Boolean flag indicating whether or not
                                plane is from Wing–and–a–Prayer

Information Returned: Appropriately updated front and rear
                                pointers.
                        New node added to queue.

Logic:
        Get a new node.
        Store data in the various components of the node.
        Properly assign front and rear pointers.

Module 4

Initialize Module

Data Received: None
Information Returned: Front and rear queue pointers set to point at
                                dummy header
Logic:
        Get dummy header record.
        Assign front and rear to point to it, hence performing
          create operation.

Module 5

Dequeue Module

Data Received: Front and rear pointers for queue
Information Returned: Time at which this plane was added to the
                                    queue
                            Boolean flag indicating whether or not plane
                                is from Wing-and-a-Prayer
                            Appropriately updated front and rear pointers

> *Module 6*

Logic:
      Use the front pointer to find the
         information in the appropriate node in the
         queue. Remove this node from the queue, returning
         the time and Boolean flag in appropriate parameters.
      Adjust front and rear pointers as node is removed from
         queue.

GetAndAdjustDataForSimulation Module

Data Received: None
Information Returned: Initialized arrival and departure
                                    probabilities
                            Initialized queues
                            Initialized counters
                            Initialized runway use list
Logic:
      Call on GetTerminalData to gather input of seven simulation
            parameters.
      Convert appropriate parameters to per-minute probabilities.
      Initialize queues.
      Set accumulating variables to 0.
      For each runway,
              assign runway use to 0.

> *Module 7*

LoadQueues Module

Data Received: Simulation minute
Information Returned: Queues may have additions

Logic:
      Call Random.
      If the random number < Wing-and-a-Prayer arrival per minute
         then
            Add 1 to number of Wing-and-a-Prayer arrivals.
            Call Enqueue with proper front, rear, minute, and Boolean
               flag as true.

      Repeat this procedure three times more for
            Arrival of other type of plane
               Boolean flag for this type is false.
            Departure of Wing-and-a-Prayer plane
               Boolean flag is true.
            Departure of other type of plane
               Boolean flag is false.

> *Module 8*

ComputeWaitTime Module

Data Received: Simulation minute
Information Returned: Various counters and queues may be affected
Logic:
```
     For each runway
          If it is not free, reduce its use time by 1
            else
                Call Dequeue with arrival parameters
                If queue not empty then
                   If Wing-and-a-Prayer plane arrival
                      update Wing-and-a-Prayer arrival
                      wait time
                   else other type arrival
                      update non-Wing-and-a-Prayer
                      arrival wait time
                   Assign arrival use time to this runway
                else
                   Call Dequeue with departure parameters
                   If queue not empty then
                      If Wing-and-a-Prayer plane departure
                         update Wing-and-a-Prayer
                         departure wait time
                      else other type departure
                         update non-Wing-and-a-Prayer
                         departure wait time
                      Assign departure use time to this runway
```

Module 9

EmptyQueues Module

Data Received: Simulation minute
Information Returned: Empty queues
                     Updated accumulators
Logic:
```
     Add 1 to minute.
     While arrival departure queue not empty
          Call ComputeWaitTime
```

Module 10

OutputResults Module

Data Received: All global accumulators to be output.
Information Returned: None
Logic:
```
     Repeatedly write out results.
```

Module 11

Coding for O'Hair Simulation

The Pascal code for this simulation follows, along with reference to the module specifications just presented.

```
PROGRAM OHAIR(input, output);

{This program represents the solution to a simulation of O'Hair
 airport traffic. The results printed are the average time spent
```

waiting by both the Wing-and-a-Prayer Airline planes and all other
airlines' planes for both departures and arrivals. }

```
CONST
  LengthOfSimulation = 240;

TYPE
  IntArray = ARRAY [1..10] OF Real;
  Fptr = ^Frec;
  Frec =
    RECORD
      Time : integer; { Records time plane entered its queue. }
      wp : boolean; { true if this is a Wing-and-a-Prayer flight. }
      Next : Fptr
    END;

  FlightQueue =
    RECORD
      Front, Rear : Fptr
    END;

VAR

  { Global reals to store statistical data for simulation and seed for
    random number generator. }

    AvDeptTimeWp,       {Average departure wait time for Wing-and-a-Prayer}
    AvDeptTimeNwp,      {Average departure wait time for
                          non-Wing-and-a-Prayer}
    AvArrivTimeWp,      {Average arrival wait time for Wing-and-a-Prayer}
    AvArrivTimeNwp,     {Average arrival wait time for non-Wing-and-a-Prayer}
    AvWpArriv,          {Probability of Wing-and-a-Prayer arrival in given
                          minute}
    AvNwpArriv,         {Probability of non-Wing-and-a-Prayer arrival in
                          given minute}
    AvWpDept,           {Probability of Wing-and-a-Prayer departure in given
                          minute}
    AvNwpDept,          {Probability of non-Wing-and-a-Prayer departure in
                          given minute}
    AvArrivUse,         {Average runway time for arrival}
    AvDeptUse,          {Average runway time for departure}
    Seed : real;        {Random number seed}

  { At any given minute in simulation, Runway stores length of time
    runways will be in use and hence not available for new arrival or
    departure. }

  RunWay: IntArray;

  { Global integers to store time counter for simulation and various other
    accumulating counters. }

    NumWpArriv,             {Wing-and-a-Prayer arrivals}
    NumNwpArriv,            {Non-Wing-and-a-Prayer arrivals}
    NumWpDept,              {Wing-and-a-Prayer departures}
```

```
    NumNwpDept,            {Non-Wing-and-a-Prayer departures}
    TotWaitTimeArrivWp,    {Total wait minutes for Wing-and-a-Prayer
                             arrivals}
    TotWaitTimeArrivNwp,   {Total wait minutes for non-Wing-and-a-Prayer
                             arrivals}
    TotWaitTimeDeptWp,     {Total wait minutes for Wing-and-a-Prayer
                             departures}
    TotWaitTimeDeptNwp,    {Total wait time for non-Wing-and-a-Prayer
                             departures}
    NumRunways,            {Number of Runways}
    Minute : integer;      {Minute counter}

    { Arrival and Departure queues. }

    Arrival, Departure : FlightQueue;

{----------Modules Initialize, Empty, Enqueue, Dequeue form------------------}
{----------queue routine package used by other routines in program.----------}


  PROCEDURE Initialize(VAR Queue : FlightQueue);

    { Creates empty queue as linked list with dummy header node. }

    VAR
      p : Fptr;


    BEGIN
      new(p);
      p^.Next := NIL;
      Queue.Front := p;
      Queue.Rear := p
    END; {Initialize}
```
See Module 5

```
  FUNCTION Empty(Queue : FlightQueue) : boolean;

    { Check for whether or not Queue is empty. }


    BEGIN
      Empty := (Queue.Front = Queue.Rear)
    END; { Empty }


  PROCEDURE Enqueue(VAR Queue : FlightQueue;
                        Time : integer;
                        Kind : boolean);

{ This procedure enqueues a node with time and kind in it to the
  correct queue. }

    VAR
      f : Fptr;
```
See Module 4

```
      BEGIN
        new(f);
        f^.Time := Time;
        f^.wp := Kind;
        Queue.Rear^.Next := f;
        f^.Next := NIL;
        Queue.Rear := f
      END; { Enqueue }


    PROCEDURE Dequeue(VAR Queue : FlightQueue;
                      VAR Time : integer;
                      VAR Kind : boolean);

{ Dequeue removes from the queue and puts the time found in Time
  and flags Kind if it is a Wing-and-a-Prayer plane. Assumes queue
  is not empty. }

      VAR
        f : Fptr;


      BEGIN
        f := Queue.Front^.Next;
        Time := f^.Time;
        Kind := f^.wp;
        Queue.Front^.Next := f^.Next;
        IF Queue.Rear = f THEN { Removing from a one-entry queue }
          Queue.Rear := Queue.Front;
        dispose(f)
      END; { Dequeue}

{--------------------End of Queue Routine Package--------------------}


    FUNCTION Random : real;

{ Returns a random value between 0 and 1 (inclusive). The variable
  seed is global in the calling program. Seed is modified each time
  to insure a (probably) different random number on successive
  invocations of the function. }

      CONST
        pi = 3.14159;

      VAR
        something : real;

      BEGIN { Random }
        something := Seed + pi;
        something := exp(5.0 * ln(something));
        Seed := something - trunc(something);
        Random := Seed
      END; {Random}
```

See Module 6

See Module 2

```
PROCEDURE GetTerminalData(VAR nr : integer;
                          VAR wpa, nwpa, wpd, nwpd, ause, duse :
                              real);
```

{ This procedure reads information about the number of planes per
  hour in use, the number of runways, and the average length of
  time a runway is in use for arrivals and departures. }

```
   BEGIN
      writeln('Please enter the number of runways in use.');
      readln(nr);
      writeln('Please enter average number of Wing-and-a-Prayer');
      writeln('planes expected to arrive per hour.');
      readln(wpa);
      writeln('Please enter average number of other planes');
      writeln('expected to arrive per hour.');
      readln(nwpa);
      writeln('Please enter the average number of
        Wing-and-a-Prayer');
      writeln('planes expected to depart per hour.');
      readln(wpd);
      writeln('Please enter the average number of other planes');
      writeln('expected to depart per hour.');
      readln(nwpd);
      writeln;
      writeln('Please enter the arrival use time of a runway.');
      readln(ause);
      writeln('Please enter the departure use time of a runway.');
      readln(duse)

   END; { GetTerminalData }
```

See Module 3

```
PROCEDURE GetAndAdjustDataForSimulation;
```

{ This procedure takes terminal data and adjusts it for the
  simulation. Essentially, this procedure initializes runways' use
  time; initializes proper queues; computes arrival and departure
  on per minute basis; and initializes some global variables to
  0. }

```
   VAR
      i : integer;


   BEGIN

      GetTerminalData(NumRunways, AvWpArriv, AvNwpArriv, AvWpDept,
                      AvNwpDept, AvArrivUse, AvDeptUse);

      AvWpArriv  := AvWpArriv / 60;
      AvNwpArriv := AvNwpArriv / 60;
      AvWpDept   := AvWpDept / 60;
      AvNwpDept  := AvNwpDept / 60;
```

See Module 7

```
      Initialize(Arrival);
      Initialize(Departure);
      NumWpArriv := 0;
      NumNwpArriv := 0;
      NumWpDept := 0;
      NumNwpDept := 0;
      TotWaitTimeArrivWp := 0;
      TotWaitTimeDeptWp := 0;
      TotWaitTimeArrivNwp := 0;
      TotWaitTimeDeptNwp := 0;
      FOR i := 1 TO NumRunways DO
        RunWay[i] := 0

    END; { GetAndAdjustDataForSimulation }




  PROCEDURE LoadQueues(min : integer);

{ This procedure calls on the function Random and the
  procedure Enqueue to load the proper queues with the right
  arrival/departure information. }

    VAR
      y : real;


    BEGIN

      y := Random;
      If y < AvWpArriv THEN {If Wing-and-a-Prayer planes arrive }
        BEGIN
        NumWpArriv := NumWpArriv + 1;
        Enqueue(Arrival, min, true)
        END;

      y := Random;
      IF y < AvNwpArriv THEN
          {check if non-Wing-and-a-Prayer planes arrive }
        BEGIN
        NumNwpArriv := NumNwpArriv + 1;
        Enqueue(Arrival, min, false)
        END;

      y := Random;
      IF y < AvWpDept THEN
          { Wing-and-a-Prayer plane ready to depart }
        BEGIN
        NumWpDept := NumWpDept + 1;
        Enqueue(Departure, min, true)
        END;

      y := Random;
      IF y < AvNwpDept THEN
          { Non-Wing-and-a-Prayer plane ready to depart }
```

See
Module 8

```
          BEGIN
          NumNwpDept := NumNwpDept + 1;
          Enqueue(Departure, min, false)
          END

    END; { LoadQueues}


  PROCEDURE ComputeWaitTime(min : integer);

{ This procedure computes the total wait time for various types of
  planes in use. }

    VAR
      j, Time : integer;
      Kind : boolean;


    BEGIN
      FOR j := 1 TO NumRunways DO
        IF RunWay[j] <> 0 THEN { Runway is not available }
          RunWay[j] := RunWay[j] - 1 { So decrease time before it
                                       will be }
        ELSE IF RunWay[j] = 0 THEN { Runway is available }
          IF NOT Empty(Arrival) THEN { Give priority to landing
                                       plane }
            BEGIN
            Dequeue(Arrival, Time, Kind);
            IF Kind THEN { Wing-and-a-Prayer }
              TotWaitTimeArrivWp := TotWaitTimeArrivWp - Time + min
            ELSE
              TotWaitTimeArrivNwp := TotWaitTimeArrivNwp - Time +
                                                          min;
            RunWay[j] := AvArrivUse { Runway now in use }
            END
          ELSE { departures gain access after arrivals }
          IF NOT Empty(Departure) THEN
            BEGIN
            Dequeue(Departure, Time, Kind);
            IF Kind THEN
              TotWaitTimeDeptWp := TotWaitTimeDeptWp - Time + min
            ELSE
              TotWaitTimeDeptNwp := TotWaitTimeDeptNwp - Time +
                                                        min;
            RunWay[j] := AvDeptUse
            END
    END; { ComputeWaitTime }
```

*See
Module 9*

```
  PROCEDURE EmptyQueues(min : integer);

    { After the simulation time, the queues must be emptied. While
      emptying the queues, we have to add the corresponding wait
      time. }
```

*See
Module 10*

```
      BEGIN
        WHILE (NOT Empty(Arrival)) OR (NOT Empty(Departure)) DO
          BEGIN
          min := min + 1;
          ComputeWaitTime(min)
          END { WHILE }
      END; { EmptyQueues }


    PROCEDURE OutputResults;

      { This procedure writes out the results of simulation. }


        BEGIN

          AvArrivTimeWp := TotWaitTimeArrivWp / NumWpArriv;
          AvArrivTimeNwp := TotWaitTimeArrivNwp / NumNwpArriv;
          AvDeptTimeWp := TotWaitTimeDeptWp / NumWpDept;
          AvDeptTimeNwp := TotWaitTimeDeptNwp / NumNwpDept;
          writeln(' Average wait time for Wing-and-a-Prayer arrivals,
            departures');
          writeln('            ', AvArrivTimeWp: 12: 4, AvDeptTimeWp: 12:
            4);
          writeln(' Average wait time for non-Wing-and-a-Prayer
            arrivals, departures');
          writeln('            ', AvArrivTimeNwp: 12: 4, AvDeptTimeNwp: 12:
            4)
        END; { OutputResults }
```

*See
Module 11*

A Relevant Issue . . .

Operating Systems and Scheduling Resource Use in a Time-Sharing Environment

One of the primary problems facing designers of operating systems is the allocation and scheduling of resources which must be shared by a number of users. For instance, consider a simple time-sharing system which allows multiple users, each on a video terminal, and also has one shared printer. Suppose that the currently running process, called process A, makes a request to use the printer. Then, before this process completes its task on the printer, its allotted time (often called a time burst) expires, and it is replaced by process B as the currently running process. If process B re-

quests the printer while it is running, we have a clear problem. If process B is granted the printer, its output will be interspersed with that from process A, which did not complete its printing before its time burst expired. Obviously, we cannot let process B continue to run.

The solution developed by operating systems designers to honor both of these requests is to use multiple queues—one containing those processes which have cleared access to all resources they require to run, and one for processes which have requested a resource currently owned by another process. The former

```
BEGIN { OHAIR }
  GetAndAdjustDataForSimulation;
  Seed := 4.0 { This is to start random number generation. A
              different initial value for seed produces
              different random number sequence. }
  FOR Minute := 1 TO LengthOfSimulation DO
    BEGIN
    LoadQueues(Minute);
    ComputeWaitTime(Minute)
    END; { FOR }
  EmptyQueues(LengthOfSimulation);
  OutputResults
END. { OHAIR }
```

*See
Module 1*

Sample Run.
```
Please enter the number of runways in use.
7
Please enter average number of Wing-and-a-Prayer
planes expected to arrive per hour.
15
Please enter average number of other planes
expected to arrive per hour.
20
Please enter the average number of Wing-and-a-Prayer
planes expected to depart per hour.
13
Please enter the average number of other planes
expected to depart per hour.
22
```

of these queues is often called the ready queue; the latter is termed the blocked queue. Hence the solution to the scenario described in the first paragraph involves two steps.

1. Move process A from its currently running state to the ready queue when its time burst expires (because it has all the necessary resources to start running again).

2. Move process B to the blocked queue when it requests the printer already owned by process A. Here it would remain until process A is done with the printer, at which time the front entry in the blocked queue for the printer (B in this case) would be moved to the ready queue.

In practice, the addition and removal of processes to and from these queues is controlled by special flags called semaphores. For a thorough exposition on operating system queues and semaphores, see H. M. Deitel's *Introduction to Operating Systems* (Reading, Mass.: Addison-Wesley, 1984).

```
Please enter the arrival use time of a runway.
5
Please enter the departure use time of a runway.
4
Average wait time for Wing-and-a-Prayer arrivals, departures
          0.1356                  0.9149
Average wait time for non-Wing-and-a-Prayer arrivals, departures
          0.1618                  1.0215
```

DESIGNER'S WORKBENCH

Increasing Program Modularization

The examples of procedures we have developed for queue operations and for the case study of this chapter present some interesting questions regarding the responsibilities of individual modules within a complex software system. Among the questions are

☐ What is the appropriate action for an individual module to take when an error condition is encountered?

☐ What kinds of data locations should be accessed globally instead of being passed as parameters?

☐ What is an appropriate length for a module? In situations in which a module may be too long, what are effective strategies for decomposing it into smaller modules?

As an example of the issues involved in the first of these questions, consider the modules that were developed in Section 5.3 for adding to and removing from a queue. In both of these modules, error messages are output when a full queue (for add operation) or empty queue (for remove operation) is encountered. Is this type of warning output what we always want a module to do when it encounters an error? In many cases, such output can be very undesirable when viewed from the perspective of the overall system. For instance, there are situations in which failure to remove an item from an empty queue is not an error but rather just a condition to be monitored by a calling module. The EmptyQueues module in the simulation case study of this chapter (Section 5.4) provides an example of such a situation. Here warning output from a module deeply embedded in the modular structure chart for the system may be completely unwanted because the calling module is itself prepared to handle such an error condition. Hence, in such situations, it may be appropriate for the module which initially detects an "error" condition such as a full or empty queue to merely use a Boolean variable to report this condition to a higher-level module. This higher-level module can then decide upon the appropriate course of action to gracefully handle the error condition.

The second modularization issue raised in this chapter's case study centers around the use of global data locations. Because the variables which kept track of the statistics in our simulation case study had to be shared by nearly all modules in the system, we used a large number of global variables. In general, however, the use of global variables should be minimized as much as possible. This is because global parameters may be erroneously altered by modules which, through careless logic, inadvertently access such global locations. Hence, removing data locations from global storage and instead treating them as procedural parameters and/or local variables is a means of protecting a system against errors which may result as side effects of a procedure or function which inappropriately accesses a global location. The issue of a module's inadvertent and accidental side effects becomes increasingly important in systems which are developed by a team of programmers. In such an environment, it is wise to protect your modules against the side effects of others even though you may have complete confidence in the other members of the team. Minor breakdowns in communications between team members can otherwise result in disastrous consequences.

The third modularization issue we consider here is the question of what constitutes appropriate module length. Gerald Weinberg has conducted experiments which show that our ability to understand a module (and hence to find bugs in it) depends on our ability to understand the entire module at once. (For Weinberg's description of these experiments and results, see his book, *The Psychology of Computer Programming* (New York: Van Nostrand Reinhold, 1971)). Given this as a premise, a rule of thumb that limits a module's length to one page makes good sense. Why? Merely reading a module longer than one page requires the physical interruption of flipping back and forth between pages, hence breaking the concentration needed to understand the module. Of course, a module's being less than one page in length does not guarantee its being a well-designed module. It must also be focused on one specific task. Recall that, in Chapter 3, we referred to a module that achieved this focus as functionally cohesive. If you find that the modules in programs you develop lack this functional cohesion or are just physically too long, it is often possible to factor out specific tasks to be done within a module and rewrite these tasks as separate procedures and/or functions.

Designer's Workbench Exercises

1. Rewrite the procedures Add and Remove of Section 5.3 so that they return an appropriate error flag instead of printing out a warning message when it is impossible to perform the operation.
2. Rewrite the case study of this chapter (Section 5.4) so that the various statistical counters and averages are not accessed globally but are instead passed as parameters from procedure to procedure. To avoid excessively long parameter lists, you could bundle all of the statistical data into one appropriate record structure.
3. The Seed variable upon which the Random function of this chapter's case study depends is a global variable that is altered within the function. Seed's being global keeps this random number generator from being a self-contained module: a quality we would very much like the module to have. Yet, if Seed is a variable local to Random, in standard Pascal its value will not be retained upon successive calls to Random. Explore the documentation for your version of Pascal to see if it provides some nonstandard way of declaring a variable which is both local

to a procedure or function and will retain its value between successive invocations. Many version of Pascal offer this type of extension to the standard. If yours does, use it to rewrite Random with Seed as a local instead of global variable.

4. Consider the module GetAndAdjustDataForSimulation in this chapter's case study. Identify various subtasks performed in this module and factor those subtasks into separate subordinate modules. Use these to rewrite GetAndAdjustDataForSimulation as a shorter and more cohesive module.

5. Consider the module LoadQueues from this chapter's case study. Within that module, identify one common subtask which is performed several times. Factor out that subtask as a module in itself (with appropriate parameters) and use this to rewrite LoadQueues in a shorter form.

6. Consider the module ComputeWaitTime from this chapter's case study. Within that module, identify one common subtask which is performed several times. Factor out that subtask as a module in itself (with appropriate parameters) and use this to rewrite ComputeWaitTime in a shorter form. ∎

Summary

A queue is a first-in, first-out (FIFO) data structure used in processing of data such as job scheduling in a large university computer environment. There are two basic pointers, front and rear, associated with this structure. New data items to be processed are added to the rear of the queue, and the data item that is about to be processed is removed from the front of the queue. The process of cars entering and leaving a car wash is a familiar analogy. Queues can be implemented with arrays or linked lists. A circular implementation of arrays will allow the queue to exist indefinitely. Primary applications of queues are in the areas of operating systems and computer simulation of events. The case study of this chapter illustrated such a simulation for the arrivals and departures at a typical airport. A Relevant Issue gives an indication of how queues are used by an operating system to schedule the use of computer resources in a time-sharing environment.

Key Terms

array implementation	priority queue
blocked queue	queue
circular implementation	random number generator
first-in, first-out (FIFO)	ready queue
front pointer	rear pointer
linked list implementation	semaphores
MOD	simulation

Exercises

1. Consider a circular array implementation of a queue in which the array is declared to have an index range of 1..5. Trace the status of the array and the Front and Rear pointers after each of the following successive operations:

```
ADD 'SMITH'
ADD 'JONES'
ADD 'GREER'
REMOVE
ADD 'CARSON'
REMOVE
ADD 'BAKER'
ADD 'CHARLES'
ADD 'BENSON'
REMOVE
ADD 'MILLER'
```

2. Develop a calling convention and associated procedure to add an item to a queue with n priorities.
3. Given the discussion of circular queues presented in this chapter, determine a valid initial setting for the Front and Rear pointers in a circular queue.
4. Why is a priority queue called by this name?
5. In the array implementation of a circular queue as described in Section 5.3, what are the conditions to be satisfied by the pointers Rear and Front for a full queue, an empty queue, and a one-entry queue?
6. Would a linked list or array implementation be better suited for a priority queue? Why?
7. Recall the example of using a priority queue to schedule batch jobs as described in Section 5.3. Suppose that we wanted to add the capability of allowing a user to withdraw his or her job from the priority queue before it reached the front. (This is a useful capability for the user who submits a job to the queue and then realizes that there is an error in it.) Explain why, in this situation, it would be advantageous to implement the queue as a doubly linked list.
8. For a circular queue implemented by a linked list, it is only necessary to separate and maintain one queue pointer. Which one: Front or Rear? Justify your answer, using a drawing to help.
9. Suppose that we adopt the following conventions for the Front and Rear pointers associated with a queue. Front is to point at the next item to be removed from the queue. Rear is to point at the first available location; that is, the next location to be filled. Explain how this change in convention would affect the operations Create(Queue), Empty-(Queue), and Full(Queue) for
    a. A noncircular array implementation.
    b. A circular array implementation.
    c. A linked list implementation.

10. Explain how a continuously maintained count of the number of elements in a circular queue could be used to implement the Create, Empty, and Full queue operations (instead of checking the relationship between Front and Rear). Write a bundled record structure for such a queue. Then write Pascal procedures to implement each of the five basic queue operations.

11. Write procedures (or functions) to implement the Create, Empty, and Full operations for a noncircular array implementation of a queue.

12. Write procedures (or functions) to implement all five queue operations for a circular array implementation of a queue.

13. Write procedures (or functions) to implement the Create, Empty, and Full operations for a linked list implementation of a queue.

14. Develop a calling convention and associated procedure to remove an item from a queue with n priorities.

15. Suppose that you are given a queue which is known to contain only positive integers. Use only the fundamental queue operations Remove and Add to write a procedure

```
Procedure Replace(VAR Queue : QueueType; Old, New : Integer);
```

which replaces all occurrences of the positive integer Old in the Queue with the positive integer New. Other than doing this, the queue is to remain unchanged. Avoid passing through the queue more than once to achieve this.

Programming Problems

1. Develop a program to simulate the processing of batch jobs by a computer system. The scheduling of these jobs should be handled via a queue (or priority queue for more of a challenge). Examples of commands that your program should be able to process are

Command	Purpose
Add	To add entry to queue.
Delete	To take an item out of the queue.
Status	To report on items currently in queue.

2. Develop a program to simulate the arrival of customers in a waiting line at a bank. Factors to consider in such a program would be the average time it takes to service one customer, the average number of customers that arrive in a given time period, and the number of service windows maintained by the bank. Statistics such as the length of time the average customer has to spend in the waiting line could be very helpful in the bank's future planning.

3. Here is a problem typically encountered in text formatting applications.

Given a file of text, that text delimited by special bracketing symbols [and] is to be considered a footnote. Footnotes, when encountered, are not to be printed as normal text but are instead stored in a footnote queue. Then, when the special symbol # is encountered, all footnotes currently in the queue are printed and the queue should be returned to an empty state. What you learn in solving this problem will allow you to make good use of string storage techniques.

4. In order to improve their services, the Fly-by-Night credit card company decided to give incentives to their customers for prompt payment. The company decided that customers who pay their bills two weeks before the due date would receive top priority and a 5 percent discount. Customers who pay their bills within one week of the due date would receive next priority and a 1 percent discount. Third priority would be given to customers who pay their bills on or within two days after the due date. The customers who pay their bills thereafter would be assigned the lowest priority. Write a program to set up a priority queue to access customer records accordingly.

5. The Bay Area Brawlers professional football team has been so successful in recent weeks that the team management is considering the addition of several new ticket windows at the team's stadium. However, before investing a sizable amount of money in such an improvement, they would like to simulate the operation of ticket sales with a variety of ticket window configurations. Develop a computer program which allows input of such data as number of ticket windows, average number of fans arriving each hour as game time approaches, and average length of time to process a ticket sale. Output from your program should include statistics such as the average waiting-line length each hour as game time approaches and the amount of time the average fan had to wait in line before having his or her ticket request processed. Use queues to represent each of the waiting lines.

Stacks and Simple Recursion

6.1

Introductory Considerations

Though a first-in, first-out structure such as a queue seems to be the obvious way of storing items that must wait to be processed, there are many natural instances in which a last-in, first-out (LIFO) strategy is more appropriate. Consider, for example, the order in which a smart traveler will pack a suitcase. To minimize shuffling, the last item packed should be the first worn. Another familiar example of such a storage strategy is that of the pop-up mechanism used to store trays for a cafeteria line. Those trays which are the first ones loaded into the mechanism may well have a long wait before they escape to a passing diner. From a data structure perspective, a list of data items processed via a last-in, first-out scheduling strategy is called a stack. As we shall see in this chapter, stacks are an extremely useful data structure. They find extensive applications in the processing of subroutine calls, the syntactical checking and translation of programming languages by compilers, and the powerful programming technique called recursion.

The Stack as an Abstract Data Structure

The queue data structure which was presented in the previous chapter is a special type of list in which all data processing activity occurs at the two ends: the front and the rear. A stack may also be viewed as such a specialized list. However, a stack is even more restricted in that all activity occurs at one designated end called the top.

> **Stack** A stack is a restricted list in which entries are added to and removed from one designated end called the top.

The operations to be performed on a stack are shown in Table 6.1.

Operation	Explanation
Create(Stack)	Initialize the parameter Stack.
Empty(Stack)	A Boolean-valued function to determine if the parameter Stack is empty.
Full(Stack)	A Boolean-valued function to determine if the parameter Stack is full.
Push(Item, Stack)	A procedure which adds Item to the top of Stack. The term *push* has become conventional terminology for this operation.
Pop(Item, Stack)	A procedure which removes the top entry on Stack and returns it in Item. The term *pop* has become conventional terminology for this operation.
OnTop(Item, Stack)	A procedure which returns in Item the entry on top of Stack but does not remove it from the Stack (like Pop does).

TABLE 6.1

Operations on stacks

Conceptually, it is easiest to develop a mental image of the push and pop operations if you picture a stack as a vertical list with the first entry at the bottom and the last at the top. Then, as indicated in Figure 6.1, adding to the stack—that is, pushing—essentially makes this stack become taller, and removing from the stack—that is, popping—results in a shorter stack.

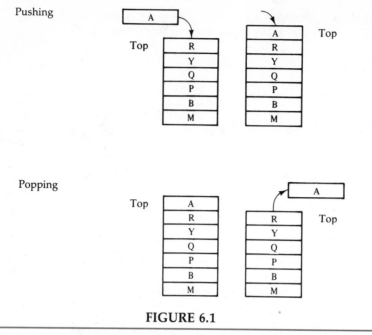

FIGURE 6.1

Pushing onto and popping from the stack

Stacks and Subroutine Calls

Before we discuss methods of implementing a stack, we shall give some hint of their importance in the processing of subroutine calls. Of key importance to the processing of subroutines in any language is that the return from a subroutine must be to the instruction immediately following the call that originally transferred control to the subroutine. For example, in the partial coding that follows:

```
PROGRAM Main;
   .
   .
   .
   PROCEDURE Sub3;
      .
      .
      .
   END; {Sub3}

   PROCEDURE Sub2;
      .
      .
      .
   Sub3; {Call Sub3}
   P := P - Q;
      .
      .
      .
   END; {Sub2}
```

```
    PROCEDURE Sub1;
        .
        .
        .
    Sub2; {Call Sub2}
    A := A + B;
        .
        .
        .
    END; {Sub1}

BEGIN {MAIN}
    .
    .
    .
Sub1; {Call Sub1}
writeln(Q);
    .
    .
    .
END. {MAIN}
```

the order of operation would be

   1. Leave Main and transfer to Sub1.

   2. Leave Sub1 and transfer to Sub2.

   3. Leave Sub2 and transfer to Sub3.

   4. Return from Sub3 to the instruction $P := P-Q$ in Sub2.

   5. Return from Sub2 to the instruction $A := A+B$ in Sub1.

   6. Return from Sub1 to the instruction writeln(Q) in Main.

   7. End of Main.

Each time a call is made, the machine must remember where to return upon completion of that procedure.

A stack is precisely the structure capable of storing the data necessary to handle calls and returns in this sequence. Hence the preceding partial coding would generate a stack that develops as illustrated in Figure 6.2. (The numbers in the figure correspond to the order of operations just shown.) Each time a call to a procedure is made, a return address is pushed on top of the stack. Each time a procedure is completed, the top item on the stack is popped to determine the memory address to which the return operation should be made. The nature of the leave-return sequence for procedures makes it crucial that the first return address accessed be the last one that was remembered by the computer. Because there is only one point, the top, at which data may enter or exit a stack, it is the ideal data structure to be used for this "last-stored, first-recalled" type of operation.

This description of the method by which a compiler actually imple-ments procedure calls is just one illustration of the utility of stacks. Later in this chapter we shall discuss a more difficult type of procedure usage called

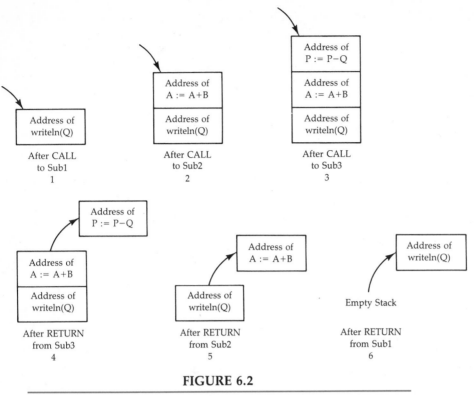

FIGURE 6.2

Memory stack generated by previous partial coding

recursion, and we will examine in detail the role of the stack in handling such a recursive call. Now, however, we will consider two ways of implementing a stack.

_____ 6.3

Implementations of a Stack

Two possible implementations of stacks will now be discussed: array implementation and linked list.

Array Implementation of a Stack

A strategy similar to that used for an array implementation of a queue can be followed for an array implementation of a stack. However, because insertions and deletions occur at the same end of a stack, only one pointer will be needed instead of the two required for a queue. We will call that pointer Top and use Figure 6.3 to trace it through the subroutine example of the previous section.

As indicated by this figure, the empty stack is signaled by the condition Top = 0. If we think of Top as pointing to the last entry pushed, then the

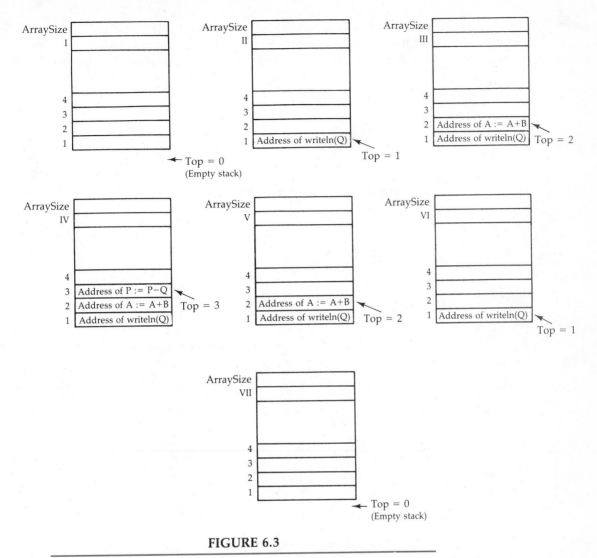

FIGURE 6.3

An array implementation of stack from Figure 6.2

two instructions

```
Top := Top + 1;
Stack[Top] := Item;
```

will push the contents of Item onto the stack. Popping an entry from the stack into Item requires

```
Item := Stack[Top];
Top := Top - 1;
```

Complete procedures for the Push and Pop operations follow. These procedures use a record to bundle the top pointer and data array into one unified StackType. These procedures also assume the existence of Empty and Full functions to test for these special boundary conditions. You will be asked to write these functions in the Exercises at the end of the chapter.

```
{Global declarations}

CONST
  StackSize = {Appropriate size};

TYPE
  StackType = RECORD
                List : ARRAY [1..StackSize] OF {Appropriate type};
                Top : integer    .
              END;

PROCEDURE Push  (Item : {Appropriate type};
                 VAR Stack : StackType);

{Push Item onto Stack.  Error message is output if this is not possible.}


  BEGIN
    IF Full(Stack)
      writeln ('Cannot push onto full stack.')
    ELSE
      BEGIN
      Stack.Top := Stack.Top + 1;
      Stack.List[Stack.Top] := Item
      END
  END;
{End Push}

PROCEDURE Pop  (VAR Item : {Appropriate type};
                VAR Stack : StackType);

{Pop Top element on Stack into Item.  Write error message if Stack is
  empty.}

  BEGIN
    IF Empty(Stack) THEN
      writeln ('Cannot pop from empty stack.')
    ELSE
      BEGIN
      Item := Stack.List[Stack.Top];
      Stack.Top := Stack.Top - 1
      END
  END;
{End Pop}
```

Linked List Implementation of a Stack

When we choose a linked list implementation of a stack, we are paying the price of a relatively small amount of memory space needed to maintain linking pointers for the dynamic allocation of stack space. Assuming that

we do not use a dummy header for the linked list, a stack with the three
integer entries 18, 40, and 31 would appear as follows:

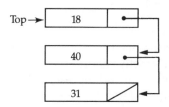

The Top pointer must be initialized to **NIL,** and, thereafter, the condition

```
Top = NIL
```

could be used to test for an empty stack. A full stack occurs only when
Pascal's **new** procedure reports that there is no available space.

   Full procedures to push and pop the stack now become nothing more
than insertions to and deletions from the beginning of a linked list. As
such, they are special cases of the procedures already developed in Chapter 4. You will write them as exercises at the end of the chapter.

_____ **6.4**

An Application of Stacks: Parsing and Evaluating Arithmetic Expressions

Often the logic of problems for which stacks are a suitable data structure
involves the necessity to backtrack, to return to a previous state. For instance, consider the problem of finding your way out of a maze. One
approach to take would be to probe a given path in the maze as deeply as
possible. Upon finding a dead end, you would need to backtrack to previously visited maze locations in order to try other paths. Such backtracking
would require recalling these previous locations in the reverse order from
which you visited them. Not many of us need to find our way out of a
maze. However, the designers of compilers are faced with an analogous
backtracking situation in the evaluation of arithmetic expressions. As you
scan the expression

$$A + B/C + D$$

in left-to-right order, it is impossible to tell upon initially encountering the
plus sign whether or not you should apply the indicated addition operation to A and the immediately following operand. Instead, you must probe
further into the expression to determine whether an operation with a
higher priority occurs. While you undertake this probing of the expression,
you must stack previously encountered operation symbols until you are
certain of the operands to which they can be applied.

   Compounding the backtracking problem just described, there are often
many different ways of representing the same algebraic expression. For

example, the assignment statements

$$Z := A * B/C + D;$$
$$Z := (A * B)/C + D;$$
$$Z := ((A * B)/C) + D;$$

should all result in the same order of arithmetic operations even though the expressions involved are written in distinctly different form. The process of checking the syntax of such an expression and representing it in one unique form is called parsing the expression. One frequently used method of parsing relies heavily upon stacks.

Infix, Postfix, and Prefix Notation

Usual algebraic notation is often termed infix notation; the arithmetic operator appears between the two operands to which it is being applied. Infix notation may require parentheses to specify a desired order of operations. For example, in the expression A/B + C, the division will occur first. If we want the addition to occur first, the expression must be parenthesized as A/(B + C).

Using postfix notation (also called reverse Polish notation after the nationality of its originator, the Polish logician Jan Lukasiewicz), the need for parentheses is eliminated because the operator is placed directly after the two operands to which it applies. Hence, A/B + C would be written as AB/C+ in postfix form. This says:

1. Apply the division operator to A and B.

2. To that result, add C.

The infix expression A/(B + C) would be written as ABC+/ in postfix notation. Reading this postfix expression from left to right, we are told to

1. Apply the addition operator to B and C.

2. Then divide that result into A.

Although relatively short expressions such as the preceding ones can be converted from infix to postfix via an intuitive process, a more systematic method is required for complicated expressions. We propose the following algorithm for humans (and will soon consider a different one for computers):

1. Completely parenthesize the infix expression to specify the order of all operations.

2. Move each operator to the space held by its corresponding right parenthesis.

3. Remove all parentheses.

Consider this three-step method as it applies to the following expression in which ^ is used to indicate exponentiation:

$$A/B^C + D*E - A*C$$

Completely parenthesizing this expression yields

$$(((A/(B^C)) + (D*E)) - (A*C))$$

Moving each operator to its corresponding right parenthesis, we obtain

Removing all parentheses, we are left with

$$ABC^/DE*+AC*-$$

Had we started out with

$$A \ / \ B^C - (D*E - A*C)$$

our three-step procedure would have resulted in

Removing the parentheses would then yield

$$ABC^/DE*AC*--$$

In a similar way, an expression can be converted into prefix form, in which an operator immediately precedes its two operands. The conversion algorithm for infix to prefix specifies that, after completely parenthesizing the infix expression according to order of priority, we move each operator to its corresponding left parenthesis. Applying the method to

$$A/B^C + D*E - A*C$$

gives us

and finally the prefix form

$$+/A^BC-*DE*AC$$

The importance of postfix and prefix notation in parsing arithmetic expressions is that these notations are completely free of parentheses. Consequently, an expression in postfix (or prefix) form is in unique form. In the design of compilers, this parsing of an expression into postfix form is crucial because having a unique form for an expression greatly simplifies its eventual evaluation. Thus, in handling an assignment statement, a compiler must

1. Parse into postfix form.

2. Apply an evaluation algorithm to the postfix form.

We shall limit our discussion here to postfix notation. The techniques we will cover are easily adaptable to the functionally equivalent prefix form.

Converting Infix Expressions to Postfix

First consider the problem of parsing an expression from infix to postfix form. Our three-step procedure is not easily adaptable to machine coding. Instead, we will use an algorithm that has as its essential data structures:

1. A stream of characters containing the infix expression and terminated by the special delimiter '#'.

2. A stack OpStack which may contain
   a. Arithmetic operators: '+', '−', '*', and '/'
   b. Parentheses: '(' and ')'
   c. The special delimiter: '#'

3. A string Postfix containing the final postfix expression.

To eliminate details that would only clutter the main logic of the algorithm, we will assume that the string representing the infix expression contains tokens (that is, incoming symbols) consisting only of the arithmetic operators '+', '−', '*', and '/'; parentheses; the delimiting character '#'; and operands that consist of a single uppercase alphabetic character each. We will also assume that these tokens may be read from a line without any intervening spaces. In the case study of the next section we will consider some of the complications introduced by tokens of varying size and type and by the exponentiation operator '^'. Thus, for the present, the algorithm we discuss will convert infix expressions of the form

$$A*B+(C-D/E)$$

into their corresponding postfix notation.

The description of the algorithm is as follows:

1. Define a function InfixPriority, which takes an operator, parentheses, or # as its argument and returns an integer as:

Character	*	/	+	−	(	)	#
Returned value	2	2	1	1	3	0	0

This function reflects the relative position of an operator in the arithmetic hierarchy and is used with the function StackPriority (defined in step 2) to determine how long an operator waits in the stack before being appended to the postfix string.

2. Define another function StackPriority, which takes the same possibilities for an argument and returns an integer as:

Character	*	/	+	−	(	)	#
Returned value	2	2	1	1	0	unde-fined	0

This function applies to operators in the operator stack as their priority in the arithmetic hierarchy is compared to that of incoming operators from the infix string. The result of this comparison deter-

mines whether or not an operator waits in the stack or is appended
to the postfix string.

3. Initialize OpStack by pushing #.

4. Read the next character Ch from the infix expression.

5. Test Ch and
   a. If Ch is an operand, append it to the Postfix string.
   b. If Ch is a right parenthesis, then pop entries form stack and
      append them to Postfix until a left parenthesis is popped. Doing
      this insures that operators within a parenthesized portion of an
      infix expression will be applied first, regardless of their priority
      in the usual arithmetic hierarchy. Discard both left and right
      parentheses.
   c. If Ch is a #, pop all entries that remain on the stack and append
      them to Postfix string.
   d. Otherwise, pop from the stack and append to the Postfix string
      operators whose StackPriority is greater than or equal to the
      InfixPriority of Ch. This comparison, keying on the priority of Ch
      from the infix string and operators which have previously been
      pushed onto the operator stack, insures that operators are ap-
      plied in the right order in the resulting postfix string. After pop-
      ping these operators, stack Ch.

6. Repeat steps 4 and 5 until Ch is the delimiter #.

The key to the algorithm is the use of the stack to hold operators from
the infix expression that appear to the left of another given operator even
though that latter operator must be applied first. The defined functions
InfixPriority and StackPriority are used to specify this priority of operators
and the associated pushing and popping operations. This entire process is
best understood by carefully tracing through an example, as shown in
Table 6.2.

The following Pascal procedure implements our algorithm for convert-
ing infix expressions of the form we have specified. The procedure uses an
array to implement the operator stack and assumes procedures InitStack
(to initialize the stack pointer), Pop, and Push to manipulate this array
implementation. Also assumed is a procedure Concatenate to append a
character to the end of the postfix string and functions StackPriority and
InfixPriority. You should study and thoroughly understand this algorithm
before moving on to the case study in the next section. In that case study,
the infix-to-postfix algorithm will be the focal point for an entire program
which must work with expressions of a slightly more complicated form.

```
{Global declarations}

CONST
  StringSize = 80;

TYPE
  PostfixString = PACKED ARRAY [1..StringSize] OF char;
```

Ch	OpStack	PostFix	Commentary
			Push #
A			Read Ch
		A	Append Ch to PostFix
*			Read Ch
	* #		Stack Ch
B			Read Ch
		AB	Append Ch to PostFix
+			Read Ch
	+ #	AB*	Pop *, append * to PostFix, push Ch
(			Read Ch
	(+ #		Push Ch
C			Read Ch
		AB*C	Append Ch to PostFix
−			Read Ch
	− (+ #		Push Ch
D			Read Ch
		AB*CD	Append Ch to PostFix
/			Read Ch
	/ − (+ #		Push Ch
E			Read Ch
		AB*CDE	Append Ch to PostFix
)			Read Ch
	+ #	AB*CDE/−	Pop and append to PostFix until (reached
#			Read Ch
		AB*CDE/−+#	Pop and append rest of stack to Ch

TABLE 6.2

Translation of infix expression A*B+(C−D/E)#

```
PROCEDURE Convert(VAR Postfix : PostfixString);
  {Convert an infix expression read from standard input
   into a Postfix string.}


  {Local declarations}
  CONST
    StackSize = 40;


  TYPE
    StackType = RECORD
                  List : ARRAY [1..StackSize] OF char;
                  Top : integer
                END;


  VAR
    Item, Ch : char;
    OpStack : StackType;
    .
    .
    .
  {Procedures/Functions Create, Pop, Push, Full, Empty, Concatenate,
   StackPriority, InfixPriority would be defined here.
   See preceding text for their description.}
    .
    .
    .
BEGIN {Convert}
Create(OpStack);
Push('#', OpStack);
REPEAT
  read (Ch);
  IF ('A' <= Ch) AND (Ch <= 'Z') THEN

    {Single character operand}

    Concatenate(Postfix, Ch)




  ELSE IF Ch = ')' THEN
    BEGIN
    Pop(Item, OpStack)
    WHILE Item <> '(' DO
      BEGIN
        Concatenate(Postfix, Item);
        Pop(Item, OpStack)
      END
    END
```

"A" <= Ch and Ch <= "Z"

Q

PostFix   Input Ch

OpStack

In this case, transfer Ch
directly to PostFix

Ch = ")"

)

PostFix   Input Ch

(

OpStack

In this case, pop stack until encounter
matching left parenthesis

```
ELSE IF Ch = '#' THEN
  BEGIN
  WHILE NOT Empty(OpStack) DO
    BEGIN
    Pop(Item, OpStack);
    Concatenate(Postfix, Item)
    END
  END
```

In this case, pop rest of stack to PostFix

```
ELSE {Operator +, -, *, /}
  BEGIN
  Pop(Item, OpStack);
  WHILE StackPriority(Item) >= InfixPriority(Ch) DO
    BEGIN
    Concatenate(Postfix, Item);
    Pop(Item, OpStack)
    END;
  Push(Item, Opstack);
  Push(Ch, OpStack)
  END
UNTIL Ch = '#'
END;
{ End Convert}
```

In this case, pop stack until encounter item of lower priority (+). Then stack incoming Ch.

Evaluating Postfix Expressions

Once an expression has been parsed and represented in postfix form, another stack plays an essential role in its final evaluation. As an example, consider the postfix expression from Table 6.2.

$$AB*CDE/-+\#$$

Let us suppose that the symbols A, B, C, D, and E had associated with them the following values:

Symbol	Value
A	5
B	3
C	6
D	8
E	2

To evaluate such an expression, we repeatedly read characters from the postfix expression. If the character read is an operand, push the value associated with it onto the stack. If it is an operator, pop two values from the stack, apply the operator to them, and push the result back onto the stack. The technique is illustrated for our current example in Figure 6.4.

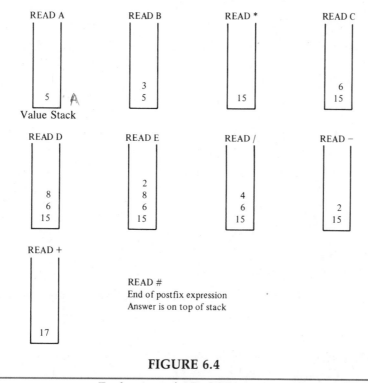

FIGURE 6.4

Evaluation of AB*CDE/−+#

Assuming functions Value which will return the value associated with a particular symbol; Eval, which will return the result of applying an operator to two values; and NextToken, which will return the next token to be read from the postfix expression, the Pascal function to evaluate a postfix expression is given by

```
{Global declarations}

CONST
  StringSize = 80;

TYPE
  PostfixString = PACKED ARRAY [1..StringSize] OF char;

FUNCTION Evaluate(Postfix: PostfixString) : real;

  {Return result of evaluating Postfix expression.}

  CONST
    StackSize = 60;
```

```
TYPE
   StackType = RECORD
                    List : ARRAY [1..StackSize] OF real;
                    Top : integer
                 END;



VAR
   Ch : char;
   v, v1, v2 : real;
   ValueStack : StackType;
        .
        .
        .
{Procedures/Functions Create, Pop, Push, Full, Value, Eval,
 and NextToken would be defined here.  See preceding text for
 their description.}
        .
        .
        .
BEGIN
   Create(ValueStack);
   Ch := NextToken(Postfix);
   WHILE Ch <> '#' {the ending delimiter} DO
     BEGIN
     IF ('A' <= Ch) AND (Ch <= 'Z') AND NOT Full(ValueStack) THEN {Operand}
        Push (Value(Ch), ValueStack)
     ELSE
        BEGIN
          Pop (v2, ValueStack);
          Pop (v1, ValueStack);
          v := Eval(v1, v2, Ch);
          Push(v, ValueStack)
        END;

     {What's left on stack is the answer we want.}

     Pop (v, ValueStack);
     Evaluate := v
   END; {Evaluate}
```

_____ 6.5

A Case Study: Evaluating Integrals

The application of the stack-oriented algorithms of the preceding sections
is not limited to the parsing and evaluation of expressions by compilers.
Many of the programs typically used by scientists, engineers, and mathematicians can be greatly enhanced by allowing the user to interactively
enter an algebraic expression as opposed to embedding the expression
inside the program. Consider, for instance, the situation described in the
following memorandum which you receive from the head of the Physics
Department at the University of Hard Knocks.

MEMORANDUM
University of Hard Knocks

TO: Director of Computer Center
FROM: Head of Physics Department
DATE: November 22, 1992
RE: Making integration program more versatile

In physics we find frequent application to take the integral of a function $f(x)$ over the interval from a to b on the real number line. As you are aware, this essentially means that we wish to find the area under the graph of the function between endpoints a and b, as indicated in the following diagram:

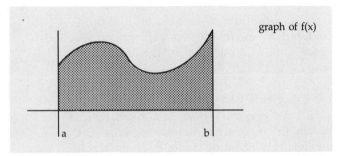

graph of f(x)

We presently have a program which obtains a good approximation of this area by adding up the areas of a large number of small rectangles, each with base along the interval from a to b and top passing through the graph of $f(x)$. This concept is highlighted in the next diagram.

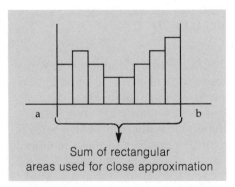

Sum of rectangular
areas used for close approximation

The user of our program can interactively enter the endpoints a and b and the number of rectangles. The result is a very good approximation when enough rectangles are used.

Our problem is not with the accuracy of the approximation but with the fact that, to change the function $f(x)$, the user must edit the definition of the function in the source program and then re-compile. Can you help us by writing a program which will allow the user to enter the function $f(x)$ interactively? The functions which we integrate in this fashion can be defined in terms of the standard arithmetic operations addition, subtraction, multiplication, division, and exponentiation. Thanks in advance for your prompt assistance.

The physics department head has presented us with a substantial task in the preceding memorandum. Consider some of the subordinate problems with which we will be faced in writing this program.

☐ The evaluation of integrals; that is, areas under graphs of functions. Obtaining numerical answers to mathematical problems of this variety will serve to introduce us to a subject known as numerical analysis.

☐ The interactive parsing and evaluation of a function will give us an opportunity to adapt the algorithms introduced in the preceding section.

☐ For the type of functions described in the memorandum, the problem of finding the next token in the expression can become complicated. Consider, for instance, a function defined by the expression

$$3.14*X^3+X^2$$

where $\hat{}$ is used to denote exponentiation. Here, from a stream of incoming characters, we must be prepared to select a token which may be a real number, the variable X, or an arithmetic operator. The problem of recognizing tokens in an incoming stream of characters is called lexical analysis. To keep our situation relatively simple, we shall specify that all tokens must be separated by a space and that no other operations such as trigonometric functions may be used in defining the function f.

Modular Structure Chart for the Integral Evaluation System

With these comments in mind, we shall turn our attention toward designing a solution to the integration problem described in the physicist's memo. Recall from the methodology developed in Chapter 3 that the first step in this design process is to develop a modular structure chart reflecting the way in which we will partition the problem into subproblems. (See Figure 6.5.) Since both conversion from infix to postfix and the evaluation of a postfix string require fundamental stack operations, we have located our stack processing modules at the deepest level of the structure chart. Here they will be accessible by both the conversion and evaluation algorithms.

Data Structures for the Integral Evaluation System

Clearly we will need a string to store the infix representation of the function to be integrated. Since this string is entered interactively by the user, it need merely be a packed array of characters. We will also need a list to store the postfix string of tokens which is built as the infix expression goes through our conversion algorithm. Here the situation demands more than a packed array of characters, however. This is because tokens which are needed from the infix string are not necessarily individual characters.

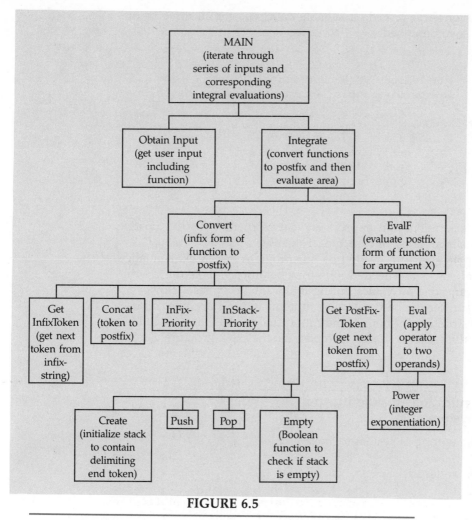

FIGURE 6.5

Modular structure chart for integration problem

Rather, such tokens will fall into one of the three following categories:

1. A real number. If the token is a real number, the lexical analysis phase of our algorithm must have converted it from the appropriate stream of digits and decimal point as typed by the user.

2. The variable X. The infix expression defines the function in terms of this general variable. When the function is evaluated, a particular value is then substituted for X.

3. An operator. We broadly include +, −, *, /, ^, (,), and the special delimiter # in this category.

The problem with a token which may be either a real number or a character is that we essentially need a data type which can assume one of several identities, depending upon the current token. This is exactly the purpose for which Pascal's variant record type is defined. Hence, the fol-

lowing declarations will provide a suitable data type for all three of the
categories we have described:

```
TYPE
   TokenType = (RealValue, VarX, Operator);
               {Number, variable, or operator/parenthesis}

   TokenRec =  RECORD
                  CASE Token : Tokentype OF
                     RealValue : (Value : real);
                     VarX : (XChar : char);
                     Operator : (OpChar : char)
                  END;
```

Given these declarations, an appropriate data structure for the postfix
string of tokens is an array of base type TokenRec.

The final data structure needed by our program is a stack. Actually,
two conceptual stacks are needed: one for operator symbols during the
parsing phase and one for values during the evaluation phase. However,
by making TokenRec the base data type of items in the stack, we can use
just one stack structure for both of the conceptual stacks that are needed.
In this case study, we have chosen to implement the stack structure using a
linked list.

Module Specifications for the Integral Evaluation System

The specifications for this system follow:

```
Main Program Module
     Logic:
        Repeatedly call on modules to obtain input specifications
            and then evaluate integral.
```
} *Module 1*

```
ObtainInput Module
     Data Received: None
     Information Returned: Interval endpoints a and b
                           Infix representation of function
                           NumberOfRectangles to use in
                               approximating area


     Logic:
        Issue appropriate prompts and read user input.
        When reading infix string, append delimiter '#' to end.
```
} *Module 2*

```
  Integrate Module
       Data Received: Endpoints a and b
                      Infix representation of function
                      NumberOfRectangles for which area is to be
                          accumulated
       Information Returned: Approximation to area under graph of
                             function
```
} *Module 3*

```
Logic:
  Compute Width of each rectangle as
      (b–a)/Number of Rectangles.
  Call on module Convert to convert Infix to Postfix
      notation.
  Initialize Area to zero.
  Repeatedly evaluate f at the midpoint of the base of
      the current rectangle, multiply this by the width of
      the base, add resulting product to Area accumulation.
```

```
Convert Module
    Data Received: Infix string delimited by special end token '#'
    Information Returned:  Postfix string of TokenRec records
                              delimited by '#'
    Logic:
      Follow algorithm described in Section 6.4 of text.
```
⎫ *Module 4*

```
GetInfixToken Module   {Note: This module responsible for lexical
                          analysis.}
    Data Received:  Infix string
    Information Returned:  FromInfix, a TokenRec containing the
                              next token
                          Appropriately updated InPointer
    Logic:
      {Note: We assume all tokens separated by one space.}
      Initialize Value field of FromInfix to zero.
        {In case token is a real number.}
      REPEAT
        Let c be next character in Infix
        CASE c OF
          1. c is a space: We are done.
          2. c is a 'X': Set FromInfix to c.
          3. c is '+', '–', '*', '/', '^', '(', ')', '#':
                Set FromInfix to c.
          4. c is decimal point: Set a Multiplier to 0.1 for
                future accumulation.
          5. c is a digit: IF left of decimal THEN Set
                Value to 10 * Value plus numeric
                  form of c.
              ELSE Set Value to Value +
                  Multiplier times numeric form of c.
                  Divide Multiplier by 10 for next iteration.

      UNTIL c is a space
```
⎫ *Module 5*

```
Concat Module
    Data Received: t, a TokenRec record
                Postfix string
                PostPointer, pointer to current position in
                    Postfix
    Information Returned: Postfix with t appended to it, and
                    PostPointer appropriately updated
    Logic:
      Update PostPointer to next location in PostFix.
      Assign t to this location.
```
⎫ *Module 6*

InfixPriority Module
    Data Received: t, a TokenRec record
    Information Returned: Infix priority rank of t
    Logic:
      See Section 6.4 of text.

Module 7

InStackPriority Module
    Data Received: t, a TokenRec record
    Information Returned: InStack priority rank of t
    Logic:
      See Section 6.4 of text.

Module 8

EvalF Module
    Data Received: Postfix string representation of function f
                x, the real number at which f is to be
                       evaluated
    Information Returned: The real number $f(x)$
    Logic:
      See evaluation algorithm in Section 6.4 of text.

Module 9

GetPostfixToken Module
    Data Received: Postfix string
                 PostPointer, a pointer to current position in
                     Postfix
    Information Returned: t, a TokenRec record containing next
                         token in Postfix.
    Logic:
      Use PostPointer to access next token, then update
        PostPointer.

Module 10

Eval Module
    Data Received: vl, v2: the values of two operands
                 Op: character containing operator +, −, *, /, ^
    Information Returned: Numeric result of applying Op to
                     vl and v2.
    Logic:
      Select the appropriate Pascal operation based on Op.

Module 11

Power Module
    Data Received: b, a base, and p, an integer exponent
    Information Returned: b^p
    Logic:
      Use loop to perform appropriate number of multiplications.

Module 12

Create Module
    Data Received: Uninitialized Top pointer for stack
    Information Returned: Appropriately initialized stack pointed
                       to by Top
    Logic:
      Initialize top and push delimiter '#' onto stack.

Module 13

Push, Pop, Empty Modules
    Standard stack manipulation modules
      for linked list implementation of
      stack

Modules 14

Coding for the Integral Evaluation System

The complete Pascal program for the integral evaluation system follows, with reference to the module specifications. Also included are graphic documentation and sample runs to give you a more detailed grasp of how the program functions in its interaction with a user.

```
PROGRAM TakeIntegral(input, output);

{ Program to compute area under curve of function entered interactively.
  Stack is used to convert function expression to postfix notation and
  then to evaluate. Valid function expressions can contain the variable
  X, numeric constants, operators +,-,*,/,^(for exponentiation) and
  appropriate parentheses. }

  CONST
    LineLength = 82; { Width of standard terminal plus two for end token }
    EndToken = '#'; { End token corresponding to algorithm described in text }

  TYPE
    InfixString = PACKED ARRAY [1..LineLength] OF char;

  VAR
    Infix : InfixString;
    a, b : real;
    NumberOfRectangles : integer;
    Area : real;


PROCEDURE ObtainInput(VAR Infix : InfixString;
                      VAR a, b : real;
                      VAR NumberOfRectangles : integer);

{ Returns infix function string from user at terminal.
  Additionally, inserts EndToken at the end of this string, so
  that user doesn't have to.  a and b return interval endpoints
  for area calculation.  NumberOfRectangles determines how many
  rectangular areas should be accumulated in approximating
  area. }

  VAR
    i : integer;


  BEGIN
    write('Enter left and right endpoints (left >= right to
        quit)-->');
    readln(a, b);
```

*See
Module 2*

```
    If a < b THEN
      BEGIN
      writeln('Enter function with spaces separating all terms.');
      readln(Infix);
      { Starting from right, determine last nonblank position. }
      i := LineLength;
      WHILE Infix[i] = ' ' DO
        i := i - 1;
      { Add EndToken to correspond to algorithm described in
            Section 6.4.}
      Infix[i + 2] := EndToken;
      write('Enter number of rectangles for computing area-->');
      readln(NumberOfRectangles)
      END
  END; {ObtainInput}
```

Infix

Want blank here

| X*3.1 | 4 | | | |

i points
at last
non-blank

Want end
token # here

```
PROCEDURE Integrate(Infix : InfixString;
                    a, b : real;
                    NumberOfRectangles : integer;
                    VAR Area : real);

{ Receives function in infix notation, endpoints, and number of
  rectangles for area approximation.  Area is returned in last
  parameter. }

  TYPE
    TokenType = (RealValue, VarX, Operator); { Number, X, or
                    operator/paren }
    TokenRec =
      RECORD
        CASE Token : TokenType OF
          RealValue :
            (Value : real);
          VarX :
            (XChar : char);
          Operator :
            (OpChar : char)
      END;
    StackType = ^StackRec;
    StackRec =
      RECORD
        Next : StackType;
        Data : TokenRec
      END;
    PfString = ARRAY [1..LineLength] OF TokenRec; { To store
                                    postfix form }
```

Token
Field

Value Field

RealValue →

XChar Field

VarX →

Operator

OpChar Field

Rest of record structure
depends on Token field

See
Module 3

```
VAR
   TokenStack : StackType;
   Postfix : PfString;
   Count : integer;
   Width, x : real;
```

```
{-----------Next four procedures centralize stack operations--------------}
{-------------Called by conversion and evaluation algorithm---------------}
```

```
PROCEDURE Create(VAR Stack : StackType);

 { Initialize stack by pushing EndToken, corresponding to algorithm
   described in text. }

  BEGIN
    new(Stack);
    Stack^.Next := NIL;
    Stack^.Data.Token := Operator;
    Stack^.Data.OpChar := EndToken
  END; { Create }
```

See
Module 13

```
FUNCTION Empty(Stack : StackType) : boolean;

     { Check for empty stack.}

  BEGIN
    Empty := (Stack = NIL)
  END; { Empty }
```

```
PROCEDURE Push(VAR Stack : StackType;
               t : TokenRec);

     { Push t onto stack. }

  VAR
    s : StackType;

  BEGIN
    new(s);
    s^.Next := Stack;
    s^.Data := t;
    Stack := s
  END;
```

See
Modules 14

```
PROCEDURE Pop(VAR Stack : StackType;
              VAR t : TokenRec);

    { Pop stack, returning result in t.}

  VAR
    s : StackType;
```

```
  BEGIN
    IF NOT Empty(Stack) THEN
      BEGIN
      t := Stack^.Data;
      s := Stack;
      Stack := Stack^.Next;
      dispose(s)
      END
    ELSE
      writeln('Error - Empty stack in Pop.')
  END; { Pop }

{---------------End of stack manipulation procedures---------------}


PROCEDURE Convert(Infix : InfixString;
                  VAR PostFix : PfString);

    { Receives Infix string, returns equivalent Postfix form. }

  VAR
    FromStack, FromInfix : TokenRec;
    Inpointer, PostPointer : integer;
```
                                    'Index'

```
PROCEDURE GetInfixToken(Infix : InfixString;
                        VAR InPointer : integer;
                        VAR FromInfix : TokenRec);

  { Gets next token from Infix string, returning it in FromInfix.
    Assumes all tokens are separated by spaces. }

  CONST Space = ' ';

  VAR
    c : char;
    Multiplier : real;
    LeftOfDecimal : boolean;


  BEGIN
    FromInfix.Value := 0;
    LeftOfDecimal := true;
    REPEAT
      c := Infix[InPointer];
      InPointer := InPointer + 1;
      CASE c OF
        '.':                    { Encountered decimal point } → 3.14
          BEGIN
          LeftOfDecimal := false;
          Multiplier := 1.0E-1
          END;
        '+', '-', '*', '/', '^', '(', ')', EndToken:
          { Operator }
          BEGIN
          FromInfix.Token := Operator;
```

We are currently here. Must prepare to accumulate digits to right of decimal.

See
Module 4

See
Module 5

```
                FromInfix.OpChar := c
                END;
           '0', '1', '2', '3', '4', '5', '6', '7', '8', '9':
                { Digit }
                BEGIN
                FromInfix.Token := RealValue;
                IF LeftOfDecimal THEN ──────────────→
```

> 23.14
> For digits to left of decimal,
> must multiply accumulated value
> by 10 and add digit.

```
                FromInfix.Value := FromInfix.Value * 10.0 + (ord(c) -
                                          ord('0'))
                ELSE ──────────────────────────────────→
```

> 23.14
> For digits to right of decimal,
> add digit scaled to appropriate
> decimal value by Multiplier.

```
                BEGIN
                FromInfix.Value := FromInfix.Value + (ord(c) -
                                       ord('0')) * Multiplier;
                Multiplier := Multiplier / 10.0
                END
                END;
           'X':    { Variable X }
                BEGIN
                FromInfix.Token := VarX;
                FromInfix.XChar := c
                END;
           Space:                  { Blank signals end of current token. }
                BEGIN   END         { So we do nothing. }
           END { CASE }
     UNTIL (c = Space) OR (c = EndToken)
END; { GetInfixToken }


PROCEDURE Concat(t : TokenRec;
                 VAR Postfix : PfString;
                 VAR PostPointer : integer);

    { Concatenate token t to Postfix string. }

  BEGIN
    Postfix[PostPointer] := t;
    PostPointer := PostPointer + 1
  END;
```

*See
Module 6*

```
FUNCTION InfixPriority(t : TokenRec) : integer;

    { Infix priority function as described in text. }

  BEGIN
    CASE t.OpChar OF
      '^':
        InfixPriority := 4;
      '*', '/':
        InfixPriority := 2;
```

*See
Module 7*

```
        '+', '-':
          InfixPriority := 1;
        '(':
          InfixPriority := 3;
        ')', EndToken:
          InfixPriority := 0
      END
   END;


FUNCTION InStackPriority(t : TokenRec) : integer;

    { In stack priority function, as described in text. }

   BEGIN
     CASE t.OpChar OF
       '^':
         InStackPriority := 4;
       '*', '/':
         InStackPriority := 2;
       '+', '-':
         InStackPriority := 1;
       '(', EndToken:
         InStackPriority := 0
      END
   END;
```

See Module 8

```
BEGIN { Convert }
   Create(TokenStack); { Pushes EndToken }
   InPointer := 1; { Initialize infix string }
   PostPointer := 1; { Initialize postfix string }
   REPEAT
     GetInfixToken(Infix, InPointer, FromInfix);
     IF (FromInfix.Token = RealValue) OR (FromInfix.Token = VarX) THEN
       { We have an operand: variable or number. }
       Concat(FromInfix, Postfix, PostPointer)
     ELSE IF FromInfix.OpChar = ')' THEN
       BEGIN
       Pop(TokenStack, FromStack);
       WHILE FromStack.OpChar <> '(' DO
         BEGIN
         Concat(FromStack, Postfix, PostPointer);
         Pop(TokenStack, FromStack)
         END
       END
     ELSE IF FromInfix.OpChar = EndToken THEN
         WHILE NOT Empty(TokenStack) DO
           BEGIN
           Pop(TokenStack, FromStack);
           Concat(FromStack, Postfix, PostPointer)
           END
     ELSE
         { We have one of arithmetic operators +,-,*,/,^ }
         BEGIN
```

See Module 4

```
          Pop(TokenStack, FromStack);
          WHILE InStackPriority(FromStack) >= InfixPriority(FromInfix) DO
            BEGIN
            Concat(FromStack, Postfix, PostPointer);
            Pop(TokenStack, FromStack)
            END;
          Push(TokenStack, FromStack);
          Push(TokenStack, FromInfix)
          END
    UNTIL (FromInfix.Token = Operator) AND (FromInfix.OpChar = EndToken)
END; {Convert}
```

for index := 1 to Post Pointer do
  write(' The following is the post fix string:_' Postfix[index]

```
FUNCTION EvalF(Postfix : PfString;
               x : real) : real; integer
                    Integer

   { Receives function in postfix form. Returns function evaluated
     at x. }

VAR
   t, t1, t2, t3 : TokenRec;
   PostPointer : integer;
```

See
Module 9

```
                        integer
FUNCTION Eval(v1, v2 : real; integer
              Op : char) : real;
```

See
Module 11

```
   { Return result of applying operator Op to operands v1
     and v2. }
```

```
FUNCTION Power(b : real;
               p : integer) : real;

  { Return b raised to power p. }

  VAR
    Prod : real;
    i : integer;
```

See
Module 12

```
  BEGIN
    Prod := 1;
    i := 1;
    WHILE i <= p DO
      BEGIN
      Prod := Prod * b;
      i := i + 1
      END;
    Power := Prod
  END; { Power }
```

```
BEGIN {Eval}
  CASE Op OF
    '+':
      Eval := v1 + v2;
    '-':
      Eval := v1 - v2;
    '*':
      Eval := v1 * v2;
    '/':
      Eval := round(v1 / v2);
    '^':
      Eval := Power(v1, round(v2))
  END { CASE }
END; {Eval}
```

See
Module 11

```
PROCEDURE GetPostfixToken(Postfix : PfString;
                          VAR PostPointer : integer;
                          VAR t : TokenRec);

  { Return in t the next token from the Postfix string. }

  BEGIN
    t := Postfix[PostPointer];
    PostPointer := PostPointer + 1
  END;
```

See
Module 10

```
BEGIN { EvalF }
  Create(TokenStack); { Will push EndToken }        {initialize}
  PostPointer := 1; { Start at beginning of Postfix string.}
  GetPostfixToken(Postfix, PostPointer, t1);

  { We're done when encounter operator that is EndToken.  Just
    testing for EndToken is not enough because coincidentally we
    could get match for EndToken when not an operator. }

  WHILE (t1.Token <> Operator) OR (t1.OpChar <> EndToken) DO    {last}
    BEGIN
    IF t1.Token <> Operator THEN
      IF t1.Token = RealValue THEN    {Int}
        Push(TokenStack, t1)
      ELSE
        BEGIN
        t1.Token := RealValue;    {Int}
        t1.Value := x;
        Push(TokenStack, t1)
        END
    ELSE
      BEGIN
      Pop(TokenStack, t2);
      Pop(TokenStack, t3);
      t.Token := RealValue;    {Int}
      t.Value := Eval(t3.Value, t2.Value, t1.OpChar);
      Push(TokenStack, t)
      END;
```

See
Module 9

```
      GetPostfixToken(Postfix, PostPointer, t1)
      END;
  Pop(TokenStack, t);
  EvalF := t.Value
END; { EvalF }
```

```
BEGIN { Integrate }
  Width := (b - a) / NumberOfRectangles;
  Count := 0;
  x := a;
  Area := 0;
  Convert(Infix, Postfix);
  WHILE Count < NumberOfRectangles DO
    BEGIN
    Area := Area + EvalF(PostFix, x + Width / 2.0) * Width;
    x := x + Width;
    Count := Count + 1
    END
END; { Integrate }
```

See Module 3

Graph of function f

This height is f(x + Width/2)

Width

x

```
BEGIN { Main Program }
  ObtainInput(Infix, a, b, NumberOfRectangles);
  WHILE a < b DO
    BEGIN
    Integrate(Infix, a, b, NumberOfRectangles, Area);
    writeln('Approximation to area is ', Area: 10: 3);
    writeln;
    ObtainInput(Infix, a, b, NumberOfRectangles)
    END
END.
```

See Module 1

Sample Runs

```
Enter left and right endpoints (left >= right to quit)-->0 3
Enter function with spaces separating all terms.
3
Enter number of subintervals for computing area-->10
Approximation to area is       9.000

Enter left and right endpoints (left >= right to quit)-->0 3
Enter function with spaces separating all terms.
X ^ 2
```

```
Enter number of subintervals for computing area-->10
Approximation to area is        8.978

Enter left and right endpoints (left >= right to quit)-->0 3
Enter function with spaces separating all terms.
X ^ 2
Enter number of subintervals for computing area-->100
Approximation to area is        9.000

Enter left and right endpoints (left >= right to quit)-->0 1
Enter function with spaces separating all terms.
( X + 2 ) ^ 3 / ( X + 1 )
Enter number of subintervals for computing area-->100
Approximation to area is        10.526

Enter left and right endpoints (left >= right to quit)-->0 0
```

6.6

Stacks and Recursion

The notion of self-reference has long intrigued philosophers and mathematicians. Consider the so-called *antinomy of the liar* first formulated by the philosopher Epimenides of ancient Crete: If a person says "I am lying," this utterance is self-contradictory. It cannot be either true or false. Epimenides was right in his analysis of this self-referential statement. Without further qualification, it leads to the logical equivalent of a vicious circle which cannot be escaped. Nonetheless, self-reference can be a powerful descriptive technique.

What Is Recursion?

In computer science, this form of self-reference is embodied in a procedure which invokes itself: a recursive procedure. Without careful logical control, however, such recursive procedures can fall prey to the same vicious circle looping that Epimenides pondered. To illustrate this, let us suppose that we have access to an output device known as a pen plotter. Such a device is equipped with a pen held by a mechanical hand which is under control of the computer. Typical procedures to manipulate the pen could include:

Procedure	Action
Line(n)	Draw a line of length n in the current direction.
RightTurn(d)	Alter current direction by rotating d degrees in clockwise direction.

If we assume that the pen is initially set to draw a line toward the north—the top of the plotting page—then the sequence of instructions

```
Line(10);
RightTurn(90);
Line(10);
RightTurn(90);
Line(10);
Rightturn(90);
Line(10);
```

will clearly draw a square with sides of length 10.

Let us now try to predict what will happen when the following recursive procedure Draw is invoked by the initial call Draw(1):

```
PROCEDURE Draw(Side : integer);

BEGIN
   Line(Side);
   RightTurn(90);
   Draw(Side+3)   {Recursive Call}
END;
```

The initial call Draw(1) will result in a line of length 1 in a northerly direction. We then rotate the pen toward the east and, via a recursive call, generate a line of length 4. This is followed by a rotation to the south and a new invocation for a line of length 7. The emerging pattern should now be clear; the resulting right-angled spiral is shown in Figure 6.6.

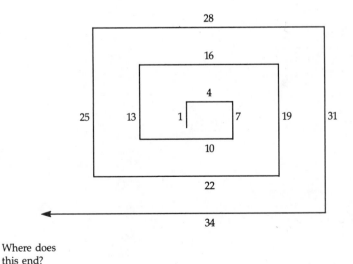

Where does
this end?

FIGURE 6.6

Runaway recursive spiral

Unfortunately, our spiral-producing procedure has tumbled into Epimenides' vicious circle loop of self-reference. There presently is no way to turn off the recursive calls made to Draw. Consider what happens, however, if we provide ourselves with a recursive out as in the following new version of Draw.

```
PROCEDURE Draw(Side : integer);

BEGIN
  IF Side <= 34 THEN {Recursive Out Test}
    BEGIN
    Line(Side);
    RightTurn(90);
    Draw(Side+3)
    END
END;
```

Now after drawing the line of length 34 in Figure 6.6, our procedure Draw will invoke itself once more, passing 37 for the parameter Side. Since the recursive out test is now false, no line of length 37 will be drawn. More importantly, no further recursive invocation of Draw will be made. Hence, we return immediately from the call to Draw with Side being 37. Moreover, that return triggers (in reverse order) returns from all the other invocations of Draw, eventually ending up at the instruction following our initial call: that is, Draw(1). The important point to stress here is that, to appropriately use recursion, we must use a recursive out conditional check to avoid an infinite series of recursive calls. If we were to view each recursive call as a descent one level deeper into an algorithm's logic, we in effect must use a recursive out to allow a corresponding ascent back to the level of the first call to the procedure. This concept is highlighted in Figure 6.7.

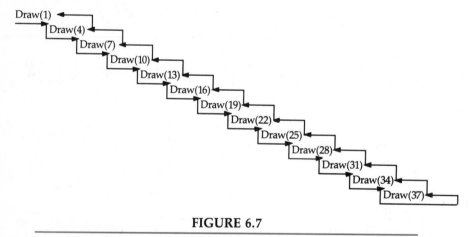

FIGURE 6.7

Unwinding from descent through recursive calls

How Is Recursion Implemented?

Our previous example has used graphics as an illustration of *what* recursion can do. However, as we progress into more complex examples, we will also need to understand in detail *how* a computer language implements recursion. Here again we encounter the abstraction-implementation duality we have emphasized throughout the book. Recursion is a powerful conceptual tool. But unless you understand details of how recursion is implemented, your use of it will be limited to an intuitive approach that often employs a trial-and-error strategy to reach a solution.

In Section 6.4, we indicated that the stack is an essential data structure in a compiler's implementation of procedure calls. The role of a system stack being manipulated by the procedure calls in your program becomes even more crucial as we use recursion. To illustrate this, let us consider a problem more computationally oriented than our previous graphics example. N factorial, denoted N!, is defined by

$$N! = N \times (N - 1) \times (N - 2) \times \ldots \times 2 \times 1$$

That is, N! is the product of the first N integers. We note that the alternate way of defining N! is by means of using $(N - 1)!$

$$N! = \begin{cases} 1 \text{ if } N = 1 \text{ or } N = 0 \\ N * (N - 1)! \text{ otherwise} \end{cases}$$

Notice that this alternate definition is a recursive definition because it uses the notion of factorial to define factorial. Such a recursive definition may seem to violate a principle learned early in any English composition course: avoid circularity in defining terms. However, despite your English teacher's concerns, we have a perfectly valid definition because of the recursive out in the special definition of 1!.

To see how recursion works, think of the preceding definition as a series of clues which eventually will allow us to unravel the mystery of how to compute N!. That is, to compute N!, the recursive definition really tells us to

1. Remember what N is.

2. Go compute $(N - 1)!$.

3. Once we've computed $(N - 1)!$, multiply that by N to get our final answer.

Of course, when we use the definition to determine how to compute $(N - 1)!$, we find out that we must, in turn, compute $(N - 2)!$. Computing $(N - 2)!$ will involve finding $(N - 3)!$. This downward spiral will eventually end with 1!, allowing us to begin the actual series of multiplications that will bring us to the appropriate answer. Figure 6.8 illustrates the logic of the recursive method for computing N factorial. In particular, if N were 4, the sequence of recursive invocations of the definition and resulting computations would be as shown in Figure 6.9.

Algorithms which are recursively defined may be easily programmed in a language such as Pascal, which allows a procedure or function to call itself. For example, the following Pascal program with its associated run calls a function Factorial to compute the value of 4!. The **writeln** statements upon entry to and exit from the function are not necessary but have been included to demonstrate the precise call and return sequence triggered by the initial call of Factorial(4) in the main program. It is crucial to note that

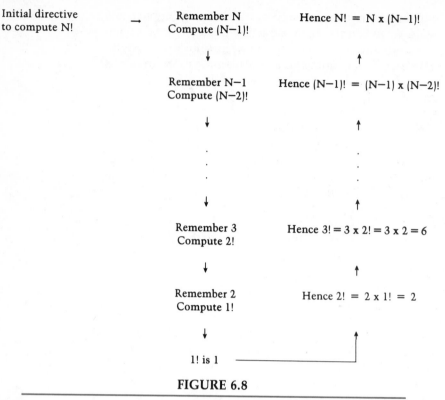

FIGURE 6.8

Recursive computation of N!

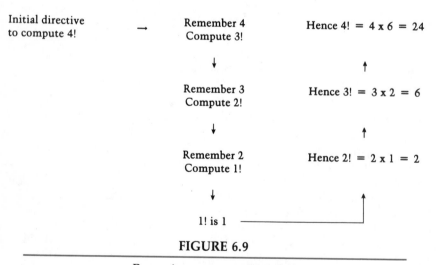

FIGURE 6.9

Recursive computation of 4!

the output from **writeln** statements implies that we must in some sense have multiple copies of the variable *n*, one copy for each descent to a recursively deeper level. As we shall see, it is a stack which keeps track of these multiple copies of *n* in the appropriate fashion.

```
PROGRAM RecursiveDemo(input, output);

   {Illustrate how recursion may be used to compute factorial.}

VAR
   m : integer;

FUNCTION Factorial(n : integer) : integer;

   BEGIN
    writeln ('ENTERING FACTORIAL WITH N = ', n);
    IF (n = 1) OR (n = 0) THEN
      Factorial := 1
    ELSE
      Factorial := n * {Return Point 2} Factorial(n-1);
    writeln ('LEAVING FACTORIAL WITH N = ', n)
    END; {Factorial}

BEGIN {Main}
   write ('ENTER NUMBER FOR FACTORIAL COMPUTATION-->');
   readln(m);
   writeln(Factorial(m)) {Return Point 1}
END.
```

Sample Run.

```
ENTER NUMBER FOR FACTORIAL COMPUTATION-->4
ENTERING FACTORIAL WITH N = 4
ENTERING FACTORIAL WITH N = 3
ENTERING FACTORIAL WITH N = 2
ENTERING FACTORIAL WITH N = 1
LEAVING FACTORIAL WITH N = 1
LEAVING FACTORIAL WITH N = 2
LEAVING FACTORIAL WITH N = 3
LEAVING FACTORIAL WITH N = 4
      24
```

The comments {Return Point 1} and {Return Point 2} have been inserted into the preceding code to allow us to see the role played by a stack as this program is run. We have already alluded to the existence of a general system stack onto which return addresses are pushed each time a function or procedure call is made. Let us now explain it more fully. Each time a procedure/function call is made, an item called a stack frame will be pushed onto the system stack. The data in this stack frame consist of the return address and a copy of each local variable and parameter for the procedure/function. Figure 6.10 illustrates how stack frames are pushed and popped from the system stack when Factorial(4) is invoked. Return

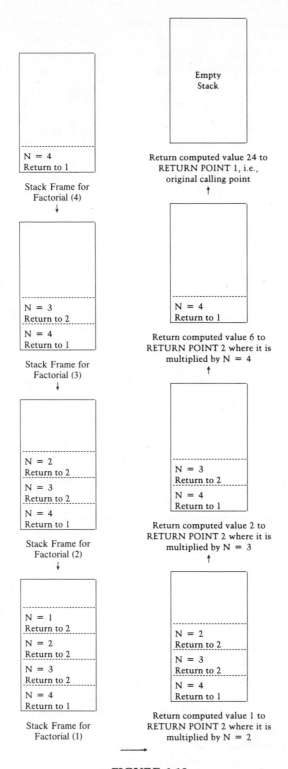

FIGURE 6.10

Sequence of pushes and pops in computing 4!

addresses have been indicated by referring to the appropriate comments in the Pascal code.

In the preceding graphic and factorial examples, the type of recursion illustrated is known as tail recursion. In tail recursion, once an initial return operation is made, an uninterrupted series of returns is triggered. This unwinding continues until it reaches the original calling point. Many times algorithms which use tail recursion may be implemented in a fashion which is just as easy (and does not consume system stack space) by using an ordinary loop structure. You may already have realized how to do this for our factorial example. The value of recursion, as we shall see, is that it represents a "natural" way of expressing the solution to certain types of problems. Moreover, as the problems which we solve by recursive algorithms become more complex, we shall see that tail recursion is often replaced by a more involved form of recursion which requires a much more complicated pattern of pushing and popping frames from the system stack.

Towers of Hanoi Problem

We introduce this more complex type of recursion with a problem that, although impractical, is excellent for illustrating the technique involved. According to legend, there existed in ancient Hanoi a monastery where the monks had the painstaking task of moving a collection of N stone disks from one pillar, designated as pillar A, to another, designated as pillar C. Moreover, the relative ordering of the disks on pillar A had to be maintained as they were moved to pillar C. That is, as illustrated in Figure 6.11, the disks were to be stacked from largest to smallest, beginning from the bottom. Additionally, the monks were to observe the following rules in moving disks:

□ Only one disk could be moved at a time.

□ No larger disk could ever be placed on a pillar on top of a smaller disk.

□ A third pillar B could be used as an intermediate to store one or more disks while they were being moved from their original source A to their destination C.

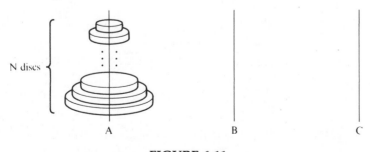

FIGURE 6.11

Towers of Hanoi

Language Definition

In the *Pascal User Manual and Report* (Berlin: Springer-Verlag, 1974). Kathleen Jensen and Niklaus Wirth made famous a diagrammatic way of representing Pascal syntax. By way of example, a syntax diagram which defines a Pascal statement is presented here. One interesting feature to note about this diagram is that the term *statement* is used eight times in defining statement. (Where are the recursive outs in this diagram?) Jensen and Wirth's diagrams are recursive in nature, and they point out the fact that the syntax of most computer languages can be recursively defined. This is of tremendous importance in the writing of compilers, most of which rely heavily upon stacks and recursion to parse source programs.

A broader question than the definition and parsing of programming languages is the ability of the computer to process natural languages such as English. Researchers in the field of artificial intelligence are attempting to use more general recursive techniques to define the syntax of natural languages and, consequently, program the computer to cope with this more complex type of language. To date, their work has met with success in only highly restricted domains of natural language such as that used to express word problems in algebra. However, despite these present limitations, research in the areas of language definition and the consequent processing of that language by computer should be one of the most intensely explored fields within computer science in the coming years.

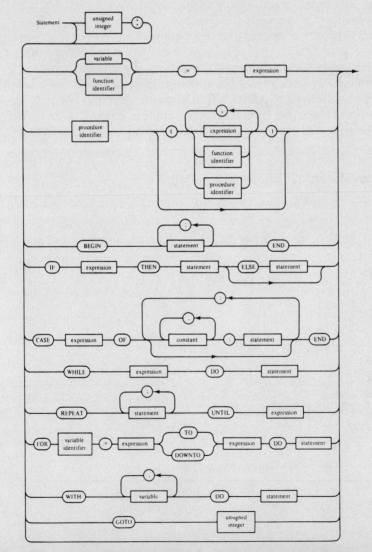

Consider the following recursive solution to this problem:

1. If N = 1, merely move the disk from A to C.

2. If N = 2, move first disk from A to B. Then move second disk from A to C. Then move first disk from B to C.

3. If N = 3, call upon the technique already established in step 2 to move the first two disks from A to B using C as an intermediate. Then move the third disk from A to C. Then use the technique in step 2 to move the first disks from B to C using A as an intermediate.

.

.

.

N. For general N, use the technique in the previous step to move N-1 disks from A to B using C as an intermediate. Then move one disk from A to C. Then use technique in the previous step to move N-1 disks from B to C using A as an intermediate.

Notice that the technique described here calls upon itself but switches the order of parameters in so doing. This can be formalized in the following Pascal procedure. The labels which appear in the procedure are included only for discussion purposes.

```
PROCEDURE Hanoi (n : integer;
                 Source, Destination, Intermediate : char);


   LABEL
     1,2;

   BEGIN
     IF n = 1 THEN
       write ('MOVE DISK FROM ', Source, 'TO', Destination)
     ELSE
       BEGIN
       Hanoi (n-1, Source, Intermediate, Destination);
```

The first recursive call transfers N − 1 disks from SOURCE to INTERMEDIATE using DESTINATION

```
    { In every recursive call Hanoi works with value of n less one. }

  1:
     write('MOVE DISK FROM ', Source 'TO', Destination);
     Hanoi(n-1, Intermediate, Destination, Source)
     END;
  2:
   END;
{End Hanoi}
```

Then transfer the single disk
from SOURCE to DESTINATION

SOURCE   INTERMEDIATE   DESTINATION

The second recursive call transfers
N − 1 disks from INTERMEDIATE
to DESTINATION using SOURCE

SOURCE   INTERMEDIATE   DESTINATION

Because we have a call to Hanoi within the procedure Hanoi, this represents a recursive call. Although such a procedure is easy to write in Pascal, it is somewhat more difficult to understand thoroughly.

The key to understanding this procedure is to be aware of what a compiler must do when the recursive call is made. The difficulty with handling recursion is that, because we call a procedure from within that procedure, eventually a return will be made to that same procedure. However, because the call also involves changing the values of the procedure's parameters, the old values of the parameters will have been destroyed upon return unless they were preserved before the recursive call. The best way of preserving them is to stack them along with other local variables and the return address. Thus, a recursive call involves stacking not only a return address but also the values of all parameters essential to the current state of the procedure. To illustrate, we will trace through the actions taken when a call of the form

```
Hanoi(3, 'A', 'C', 'B')
```

is initiated. The values in the return address portion of the stack are the statement labels in our Hanoi procedure.

1. n is not 1, so the condition in the **IF** statement is **false**.

2. Hanoi(n-1, Source, Intermediate, Destination) is encountered with A, B, and C as first, second, and third arguments. Because this represents a recursive call, some stacking must be done.

1	3	A	C	B
Return Address	N	Source	Destination	Intermediate
			Parameters	

Stack Frame(s)

3. Reenter Hanoi. Notice that as we enter this time, the procedure's view of the parameters is $n = 2$, Source = A, Destination = B, and Intermediate = C. Because n is not 1, the condition in the **IF** statement is **false**.

4. Hanoi(n-1, Source, Intermediate, Destination) is encountered. Because this is a recursive call, stacking occurs.

1	2	A	B	C
1	3	A	C	B
Return Address	N	Source	Destination	Intermediate
			Parameters	

Stack Frame(s)

5. We reenter Hanoi with $n = 1$, Source = A, Destination = C, and Intermediate = B. Because $n = 1$, the condition in the **IF** statement is **true**.

6. Hence

MOVE DISK FROM A TO C

is printed and a return triggers a popping of a return address (1) and four parameters ($n = 2$, Source = A, Destination = B, and Intermediate = C).

1	3	A	C	B
Return Address	N	Source	Destination	Intermediate
			Parameters	

Stack Frame(s)

7. Because the return address popped was 1

MOVE DISK FROM A TO B

is printed and

Hanoi(n-1, Intermediate, Destination, Source)

is encountered with $n = 2$, Source = A, Destination = B, and Intermediate = C.

8. The call pushes a return address and four parameters onto the stacks.

Return Address	N	Source	Destination	Intermediate
2	2	A	B	C
1	3	A	C	B

| | | | Parameters | |

Stack Frame(s)

9. We reenter Hanoi, this time with $n = 1$, Source = C, Destination = B, and Intermediate = A.

10. Because $n = 1$, the **IF** statement generates the output

```
MOVE DISK FROM C TO B
```

and a return.

11. The return pops values from both stacks and we return to statement 2 with $n = 2$, Source = A, Destination = B, and Intermediate = C.

12. But statement 2 triggers a return itself, so both stacks are popped again and we return to statement 1 with $n = 3$, Source = A, Destination = C, Intermediate = B, and both stacks temporarily empty.

13. Statement 1 triggers the output

```
MOVE DISK FROM A TO C
```

and we are immediately at another call:

```
Hanoi(n-1, Intermediate, Destination, Source)
```

Hence the temporary empty status of the stacks is changed to

Return Address	N	Source	Destination	Intermediate
2	3	A	C	B

| | | | Parameters | |

Stack Frame(s)

14. We reenter Hanoi with $n = 2$, Source = B, Destination = C, and Intermediate = A. Because n is not 1, another call is executed and more values are stacked.

Return Address	N	Source	Destination	Intermediate
1	2	B	C	A
2	3	A	C	B

| | | | Parameters | |

Stack Frame(s)

15. Reenter Hanoi with $n = 1$, Source = B, Destination = A, and Intermediate = C. Because $n = 1$, we print

```
MOVE DISK FROM B TO A
```

and return.

16. The return prompts the popping of both stacks. The return address popped is statement 1 with parameters $n = 2$, Source = B, Destination = C, and Intermediate = A. Statement 1 causes output

```
MOVE DISK FROM B TO C
```

with the stack frames left at

2	3	A	C	B
Return Address	N	Source	Destination Parameters	Intermediate

Stack Frame(s)

17. The output from statement 1 is followed by

```
Hanoi(n-1, Intermediate, Destination, Source)
```

Hence pushed onto the stack frames are

2	2	B	C	A
2	3	A	C	B
Return Address	N	Source	Destination Parameters	Intermediate

Stack Frame(s)

18. Reenter (for the last time) Hanoi with $n = 1$, Source = A, Destination = C, and Intermediate = B. Because $n = 1$, output

```
MOVE DISK FROM A TO C
```

and return.

19. But now the return pops return address 2 from the stack, so return to statement 2 with $n = 2$, Source = B, Destination = C, and Intermediate = A.

2	3	A	C	B
Return Address	N	Source	Destination Parameters	Intermediate

Stack Frame(s)

20. Statement 2 is another return, so pop the stacks again. Return address popped is 2, the same return statement. But this time the return will transfer control back to the original calling location and WE ARE DONE!

Long-winded as this narrative is, it is essential that you understand it. Recursive procedures are crucial to many of the algorithms used in computer science, and you can acquire the necessary familiarity with recursion only by convincing yourself that it really works. If you have some doubt or are not sure you understand, we recommend that you trace through the Hanoi procedure with $n = 4$ (be prepared to go through a lot of paper).

The key to writing recursive procedures is *always to leave a recursive out*. Suppose, for instance, that the **IF** statement were to be left out of our previous Hanoi procedure. This would trigger an endless sequence of procedure calls never interrupted by a return operation. The outcome is predictable: the program soon runs out of stack space. Such erroneous recursive calls are typically met with a "stack overflow" error message.

Efficiency Considerations for Recursion

The value of recursion lies in the way in which it enables us to express algorithms compactly and elegantly for a certain class of problems. Since we use recursion frequently throughout the rest of this text, you will learn to acquire a feel for the type of problems particularly suitable to this powerful technique. In the next chapter, we will see that recursion is an indispensable strategy for manipulating a data structure known as a tree. In later chapters, recursion will be explored as a means of sorting, searching, and simulating nested loops to an arbitrary depth.

One caution should be stressed, however, before we proceed with these applications of recursion. Do not be misled into thinking that recursion is necessarily the most efficient programming technique because the code which expresses it is often compact and lacking in any explicit loop control statements such as **WHILE** or **REPEAT**. The very nature of a recursive call generates iteration without any need for **WHILE** or **REPEAT**. The iteration control mechanism in recursion is the recursive out condition which triggers a series of returns before another recursive call is made. Hence, from a time-efficiency perspective, a recursive algorithm's measure of effectiveness is closely tied to the number of times it must iterate its recursive call-and-return pattern. Moreover, with recursion, we pay a price in memory efficiency that is not present in other iterative control structures. This price is system stack space. For instance, no matter what computer you may be using, you can easily find a value for the parameter n which will cause our Hanoi procedure to terminate with an "Out of stack space" error message. This error will inevitably occur for values of n which are too large for the system stack despite the fact that we have an appropriate recursive out in our procedure. All computers are finite machines, and a recursive out can't save us from a situation in which the algorithm would have worked had the system allocated 1K (or 10K or 100K . . .) more bytes for its stack space.

Because of the potentially enormous price which might be paid when using recursion, we will later explore ways of removing recursion from algorithms. (See Chapter 8.) A viable strategy that will emerge is to use recursion to initially express an algorithm because the recursive approach is most natural and then convert it to a nonrecursive implementation.

However, before doing this, we will use the next chapter to hone our recursive skills by studying a data structure which is inherently recursive in nature.

DESIGNER'S WORKBENCH

Robust Programs

In Chapter 3 we defined a robust module as one which guards against harmful side effects when it receives invalid data. In a robust module we must be concerned with the following issues:

1. Guiding the user through the entry of data in its appropriate form.

2. Trapping errors in data entry to insure that the module does not return invalid or inaccurate data.

3. Insuring that an error in a data entry module does not "crash" the entire program, leaving crucial pointer references and other computations in a half-finished (and hence totally unreliable) state.

4. Making it as easy as possible for a user to recover from an error in data entry. One of the main issues in this regard is how much the user must retype when a data entry error is detected. Must the user retype all data that have been previously entered, including those values that were valid? Or is it sufficient for the user to retype merely the data item which triggered the error?

As an example of a module which should be robust, consider Pascal's supplied **read** procedure. Do some testing for your version of Pascal and determine how robust its **read** procedure is for entry of integer and real data. For instance, how does **read**(X) respond when X is a real variable and the user accidentally enters O.642 for X instead of 0.642? Typing the letter O instead of the digit 0 or the lowercase letter l instead of the digit 1 are data entry errors frequently made by naive computer users. In many versions of Pascal, such an error in numeric data entry encountered during execution of a **read** statement can "crash" a program or result in the wrong numeric value being returned. In such versions of Pascal, the **read** procedure is not very robust. Hence you may have to write your own procedures to allow a user to enter a numeric value in an error-proof fashion. The basis for such procedures employs logic similar to that used in the GetInfixToken module of this chapter's case study (Section 6.5). Read the user input as a character stream and convert incoming digits to their numeric values as they are read. This will allow you to catch a character which is not an appropriate digit before it can lead to a problem.

In discussing this chapter's case study, we identified the role of the lexical analysis module as being responsible for returning the next token from the infix string. Since the lexical analysis module GetInfixToken is the primary interface between the user and the program, it is here that we must concentrate our efforts at making the program robust. Among the specific robustness issues which might be considered in this chapter's case study are

☐ How does our program react when a nondigit is accidentally entered as part of a number?

☐ How does our program react when the user does not leave a space between tokens?

☐ How does our program react when an invalid operator is entered?

☐ How does our program react when a variable other than X is entered? For example, what happens when the user enters a function in terms of Y instead of X?

Making a program completely robust is a difficult and time-consuming task. In the exercises which follow, you will be asked to explore more deeply the robustness issues connected to the lexical analysis module of this chapter's case study.

Designer's Workbench Exercises

1. Write a Pascal procedure ReadInteger to read a stream of characters which should represent an integer number. Return the integer value corresponding to that stream of characters. If the stream of characters does not represent a valid integer, have your procedure return an appropriate error flag.
2. Write a Pascal procedure ReadReal to read a stream of characters which should represent a real number. Allow for both decimal and exponential E notation. Return the real value corresponding to that stream of characters. If the stream of characters does not represent a valid real, have your program return an appropriate error flag.
3. Make the GetInfixToken module of this chapter's case study more robust by allowing the user to separate individual tokens with an arbitrary number of zero or more spaces.
4. Make the GetInfixToken module of this chapter's case study more robust by guarding against input of an invalid arithmetic operator.
5. Make the GetInfixToken module of this chapter's case study more robust by guarding against an invalid character in a stream of characters intended to be a real number. When such an invalid character is detected, allow the user to recover from the point of the error rather than forcing the user to retype the entire line.   ■

Summary

In this chapter we have discussed the stack as an abstract data structure. Conceptually, a stack is simpler than a queue since all additions and deletions are limited to one end of the structure, the top. For this reason, a stack is also known as a last-in, first-out (LIFO) list. Like a queue, a stack may be implemented using either an array or a linked list.

The simplicity of the stack as an abstract structure belies the importance of its applications. The first application studied was the parsing and evaluation of arithmetic expressions. This application is indicative of the crucial role a stack plays in the parsing done by language compilers. As a second application, we examined how a stack is used to process procedure calls when a program executes. Understanding the role of the stack in this application is essential to effectively using the programming technique known as recursion. Finally, we began exploring recursion; it is an important algorithmic strategy that we will frequently employ in the remainder of the book.

Key Terms

factorial
infix
infix priority
integral
last-in, first-out (LIFO)
lexical analysis
numerical analysis
parsing
pop procedure
postfix
prefix
push procedure
recursion

recursive call
recursive definition
recursive out
recursive procedure
stack
stack frame
stack priority
tail recursion
tokens
top
Towers of Hanoi
variant record

Exercises

1. What are the infix, postfix, and prefix forms of the expression

$$A + B * (C - D)/(P - R)?$$

2. Trace the contents of the stack as the postfix form of the expression in Exercise 2 is evaluated. Assume that A = 6, B = 4, C = 3, D = 1, P = 12, and R = 11.
3. How would the stack and infix priority functions in the case study dictate that

$$3^{2^3}$$

be evaluated? Is this appropriate? If not, how should these functions be adjusted to assure appropriate evaluation of such infix expressions?
4. Each of the following programs is intended to read a string character-by-character, put each character on the system stack, and then print out the string of characters in reverse order. Which one(s) actually achieve this intent? Which one(s) don't? Why not? What will be the output of each program for input of MADAM?

a. PROGRAM Palindrome {input, output};

```
      {Print out a string in reverse order to check if
         palindrome.}

      PROCEDURE Reverse;

      { Keep recursively stacking characters until end of
          string. Then print it out in reverse by popping the
          stack. }

      VAR
          c : char; { Here c is local to Reverse. }

        BEGIN
          read(c);
          IF NOT eoln THEN
            Reverse;
          write(c)
        END; { Reverse }

    BEGIN
      Reverse
    END.
```

b. PROGRAM Palindrome (input, output);

```
    { Print out a string in reverse order to check if
        palindrome. }

    VAR
      c : char; {Here c is global.}

    PROCEDURE Reverse;

      { Keep recursively stacking characters until end of
          string. Then print it out in reverse by popping the
          stack. }

        BEGIN
          read(c);
          IF NOT eoln THEN
            Reverse;
          write(c)
        END; { Reverse }

    BEGIN
      Reverse
    END.
```

5. Consider the following recursive function and associated top-level call.
   Comments of the form { Return Point N } have been used to label

possible return points from recursive calls. What would a stack frame
for this function contain? Show by a series of stack "snapshots" how
the stack would be manipulated for the calls indicated. Finally, use this
to assist you in providing the output that would be produced by these
calls.

```
PROGRAM Mystery(input, output);

   VAR
      i, j : integer;

   FUNCTION Weird(m, n : integer) : integer;

      BEGIN
         writeln(m, n);
         IF m = 0 THEN
            Weird := n + 1
         ELSE IF n = 0 THEN
            Weird := Weird(m - 1, 1)

                        { Return Point 2 }

         ELSE
            Weird := Weird(m - 1,          Weird(m, n - 1))

                     { Return Point 4 } { Return Point 3 }

      END; { Weird }

BEGIN

   writeln(Weird(1, 3))
                  { Return Point 1 }
END.
```

6. Consider the expression with the infix notation P+(Q−F)/Y. Using the
   algorithm discussed in this chapter to transform this into a postfix
   expression, trace the state of both the operator stack and postfix string
   as each character of the infix expression is processed.

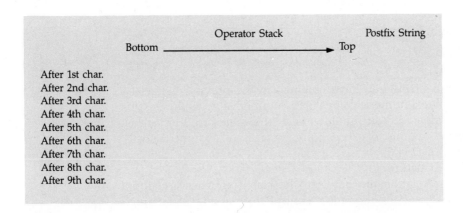

7. Using the postfix expression you have obtained in the previous exercise, trace the stack of real values that would develop as the postfix expression is evaluated. You should indicate the numeric values on the stack as each character in the postfix expression is processed. Assume the values P = 10, Q = 18, F = 4, and Y = 2.

8. Parse the infix expression

$$P * (Q/Y) + A - B + D * Y\#$$

using the following definitions of InfixPriority and StackPriority:

	$*$	/	+	−	(	)	#
Infix Priority	2	2	4	4	5	0	0
Stack Priority	1	1	3	3	0	unde-fined	0

Trace this parsing operation by filling in the following table to indicate the contents of the operator stack and postfix string after each character is read in.

	Operator Stack	Postfix String
	Bottom ————————————————→ Top	
After 1st char.		
After 2nd char.		
After 3rd char.		
After 4th char.		
After 5th char.		
After 6th char.		
After 7th char.		
After 8th char.		
After 9th char.		
After 10th char.		
After 11th char.		
After 12th char.		
After 13th char.		
After 14th char.		
After 15th char.		
After 16th char.		

9. Using the postfix string you have obtained in the previous exercise, trace the stack of real numeric values that would develop as the postfix expression is evaluated. You should indicate the values on the stack as each character in the postfix expression is processed. Assume the values A = 4, B = 3, D = 2, P = 1, Q = 4, and Y = 2.

10. What is a stack structure?

11. Explain how the relationship between the stack priorities and infix priorities of (,), *, /, +, −, and # control the parsing of an infix expression.

12. Stand between two parallel mirrors and see how recursion works for you.
13. Discuss some of the trade-offs in efficiency that are made when recursion is used.
14. Discuss how the case study of this chapter would have to be modified to allow expressions to contain unary minus (that is, the negative of a single number), trigonometric, logarithmic, and exponential functions. Implement these changes.
15. Use big-O notation to express the memory utilization and run-time efficiency of the Towers of Hanoi algorithms in terms of n, the number of disks to be moved.
16. Explore the limits of system stack space on your computer by determining values of n for which the Towers of Hanoi program will fail.
17. How would the functions InfixPriority and StackPriority be extended to include the Boolean operators $<$, $>$, $<=$, $>=$, $=$, $<>$, **AND, OR, NOT**?
18. Write procedures to implement each of the following operations for an array implementation of a stack:
    a. Create(Stack)
    b. Full(Stack)
    c. Empty(Stack)
    d. OnTop(Item,Stack)
19. Write procedures to implement each of the following stack operations for a linked list implementation of a stack:
    a. Create(Stack)
    b. Full(Stack)
    c. Empty(Stack)
    d. Push(Item, Stack)
    e. Pop(Item, Stack)
    f. OnTop(Item, Stack)

Programming Problems

1. Write a program that will parse infix expressions into prefix form.
2. Write a program to call for input of a decimal number and convert it to its binary equivalent using the method described in the following flowchart.

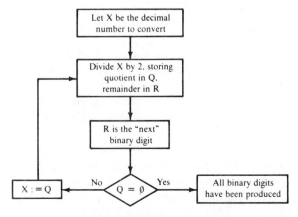

Note that this method produces the binary digits for the given number in reverse order. One strategy for printing out the digits in the correct order would be to store them in an array as they are produced and then print out the array. However, this strategy would have the drawbacks of allocating unnecessary storage for an array and then limiting the size of the binary number to the size of the array. Your program is not to employ this strategy. Rather call for input of the decimal number in your main program and then immediately transfer control to a procedure that in turn is called recursively, stacking the binary digits as they are produced. Once division by 2 yields 0, the succession of returns can be used to print out the digits one by one as they are popped from this stack.

3. The Nth Fibonacci number is defined by

> 1 if N is 1.
> 1 if N is 2.
> The sum of the previous two Fibonacci numbers otherwise.

Write a recursive procedure to compute the Nth Fibonacci number.

4. Euclid devised a clever algorithm for computing the greatest common divisor of two integers. According to Euclid's algorithm,

$$GCD(M,N) = \begin{cases} GCD(N,M) \text{ if } N > M \\ M \text{ if } N = 0 \\ GCD(N,M \text{ MOD } N) \text{ if } N > 0 \end{cases}$$

Write a recursive procedure to compute greatest common divisors via Euclid's method.

5. In the Programming Problems for Chapter 4, you developed a passenger list processing system for the various flights of Wing-and-a-Prayer Airlines. Wing-and-a-Prayer management would now like you to extend this system so that it processes logical combinations of flight numbers. For example, the command

LIST 1 OR 2

should list all passengers whose name appears on the flight 1 list or the flight 2 list. Your program should also accept the logical operators **AND** and **NOT** and allow parenthesized logical expressions obeying the standard logical hierarchy

> **NOT**
> **AND**
> **OR**

6. A tax form may be thought of as a sequence of items, each of which is either a number or defined by an arbitrary mathematical formula involving other items in the sequence. To assist them in their tax-planning strategy, top management at the Fly-by-Night credit card company desire a program which would allow them to interactively enter numbers or formulas associated with given lines of a tax form. Once all such lines have been defined, users of the program may redefine the number or formula associated with a particular line, and all other lines dependent on that one should be appropriately updated. Note that, since formulas may be entered interactively, your program will have to use a stack to

evaluate them. You will in effect have written a small-scale spreadsheet program.

7. Write a program that will accept commands of the following form:

- □ **INPUT** variable name
- □ variable name = infix expression involving variables names and arithmetic operators +, −, *, /
- □ **PRINT** variable name
- □ **GO**

These commands are to be stored in an array of strings until the **GO** command is entered. Once **GO** is entered, your program should execute the previously stored commands. "Execute" here means:

- □ For an **INPUT** command: Send a question mark to the terminal and allow the user to enter a real number which is then stored in variable name.
- □ For an assignment statement: Parse the expression into postfix form and then evaluate it, storing the results in the variable name on the left of the equality sign.
- □ For a **PRINT** instruction: Write to the terminal the numerical contents of the specified variable name.

To make things relatively easy you may assume a syntax that

- □ Allows variable names consisting of one uppercase alphabetical character.
- □ Allows only one variable name following **INPUT** or **PRINT**.
- □ Allows one blank space after the keywords **INPUT** and **PRINT** and no blank spaces anywhere else.

For an additional challenge, enable your program to handle successfully the exponentiation operator ^ within assignment statement expressions. The following example should illustrate the need for care in handling this exponentiation operator:

$$3^{2^3} = 3^8, \text{ not } 9^3$$

8. This problem is an extension of Problem 7 for a "compiler" for a primitive programming language. Write a program that will accept commands of the following form:

- □ **INPUT** variable name
- □ **PRINT** variable name
- □ variable name = infix arithmetic expression involving variable names and arithmetic operators +, −, *, /, ^
- □ **GOTO** line $\begin{cases} \textbf{ALWAYS, or} \\ \\ \textbf{IF} \text{ infix logical expression involving variable names} \\ \quad \text{and operators } +, -, *, /, \char`\^, \&(\text{for AND}), !(\text{for} \\ \quad \text{OR}), \sim(\text{for NOT}), <, >, = \end{cases}$
- □ **STOP**
- □ **RUN**

These commands are to be stored in an array of strings until the **RUN** command is entered. Upon encountering **RUN**, your program should execute the previously stored commands. "Execute" here means:

- For an **INPUT** command: Send a question mark to the terminal and allow the user to enter a real number, which is stored in variable name.
- For a **PRINT** command: Write to the terminal the numerical contents of the specified variable name.
- For an assignment command: Parse the expression into postfix form and then evaluate it. Store the result in the variable name on the left of the equality sign.
- For a **GOTO** command: Branch to the line number specified when **ALWAYS** follows the line number or when the infix expression which follows the **IF** evaluates to true. Here "line number" refers to the relative position of the line in the sequence of lines which were entered prior to the **RUN** command. The first line number in this sequence is "00".
- For a **STOP** command: Halt execution.

To make things relatively easy, you may assume a syntax that

- Specifies that one and only one blank space follows **INPUT**, **PRINT**, **GOTO**, and line number. No other blanks appear anywhere.
- Allows only one variable name to follow **INPUT** or **PRINT**.
- Only allows variable names consisting of one uppercase alphabetical character.
- Only allows line numbers consisting of two digits: 00 through 99.

The usual hierarchy for operators is assumed.

9. If you have access to an appropriate graphics device, write the procedures Line and RightTurn described in Section 6.6. Then experiment by writing recursive procedures which call on these procedures (and others you may develop) to produce a variety of interesting figures.

Binary Trees, General Trees, and Graphs

Except during the nine months before he draws his first breath, no man manages his affairs as well as a tree does.

George Bernard Shaw

Introductory Considerations

Human beings organize much of the world around them into hierarchies. For instance, an industrial or governmental body functions effectively only by defining a collection of supervisor-subordinate relationships among its participants. We have seen in Chapter 3 that computer scientists design a software system by breaking it down into modules and defining hierarchical boss-worker relationships among those modules. The familial parent-child relationship allows a natural breakdown of a family's history into a genealogical tree. In computer science, a tree is a data structure that represents such hierarchical relationships between data items.

To introduce some of the terminology of tree structures, we will consider the record of a student at a typical university. In addition to the usual statistical background information such as social security number, name, and address, a typical student record contains listings for a number of courses, exams and final grades in each course, overall grade point average, and other data relating to the student's performance at the college. Figure 7.1 is an example of a tree structure representing such a student record. As in genealogical trees, at the highest level (0) of a tree is its root (also called the *root node*). Here STUDENT is the root node. The nodes NAME, ADDRESS, SSN, COURSE, and GPA, which are directly connected to the root node, are the child nodes of the parent node STUDENT. The child nodes of a given parent constitute a set of siblings. Thus NAME, ADDRESS, SSN, COURSE, and GPA are siblings. In the hierarchy represented by a tree, the child nodes of a parent are one level lower than the parent node. Thus NAME, ADDRESS, SSN, COURSE, and GPA are at level 1 in Figure 7.1.

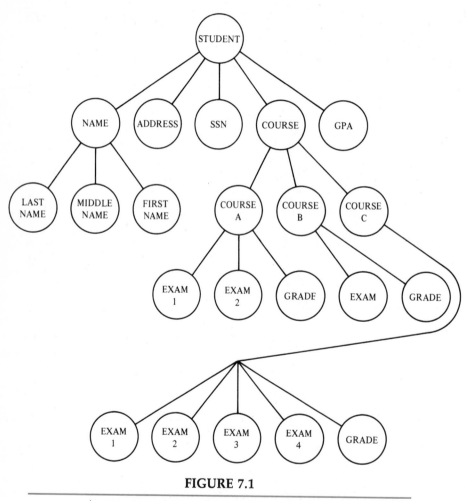

FIGURE 7.1

A tree structure representing a student record

A link between a parent and its child is called a branch in a tree structure. Each node in a tree except the root must descend from a parent node via a branch. Thus LASTNAME, FIRSTNAME, and MIDDLENAME descend from the parent node NAME. The root of the tree is the ancestor of all the nodes in the tree. Each node may be the parent of any number of nodes in the tree. A node with no children is called a leaf node. In Figure 7.1, GPA is a leaf node. LASTNAME, FIRSTNAME, MIDDLENAME, EXAM1, and EXAM2 also are leaf nodes.

A subtree is a subset of a tree that is itself a tree; the tree in Figure 7.2 is a subtree of the tree in Figure 7.1. This subtree has the root node NAME.

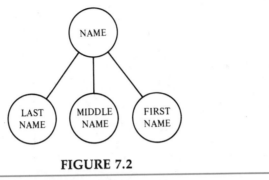

FIGURE 7.2

A subtree of Figure 7.1

Similarly, the tree in Figure 7.3 is another subtree of the tree in Figure 7.1.

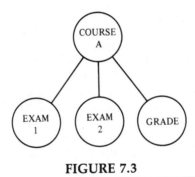

FIGURE 7.3

Another subtree of Figure 7.1, also a subtree of Figure 7.4

Notice that the tree in Figure 7.3 is a subtree of both the tree in Figure 7.1 and the tree in Figure 7.4.

_____ **7.2**

General Trees and Binary Trees as Abstract Data Types

It is evident from the preceding discussion that a tree has the following interesting property: Any given node within a tree is itself the root node of a completely analogous tree structure. That is, a tree is composed of a

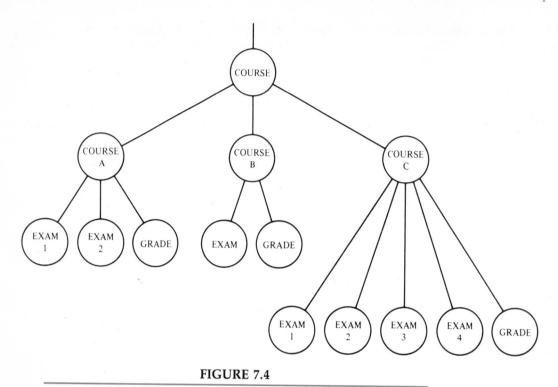

FIGURE 7.4

Another subtree of Figure 7.1

collection of substructures, each of which also meets the criteria for being a tree. This sounds dangerously circular, and, to formally describe a tree in this fashion, we must be sure to give ourselves a recursive out. This is done via the following definition of a tree as an abstract data type:

Tree A general tree is a set of nodes that is either empty (the recursive out), or has a designated node called the root from which (hierarchically) descend zero or more subtrees. Each subtree itself satisfies the definition of a tree.

The operations we wish to perform on a tree include those shown in Table 7.1.

Two points about this definition should be emphasized. First, the recursive fashion in which a tree is defined should provide a strong hint that most tree-processing algorithms will also be recursive. Second, most operations on the tree data structure are closely linked to the hierarchical relationship among nodes for that particular tree. This hierarchical relationship may vary greatly from tree to tree. To consider some examples of such

Operation	Explanation
Create(Root)	Initialize the tree referenced by Root.
Empty(Root)	Boolean-valued function to determine whether tree referenced by Root is empty.
Find(Root, Target, TargetLoc)	For the tree referenced by Root, return in TargetLoc the location of the Target data item. If Target cannot be found, return appropriate flag in TargetLoc.
Add(Root, Node)	Add to the tree referenced by Root, the data in Node (while maintaining the appropriate hierarchical relationships within the tree).
Delete(Root, Node)	Delete from the tree referenced by Root the data referenced by Node (while maintaining the appropriate hierarchical relationships within the tree).
Traverse(Root)	In the tree referenced by Root, visit every node in a specified order relative to the hierarchical relationships within the tree.

TABLE 7.1

Operations on trees

relationships which are found quite often in computer science applications, let us restrict our attention for the moment to binary trees.

> **Binary tree** A binary tree is a tree in which each node has no more than two subtrees; that is, it has no more than two child nodes.

For example, the tree of Figure 7.5 is a binary tree. Each node of this tree has two subtrees (null or non-null) designated as the left subtree and the right subtree. The particular hierarchical relationship underlying this tree is that the data in any given node of the tree is greater than or equal to the data in its left *and* right subtrees. A tree with this property is said to be a heap and to have the heap property. (This notion is not to be confused with the heap maintained by Pascal for allocating space to pointer variables as described in Chapter 4.) Although we will not discuss heaps in great detail in this chapter, they will prove particularly important in our discussion of more powerful sorting methods in Chapter 9. The Programming Problems at the end of the chapter also indicate how a heap may be used to implement the priority queue abstract data structure introduced in Chapter 5. The heap property is one example of a hierarchical relationship which can underlie a tree and hence must be preserved when various operations are performed upon the tree.

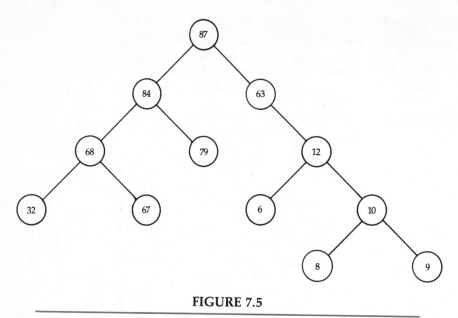

FIGURE 7.5

A binary tree with the heap property

A second example of a hierarchical relationship underlying a binary tree structure is shown in Figure 7.6.

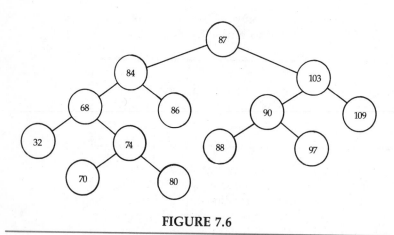

FIGURE 7.6

A binary tree with the ordering property

This binary tree exhibits the property known as the ordering property: the data in each node of the tree is greater than or equal to all of the data in that node's left subtree and less than or equal to all the data in the right subtree. We shall see the importance of trees possessing this property when we explore binary trees as a means of implementing a general list in Section 7.5.

As a final example of a hierarchical relationship which can determine the arrangement of data in a binary tree, consider Figure 7.7.

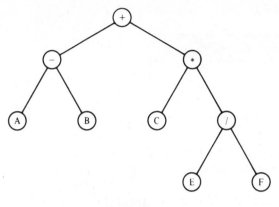

post
A B − E F I c * +

FIGURE 7.7

A binary expression tree for (A − B) + C * (E/F)

Here we have a binary tree representation of the infix algebraic expression

$$(A - B) + C * (E/F)$$

The hierarchical relationship of parent to children in this tree is that of algebraic operator to its two operands. Note that an operand may itself be an expression (that is, a subtree) which must be evaluated before the operator in the parent node can be applied. Note also that, if the order of evaluation in the expression changes as in

$$(A - B) + C * E/F$$

then the corresponding binary expression tree must also change as reflected in Figure 7.8.

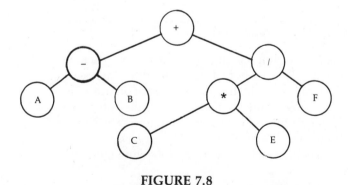

FIGURE 7.8

Binary expression tree for (A − B) + C * E/F

Contemporary compilers make use of tree structures in obtaining forms of an arithmetic expression for efficient evaluation. As discussed in Chapter 6, there are basically three forms for an arithmetic expression such as that corresponding to Figure 7.7: infix, prefix, and postfix:

Expression	Form
(A − B) + C * (E/F)	infix
+−AB*C/EF	prefix
AB−CEF/*+	postfix

All three of these forms are immediately available to us if we know exactly how the corresponding tree should be traversed. Traversing a tree means processing it in such a way that each node is visited for processing only once. The inorder traversal of the binary tree for an arithmetic expression gives us the expression in unparenthesized infix form. The preorder traversal of the same tree leads us to the prefix form of the expression, whereas the postorder traversal of the tree yields the postfix form of the expression. We shall study these three traversals in Section 7.4, after we discuss methods of implementing a binary tree.

7.3

Implementation Strategies for Binary Trees

Consistent with the way in which we have studied other data structures, we now have a very good idea of *what* a tree is without any consideration of *how* we will implement it. This latter issue must now be explored. There are two common methods for implementing binary trees; implementation techniques for general trees will not be discussed until Section 7.6. One method, which does not require the overhead of maintaining pointers, is called a linear representation; the other, known as a linked representation, uses pointers.

Linear Representation of a Binary Tree

The linear representation method of implementing a binary tree uses a one-dimensional array of size $(2^{(d+1)} − 1)$ where d is the depth of the tree, that is, the maximum level of any node in the tree. In the tree of Figure 7.7, the root + is at the level 0, the nodes − and * are at level 1, and so on. The deepest level in this tree is the level of E and F, level 3. Therefore, $d = 3$ and this tree will require an array of size $2^{(3+1)} − 1 = 15$.

Once the size of the array has been determined, the following method is used to represent the tree:

1. Store the root in the first location of the array.

2. If a node is in location n of the array, store its left child at location $2n$, and its right child at location $(2n + 1)$.

With the aid of this scheme, the tree of Figure 7.7 is stored in the array ImpBin of size 15 shown in Figure 7.9. Locations ImpBin[8] through ImpBin[13] are not used.

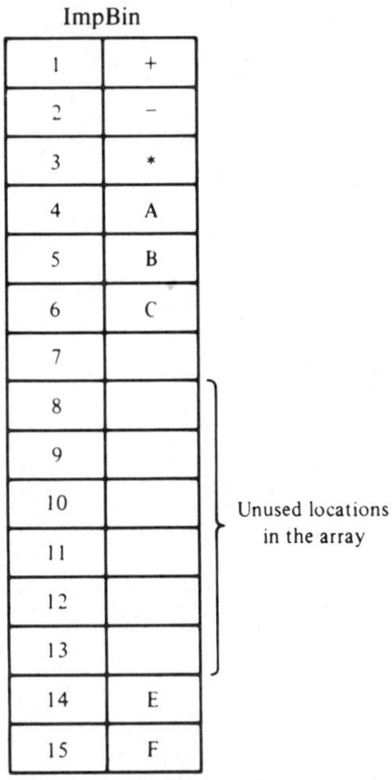

ImpBin

1	+
2	–
3	*
4	A
5	B
6	C
7	
8	
9	
10	
11	
12	
13	
14	E
15	F

Unused locations
in the array

FIGURE 7.9

The tree of Figure 7.7 stored in a linear representation of
an array

Efficiency Considerations for the Linear Representation. The main advantages of this method lie in its simplicity and the fact that, given a child node, its parent node can be determined immediately. If a child node is at location n in the array, then its parent node is at location $n/2$ (integer division).

In spite of its simplicity and ease of implementation, the linear representation method has all the overhead that comes with physically ordering items. Insertion or deletion of a node in a fashion which maintains the hierarchical relationships within the tree may cause considerable data movement up and down the array and hence use an excessive amount of processing time. Also, there usually are wasted memory locations (such as locations 8 through 13 in our example) due to partially filled trees.

Linked Representation of a Binary Tree

Because each node in a binary tree may have two child nodes, a node in a linked representation has two pointer fields, one for each child, and one or more data fields. When a node has no children, the corresponding pointer fields are **NIL**. Figure 7.10 is a linked representation of the binary expression tree of Figure 7.7. The LeftChild and RightChild fields are pointers to (that is, memory addresses of) the left child and the right child of a node.

For the moment, let us give a detailed description of the linked representation of the binary tree of Figure 7.7 using an array of records. This is similar to the way in which we first discussed linked lists in Chapter 4. By

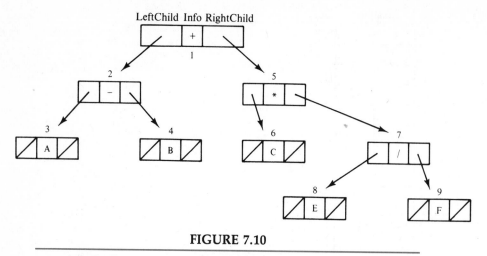

FIGURE 7.10

A linked representation of the binary expression tree of
Figure 7.7

doing this, we will actually be able to trace the values of the pointers. Once
the concept is thoroughly understood, we will then return to using Pascal
pointer variables for the actual implementation of binary trees. For example, we can implement the tree of Figure 7.10 as shown in Table 7.2, using
the strategy of building the left subtree for each node before considering
the right subtree. The numbers on top of the cells in Figure 7.10 represent
the addresses given in the LeftChild and RightChild fields.

Node	Info	LeftChild	RightChild
1	+	2	5
2	−	3	4
3	A	NIL	NIL
4	B	NIL	NIL
5	*	6	7
6	C	NIL	NIL
7	/	8	9
8	E	NIL	NIL
9	F	NIL	NIL

TABLE 7.2

Implementation of Figure 7.10 using array of records

In the linked representation, insertions and deletions involve no data
movement except the rearrangement of pointers. Suppose we wish to
modify the tree in Figure 7.7 to that which appears in Figure 7.11. (This
change might be needed due to some recent modification in the expression
represented by Figure 7.7.) The insertion of the nodes containing − and P
into the tree structure can be achieved easily by simply adding the nodes −
and P in the next available spaces in the array and adjusting the corresponding pointers.

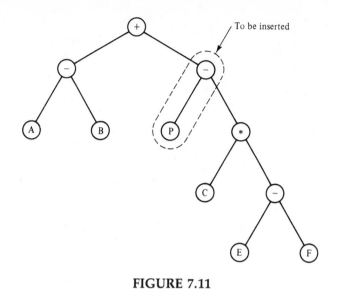

FIGURE 7.11

Desired modification of Figure 7.7

For the implementation of the tree shown in Figure 7.10, the effect of this insertion is given by Table 7.3. The adjusted pointers and data fields have been underscored. Notice that the change in row 1 of RightChild and the additional rows 10 and 11 are all that is necessary. No data were moved.

	Info	LeftChild	RightChild
1	+	2	10
2	−	3	4
3	A	NIL	NIL
4	B	NIL	NIL
5	*	6	7
6	C	NIL	NIL
7	/	8	9
8	E	NIL	NIL
9	F	NIL	NIL
10	−	11	5
11	P	NIL	NIL

TABLE 7.3

Modification of Table 7.2 by insertions into the tree of
Figure 7.7.

Similarly, if we wish to shorten the tree in Figure 7.7 by deleting the nodes * and C, then all we must do is rearrange the pointers to obtain the altered tree, as shown in Figure 7.12. The effect of this deletion is given in Table 7.4. As before, the adjusted pointers and data fields have been underscored.

A more formal statement of the algorithm underlying such insertions and deletions will be given later in this chapter, when we discuss list

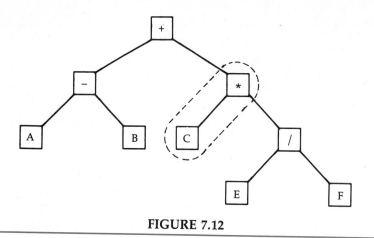

FIGURE 7.12

Another modification of Figure 7.7

	Info	LeftChild	RightChild	Modified tree
1	+	2	7	
2	−	3	4	
3	A	NIL	NIL	
4	B	NIL	NIL	
5	*			unused space after
6	C			deletion of '*' and
				'C'
7	/	8	9	
8	E	NIL	NIL	
9	F	NIL	NIL	

TABLE 7.4

Modification of tree of Figure 7.7

maintenance using a binary tree. Now that we have explained the linked representation of a binary tree by using arrays to contain pointer values which can be explicitly traced, we will use the following general record description with Pascal pointer variables to implement this structure in the remainder of the chapter.

```
TYPE
  Pointer = ^TreeNode;
  TreeNode = RECORD
               LeftChild : Pointer;
               Info : char; {or other appropriate type}
               RightChild : Pointer
             END;
```

Efficiency Considerations for the Linked Representation. The preceding examples indicate that, as far as processing efficiency is concerned, the linked representation seems to be more efficient, particularly where frequent insertions and deletions are required. Although for most purposes the linked representation of a binary tree is most efficient, it does have certain disadvantages, namely:

1. Wasted memory space in **NIL** pointers. For instance, the representation in Figure 7.10 has 10 **NIL** pointers.

2. Given a node, it is difficult to determine its parent.

The first disadvantage can be offset by threading the tree, a technique we'll discuss in Chapter 8. The second drawback can be easily overcome at the expense of more memory by adding a parent pointer field to each node.

Binary Tree Traversals

As noted in our definition of a tree as an abstract data structure, a tree traversal requires an algorithm which visits (and processes) each node of a tree exactly once. Just as the only way into a linked list is through the head node, so the only way into a tree is through the root. However, any attempt to draw an analogy between traversing a singly linked list and a binary tree is limited to the preceding statement. Although both structures have only one entry point, from any given node in a linked list there is no choice about where to proceed. After entering a binary tree, we are faced with a threefold dilemma at each node:

1. Do we process the data contained in the node at which we are currently located?

2. Do we remember the location of the current node (so that we can return to process it) and visit (and process) all nodes in its left subtree?

3. Do we remember the location of the current node (so that we can return to process it) and visit (and process) all nodes in its right subtree?

Here the generic term *process* has been used to apply to whatever operation is to be performed on the data at a given node; for example, print it or update it. What is actually done to the data is not as relevant to our discussion as the order in which the nodes are processed. Each of the three preceding choices represents a valid choice. The route chosen out of the three-way dilemma dictates the order in which the nodes are visited and processed. Though various arrangements of these three choices allow for many different traversals, three particular traversal techniques have come to be regarded as standard. They are the preorder traversal, inorder traversal, and postorder traversal.

Preorder Traversal of a Binary Tree

In a preorder traversal, the three options are combined in the following order:

1. First, process the root node.

2. Then, recursively visit all nodes in the left subtree.

3. Finally, recursively visit all nodes in the right subtree.

These three ordered steps are recursive. Once the root of the tree is processed, we go to the root of the left subtree, and then to the root of the left subtree of the left subtree, and so on until we can go no farther. Following these three steps, the preorder traversal of the tree of Figure 7.7 would process nodes in the order

$$+ - AB * C/EF$$

which is the prefix form of the expression

$$(A - B) + C * (E/F)$$

Hence we conclude that if to process a node means to print it, then a preorder traversal of a binary expression tree will output the prefix form of the expression.

The preorder traversal of an existing binary tree implemented via the linked representation and with a root node at location Root can be accomplished recursively using the following procedure:

```
{Global declarations}

TYPE
  Pointer = ^TreeNode;
  TreeNode =
    RECORD
      LeftChild : Pointer;
      Info : char;
      RightChild : Pointer
    END;

PROCEDURE PreorderTrav(Root : Pointer);

{ LeftChild and RightChild are pointers to the left and right children
  respectively. Info is a one-character data field.}

  BEGIN
    IF Root <> NIL THEN
    BEGIN
    Process(Root^.Info);

        { Process represents an arbitrary procedure designed to
          process a given node.}

    PreorderTrav(Root^.LeftChild);
    PreorderTrav(Root^.RightChild)
    END
  END;
{ End PreorderTrav }
```

1st, process Root node

2nd, traverse left subtree

3rd, traverse right subtree

Inorder Traversal of a Binary Tree

The inorder traversal of a binary tree proceeds as outlined in the following three ordered steps:

1. First, recursively visit all nodes in the left subtree.

2. Then, process the root node.

3. Finally, recursively visit all nodes in the right subtree.

By carefully following these steps for the tree of Figure 7.7 and assuming "process" means "print," we obtain the readily recognizable infix expression

$$A - B + C * E/F$$

Unless we add parentheses, this infix expression is not algebraically equivalent to the order of operations reflected in the tree of Figure 7.7. The fact that prefix and postfix notations do not require parentheses to avoid such ambiguities makes them distinctly superior to infix notation for evaluation purposes.

A more formal statement of the recursive algorithm for an inorder traversal is given in the following procedure for a linked representation of a binary tree:

```
{Global declarations}

TYPE
  Pointer = ^TreeNode;
  TreeNode =
    RECORD
      LeftChild : Pointer;
      Info : char;
      RightChild : Pointer
    END;

PROCEDURE InorderTrav(Root : Pointer);

{ LeftChild and RightChild are pointers to the left and right children
  respectively. Info is a one-character data field.}

    BEGIN
      IF Root <> NIL THEN
      BEGIN
      InorderTrav(Root^.LeftChild);
      Process(Root^.Info);
      InorderTrav(Root^.RightChild)
      END
    END;
{ End InorderTrav }
```

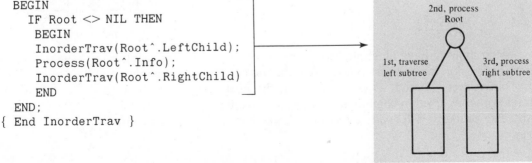

Postorder Traversal of a Binary Tree

The third standard traversal of a binary tree, the postorder traversal, entails an arrangement of options which postpones processing the root node until last.

1. First, recursively visit all nodes in the left subtree of the root node.

2. Then, recursively visit all nodes in the right subtree of the root node.

3. Finally, process the root node.

The postorder traversal can be implemented recursively by the following procedure PostorderTrav:

```
{Global declarations}
TYPE
  Pointer = ^TreeNode;
  TreeNode =
    RECORD
      LeftChild : Pointer;
      Info : char;
      RightChild : Pointer
    END;

PROCEDURE PostorderTrav(Root : Pointer);

{ LeftChild and RightChild are pointers to the left and right children
  respectively. Info is a one-character data field.}

  BEGIN
    IF Root <> NIL THEN
    BEGIN
    PostorderTrav(Root^.LeftChild);
    PostorderTrav(Root^.RightChild);
    Process (Root^.Info)
    END
  END;
{ End PostorderTrav }
```

Although we have illustrated the three traversal algorithms using binary expression trees, we emphasize that the traversals apply in general to *any* binary tree. Indeed, as we shall see in the next section, the inorder traversal when used in combination with a tree exhibiting the hierarchical ordering property will neatly allow us to implement a general list using a binary tree.

_____ 7.5

Binary Tree Implementation of a General Sorted List

The two implementations which we have considered for the general list of records needed by the registrar's system (see Chapter 1) have both been found lacking in certain respects. The array implementation of Chapter 3 allowed for the fast inspection of records via the binary search algorithm but necessitated excessive data movement when records were added to or deleted from the list. The linked list implementation suggested in Chapter 4 handled adds and deletes nicely but presented us with undesirable $O(n)$ search efficiency because the lack of direct access into a linked list forced a sequential search strategy. In this section we shall see that by implementing a general list using a binary tree, we can achieve efficiency in both searching and adding/deleting while at the same time maintaining the list in order. Moreover, we do not have to pay too great a price in other trade-offs to achieve this best of both worlds.

A binary tree implementation of a list is organized via the hierarchical ordering property discussed in Section 7.2. Recall that this ordering property stipulates as follows:

> For any given data item X in the tree, every node in the left subtree of X contains only items that are less than or equal to X with respect to a particular type of ordering. Every node in the right subtree of X contains only items that are greater than or equal to X with respect to the same ordering.

For instance, the tree of Figure 7.13 illustrates this property with respect to alphabetical ordering of binary trees.

You can quickly verify that an inorder traversal of this tree (in which the processing of each node consists merely of printing its contents) leads to the following alphabetized list:

ARPS
DIETZ
EGOFSKE
FAIRCHILD
GARTH
HUSTON
KEITH
MAGILLICUDDY
NATHAN
PERKINS
SELIGER
TALBOT
UNDERWOOD
VERKINS
ZARDA

This allows us to reach the following important conclusion. That is, an inorder traversal of a binary tree which has the ordering property will visit

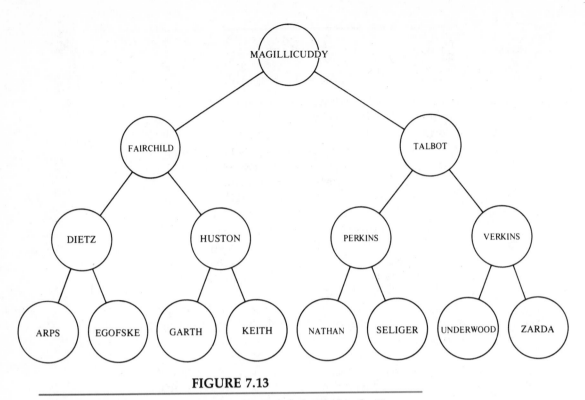

FIGURE 7.13

Ordering property with respect to alphabetical ordering

nodes in ascending order. Hence such a tree may be viewed as an ordered general list. The first list element is the first item visited by the inorder traversal. More generally, the nth element visited by the inorder traversal corresponds precisely to the nth element in the list. Given this view of a binary tree as an implementation of a general list, let us now consider the operations of adding, deleting, and finding (inspecting) nodes in the list.

Adding Nodes to the Binary Tree Implementation of a List

Insertion of a new string into such an ordered tree is a fairly easy process that may well require significantly fewer comparisons than insertion into a linked list. Consider, for example, the steps necessary to insert the string 'SEFTON' into the tree of Figure 7.13 in such a fashion as to maintain the ordering property. We must

1. Compare SEFTON to MAGILLICUDDY. Because SEFTON is greater than MAGILLICUDDY, follow the right child pointer to TALBOT.

2. Compare SEFTON to TALBOT. Because SEFTON is less than TALBOT, follow the left child pointer to PERKINS.

3. SEFTON is greater than PERKINS. Hence follow the right child pointer to SELIGER.

4. SELIGER is a leaf node, so SEFTON may be added as one of its children. The left child is chosen because SEFTON is less than SELIGER.

The resulting tree for the sample insertion is given in Figure 7.14.

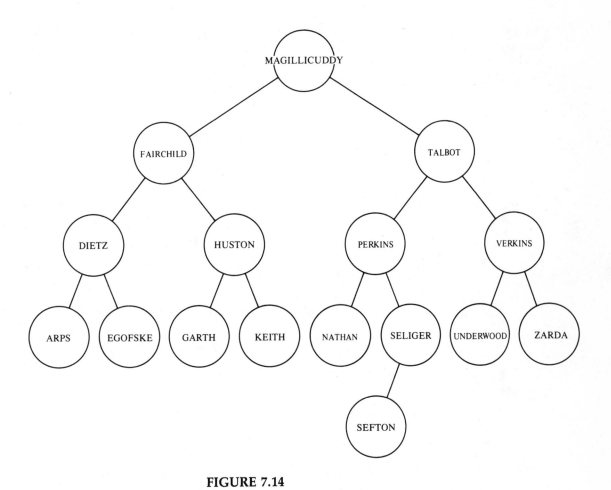

FIGURE 7.14

The tree in Figure 7.13 with the insertion SEFTON

The preceding algorithm implies that insertion of new nodes will always occur at the leaf nodes of a tree. As with insertion into a linked list, no data are moved; only pointers are manipulated. However, unlike the steps required by a linked list representation, we do not have to traverse the list sequentially to determine where the new node belongs. Instead, using the insertion rule—if less than, go left; otherwise, go right—we need merely traverse one branch of the tree to determine the position for a new node. Provided that the tree maintains a full shape, the number of nodes on a given branch will be at most

$$\log_2 n + 1$$

Computer Security and Tree-Structured File Systems

One of the prime concerns in developing operating systems for multiuser computers is to insure that a user cannot, in an unauthorized fashion, access system files or the files of other users. A convenient data structure to implement such a file directory system is a tree such as that pictured here.

Each interior node of the tree can be

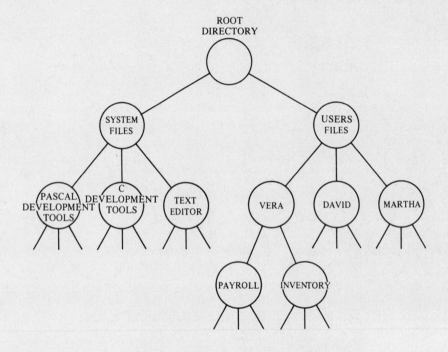

where n is the total number of nodes in the tree. By *full* we mean that all nodes with fewer than two children must occur at level m or $m - 1$ where m is the deepest level in the tree. In other words, all nodes above level $m - 1$ must have exactly two children. Hence, adding ROBERTS to the tree of Figure 7.14 by the insertion rule would destroy its fullness.

Given this definition of full, the $(\log_2 n + 1)$ figure for the maximum number of nodes on a branch emerges immediately upon inspection or, more formally, using a proof by mathematical induction. Our purpose here, however, is not to give the details of such a proof but rather to emphasize that a binary tree presents an alternative to a linked list structure for the type of processing involved in maintaining ordered lists. Moreover, it is a particularly attractive alternative when the tree is full, because substantially fewer comparisons are needed to locate where in the structure an insertion is to be made. For instance, if n is 1,024, the linked list may require as many as 1,024 comparisons to make an insertion. Because

viewed as a directory containing various system information about those files or subdirectories that are its descendants. Leaf nodes in the tree are the actual files. Hence, in the diagram, files can be broken down into system files and user files. System files consist of the Pascal development tools, the C development tools, and the text editor. User directories are called VERA, DAVID, and MARTHA. One of the very convenient features of such a system is that it allows the user to extend this tree structure as deeply as desired. For instance, in the given tree directory structure, we see that user VERA has created subdirectories for files related to PAYROLL and INVENTORY. DAVID and MARTHA could have similarly partitioned subdirectories to organize their work.

In addition to offering users the convenience of being able to appropriately group their files into subdirectories, such a file system offers a very natural solution to the problem of file security. Since each individual user is, in effect, the root of a miniature subordinate file system within the overall system, a user is given, by default, free access to every node in his or her subtree. That is, the user is viewed as the owner of every node in the subtree. To jump outside of this subtree of naturally owned files and directories requires that special permissions be given the user by other users or by the operating system itself. Hence the tree structure offers convenience as well as a means of carefully monitoring the integrity of the file system.

AT&T's UNIX operating system, developed at Bell Laboratories in the early 1970s, was one of the first to use such a tree-structured directory system. The widespread popularity of UNIX today and the adoption of this scheme by a significant number of other operating systems is evidence of the attractive way in which it combines user convenience with system security. However, this is not to say that such systems are completely free of security problems. Once the security of such a system is slightly compromised, the tree structure lends itself to a cascade of far-reaching security breaks. Brian Reid's article "Reflections on Some Recent Widespread Computer Break-ins" in the February 1987 issue of *Communications of the ACM* provides an interesting account of how such security problems recently surfaced at Stanford University and spread to an entire network of computers.

$\log_2 1024$ is 10, the full binary tree method will require at most 11 comparisons. This difference becomes even more dramatic as n gets larger. For an ordered list with 1,000,000 entries, a linked list may require that many comparisons, but the full binary tree requires a mere 21 comparisons.

What happens when the tree is not full? We will comment on that situation at the end of this section, when we discuss the overall efficiency considerations for this implementation of a list. Before that, however, consider the operations of finding and deleting data in a binary tree with the ordering property.

Searching for Data in a Binary Tree Implementation of a List

The insertion rule introduced earlier also dictates the search path followed through an ordered binary tree when we are attempting to find a given data item. Interestingly, if we trace the nodes visited on such a search path for a full binary tree, we will probe exactly the same items that we would in conducting a binary search on a physically ordered array containing the same data. For instance, if we are searching for SMITH in the tree of Figure 7.13, we will have to probe MAGILLICUDDY, TALBOT, and PERKINS. These are precisely the items that would be probed if the binary search algorithm were applied to the physically ordered list that follows Figure 7.13. Because of this, a binary tree representation of a list is often called a binary search tree. Our analysis of such a tree has allowed us to conclude that, as long as the binary tree remains full, search efficiency for this method of implementing a list matches that of the array implementation. That is, the search efficiency is $O(\log_2 n)$.

Deleting Data in a Binary Tree Implementation of a List

The deletion algorithm for an ordered binary tree is conceptually more complex than that for a linked list. Suppose, for instance, that we wish to remove TALBOT from the list represented by the tree of Figure 7.13. Two questions arise.

1. Can such a deletion be achieved merely by manipulating pointers?

2. If so, what does the resulting tree look like?

To answer these questions, begin by recalling that all that is necessary to represent an ordered list with a binary tree is that, for each node in the tree

1. The left subtree must contain only items less than or equal to it.

2. The right subtree must contain only items greater than or equal to it.

With the preservation of this ordering property as the primary goal in processing a deletion, one acceptable way of restructuring the tree of Figure 7.13 after deleting TALBOT appears in Figure 7.15; essentially, SELIGER moves up to replace TALBOT in the tree. The choice of SELIGER to replace TALBOT is made because SELIGER represents the greatest data item in the left subtree of the node containing TALBOT. As long as we choose this greatest item in the left subtree to replace the item being deleted, we guarantee preservation of the crucial ordering property that enables the tree to represent the list accurately.

Given this general motivation for choosing a node to replace the one being deleted, let us now outline a case-by-case analysis of the deletion algorithm. Throughout this analysis, we assume that we have a pointer p to the item that we wish to delete. The pointer p may be one of the following:

1. The root pointer for the entire tree.

2. The left child pointer of the parent of the node to be deleted.

3. The right child pointer of the parent of the node to be deleted.

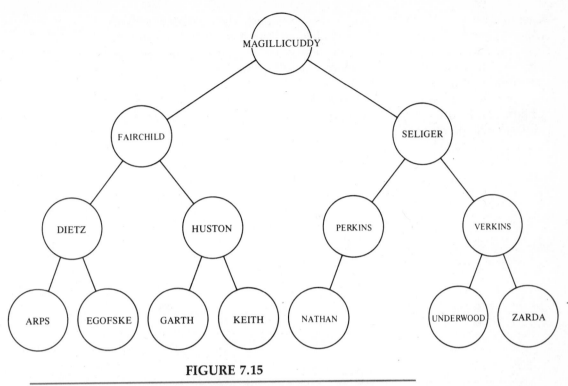

FIGURE 7.15

Restructuring the tree in figure 7.13 after deleting
TALBOT

Figure 7.16 highlights these three possibilities; the algorithm applies
whether 1, 2, or 3 holds.

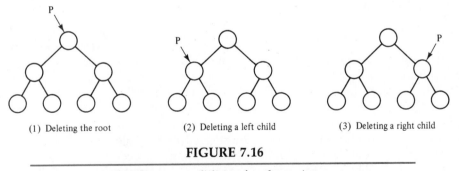

(1) Deleting the root   (2) Deleting a left child   (3) Deleting a right child

FIGURE 7.16

The three possibilities for the pointer p

We will examine three cases of node deletion on a binary tree.

1. The node to be deleted has a left child.

2. The node to be deleted has a right child but no left child.

3. The node to be deleted has no children.

Case 1. The node pointed to by *p*, that is, the node to be deleted, has a left child. In Figure 7.17, node M is to be deleted, and has left child K. In this case, because we have a non-null left subtree of the node to be deleted, our previous discussion indicates that we must find the greatest node in that left subtree. If the node pointed to by p^.LeftChild (node K in the figure) has no right child, then the greatest node in the left subtree of *p* is p^.Left-Child itself. Figure 7.17 pictorially describes this situation; the dotted lines indicate new pointer values.

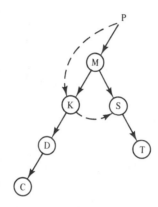

FIGURE 7.17

Case 1 with p^.LeftChild (node K) having no
right children

The partial coding to achieve this pointer manipulation is given by:

```
x := p;
p := x^.LeftChild;
p^.RightChild := x^.RightChild;
dispose(x);
```

where LeftChild and RightChild refer to the left and right child pointers described earlier in this chapter.

If the node pointed to by p^.LeftChild does have a right child, then to find the greatest node in the left subtree of *p* we must follow the right branch leading from p^.LeftChild as deeply as possible into the tree. In Figure 7.18, node R is the one chosen to replace the deleted node. This figure gives the schematic representation, with the pointer changes necessary to complete the deletion. The coding necessary for this slightly more complicated version of Case 1 is

```
x := p;
q := x^.LeftChild^.RightChild
Qparent := x^.LeftChild

{ q will eventually point to node which will replace p.
  Qparent will point to q's parent. }
```

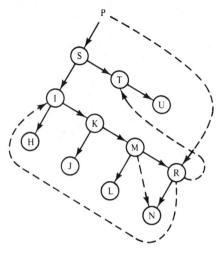

FIGURE 7.18

Case 1 with p^.LeftChild having a right child

```
{ The following loop forces q as deep as possible
  along the right branch from p^.LeftChild. }

WHILE q^.RightChild <> NIL DO
BEGIN
     q := q^.RightChild;
     Qparent := Qparent^.RightChild
END;

{ Having found node q to replace p, adjust
  pointers to appropriately link it into the
  tree. }

q^.RightChild := x^.RightChild;
p := q;
Qparent^.RightChild := q^.LeftChild;
q^.LeftChild := x^.LeftChild;
dispose(x);
```

Case 2. The node pointed to by p, that is, the node to be deleted, has a right child but no left child. This case is substantially easier than Case 1 and is described in Figure 7.19. The node to be deleted is merely replaced by its right child. The necessary Pascal coding is

```
x := p;
p := x^.RightChild;
dispose(x);
```

Case 3. The node pointed to by p, that is the node to be deleted, has no children. This is the easiest of all the cases. It can be compactly handled by

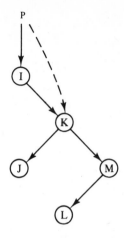

FIGURE 7.19

In Case 2 the node pointed to by p has a right but no
left child

the same coding used for Case 2 or, more directly, by

```
x := p;
p := NIL;
dispose(x);
```

Efficiency Considerations for Binary Tree Implementation of a List

It is important to note that, in all three cases, the deletion of a node from
the tree involved only pointer manipulation and no actual data movement.
Hence, in a list maintained with a binary tree, we are able to process both
insertions and deletions by the same pure pointer manipulation that makes
linked lists so desirable. Moreover, the binary tree approach apparently
allows us to locate data for inspection, insertion, or deletion much faster
than a linked list representation would. However, there are aspects of the
binary tree method that tarnish its performance in comparison to a linked
list. In particular:

☐ The binary tree implementation requires more memory in two respects. First, each node has two pointers instead of the one required
in a singly linked list. This proliferation of pointers is particularly
wasteful because many of the pointers may be **NIL**. Second, we
presently can traverse the tree in order only by using recursive techniques. Even in a language that allows recursion, a substantial
amount of overhead is needed to maintain the stack used by recursive calls.

☐ The $O(\log_2 n)$ efficiency of the binary tree method is only an optimal,
not a guaranteed, efficiency. It is contingent upon the tree's remain-

ing nearly full. The tree's remaining full is in turn contingent upon the order in which data are added and deleted. In the worst possible case, data entering the tree structure in the wrong order can cause the tree to degenerate into a glorified linked list with a corresponding $O(n)$ efficiency. (The Exercises at the end of the chapter will have you explore this relationship between the order in which data arrives for insertion and the resulting search efficiency of the ordered binary tree.)

Both of these drawbacks can be overcome. We shall see in the next chapter that we can actually avoid the overhead associated with recursion if we use a technique known as *threading* which puts to good use the pointers that are otherwise wasted as **NIL**. Moreover, by using a technique known as height balancing, the binary tree may be maintained in a fashion which approaches fullness at all times, regardless of the order in which data arrive for entry. This nearly full form is enough to completely guarantee the $O(\log_2 n)$ search efficiency. Originally devised by G. M. Adelson-Velskii and Y. M. Landis, the height-balancing algorithm is sufficiently complex to be beyond the scope of this book. An in-depth treatment of it is given in *Fundamentals of Data Structures* by Ellis Horowitz and Sartaj Sahni (Rockville, Md.; Computer Science Press, 1977) and in our earlier pseudocode-based *Introduction to Data Structures* (St. Paul, Minn.: West Publishing, 1985).

Overall, the binary tree implementation of a list would seem to be the best of the three implementations we have studied for situations in which additions, deletions, and searches must all be processed efficiently. Even when steps are not taken to correct the two disadvantages we have cited, it offers the addition/deletion advantages of a linked list with a search efficiency that is bounded between $O(\log_2 n)$ and $O(n)$.

_____ **7.6**

General Trees

We began this chapter with a discussion of the many ways in which hierarchical structures are used to organize information around us. We then quickly imposed a birth control dictate of at most two children which focused all of our attention on the seemingly restricted case of the binary tree. What about all of those applications which require a hierarchical relationship where a parent may have an unrestricted number of children? You may have become suspicious that we are avoiding such considerations because they are too difficult. Fortunately, we have a much more educationally sound reason. That is, we may use a binary tree to implement a general tree. The nice implication of this rather surprising statement is that we will not have to spend a significant amount of time discussing general trees because we have unknowingly studied them in our thorough analysis of binary trees.

The real key to using a restricted type of tree such as a binary tree to implement a more general type of tree is to adjust our perspective. For example, consider the general genealogical tree of Figure 7.20.

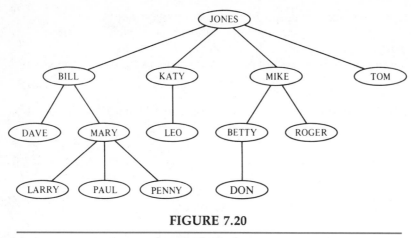

FIGURE 7.20

A genealogical tree

Here BILL is the first child of the JONES family, with KATY, MIKE, and TOM as BILL's siblings. Similarly, LARRY is the first child of MARY, with PAUL and PENNY as siblings. Now, in a linked representation of a binary tree, we have two pointer fields associated with each node. We have called these pointer fields LeftChild and RightChild because it suited our perspective at the time. However, we shall now switch that perspective in the following way. One of the pointer fields is to be viewed as pointer to the leftmost child of a node in a general tree. The second pointer identifies the next sibling to the right of the node under consideration in the general tree. Since the children of a node taken in this context form an ordered set of nodes, we can regard the leftmost child of a node as FirstChild and the sibling to the right of this node as Sibling. We will henceforth adopt this terminology for the two link fields involved with the binary tree representation of a general tree. Figure 7.21 gives the binary representation of the general genealogical tree shown in Figure 7.20.

   Although we will typically use Pascal pointer variables for such a binary tree implementation of a general tree, it is worth noting that an array of records with integer pointer fields can still be used just as it was for a linked list in Chapter 4. Indeed, because this array perspective allows us to specify some actual values for pointers, we have portrayed the tree of Figure 7.20 as an array of records in Table 7.5. You should carefully check all FirstChild and Sibling values to convince yourself that the scheme used to fill this array was to store a node before any of its children, and then recursively store the leftmost child. The analogous representation in terms of Pascal pointer variables (and the representation we shall henceforth use) requires the following type declarations:

```
GenTreePtr : ^GenTreeNode;
GenTreeNode :   RECORD
                    Data : {Appropriate Type};
                    FirstChild : GenTreePtr;
                    Sibling : GenTreePtr
                END;
```

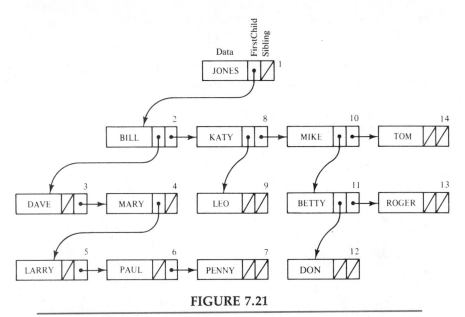

FIGURE 7.21

A binary tree representation of the genealogical tree in
Figure 7.20

Location	Data	FirstChild	Sibling
1	JONES	2	0
2	BILL	3	8
3	DAVE	0	4
4	MARY	5	0
5	LARRY	0	6
6	PAUL	0	7
7	PENNY	0	0
8	KATY	9	10
9	LEO	0	0
10	MIKE	11	14
11	BETTY	12	13
12	DON	0	0
13	ROGER	0	0
14	TOM	0	0

TABLE 7.5

The tree in Figure 7.20 stored in array of records for data
and pointers

Traversals of a General Tree Implemented via a Binary Tree

Since this implementation scheme for a general tree is nothing more than a special interpretation of a binary tree, all of the traversals defined for a binary tree clearly exist for the general tree. A more relevant question than the mere existence of a traversal, however, is the significance of the order in which the nodes of a general tree are visited when its corresponding binary tree is traversed. Of particular interest in this regard are the preorder and postorder traversals.

It should be verified at this point that the preorder traversal algorithm for a binary tree applied to Figure 7.21 yields the following listing:

```
JONES
     BILL
          DAVE
          MARY
               LARRY
               PAUL
               PENNY
     KATY
          LEO
     MIKE
          BETTY
               DON
          ROGER
     TOM
```

The indentation here has been added to highlight the fact that the preorder traversal will recursively process a parent node, and then process the child nodes from left to right.

Relative to the general tree pictured in Figure 7.20, we see that the effect of the preorder traversal is to fix on a node at one level of the tree and then run through all of that node's children before progressing to the next node at the same level (the sibling). There is a hint here of a generalized nested loop situation which, as you will see, has some interesting applications in the Programming Problems and again in the next chapter.

The other traversal of interest in a binary tree representation of a general tree is the postorder traversal. In this regard, it should first be verified that the postorder traversal applied to Figure 7.21 yields the following listing:

PENNY
PAUL
LARRY
MARY
DAVE
LEO
DON
ROGER
BETTY
TOM
MIKE
KATY
BILL
JONES

In general, the postorder traversal works its way up from the leaf nodes of a tree, insuring that no given node is processed until all nodes in the subtree below it have been processed.

Graphs and Networks: Bidirectional Trees

The key defining characteristic of a tree is the hierarchical relationship between parent and child nodes. In a tree, this hierarchical relationship is a one-way relationship. That is, within the tree there is pointer information that allows us to descend from parent to child. However, there is generally no pointer information within the tree which allows us to ascend from a child node to its parent. In many information storage applications such a one-way relationship is not sufficient.

Consider, for instance, the relationship between students and courses at a university. Each student is enrolled in several courses and could thus be viewed as a parent node with children consisting of the courses he or she is taking. Conversely, each course enrolls many students and could thus be viewed as a parent node with children consisting of the students enrolled in that particular course. The data structure which emerges from this type of bidirectional relationship is pictured in Figure 7.22.

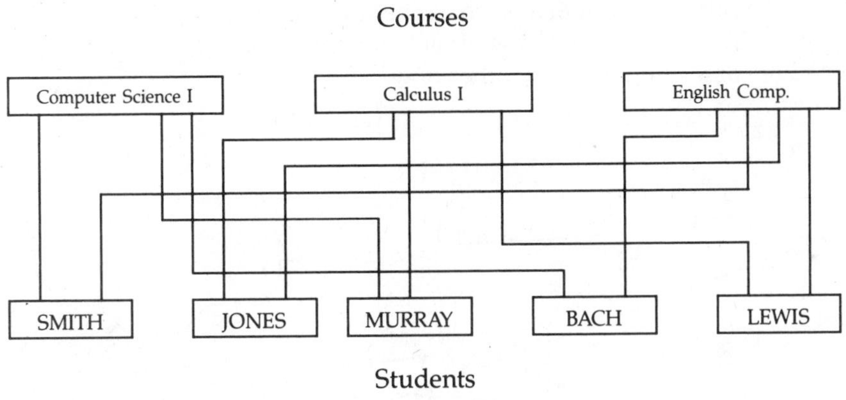

Courses

Students

FIGURE 7.22

Bidirectional relationship between students and courses

In terms of an abstract data type, the representation of such a bidirectional relationship between nodes is called a graph.

> **Graph**   A graph is a set of objects called nodes and edges. A node is a data element of the graph, and an edge is a path between two nodes.

The operations we wish to perform on a graph are shown in Table 7.6. Notice that, as it relates to Figure 7.22, the formal definition of a graph does not rule out the possibility of an edge connecting two courses or connect-

Operation	Explanation
Create(Graph)	Procedure to initialize Graph.
AddEdge(Graph, i, j))	Add to Graph an edge connecting nodes i and j.
RemoveEdge(Graph, i, j)	Remove from Graph the edge connecting i and j.
Connected(Graph, i, j)	A Boolean function which returns **true** if Graph contains a path connecting nodes i and j and **false** otherwise.
Traverse(Graph)	Visit (and process) every node in Graph in an order determined by the edge connections between nodes.

TABLE 7.6

Operations on graphs

ing two students. It is merely the nature of this course-student relationship which makes the existence of such a course-to-course edge or student-to-student edge impractical. In other applications, such as the transportation network pictured in Figure 7.23, it may be entirely feasible for any node in the graph to have an edge connecting it to any other node.

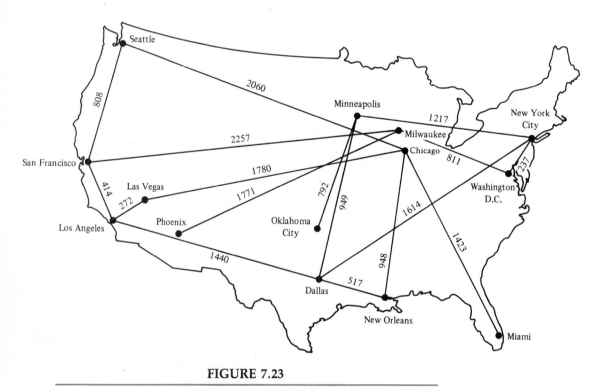

FIGURE 7.23

Transportation network as graph in which edges have weights (distances)

The graph of Figure 7.23 is somewhat special in that the edges have weights associated with them, here representing distances between nodes (cities). Such a graph is an example of the network abstract data type.

Network   A network is a set of objects called nodes and edges. A node is a data element of the graph, and an edge is a path between two nodes. Unlike a pure graph, edges in a network have weight values associated with them.

The operations we wish to perform on a network are shown in Table 7.7.

Operation	Explanation
Create(Network)	Procedure to initialize Network.
AddEdge(Network, i, j, Wt)	Add to Network an edge of weight Wt connecting nodes i and j.
RemoveEdge(Network, i, j)	Remove from Network the edge connecting nodes i and j.
Weight(Network, i, j)	A function which returns the weight of the edge connecting nodes i and j in Network or an appropriate flagging value if no such edge exists.
Traverse(Network)	Visit every node in Network in an order determined by the edge connections between nodes.

TABLE 7.7

Operations on networks

Graphs and networks provide excellent examples of how a theoretical area of mathematics has found very relevant application in computer science. It is beyond the scope of this text to provide a comprehensive treatment of graphs and networks. Rather, our purpose in the rest of this section is to provide you with an overview of a data structure which you will no doubt encounter again as you continue your study of computer science. More in-depth treatments of graphs and networks can be found in numerous advanced texts on data structures such as *Fundamentals of Data Structures* by Ellis Horowitz and Sartaj Sahni (Rockville, Md.: Computer Science Press, 1977) and *Data Structures and Algorithms* by Alfred V. Aho, John E. Hopcroft, and Jeffrey D. Ullman (Reading, Mass.: Addison-Wesley, 1983).

Implementation of Graphs and Networks

A graph may be conveniently implemented using a two-dimensional table of Boolean values. For instance, the information in the graph of Figure 7.22 is contained in the following two-dimensional table: (Table 7.8). In this table, the value **true** indicates the presence of an edge between two nodes and the value **false** indicates the absence of such an edge.

	SMITH	JONES	MURRAY	BACH	LEWIS
Computer Science I	true	false	true	true	false
Calculus I	false	true	true	false	true
English Comp.	true	true	false	true	true

TABLE 7.8

Two-dimensional table implementation of graph from
Figure 7.22

In the case of a network, the two-dimensional table implementation still applies. Now, however, the data stored in the table is of a type compatible with edge weights. Such a two-dimensional table implementation of the transportation network from Figure 7.23 is given in Table 7.9. Note that the data are mirrored across the diagonal of the table.

	NY	Wash	Miam	Milw	Chi	NOrl	Mpls	OklC	Dals	LVeg	Phex	Stl	SFran	LA
N York		237		1217					1614					
Wshngtn	237			811										
Miami					1423									
Milwauk		811									1771		2257	
Chicago			1423			948				1780		2060		
N Orlea					948				517					
Mpls	1217							792	949					
OklaCty						792								
Dallas	1614					517	949							1440
LsVegas					1780									272
Phoenix				1771										
Seattle					2060								808	
SanFran				2257								808		414
L A									1440	172			414	

TABLE 7.9

Two-dimensional table implementation of network from
Figure 7.23

Table 7.9 illustrates a quality typically found in two-dimensional table implementations of large graphs and networks: the sparseness of nontrivial data. Hence, the methods we have discussed for implementing sparse tables in Chapters 3 and 4 (and which we will discuss in the Programming Problems for Chapter 10) actually provide alternative implementation strategies for graphs and networks. In fact, the pilot/flight data-base problem of Wing-and-a-Prayer Airlines which was introduced in Chapter 1 may now actually be viewed as a graph problem. This problem presented us with a bidirectional tree in which each pilot could have multiple flights as child nodes and, conversely, each flight could have multiple pilots as child nodes. In the discussion of the two graph/network algorithms which follow, we shall not tie ourselves to a particular implementation strategy for representing the underlying data structure. Rather, we will discuss the algorithms in terms of the operations associated with the abstract data type involved and leave implementation considerations for the Exercises and Programming Problems at the end of the chapter.

Example of a Graph Algorithm: Depth-First Traversal

In many practical applications of graphs, there is frequently a need to systematically visit all the nodes on a graph. One such application occurs in a political campaign when the organizers of the campaign are interested in having their candidate visit all important political centers. The presence or absence of direct transportation routes (that is, edges) between such centers will determine the possible ways in which all the centers could be visited. At the moment, our only concern is the development of an algorithm which insures that all nodes are visited. Later in the chapter we shall investigate how to determine the shortest possible distances from one node to all others. The main logic of the depth-first search algorithm is analogous to the preorder traversal of a tree. It is accomplished recursively as follows:

1. Choose any node in the graph. Designate it as the search node and mark it as visited.

2. Find a node adjacent to the search node (that is, connected by an edge from the search node) which has not yet been visited. Designate this as the new search node (but remember the previous one) and mark it as visited.

3. Repeat step 2 using the new search node. If no nodes satisfying step 2 can be found, return to the previous search node and continue from there.

4. When a return to the previous search node in step 3 is impossible, the search from the originally chosen search node is complete.

5. If the graph still contains unvisited nodes, choose any node that has not been visited and repeat steps 1 through 4.

This algorithm is called a depth-first search because the search continues progressively deeper into the graph in a recursive manner.

To illustrate this procedure more clearly, we consider the graph Figure 7.24. The table implementation of this graph is shown in Table 7.10.

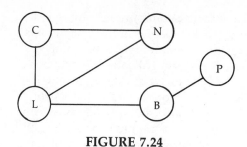

FIGURE 7.24

Graph to illustrate depth-first search

Suppose we have a procedure called SearchFrom which is invoked to begin a depth-first search from a given node on the graph. The steps followed by the algorithm are:

1. We begin by marking C visited and invoke SearchFrom(C).

2. Since both N and L are adjacent to C according to the matrix implementation of the graph, but L is encountered first on a left-to-right scan of the row for C, the search goes to L. We invoke SearchFrom(L) and L is marked as visited.

3. Since N is the first unvisited node adjacent to L, the search now goes to N, SearchFrom(N) is invoked, and N is marked as visited.

4. Since there is no unvisited node adjacent to N, we say that N has exhausted the search; the search goes back to its predecessor, that is, to L.

5. From L, we visit B.

6. From B, we proceed to P. All nodes have now been visited, and the depth-first traversal is complete.

Use Table 7.10 to verify the steps above.

	C	L	N	B	P
C	FALSE	TRUE	TRUE	FALSE	FALSE
L	TRUE	FALSE	TRUE	TRUE	FALSE
N	TRUE	TRUE	FALSE	FALSE	FALSE
B	FALSE	TRUE	FALSE	FALSE	TRUE
P	FALSE	FALSE	FALSE	TRUE	FALSE

TABLE 7.10

Table implementation of Figure 7.24

We note that the order in which nodes are visited in a depth-first traversal is not unique. This is because the order is dependent upon the manner in which "adjacent" nodes are chosen. That is, given two unvisited nodes adjacent to another node, which one should be chosen to invoke the SearchFrom procedure? In practice, this will usually be determined by the ordering of the data type used to represent the nodes in the graph. In the Pascal procedure DepthFirstSearch given next, this data type is assumed to be an appropriate user-defined enumerated type NodeType. Of course, NodeType could just as easily be **integer** or **char** data.

```
{ Global declarations }

TYPE
   NodeType = (FirstNode, {Appropriate other values}, LastNode);
   GraphType = {Appropriate implementation of abstract
                      data type graph};

PROCEDURE DepthFirstSearch (Graph : GraphType)

    { Depth-first search of graph starting at FirstNode }

   VAR i : NodeType;
       Visited : ARRAY [NodeType] OF boolean;

   PROCEDURE SearchFrom (k : NodeType);

       { Conduct depth-first search from node k until all
         possibilities have been exhausted. }

      VAR j : NodeType;

      BEGIN
        Visited[k] := true;
        Process(k); { Assume procedure to process node k }
        FOR j := FirstNode TO LastNode DO
            IF NOT Visited[j] and Connected(Graph, k, j) THEN
                SearchFrom(j) { Recursively progress deeper into graph }

      END; { SearchFrom }

   BEGIN { DepthFirstSearch }
       FOR i := FirstNode TO LastNode DO
           Visited[i] := false; { Initially no nodes visited }
       { Begin searching from unvisited nodes. }
       FOR i := FirstNode TO LastNode DO
          IF NOT Visited[i] THEN
             SearchFrom(i)

   END; { DepthFirstSearch }
```

An alternate graph traversal to the depth-first search is the breadth-first search. You will be asked to explore this strategy in the Programming Problems at the end of the chapter.

Example of a Network Algorithm: Finding Shortest Paths

If the graph under consideration is a network in which edge weights represent distances, then an appropriate question is: From a given node called the Source, what is the shortest distance to all other nodes in the network?

For instance, the network of Figure 7.25 could be thought of as showing airline routes between cities. An airline would be interested in finding the most economical route between any two given cities in the network. The numbers listed on the edges would, in this case, represent distances between cities. Thus, the airline wishes to find the shortest path that can be flown from node 3 in order to reach nodes 1, 2, 4, and 5.

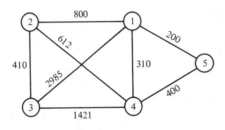

FIGURE 7.25

Network with edge weights representing distances

Suppose we want to find the shortest path from node 1 to node 3. From Figure 7.25, we note that this path would be 1→2→3, yielding a total weight of 800 + 410 = 1,210. An algorithm to find such a path was discovered by E. W. Dijkstra. For convenience in discussing Dijkstra's algorithm, often called the shortest-path algorithm, let us assume that the nodes in the network under consideration are numbered 1,2, . . . , NumberOfNodes.

Given such a collection of nodes, Dijkstra's algorithm requires three arrays in addition to a suitable implementation of the network M. These three arrays are identified as follows:

```
VAR Distance, Path : ARRAY[1..NumberOfNodes] OF integer;
         Included: ARRAY[1..NumberOfNodes] OF boolean;
```

Identifying one node as the Source, the algorithm proceeds to find the shortest distance from Source to all other nodes in the network. At the conclusion of the algorithm, the shortest distance from Source to node J is stored in Distance[J] while Path[J] contains the immediate predecessor of node J on the path determining this shortest distance. While the algorithm is in progress, Distance[J] and Path[J] are being continually updated until Included[J] is switched from **false** to **true**. Once this switch occurs, it is definitely known that Distance[J] contains the shortest distance from Source to J. The algorithm progresses until all nodes have been so included. Hence it actually gives us the shortest distance from Source to every other node in the network.

Given the Source node in the network M, the algorithm may be divided into two phases: an initialization phase followed by an iteration phase in which nodes are included one by one in the set of nodes for which the shortest distance from Source is definitely known.

During the initialization phase, we must

1. Initialize Included[Source] to **true** and Include[J] to **false** for all other J.

2. Initialize the Distance array via the rule

$$\text{Distance[J]} = \begin{cases} 0 \text{ if J} = \text{Source} \\ \text{Weight(M,Source,J) if Weight(M,Source,J)} <> 0 \\ \text{Infinity if J is not connected to Source by a} \\ \quad \text{direct edge (that is, if} \\ \quad \text{Weight(M,Source,J)} = 0) \end{cases}$$

3. Initialize the Path array via the rule:

$$\text{Path[J]} = \begin{cases} \text{Source if Weight (M,Source,J)} <> 0 \\ \text{Undefined otherwise} \end{cases}$$

Given this initialization, the iteration phase may be expressed in a generalized pseudocode form as follows:

```
REPEAT
      Find the node J which has the minimal Distance
             among those nodes not yet Included;
      Mark J as now Included;
      FOR each R not yet Included
            IF R is connected by an edge to J THEN
                  IF Distance[J] + Weight (M,R,J) < Distance[R] THEN
                        BEGIN
                           Distance[R] := Distance[J] + Weight (M,R,J)
                           Path[R] := J
                        END
UNTIL All nodes are Included
```

The crucial part of the algorithm occurs within the innermost **IF** of the **FOR** loop. Figure 7.26 provides a pictorial representation of the logic involved here. The circled nodes represent those nodes already included prior to a given iteration of the **REPEAT** loop. The node J in Figure 7.26 represents the node found in the first step of the **REPEAT** loop; R represents another arbitrary node which has not yet been Included. The lines emanating from Source represent the paths corresponding to the current entries in the Distance array. For nodes within the circle—that is, those already Included—these paths are guaranteed to be the shortest-distance paths. If J is the node having the minimal entry in Distance among those not yet Included, we will add J to the circle of Included nodes and then check to see if J's connections to other nodes in the network which are not yet Included may result in a newly found shorter path to such nodes.

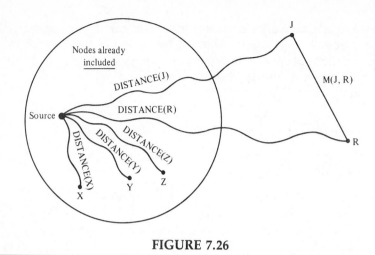

FIGURE 7.26

REPEAT loop logic in shortest-path (Dijkstra's) algorithm

Referring to Figure 7.26 again, the sum of two sides of a triangle

$$\text{Distance}[J] + \text{Weight}(M,J,R)$$

may in fact be shorter than the third side,

$$\text{Distance}[R]$$

This geometric contradiction is possible because these are not true straight-sided triangles, but "triangles" whose sides may be very complicated paths through a network.

It is also apparent why Dijkstra's algorithm works. As the node J in this figure is found to have the minimal Distance entry from among all those nodes not yet Included, we may now Include it among the nodes whose minimal distance from the source is absolutely known. Why? Because the very fashion in which we update the Distance and Path arrays guarantees that nodes which will be Included in the future could never alter Distance[J] and Path[J]. Distance[J] is already minimal among Distance[X] for X which have not yet been Included.

To be sure you understand Dijkstra's complicated algorithm before you attempt to implement it, trace it through on the network of Figure 7.25 with Source = 1. Initially, we would have

$$\begin{array}{ll} \text{Distance}[2] = 800 & \text{Path}[2] = 1 \\ \text{Distance}[3] = 2985 & \text{Path}[3] = 1 \\ \text{Distance}[4] = 310 & \text{Path}[4] = 1 \\ \text{Distance}[5] = 200 & \text{Path}[5] = 1 \end{array}$$

in accordance with steps 2 and 3 of the initialization phase. According to the iteration phase of the algorithm, we would then, in order

1. Include node 5; no change in Distance and Path needed.

$$\begin{array}{ll} \text{Distance}[2] = 800 & \text{Path}[2] = 1 \\ \text{Distance}[3] = 2985 & \text{Path}[3] = 1 \\ \text{Distance}[4] = 310 & \text{Path}[4] = 1 \\ \text{Distance}[5] = 200 & \text{Path}[5] = 1 \end{array}$$

2. Include node 4; update Distance and Path to

$$Distance[2] = 800 \qquad Path[2] = 1$$
$$Distance[3] = 1731 \qquad Path[3] = 4$$
$$Distance[4] = 310 \qquad Path[4] = 1$$
$$Distance[5] = 200 \qquad Path[5] = 1$$

(Note that it is shorter to go from node 1 to node 4 to node 3 than to follow the edge directly connecting node 1 to node 3.)

3. Include node 2; update Distance and Path to

$$Distance[2] = 800 \qquad Path[2] = 1$$
$$Distance[3] = 1210 \qquad Path[3] = 2$$
$$Distance[4] = 310 \qquad Path[4] = 1$$
$$Distance[5] = 200 \qquad Path[5] = 1$$

(Now we find that traveling from node 1 to node 2 to node 3 is even better than the path determined in step 2.)

4. Finally node 3 is Included with (obviously) no changes made in Distance or Path.

DESIGNER'S WORKBENCH

White Box and Black Box Testing

In this chapter, we have introduced the binary tree as yet another means of implementing a general list. We now have at least four techniques at our disposal for this task: array with binary search, random access file with binary search, linked list, and binary tree. Put yourself in the place of someone assigned the task of testing the performance and reliability of a package of modules designed to perform the basic ACIDS operations on a general list as defined in Chapter 1. You could approach this testing with or without knowledge beforehand about how the modules implemented the general list. In the former case you would be engaged in white box testing. That is, the package of modules represents a "white box" because you are aware of the internal logic and data structure implementations in the modules. In white box testing, test cases can be partitioned into equivalence classes which specifically exercise each logical path through a module. In black box testing, the package of modules is approached without knowledge of their internal structure. You know what the modules are supposed to do but not how they do it.

This difference in perspective can greatly influence the fashion in which you design test cases. For instance, in testing the search efficiency of a package of modules to perform the ACIDS operations on a general list, the order in which data items arrive for insertion is a much more critical consideration for a tree implementation than for a linked list or array implementation. (Why?) Hence, if the modules were a white box in the sense that you were aware of an underlying tree implementation strategy, you would design your performance test cases to explore the relationships between the order of insertions and the resulting search efficiencies.

In practice, testing at the modular level tends to be white box testing. This is because a well-designed module will be compact and focused. Hence it is relatively easy to explore the internal structure of a module and create test cases geared toward that internal structure. As modules merge together into a full-fledged software system, the testing of the entire system takes on more of a black box perspective. Ultimately, the system is tested not only by technical people but by the end users who must work with the system on a regular basis. This final phase of acceptance testing carried out by end users is totally black box in nature. Typically end users neither want nor need detailed knowledge of *how* a system is implemented. However, they have a very substantial interest in *what* the system does. Does it successfully meet the specifications that were described very early in the analysis phase of the project? Consequently, end users will test and ultimately accept or reject the system based upon how it meets these specifications.

Designer's Workbench Exercises

1. Explain why the order of insertions into a general list would be especially important in white box testing the efficiency of a search module for a list which you knew to be implemented via a binary tree.

Exercises 2–5 refer to the registrar's system initially described in Chapter 1.

2. Design test cases for this system from an end user's (that is, black box) perspective.
3. Design test cases for this system based on the knowledge that an array is used to implement the general list data base.
4. Design test cases for this system based on the knowledge that a linked list is used to implement the general list data base.
5. Design test cases for this system based on the knowledge that a binary tree is used to implement the general list data base.
6. Summarize the differences in the test cases you designed for Exercises 2, 3, 4, and 5. Explain how these differences are tied to the testing perspective assumed for each exercise.
7. You are white box testing a package of modules to perform basic stack operations. Explain how knowledge of whether an array or linked list implementation is used for the stack would affect your test cases.   ∎

Summary

In this chapter we have studied trees, a data structure used to reflect a hierarchical relationship among data items. Indicative of this hierarchy is the parent-child terminology used to express the relationship between items on successive levels of the tree. Trees are by nature recursive structures, with each node of a tree being itself the root of a smaller, embedded subtree. Binary trees are trees in which each parent may have at most two child nodes. Although this seems like a major restriction, binary trees find a wide range of applications. Two such applications studied in this chapter were the representation of algebraic expressions and general lists. Two ways of implementing a binary tree are the linear representation and the linked representation. The former method uses an array and requires no pointers but is prone to wasting a large number of array locations. The latter uses pointers and consequently is able to take advantage of Pascal's dynamic memory allocation.

There are three standard ways of traversing a binary tree; that is, visiting all nodes exactly once. These are the preorder, postorder, and inorder traversals. In a preorder traversal, the current root node is processed, followed recursively by the nodes in its left subtree and then its right subtree. In a postorder traversal, all nodes in the left subtree of the current root are recursively processed. Then all nodes in the right subtree are processed, and the root itself is processed last. In an inorder traversal, the nodes in the left subtree are processed first, followed by the root node, and finally the nodes in the right subtree of the root. The inorder traversal is critical in the binary tree implementation of a list since the order in which it visits nodes corresponds precisely to the ordering of items as 1st, 2nd, 3rd, . . . , within the list represented by the tree.

The binary tree implementation of a general list is the third general list implementation we have studied. The other two were the array implementation (Chapter 3) and the linked list implementation (Chapter 4). The following table summarizes the relative advantages and disadvantages of the three methods.

Method	Search	Additions/ Deletions	Other Comments
Array	$O(\log_2 n)$ with binary search	Excessive data movement	Data must be physically ordered
Linked List	Requires sequential search, hence $O(n)$	Only pointer manipulation required	
Binary tree	Bounded between $O(\log_2 n)$ and $O(n)$ though advanced methods can guarantee the former	Only pointer manipulation required	May necessitate the overhead associated with recursive traversals

From this table it is apparent that the binary tree implementation of a general list will offer the best overall run-time performance relative to the ACIDS criteria for general list manipulation.

We also showed that the binary tree may actually be used to implement the general tree structure. The preorder and postorder traversals emerge as the most important for this particular application.

Finally, we introduced graphs and networks as abstract data structures which are more complex than trees because they reflect bidirectional rather than hierarchical relationships. Depth-first traversal and finding the shortest path are examples of algorithms which manipulate graphs and networks.

Key Terms

acceptance testing	inorder traversal
ancestor	insertion rule
binary search tree	leaf node
binary tree	level
binary tree implementation of general tree	linear representation
	linked representation
binary tree implementation of list	network
black box testing	ordering property
branch	parent node
breadth-first search	postorder traversal
child node	preorder traversal
depth-first traversal	root
general tree	siblings
graph	subtree
heap	tree
height balancing	tree traversal
hierarchy	white box testing

Exercises

1. Draw a binary tree for the expression:

$$A * B - (C + D) * (P/Q)$$

2. Using a preorder traversal of the tree from Exercise 1, obtain the prefix form of the expression.
3. Represent the StudentRec described here as a binary tree.

```
Name = RECORD
        FirstName : ARRAY [1..10] OF char;
        LastName : ARRAY [1..10] OF char
        END;

Year = RECORD
        FirstSem : ARRAY [1..2] OF char;
        SecondSem : ARRAY [1..2] OF char
        END;
```

```
StudentRec = RECORD
        StudentName : Name;
        YearOfStudy : Year
      END;
```

4. What is the output produced by the following procedure for the pictured tree?

```
PROCEDURE TreeWalk(Root : TreePointer);

BEGIN
IF Root = NIL THEN
   writeln('OOPS')
ELSE
  BEGIN
  TreeWalk(Root^.RightChild);
  TreeWalk(Root^.LeftChild);
  writeln (Root^.Data)
  END
END;
```

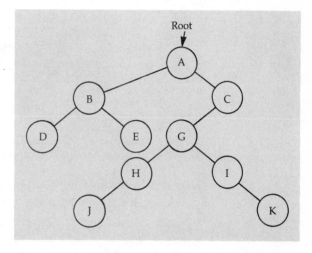

5. How does the output from Exercise 4 change if the statement
   writeln(Root^.Data) is moved ahead of the recursive calls to TreeWalk?
6. How does the output from Exercise 4 change if the statement
   writeln(Root^.Data) is located between the recursive calls to TreeWalk?
7. Repeat the three previous exercises for the following tree:

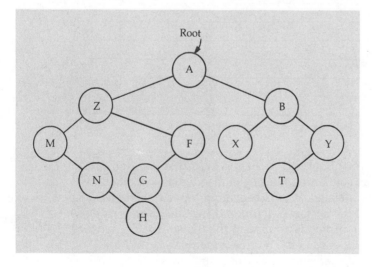

8. Given the following traversals of a binary tree,

   Postorder: ABCDEFIKJGH
   Inorder: CBAEDFHIGKJ

draw the tree. Attempt to deduce your answer in a systematic (and recursive) fashion, not by trial-and-error methods.

9. You are writing a program which uses a binary tree. To make it easy to trace the structure, you use an array of records instead of pointer variables. Consider the following binary tree:

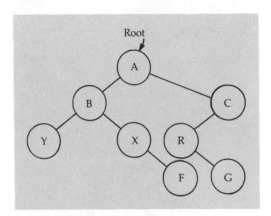

a. Indicate the contents of Root and Avail pointers and LeftChild and RightChild fields in the following array Tree:

Tree

Location	Data	LeftChild	RightChild	
1	C			Root
2	R			
3	G			
4	F			
5	X			Avail
6	Y			
7	B			
8	A			
9				

b. Show the contents of Root and Avail and LeftChild and RightChild fields after a node containing J has been inserted as the left child of X and R has been deleted with G becoming the left child of C.

10. Trace the contents of the Distance, Path, and Included arrays as Dijkstra's shortest-path algorithm is applied to the transportation network of Figure 7.23. Use Phoenix as the Source node.

11. Repeat Exercise 10 with Milwaukee as the Source node.

12. Indicate the order that nodes would be visited if a depth-first traversal of the network in Figure 7.23 were initiated from Seattle. Use the adjacency relationships from Table 7.9.

13. Repeat Exercise 12, but initiate the traversal from Miami.

14. Suppose that integers in the following order arrive for insertion into a binary tree with the ordering property. Discuss the resulting fullness of the tree and categorize its search efficiency in big-O terms.

    100
    90
    80
    70
    60
    50
    40
    30
    20
    10

15. Repeat Exercise 14, but assume that the numbers arrive in the following order:

    60
    80
    30
    90
    70
    100
    40
    20
    50
    10

16. Repeat Exercise 14, but assume that the numbers arrive in the following order:

    60
    50
    70
    40
    80
    30
    90
    20
    100
    10

17. What, in an abstract sense, does a tree structure represent?
18. Describe a full binary tree.
19. How is a linked representation of a binary tree an improvement over its linear representation?
20. How could the inorder traversal of a binary tree be used to logically sort data?
21. Which of the three traversal schemes of a binary tree leads to the postfix notation for evaluating an arithmetic expression?
22. Discuss the relative merits of maintaining an ordered list by a binary tree, a singly linked list, and a doubly linked list.

23. Discuss how the order in which data are entered into a binary tree representation of a list affects the fullness of the tree. Identify the best and worst possible cases.

24. Develop a complete Pascal procedure to process the insertion of a node into the binary tree representation of an ordered list. Can you write both recursive and nonrecursive versions?

25. Develop a complete Pascal procedure to process the deletion of a node from a binary tree representation of an ordered list. This will essentially require that you combine into one module the three cases discussed in this chapter. For an added challenge, try writing the procedure so that it handles deletion by using the mirror image of these three cases.

26. Develop recursive and nonrecursive versions of a procedure which will search for a specified node in a binary tree with the ordering property.

27. How would you implement a preorder traversal to achieve the indentation in the output for Figure 7.21 (which appears after Table 7.5)?

28. Write procedures which employ a linear implementation for each of the following binary tree operations:
    a. Create
    b. Empty
    c. Add
    d. Delete
    e. Find

    Assume the ordering property underlies the hierarchical structure of the tree.

29. Repeat Exercise 28 for a linked implementation of the binary tree.

30. Implement the binary tree operations Add and Delete for a tree with the heap property.

31. Consider the following abstract graphic representation of a general tree:

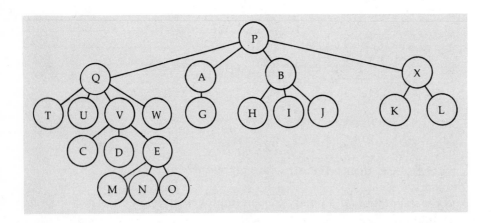

Provide a specific Pascal record description for a node in this tree as you would represent it. (Do not make any assumption about maximum possible number of children.) Then draw a specific picture of how this tree would actually be stored using the record description you have chosen.

32. Using a two-dimensional table, write procedures to implement each of the basic operations for the graph abstract data type.
33. Using a two-dimensional table, write procedures to implement each of the basic operations for the network abstract data type.
34. Suppose you are given a list of data in increasing order of keys. Develop a Pascal algorithm which will load this list into an optimal binary search tree.

Programming Problems

1. Use a binary tree to implement the general list in the registrar's system.
2. Using a linear representation of a binary tree, write a program to achieve inorder, preorder, and postorder traversals of the tree.
3. Modify the airline reservation system you developed for Wing-and-a-Prayer Airlines in Chapter 4 so that the alphabetized lists are maintained with binary trees instead of linked lists.
4. Write a program that sorts the records of the Fly-by-Night credit card company file in alphabetical order by the last name and then the first name of the customer. Use a binary tree and its inorder traversal to accomplish the sort.
5. Recall the roster maintenance system which you wrote for the Bay Area Brawlers in the Programming Problems for Chapter 4. The system has been so successful that the league office would like to expand the system to include all the players in the league. Again the goal is to maintain the list of players in alphabetical order, allowing for frequent insertions and deletions as players are cut, picked up, and traded among teams. In addition to storing each player's height, weight, age, and university affiliation, the record for each player should be expanded to include team affiliation, years in league, and annual salary. Because the data base for the entire league is many times larger than that for just one team, maintain this list as a binary tree to increase efficiency.
6. Write a program that reads an expression in its prefix form and builds the binary tree corresponding to that expression. Then write procedures to print the infix and postfix forms of the expression using inorder and postorder traversals of this tree. Then see if you can write a program to evaluate the expression represented by the tree.
7. Given a file containing some arbitrary text, determine how many times each word appears in the file. Your program should print out in alphabetical order the words that appear in the file, with their frequency counts. For an added challenge, do not assume any maximum word length; this will enable you to combine trees with the string handling methods you have already learned.
8. Here is a problem you will encounter if you write statistical analysis software. Given an arbitrarily long list of unordered numbers with an arbitrary number of different values appearing in it, determine and print out the marginal distribution for this list of numbers. That is, count how many times each different value appears in the list and then

print out each value along with its count (frequency). The final output should be arranged from smallest to largest value. This problem can be solved in elegant fashion using trees.

An example of such output as produced by the COSAP (Conversationally Oriented Statistical Analysis Package) of Lawrence University follows:

```
Command?  Marginals Judge
                   Outagame County Criminal Cases

                  M A R G I N A L   F R E Q U E N C I E S
     Variable Judge      JUDGE BEFORE WHOM CASE BROUGHT (2)
     Value label            Value       Absolute        Relative
                                        Frequency       Frequency

     SHAFER                   1             677            80.8%
     CANE                     2              88            10.5%
     VANSUS                   3              26             3.1%
     MYSE                     5              47             5.6%

          838 Valid  0 Missing  838 Total Observations
```

Here the data file contained 838 occurrences of the values 1, 2, 3, and 5. Each value was a code number assigned to a particular judge.

9. Many compilers offer the services of a cross-referencing program to aid in debugging. Such a program will list in alphabetical order all the identifiers that appear in a program and the various lines of the program that reference them. Write such a cross-referencer for your favorite language using a binary tree to maintain the list of identifiers that are encountered.

10. A relatively easy game to implement with a binary tree is to have the computer try to guess an animal about which the user is thinking by asking the user a series of questions that can be answered by yes or no. A node in the binary tree to play this game could be viewed as

   YES/NO pointers leading to

   1. Another question.
   2. The name of the animal.
   3. **NIL**.

If **NIL**, have your program surrender and then ask the user for a new question that uniquely defines the animal being thought of and then add this new question to the growing binary tree data base.

11. For this problem, you are to write a program which will differentiate expressions in the variable X. The input to this program will be a series of strings, each representing an infix expression to be differentiated. Each such expression is to be viewed as a stream of tokens. Valid tokens are integers, the variable X, the binary operators (+, −, *, /, ^), and parentheses. To make scanning for tokens easy, you may assume

that each token is followed by exactly one space, with the exception of the final token which is followed by **eoln**.

First your program will have to scan the infix expression, building up an appropriate binary tree representation of it. For this you should be able to borrow significantly on the work you did in parsing expressions in Chapter 6. The major difference here is that the end result of this parse is to be a binary tree instead of a postfix string.

Once the binary expression tree is built, traverse it, building up another binary expression tree which represents the derivative of the original expression. The following differentiation rules should be used in this process:

Suppose C is a constant, and S and T are expressions in X

Diff(C) = 0

Diff(X) = 1

Diff(S+T) = Diff(S) + Diff(T)

Diff(S−T) = Diff(S) − Diff(T)

Diff(S*T) = S*Diff(T) + T*Diff(S)

Diff(S/T) = ((T*Diff(S)) − (S*Diff(T)))/(T^2)

Diff(S^C) = (C*S^(C−1)) * Diff(S) {the infamous Chain Rule}

Finally, once the binary expression tree for the derivative has been built, print the expression. Print it in completely parenthesized infix notation to avoid ambiguity.

Note that there are three distinct phases to this problem: parsing of the original infix expression into a binary tree representation, then building a binary tree representation of the derivative, and finally printing out the derivative in completely parenthesized infix notation.

For an added challenge on this problem, simplify the derivative before printing it out. Simplify the expression for the derivative according to the following rules:

```
S + 0 = S
0 + S = S
S − 0 = S
S * 0 = 0
0 * S = 0
S * 1 = S
1 * S = S
0 / S = 0
S ^ 0 = 1
S ^ 1 = S
S − S = 0
S / S = 1
S / 0 = 'DIVISION BY ZERO'
0 / 0 = 'UNDEFINED'
```

12. Wing-and-a-Prayer Airlines is expanding their recordkeeping data base. This data base may now be pictured hierarchically as

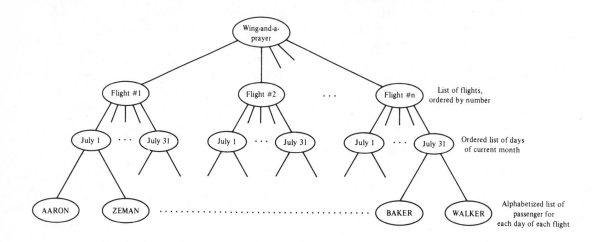

Write a program to maintain this data base. Your program should process requests to add, delete, or list the following:

☐ Specified flight number.

☐ Specified day of the month (for a given flight number).

☐ Specified passenger or all passengers (for a given flight number and day of the month).

13. Many statistical analysis packages support a "cross-tabulation" command designed to explore the relationship between statistical variables. A cross-tabulation between two variables produces a two-dimensional table containing a frequency count for each possible ordered pair of values of the two variables. However, these statistical packages typically allow this type of analysis to proceed even further than merely exploring two variables. For instance, in a legal-system data base, we might be interested in cross-tabulating a defendant's age with the judge before whom the defendant stood trial. We may then wish to cross-tabulate this result with the sex of the defendant. Sex in this case is called the control variable. We would output one such cross-tabulation table for each possible value of sex. Note that this type of output is not limited to just one control variable. There may be an arbitrary number of control variables and tables to cycle through. Moreover, the variables have an arbitrary number of observations and are all in arbitrary order. Yet for each variable the list of possible values is always printed out in smallest to largest order. The general tree structure that emerges for handling cross-tabulations is

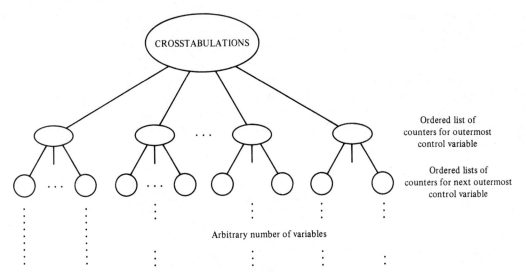

Ordered list of
counters for outermost
control variable

Ordered lists of
counters for next outermost
control variable

Arbitrary number of variables

Final level of tree contains lists of counters
for the innermost variable

Write a program to handle the task of producing statistical cross-tabulations.

14. Write a program to print out the nodes of a tree level by level; that is, all level 0 nodes, followed by all level 1 nodes, followed by all level 2 nodes, and so on. As a hint in getting started, note that this program will afford an excellent opportunity to practice using a queue in addition to a tree.

15. Operating systems often use general trees as the data structure on which their file directory system is based. Leaf nodes in such a system represent actual files or empty directories while interior nodes represent nonempty directories. For instance, consider the following situation:

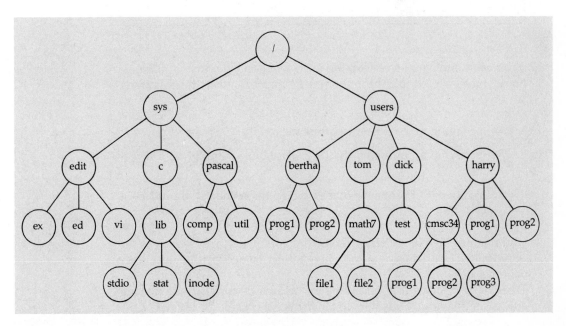

A directory entry is specified by its pathname. A pathname consists of tree node names separated by slashes. Such a pathname is absolute if it starts at the root; that is, it starts with a slash (/). It is relative to the current directory if it does not start with a slash.

In this assignment, you are to write a command processor that will allow a user to manipulate files within such a directory structure. The commands accepted by your processor will be in the form of numbers associated with particular operations and pathnames, as shown in the following table:

Number	Operation	Pathname
1	Change directory	Absolute pathname, relative pathname, or ".." for parent
2	Make a new directory	Absolute or relative pathname
3	Make a new file	Absolute or relative pathname
4	Remove a file	Absolute or relative pathname
5	Remove a directory, but only if it is empty	Absolute or relative pathname
6	Remove a directory and, recursively, everything below it	Absolute or relative pathname
7	Print directory entries in alphabetical order	Absolute or relative pathname
8	Recursively print directory entries in alphabetical order	Absolute or relative pathname
9	Print current directory name	
10	Quit processing commands	

Since even intelligent tree-walking users can easily get lost, your command processor should be prepared to trap errors of the following variety:

☐ Specifying a nonexistent pathname.

☐ Specifying a pathname that is a file when it should be a directory.

☐ Specifying a pathname that is a directory when it should be a file.

Upon detecting such an error, have your command processor print an appropriate error message and then return to accept the next user command.

16. Trees have significant applications in the area of artificial intelligence and game playing. Consider, for instance, the game of FIFTEEN. In

this game, two players take turns selecting digits between 1 and 9 with the goal of selecting a combination of digits that add up to 15. Once a digit is chosen, it may not be chosen again by either player.

Rather than immediately considering a tree for the game of FIFTEEN, let us first consider a tree for the simpler game of SEVEN with digits chosen in the range 1 to 6. A tree which partially represents the states that may be reached in this game follows:

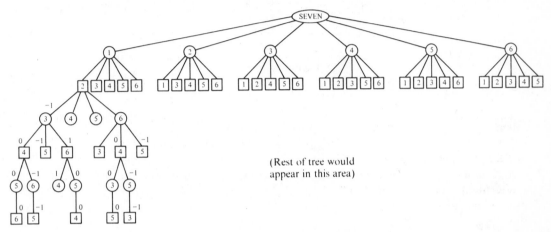

(Rest of tree would appear in this area)

**Some of the nodes appearing in tree
for game of SEVEN using 1–6**

In this tree, circular nodes represent the states that may be reached by the player who moves first (the computer), and square nodes represent the states that may be reached by the player who moves second (a human opponent). The +1, 0, or −1 attached to each node represent weighting factors designed to help the computer choose the most advantageous move at any given stage of the game. The rules used to compute these weighting factors are

- If the node is a leaf node, its weight is determined by some static weighting function. In this case, the static weighting function used was to assign +1 to a leaf node representing a computer win, 0 to a leaf node representing a draw, and −1 to a leaf node representing a human win.

- If the node is a node in which the computer will move next (that is, a state occupied by the human opponent), then the weighting factor of the node is the maximum of the weighting factors of its children.

- If the node is a node in which the human opponent will move next, then the weighting factor of the node is the minimum of the weighting factors of its children.

In its turn, the computer should always choose to move to the node having the maximum possible weighting factor. The rationale behind this technique, called the minimax technique, is that the computer will move in such a way as to always maximize its chances of winning. The human opponent, if playing intelligently, will always move to a node having a minimum weighting factor. Thus in the partial game tree shown, the computer would choose 4 if the human had been naive enough to select the 6 node with the weighting factor of +1.

Write a program to build a weighted game tree for the game of FIFTEEN and then have the computer play against a human opponent. Note that this game is really the game of tick-tack-toe if one considers the following matrix:

4	9	2
3	5	7
8	1	6

All winning tick-tack-toe paths add up to 15

Give some consideration as to the time and efficiency of your algorithm. Many games simply cannot be completely represented via a general tree because of space limitations. Consequently, a partial game tree is built in which the leaf nodes may not actually be the final moves made in the game. In such situations, the static weighting function applied to the leaf nodes in the game tree requires a bit more insight to develop.

17. Consider a priority queue (see Chapter 5) in which each item is assigned a different priority. Discuss how a binary tree with the heap property could be used to maintain such a priority queue. Write procedures for a heap implementation of the basic priority queue operations.

    Create(PriorityQueue)
    Empty(PriorityQueue)
    Add(Item, PriorityQueue)
    Remove(Item, PriorityQueue)

Categorize the run-time efficiency of the Add and Remove operations in big-O terms. Would a linear implementation or linked list implementation of the binary tree be most advantageous for this application? Explain why.

18. Implement Dijkstra's shortest-path algorithm using a suitable sparse table representation scheme to store the network data. Test your program with the transportation network pictured in Figure 7.23.

19. A breadth-first traversal of a graph involves the following steps:
    a. Begin with any node, and mark it as visited.
    b. Proceed to the next node having an edge connection to the node in step a. Mark it as visited.
    c. Come back to the node in step a, descend along an edge toward an unvisited node, and mark the new node as visited.
    d. Repeat step b until all nodes adjacent to the node in step a have been marked as visited.
    e. Repeat steps a–d starting from the node visited in b, then starting from the nodes visited in step c in the order visited. Keep this up as long as possible before starting a new scan.

Implement this algorithm as a Pascal procedure. *Hint:* Use a queue.

Unit **III**

The Techniques: Recursion, Sorting, and Searching

for a specified goal. Hence, recursion will emerge as an even more powerful programming technique than we have already witnessed.

Second, we will explore more closely the overhead associated with recursion in terms of processing time and memory consumed by the stack which lies at the foundation of this technique. This will lead us to considerations of how we can implement recursive algorithms in a nonrecursive fashion. In effect, we will show that it is often possible to approach a problem recursively at a conceptual level and then eliminate some of the overhead of recursion when we actually implement a solution to the problem.

8.2

Recursion and Generalized Nested Loops

As an example of the class of problems we will study in this section and the next, consider the notion of a permutation.

> **Permutation**   A permutation of the integers 1, 2, . . . , n is an ordered arrangement of these integers in which each integer appears exactly once.

For instance, two possible permutations of the integers 1, 2, 3, 4 are

```
3  2  1  4
2  4  3  1
```

The Permutation Problem

We now pose the following problem: For input of n, devise a program which outputs all permutations of the integers 1, 2, . . . , n. The following program solves this problem, but only for the special case where $n = 4$.

```
PROGRAM LimitedPermutations(input, output);

    {Produce all permutations of 1,2,3,4}

VAR il, i2, i3, i4 : integer;

BEGIN
FOR il := 1 TO 4 DO
  FOR i2 := 1 TO 4 DO
   IF i2 <> il THEN
    FOR i3 := 1 TO 4 DO
     IF (i3 <> i2) AND (i3 <> il) THEN
      FOR i4 := 1 TO 4 DO
       IF (i4 <> i3) AND (i4 <> i2) AND (i4 <> il) THEN
          writeln (il:2, i2:2, i3:2, i4:2)
END.
```

A Closer Look at Recursion

When you look into a mirror you do not see your reflection—your reflection sees you.

Anonymous Japanese poet
Daedalus

Introductory Considerations

The previous two chapters have intimately tied recursion to two data structures—stacks and trees. However, the relationships between recursion and these two data structures are quite different. A stack is a data structure necessary for the implementation of recursive algorithms. Trees are data structures which seem to naturally lend themselves to processing by recursive algorithms. In this chapter, we shall explore both of these relationships more deeply.

First, we shall examine the use of recursion to solve a general class of problems using a trial-and-error type of backtracking algorithm. It will turn out that this trial-and-error technique may be identified with two other algorithmic strategies: the nesting of loops to arbitrarily deep levels and the searching of a conceptual tree (which may never actually exist in memory)

The strategy of this program is to use a **FOR** loop to control a variable which runs through the four possibilities for each of the four permutation positions. Hence four loops emerge, nested within each other. When an inner loop generates a number that matches one at a previously generated position, the **IF** statement is used to reject that number.

This constitutes a simple and straightforward approach. But it falls far short of solving the general problem as originally posed because it only works for the number 4, not for a general n to be input when the program runs. Note that the requirement that n be entered at run-time is what causes the major complication. Certainly, the strategy of using nested loops would allow us to write one program that works for $n = 2$, another that works for $n = 3$, another for $n = 4$, and so on. However, in addition to having a ridiculous number of nested **FOR** loops for reasonably large n, the decision as to which permutations to generate would instead be made at the time the appropriate program is compiled and not when it runs. Computer scientists typically call this a binding time problem. Here we would prefer to bind a value to n when our program runs instead of when it compiles. Clearly, the later the binding time, the more versatile the program. To do this, we need some means of simulating arbitrarily deep nested loops when the program runs.

To see how we can use recursion to achieve such a simulation, consider the tree-like diagram of permutation possibilities in Figure 8.1.

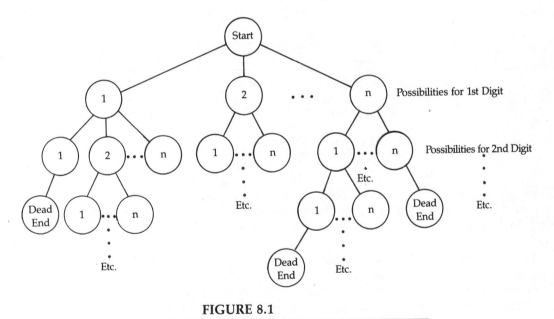

FIGURE 8.1

_____

Candidates for permutations

Interpret this diagram by viewing any given path down to the base of the tree as a potential candidate for a permutation of 1, 2, . . . , n. Although our solution will never actually store this tree as a data structure existing in memory, conceptually we must use recursion to generate all the paths that appear in the figure. As soon as we generate a path which has two equal numbers on it, we abandon that dead-end path and backtrack one level to continue the path along a potentially more fruitful route. If we ever complete one entire permutation along a path, we will output it, backtrack a level, and continue looking for more permutations that share the beginning of this path. Rather than ever storing the entire tree of Figure 8.1 in memory, we need only store the current path. For this, a simple global array will do. Thus, the array CurrentPermutation of Figure 8.2 will store in its ith subscript the number in the ith position of the permutation currently being generated. The limiting factor on the size of permutations generated by our program will be the dimension of this array.

CurrentPermutation   MaxPermutation

1	2	3	4	5	•	•	•	Size
2	1	4	undefined	undefined	•	•	•	undefined

FIGURE 8.2

Current exploration of permutations beginning with 2 1 4

A complete program to solve our permutation problem follows. The heart of the program is the recursive procedure Try. Try receives three parameters.

Parameter	Explanation
n	The number of numbers to be permuted in the current run.
Level	The level in the tree of Figure 8.1; that is, position in CurrentPermutation at which Try is to attempt placement of a new value.
Possibility	The new value to be placed at this Level.

Try initially calls on a procedure AddToCurrentPath to actually place Possibility at the appropriate Level. Once this placement is made, there are three states in which the CurrentPermutation array could be.

1. The placement of the value Possibility at the designated Level could have completed a successful permutation. In this case, call on a procedure to print out the permutation and then remove Possibility from CurrentPermutation at the given Level so that we may continue seeking additional permutations.

2. The placement of the value Possibility at the designated Level did not complete a permutation but does represent a valid beginning of length Level for a potential permutation. For instance, this case would occur if n, Level, and Possibility were 6, 4, and 5 respectively and we called Try with CurrentPermutation as pictured in Figure 8.2. The CurrentPermutation array would be extended to contain 2 1 4 5. Here what we must do is to test the possible candidates for a

value at the next position; that is, at depth (Level + 1). This is done by an iterative series of recursive calls to Try, passing a variety of values for Possibility at (Level + 1). This iterative series of recursive calls is what achieves the desired simulation of nested looping. After all of these deeper-level possibilities (the subtree below the beginning of the current permutation in Figure 8.1) have been explored, we return and can remove Possibility from CurrentPermutation at position Level since (recursively) all permutations with this beginning arrangement will have been generated.

3. The placement of the value Possibility at Level destroys the viability of the current path by adding a number which appeared earlier in the permutation. For instance, calling on Try with $n = 6$, Level = 4, and Possibility = 1 would cause an invalid path for the state of CurrentPermutation given in Figure 8.2. In this case we do nothing but retract from the placement of this invalid Possibility before attempting to place other possible values.

You should carefully study how these three potential cases are handled in our recursive procedure Try which appears in the program VersatilePermutations. In the next section, we will adapt the technique illustrated here to a broader class of problems.

```
PROGRAM VersatilePermutations(input, output);

{ Use recursion to find all permutations of 1,2, . . . n. }

  CONST
    MaxPermutationSize = 100;
    Undefined = MaxInt;

  VAR
    n, i : integer;
    CurrentPermutation : ARRAY [1..MaxPermutationSize] OF integer:


  PROCEDURE InitializeCurrentPath;

    { Set all locations in CurrentPermutation to Undefined flag. }

    VAR
      i : integer;

    BEGIN
      FOR i := 1 TO MaxPermutationSize DO
        CurrentPermutation[i] := Undefined
    END;


  PROCEDURE Try(n, Level, Possibility : integer);

    { Try given Possibility at specified Level of potential solution tree.
      Permutation has been found if Possibility does not match a previous
      entry in CurrentPermutation and Level equals n. }
```

```
VAR
  i : integer;


PROCEDURE AddToCurrentPath(Level, Possibility : integer);

  { Add Possibility to CurrentPermutation at given Level. }

  BEGIN
    CurrentPermutation[Level] := Possibility
  END;


PROCEDURE RemoveFromCurrentPath(Level, Possibility : integer);

  { Remove Possibility from CurrentPermutation at given Level. }

  BEGIN
    CurrentPermutation[Level] := Undefined
  END;


FUNCTION CurrentPathSuccess(n, Level : integer) : boolean;

  { Return true if CurrentPermutation actually contains a
    permutation of length n. }

  VAR
    Success : boolean;
    i : integer;


  BEGIN
    Success := true;
    IF n > Level THEN   {Level must be n for successful permutation.}
      Success := false
    ELSE   {Are all entries different from that at index Level?}
      BEGIN
      i := 1;
      WHILE (i <= (Level - 1)) AND Success DO
        BEGIN
        Success := (CurrentPermutation[i] <> CurrentPermutation[Level]);
        i := i + 1
        END
      END;
    CurrentPathSuccess := Success
  END;


FUNCTION CurrentPathStillViable(Level : integer): boolean;

  { Return true if CurrentPermutation still contains a viable
    beginning for a permutation. }

  VAR
    Viable : boolean;
    i : integer;
```

```
BEGIN
  Viable := true;
  i := 1;
  WHILE (i <= (Level - 1)) AND Viable DO
    BEGIN
    Viable := (CurrentPermutation[i] <> CurrentPermutation[Level]);
    i := i + 1
    END;
  CurrentPathStillViable := Viable
END;


PROCEDURE ProcessSuccessfulPath(n : integer);

  { Output a permutation that has been found. }

  VAR
    i : integer;


  BEGIN
    FOR i := 1 TO n DO
      write(CurrentPermutation[i]: 3);
    writeln
  END;


    BEGIN { Try }
      AddToCurrentPath(Level, Possibility);
      IF CurrentPathSuccess(n, Level) THEN
        ProcessSuccessfulPath(n)
      ELSE IF CurrentPathStillViable(Level) THEN
        FOR i := 1 TO n DO
          Try(n, Level + 1, i);
      RemoveFromCurrentPath(Level, Possibility)
    END; { Try }


  BEGIN { Main }
    InitializeCurrentPath;
    write('Permutation of integers from 1 to ? ');
    readln(n);
    FOR i := 1 TO n DO
      Try(n, 1, i)
  END.
```

You may have noticed that certain economies could have been taken in writing the previous program. For example, the initialization of the CurrentPermutation array actually is unnecessary in this particular implementation. Also, the call to RemoveFromCurrentPath could have been eliminated since the Undefined flag that this procedure assigns is quickly replaced without ever being explicitly used. You will be asked to rewrite this procedure taking these economies into account in the Exercises. Our purpose in this section has not been to present the most compact version of a permutations program, but rather to illustrate how recursion can be used to simulate generalized nested loops whose nesting depth can be established at run-time. In this context, we have intended the program to be illustrative of a general problem-solving approach rather than a solution to a particular problem. We shall see that our being able to simulate such a looping structure via recursion allows us to solve a whole new class of problems.

Trial-and-Error Backtracking as a Problem-Solving Technique

We have emphasized throughout this text that computer scientists must work at varying levels of abstraction. With this in mind, consider the program of the last section not merely as a permutation printer but rather as illustrative of a more abstract problem-solving technique. The tree of Figure 8.1 presents the problem of finding permutations as a problem in finding certain types of paths through an implicit tree structure. In this context, the permutation problem could be viewed as finding our way out of a maze. We probe deeper and deeper along a given path (that is, add new numbers to the current permutation) until we reach a predefined goal or reach a dead end. That is, we take a new step along the current path and analyze the state in which it has placed us.

1. Have we reached a goal state?
2. Have we reached a state that, though not itself a goal, is still a viable start toward that goal?
3. Have we reached a dead end?

For each of the three cases we take appropriate action such as

1. Processing a goal state; for example, printing it out, tallying a counter, or setting a flag signaling we are done.
2. Probing further along a viable path by recursively taking another step.
3. No action in the case of a dead end.

After taking the appropriate action, we then retract from the step that led us to the current state, possibly returning to a higher recursive level where we may find ourselves in the midst of a similar three-state analysis. The concept of this trial-and-error backtracking logic is illustrated in Figure 8.3. Upon reaching a dead end for path A, you must retrace steps $9 \rightarrow 8 \rightarrow 7 \rightarrow 6 \rightarrow 5$ before you can try new path B. The retracing of states which have been visited previously is conveniently done by unwinding from recursive calls.

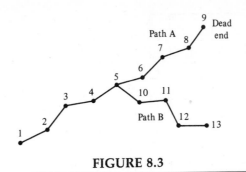

FIGURE 8.3

Backtracking problem illustrated by maze solution

The Eight Queens Problem

As an example of another problem which, in an abstract sense, could be considered analogous to the permutation problem, consider what has come to be known as the Eight Queens Problem. This is a problem which has long intrigued chess fanatics. It requires determining the various ways in which eight queens could be configured on a chessboard so that none of them could capture any other queen. (The rules of chess allow a queen to move an arbitrary number of squares in a horizontal, vertical, or diagonal fashion.) Figure 8.4 illustrates one such configuration.

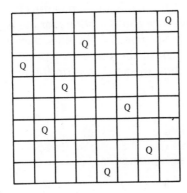

FIGURE 8.4

One successful eight queens configuration

Applying backtracking logic to this problem we could attempt to find a path to a configuration by successively trying to place a queen in each column of a chessboard until we reach a dead end: a column in which the placement of queens in prior columns makes it impossible to place the queen being moved. This situation is pictured in Figure 8.5. When we reach this dead end, we must backtrack one column (to column 5 in the case of Figure 8.5), and attempt to find a new placement for the queen in the previous column. If placement in the previous column is impossible,

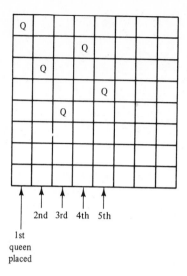

FIGURE 8.5

Dead end in queen placement

we must backtrack yet another column to attempt the new placement. This backtracking through previous columns continues until we finally are able to reposition a queen. At that point, we can begin a new path by again attempting to position queens on a column-by-column basis until another dead end is reached or until a fully successful configuration is developed.

The key to a program that finds all possible configurations for the eight queens is a procedure that attempts to place a queen in a given square and, if successful, recursively calls itself to attempt the placement of another queen in the next column. Such a procedure in skeleton form follows:

```
PROCEDURE  TryQueen(i,j)

    {Place a queen in row i, column j.  Analyze
     state reached by this placement.  If appropriate,
     recurse to place queen in next column.}

Actually put queen at position i,j
IF this results in successful configuration THEN
        Tally this configuration

ELSE IF no queen in immediate danger THEN
        FOR k := 1 to 8 DO
            TryQueen(k,j+1)

Retract from position i,j

END    {TryQueen}
```

The similarities between this sketch of a solution to the Eight Queens Problem and our complete solution to the permutation problem should convince you that, from an abstract perspective, both problems are really the same. We have intentionally left the Eight Queens Problem unfinished. Still to be resolved are such issues as:

- ☐ The initial call(s) to TryQueen.

- ☐ How to represent the chessboard.

- ☐ How to check whether placing a queen at position i, j puts it in immediate danger. That is, how to determine whether there is currently another queen sharing the same row, column, or diagonal.

The resolution of these issues is left for your enjoyment in the Programming Problems at the end of the chapter. Additional problems which are given there further illustrate the far-reaching applicability of the trial-and-error backtracking method.

_____ 8.4

The Costs Associated with Recursion

In Chapter 6, we have already hinted that recursion does not come cheaply. We have now seen what a powerful problem-solving method it is. Consequently, we should not be surprised if the costs associated with recursion can often be very steep. With the added experience we have acquired in using recursion, we are now in a better position to analyze these costs more precisely. To do so, consider our old friend, the Towers of Hanoi algorithm, as an example.

Our familiarity with trees now allows us to conveniently picture the procedure calls made for Hanoi (3, A, C, B) in terms of the tree in Figure 8.6.

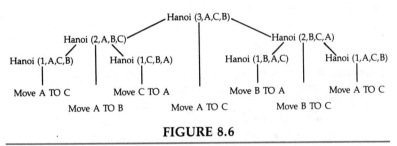

FIGURE 8.6

Tree of procedure calls for Hanoi

We emphasize that the Towers of Hanoi algorithm itself does not work with such a binary tree as a data structure, but rather the binary tree diagram of Figure 8.6 will merely serve as an aid in our analyzing the efficiency of the algorithm.

If we were to draw a similar binary tree of procedure calls for the general parameter n, we immediately see that it would contain n levels and $2^n - 1$ nodes. This is because it will always be a full binary tree for any given value of n. This analysis of the tree of procedure calls leads us to two important conclusions about the algorithm.

1. The maximum depth reached by the system stack will be n stack frames. Thus, in terms of a space analysis with respect to the stack, it is an $O(n)$ algorithm.

2. $2^n - 1$ calls to Hanoi will be made during the overall execution of the algorithm. Thus, in terms of a time analysis with respect to the stacking operations associated with a procedure call, it is an $O(2^n)$ algorithm.

This is the first $O(2^n)$ algorithm we have encountered. The sorting algorithms we discussed in Chapter 2 were $O(n^2)$, and, until now, they have been the slowest algorithms we have studied. An $O(2^n)$ algorithm is significantly slower than an $O(n^2)$ algorithm. In fact, it can be mathematically demonstrated that an $O(2^n)$ algorithm is significantly slower than an $O(n^m)$ algorithm for any fixed value of m. Such algorithms are often called exponential algorithms. To give you some idea of how slow an $O(2^n)$ algorithm can be, consider a machine that executes an instruction each microsecond; that is, one million instructions per second. Such a machine will require 1 second to execute an $O(2^n)$ algorithm for $n = 20$, 10^6 seconds (or 116 days) for $n = 40$, and 10^{24} seconds (approximately 30,000,000,000,000,000 years) for $n = 80$. Clearly, it is not realistic to think that such a computer will ever actually implement a solution for this Hanoi algorithm with $n = 80$.

This analysis of the Hanoi algorithm allows us to draw the following conclusion about the cost of recursion. This cost is a twofold cost. It is paid partially in terms of stack space. This aspect of the cost is measured by the depth of the tree of procedure calls. The other part of the cost is paid in terms of the run-time associated with the stacking operations required when a recursive call is made. This run-time cost is usually much greater than the space cost because it is measured by the number of nodes in the tree of recursive calls.

We do not mean to imply that the high space/time price of recursion makes it an impractical technique, however. Often, recursive programs which solve significant problems can be implemented with a tree of procedure calls which is small enough to allow a practical run-time efficiency. Moreover, even in situations where the run-time costs of recurison become quite steep, we may want to express an algorithm recursively because that is the "natural" way of looking at the problem. Then, when we attempt to implement that algorithm on an actual machine, perhaps we can devise ways of eliminating or reducing the costs of recursion. Hence, we may be able to implement the algorithm nonrecursively and achieve a practical time/space performance even though the algorithm itself is recursive in nature. In the remainder of this chapter, we shall examine some of the techniques used to eliminate recursion from the implementation of a recursive algorithm. We are not advocating that such techniques always be employed. However, in situations where the actual time or space cost of a recursive implementation is too great for practical use, these techniques may achieve a worthwhile savings.

Elimination of Recursion

Perhaps another reason for knowing how to eliminate recursion should be cited at this point. That is, some languages which are in quite wide use simply do not support recursion as a programming technique. FORTRAN, COBOL, and BASIC are examples of such languages. It is distinctly possible that you may sometime have no choice but to use such a language and yet you still want to implement a conceptually recursive algorithm. The techniques we will discuss in this section will be of help in this regard.

Elimination of Tail Recursion

Recall from Section 6.6 that, in a tail recursive algorithm such as the computation of a factorial, a sequence of recursive calls is followed by an uninterrupted series of returns back to the original calling point. The reason for this pattern of calls and returns is that the recursive call is made at the end of the procedure or function in which it appears. In such a case, recursion is really doing nothing more than controlling an iterative loop. Hence it is usually a trivial matter to rewrite the procedure using a standard loop control structure. Occasionally you will need to use a local variable to compensate for data that would have been pushed on the system stack during recursive calls. For instance, our recursive factorial function may be easily recast in the following nonrecursive form:

```
FUNCTION Factorial (n : integer) : integer;

    {Computer and return n! without using recursion.}

VAR Nfact, i : integer;

BEGIN
Nfact := 1;
FOR i := 2 TO n DO   {Note this loop skipped if n < 2}
    Nfact := Nfact * i;
Factorial := Nfact
END;
```

Virtually all cases of tail recursion are equally easy to eliminate. Hence we comment on it no further here. Instead we turn our attention to those types of algorithms for which recursion is more appropriately suited—those in which there is an ebb and flow to the system stack caused by a pattern of recursion significantly more complex than a standard loop control structure.

Elimination of Recursion by Simulating the System Stack

The two motivating factors we have cited for eliminating recursion are time/space efficiency and being able to implement recursive algorithms in a language environment that doesn't support recursion. The technique we are about to describe will have us using a local stack. Essentially it requires that we do ourselves what the system would normally do for us upon a recursive call. Hence it is a technique that, though sometimes messy, will always allow us to implement a recursive algorithm in a nonrecursive environment. With respect to the time/space efficiency question, we will not be able to achieve an order of magnitude improvement since we will just be simulating what the operating system would do anyway. However, it will turn out that we can achieve certain small scale economies since we may not have to do as much stack manipulation as the operating system would. We will discuss these economies in greater detail after looking at some examples of the method.

As an aside, we might mention a third motivation for learning this particular scheme of eliminating recursion. That motivation is more one of understanding than any pragmatic operational goal. If we can simulate what the run-time system of Pascal does for us in recursion, then certainly our understanding of recursion will be much deeper than it had previously been. Consequently we are likely to acquire more confidence in it as a programming technique.

The elimination of recursion by simulating the system stack can be systematically broken down into the following three operations:

☐ Substituting appropriate branching instructions for procedural call and return operations.

☐ Using local stack(s) to store return addresses and preserve necessary parameters prior to a recursive call.

☐ Using assignment statements to simulate the passage of arguments that a procedural call would generate.

To illustrate the method, we will present a nonrecursive Pascal version of the Hanoi algorithm. We will assume the existence of three stacks: IStack, CStack, LStack, composed of integer, character, and label data respectively. Label data in this example turn out to be integer in type and hence could actually be pushed onto the integer data stack IStack. However, two separate stacks are used to emphasize the distinction between integers that are pure data and those that represent return addresses. Finally, we assume the existence of appropriate push and pop procedures for these stacks as described in Chapter 6. In particular, recall that these procedures, as developed in Chapter 6, had two parameters: the item to be pushed or popped and the stack.

```
PROCEDURE NonrecursiveHanoi (n : integer;
                            Source, Destination, Intermediate : char);

{Nonrecursive implementation of Towers of Hanoi}

LABEL

    1, {Corresponds to Label 1 in earlier recursive version of Chapter 6}
    2, {Corresponds to Label 2 in earlier recursive version}
    3, {Corresponds to entry point for simulated recursive call}
    10, {End of procedure, return to higher-level calling procedure}
```

```
VAR
  ReturnPt : integer;
  Temp : char;

  {Here appropriate declarations and procedures for local stacks would
   be inserted. See discussion in preceding text.}

BEGIN {NonrecursiveHanoi}
3: {Entry}
  IF n = 1 THEN
    BEGIN
    write('MOVE DISK FROM', Source, 'TO', Destination);

     {Now simulate a Return operation}
    PopInt(n, IStack);
    PopCh(Intermediate, CStack);
    PopCh(Destination, CStack);
    PopCh(Source, CStack);
    IF  Empty(LStack) THEN
      GOTO 10 {Return to higher-level calling procedure}
    ELSE {Branch to appropriate return address}
      BEGIN
      PopInt(ReturnPt, LStack);
      CASE   ReturnPt   OF
        1:
          GOTO 1;
        2:
          GOTO 2
      END
    END
  END;
```

n
Intermediate
Destination
Source
Return Address

The first 4 POPs restore previous parameter values from the stack

The 5th POP then determines the return address

```
{Simulate first recursive call from previous version in Chapter 6.
 Stack parameters.}

  PushInt(n, IStack);
  PushCh(Source, CStack);
  PushCh(Destination, CStack);
  PushCh(Intermediate, CStack);

  {Arrange parameter passing}

  n := n - 1;
  Temp := Intermediate;
  Intermediate := Destination;
  Destination := Temp;

  {Stack return address}

  PushInt(1, LStack);

  {Actual recursive procedure Call replaced by GOTO}
```

```
      GOTO 3;


  1:
      write('MOVE DISK FROM', Source, 'TO', Destination);

      {Next simulate second recursive call in previous Hanoi.
       Stack parameters.}

      PushInt(n,IStack);
      PushCh(Source, CStack);
      PushCh(Destination, CStack);
      PushCh(Intermediate, CStack);

      {Simulate parameter passing for second call.}

      n := n - 1;
      Temp := Intermediate;
      Intermediate := Source;
      Source := Temp;

  {Stack return address}

  PushInt(2, LStack);

  {Actual recursive procedure Call replaced by GOTO.}
```

A Relevant Issue . . .

Recursion, LISP, and the Practicality of Artificial Intelligence

Artificial intelligence, the science of implementing on computers the problem-solving methods used by human beings, is one of the most rapidly expanding fields within computer science. Research in this field includes enabling computers to play games of strategy, to understand natural languages, to prove theorems in logic and mathematics, and to mimic the reasoning of human experts in fields such as medical diagnosis. Only recently has artificial intelligence become a commercially viable area of application, capable of solving some real-life problems apart from the idealized setting of a pure research environment. More and more, we are seeing artificial intelligence systems which perform such practical functions as aiding business executives in their decision-making processes and providing a "near-English" user-interface language for data-base management software.

What has sparked the sudden emergence of artificial intelligence? Why wasn't it possible to produce commercially feasible programs in this field until recently? One of the primary answers to these questions is tied to the language in which most artificial intelligence programming is done. This language is called LISP (for LISt Processor). Interestingly, the control structures of LISP are based almost entirely on recursion. What a Pascal programmer would view as normal iterative control structures (for example, **WHILE**, **REPEAT**, and **FOR** loops) appear in various versions of LISP only as infrequently used, nonstandard extensions to the language. One of the reasons that a recursively based language such as LISP is so ideally suited to this field is that most problem-solving methods in

```
GOTO 3;

{The remaining lines simulate the Return operation appearing in line
2 of the previous recursive Hanoi.
First pop parameters from the stack.}

2:

   PopInt(n, IStack);
   PopCh(Intermediate, CStack);
   PopCh(Destination, CStack);
   PopCh(Source, CStack);
   IF Empty(LStack) THEN
      GOTO 10 {Return to higher-level calling procedure}
   ELSE {Branch to appropriate return address}
     BEGIN
        PopInt(ReturnPt, LStack);
        CASE ReturnPt OF
          1:
             GOTO 1;
          2:
             GOTO 2
        END
     END;
   10:
   END;
{End NonrecursiveHanoi}
```

artificial intelligence involve searching a tree for a particular goal state; that is, searching for a path through a tree leading to a complete problem solution. This is similar to the approach we have taken in the permutation problem and the Eight Queens Problem of this chapter.

The complexity of problems studied in artificial intelligence leads to search trees of enormous size. Interestingly, LISP has been available as a recursive language ideally suited to such tree searches for a long time. It is one of the oldest high-level programming languages, having been first developed by John McCarthy in the late 1950s. Researchers who work in artificial intelligence have realized since LISP's introduction that its ability to recursively process general data structures was, on a theoretical basis, exactly what they needed. The problem through the years has been that, because of the very high overhead associated with recursion (and some other features built into LISP), computer hardware has not been fast enough to run LISP programs in practical applications. Thus, researchers were restricted not by LISP itself but rather by the ability of computer hardware to execute LISP programs in reasonable times. One of the major reasons for the recent emergence of artificial intelligence has been the increase in speed of computing hardware and the decrease in cost of this same hardware. This has made it possible for users to have dedicated computer resources capable of meeting the demands of LISP's recursive style. As hardware continues to improve, so will applications in LISP and artificial intelligence become increasingly sophisticated.

When you compare this to the previous recursive Hanoi procedure, you should note that each recursive call is replaced by a considerable number of statements. Procedure calls are replaced by a series of push operations, assignment statements, and finally a **GOTO**. Returns are replaced by a reverse series of pop operations and then, conditionally, either a **GOTO** or a true return to the original calling procedure. This increase in the number of statements should not be interpreted as meaning that the nonrecursive version of the program is less efficient; we are merely doing what the system would otherwise do for us. In fact, as we will see in our later discussion of efficiency, our simulation of the system stack can often be more efficient than the system's own stacking operation.

Unfortunately, such systematic translation of recursive algorithms into nonrecursive implementations frequently results in very unstructured code. This is because a return following a recursive procedure call may lead to any one of several possible locations in the procedure, depending upon the return address popped from the stack. In our nonrecursive Hanoi procedure we have used a **CASE** statement which dispatches control to the appropriate point via a **GOTO** statement in which the destination is a label popped from the stack. In defense of the resulting unstructured code, we note that it can almost be automatically generated from the recursive version of the algorithm. Hence it is not likely to lead to the type of errors that often occur with unstructured programs.

Moreover, it is frequently quite easy to recast the nonrecursive version of the program into a structured form. To illustrate this, we present a nonrecursive structured version of a preorder tree traversal. In this case, we only have to push onto the local stack (used in lieu of the system stack) pointers to nonempty right subtrees to which we must return after visiting all nodes in the left subtree. We have eliminated the need to push return addresses through the use of the **IF . . . THEN . . . ELSE** inside the **WHILE** loop. The pushing and popping which occurs on the local stack when this procedure executes is illustrated for a sample binary expression tree in Figure 8.7.

This figure also includes a trace of the local stack during iterations of **PROCEDURE** NonrecursivePreorder; it assumes that pointers lead to tree locations 1 through 9.

```
{Global declarations}

TYPE TreePointer = ^TreeNode;
     TreeNode  =  RECORD
                     LeftChild : TreePointer;
                     Info : char; {or other appropriate type}
                     RightChild : TreePointer
                  END;
```

```
{---------------------------------------------------------------------}
```

```
PROCEDURE NonrecursivePreorder (Root : TreePointer);
```

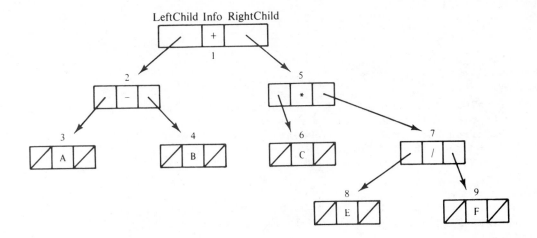

LeftChild Info RightChild

Iteration	Stack	Output
1	5	+
2	4 5	+ −
3	4 5	+ − A
4	5	+ − AB
5	7	+ − AB*
6	7	+ − AB*C
7	9	+ − AB*C/
8	9	+ − AB*C/E
9		+ − AB*C/EF

FIGURE 8.7

Pushing and popping on the local stack

```
{Nonrecursive preorder traversal of binary tree pointed to by
 Root.  We assume the existence of appropriate declarations for a
 local PointerStack of TreePointers manipulated by procedures
 CreateStack, Pop, and Push.}

VAR CurrentNode : TreePointer;
    PointerStack : {Appropriate implementation}
    Done : boolean;

BEGIN
Done := false;
CurrentNode := Root;
CreateStack(PointerStack);
IF CurrentNode = NIL THEN {Empty tree is special case}
```

```
      BEGIN
      writeln ('EMPTY TREE');
      Done := true
      END;

   WHILE NOT Done DO
     IF CurrentNode <> NIL THEN
       BEGIN
       Process(CurrentNode^.Info);  {Appropriate processing procedure}
       {Push pointer to right subtree on stack}
       Push(CurrentNode^.RightChild, PointerStack);
       {Then process the left subtree}
       CurrentNode := CurrentNode^.LeftChild
       END
     ELSE
       {No more movement left.  Start popping stack to return
        to appropriate right subtree.  If empty, we are done.}

     IF Empty(PointerStack) THEN
        Done := true
     ELSE
        Pop (CurrentNode, PointerStack)
   END;  {NonrecursivePreorder}
```

CurrentNode

This pointer, CurrentNode^.RightChild must be stacked while processing the left subtree of CurrentNode

Efficiency of System Stack Simulation. As we have indicated, we cannot expect the elimination of recursion by this method to achieve an order of magnitude improvement in stack operations because we merely do for ourselves much of what the Pascal's run-time system would do for us in processing a recursive call. This is particularly true when the translation to a nonrecursive implementation is done in the nearly automatic fashion illustrated by our nonrecursive Hanoi procedure. Here the only savings we would achieve would be found in the extra data the system might stack in addition to the return address and local parameters we have already discussed. This extra data usually take the form of special CPU registers and condition codes that are not of direct importance to a programmer in a high-level language like Pascal. Moreover, by a more judicious choice of data items to be stacked in our nonrecursive Hanoi procedure, we could have eliminated some unnecessary stack operations. In this regard, the crucial question to be asked is whether or not a parameter will change in value when a recursive call is made. If not, then there is really no need to push it onto the stack, although procedure calls handled by the system will do this anyway. In the Exercises at the end of the chapter, you will be asked to identify push operations in the nonrecursive Hanoi implementation which could be removed in order to minimize stack operations and space.

The more structured nonrecursive preorder traversal which we presented is more efficient than the Hanoi procedure because it avoids pushing a return address onto the stack. Instead, the appropriate branching is handled entirely by an **IF . . . THEN . . . ELSE.** An additional savings is achieved because **NIL** RightChild pointers are never pushed. Hence, we may actually be able to climb several levels in the tree with one pop operation. However, even in this regard, an improvement by an order of magnitude would occur only for special cases in which the tree being processed has a vast preponderance of **NIL** RightChild pointers.

Thus, our conclusion is that system stack simulation will result in incremental improvements at best over pure recursive implementations. Perhaps the greatest value of this technique is not in its slightly better efficiency but rather in its allowing recursion to be implemented in all languages and in the greater understanding of recursion which is fostered by having to do it yourself.

Threading as a Means of Eliminating Recursion in Tree Traversals

Threading is a technique of recursion elimination which applies only to tree traversal algorithms. Unlike system stack simulation, it eliminates all of the overhead associated with recursion. Moreover, it does so at a very small price because it merely utilizes leaf node pointers which would otherwise be **NIL.** Consider the linked representation of a binary tree in the preceding Figure 8.7. There are 10 wasted fields taken up by **NIL** pointers. These could be effectively used to point to significant nodes chosen according to a traversal scheme to be used for the tree. For the inorder traversal of the binary tree in Figure 8.8, note that node A comes before − and that node B is preceded by − but followed by the root node +. With an inorder traversal, we could therefore adjust the RightChild pointer field of the

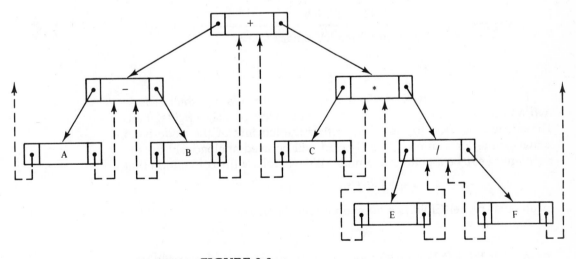

FIGURE 8.8

Threaded version of the binary tree of Figure 8.7

node containing B (presently **NIL**) to point to the node containing +, and the LeftChild pointer field of the node containing B to point to its predecessor node (−). The inorder traversal of this tree yields the expression

$$A-B+C*E/F$$

Notice that B comes after − but before +. Similarly, because E is preceded by * but followed by /, the **NIL** left link of the node containing E should, in our scheme, point to *. The **NIL** right link of E should point to /.

Because we are arranging pointers to the inorder predecessor and successor of a leaf node, we call the pointers inorder threads. Following a thread pointer allows us to ascend strategically one or more appropriate levels in the tree without relying on recursion. Figure 8.8 is the transformed version of Figure 8.7 with threads indicated by dotted lines. Threads that take the place of a left child pointer indicate the inorder predecessor, whereas those that take the place of a right child pointer lead to the inorder successor.

The two threads on the left and right of Figure 8.8 are the only loose threads at this stage. To correct this situation, we shall assume that a threaded binary tree is the left subtree of a dummy root node whose right child pointer points to itself. An empty, threaded binary tree drawn according to this convention is shown in Figure 8.9. This choice of a dummy root node for a threaded binary tree is similar to the convention that we adopted in Chapter 4 when using a dummy header for a linked list to eliminate consideration of special cases. We shall see that by initially setting the pointers as indicated in Figure 8.9, we avoid having to treat the empty tree as a special case in our algorithm to process threaded trees.

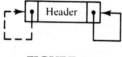

FIGURE 8.9

An empty threaded binary tree

In order to keep track of which pointers are threads, we shall include two additional Boolean fields in each node. One of these fields, Left-Thread, will be used to indicate whether the left link of the node is an actual pointer or a thread. RightThread will be used analogously for the right link. Let p be a pointer to a node. We will follow the convention that

$$p\hat{}.LeftThread = false$$

means that $p\hat{}.LeftChild$ is a normal pointer. Similarly

$$p\hat{}.LeftThread = true$$

means that the left link of the node pointed to be p is a thread pointer. Similar interpretations hold for

$$p\hat{}.RightThread = true$$

and

$$p\hat{}.RightThread = false$$

The purpose of this Boolean information as a means of identifying various pointers is only to help facilitate algorithms for different modes of traversing the tree. When we incorporate the header and Boolean information into the tree of Figure 8.8, it takes the form of Figure 8.10.

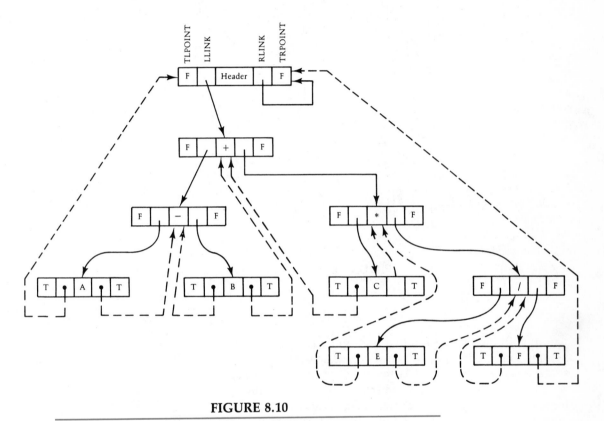

FIGURE 8.10

Threaded tree of Figure 8.8 with header and Boolean
information

To achieve an inorder traversal of the tree in Figure 8.10, we must proceed from each given node to its inorder successor. The inorder successor of a node is determined by one of two methods depending upon whether or not the right child pointer of the node in question is a thread or a normal pointer. If it is a thread, then it leads us directly to the inorder successor. If it is not a thread, then we must follow the right child pointer to the node it references and, from there, follow left child pointers until we encounter a left thread. To convince yourself of this last step, consider the threaded tree that is given in Figure 8.11. In this tree, to get the inorder successor of the node containing M, we must first follow the right child pointer from M to V and then go left as deeply as possible in the tree, finally arriving at the node containing Q. Note also that this general strategy of proceeding one to the right, then left as deeply as possible in combi-

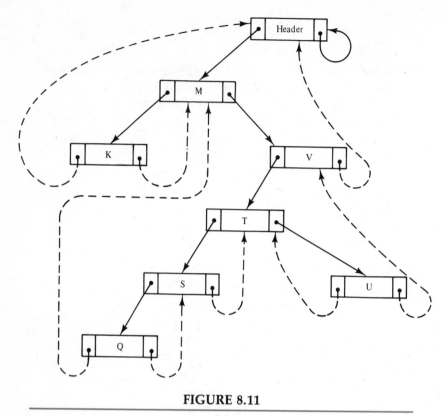

FIGURE 8.11

Threaded tree

nation with the initial setting of the right child pointer to the header node insures that the inorder traversal begins with the proper node. Trace the process shown in Figure 8.11 to find Q as the inorder successor of M.

The following Pascal procedure more formally expresses the algorithm for the threaded inorder traversal just discussed. Note that it is achieved without any need for recursion or the use of a stack to simulate recursion.

```
{Global variables and data types}

TYPE
  Pointer = ^TreeNode;
  TreeNode =
    RECORD
      LeftThread : boolean;
      LeftChild : Pointer;
      Data : char; {Or other appropriate type}
      RightChild : Pointer;
      RightThread : boolean
    END;


PROCEDURE ThreadedInorder (Root : Pointer);

{Performs a threaded inorder traversal of the tree with dummy
  root node pointed to by Root.}
```

```
{Local variables}

VAR
   p : Pointer;

BEGIN
   p := Root;
   REPEAT
```

replace ✳

p starts here

The WHILE loop in ELSE clause forces p down to inorder successor

```
{The following IF statement alters
 p to point to its inorder successor.}

   IF p^.RightThread THEN
     p:= p^.RightChild
   ELSE
     BEGIN
     p := p^.RightChild;
     WHILE NOT p^.LeftThread DO
       p := p^.LeftChild
     END;

   {p now has been changed to point to its inorder successor.}

   {Next check to see whether or not we have returned to the root; that is,
    completed the traversal.}

   IF p <> Root THEN
     writeln(p^.Data)
   UNTIL p = Root
END;
{End ThreadedInorder}
```

We encourage you to trace carefully through this procedure on the tree appearing in Figure 8.11. You should also verify that the procedure gracefully prints nothing when the Root pointer refers to an empty tree. A few minor modifications to the procedure will yield a new one

```
PROCEDURE ReverseThreadedInorder(Root)
```

which will employ the predecessor threads to perform a reverse inorder traversal. Note that, if a given application required only forward traversing of the tree, there would be no need to maintain these predecessor threads. In that case, the left child pointers of the leaf nodes could remain **NIL** or perhaps even thread the tree for a preorder traversal. (See the Exercises at the end of the chapter.)

A valid question at this stage is: "Where do the threads come from?" In our examples so far, they have merely been drawn as dotted-line pointers in the context of an already existing tree. We stress, however, that in practice, threads cannot exist unless they are continually maintained as nodes are added to the tree. In the discussion which follows, we will develop a procedure to insert a node into a threaded binary tree. In performing insertions, we will preserve the ordering property cited in Chapter 7. That is, for any given node, its left subtree contains only data less than (or equal to) it while its right subtree contains only data greater than (or equal to) it. In order to insure that this property is met for the dummy root node, we stipulate that the data portion of the dummy root node should be initialized to a value greater than any other data which will appear in the tree.

Given this criterion, insertion requires that the node to be inserted should travel down a branch of the tree following the insertion rule (which we saw in Chapter 7): Less than, go left; greater than, go right. Upon reaching a thread (that is, where a null pointer would be in an unthreaded tree), the new node is inserted appropriately as the left or right child. Figures 8.12 and 8.13 illustrate the pointer manipulations that must occur in each of these cases.

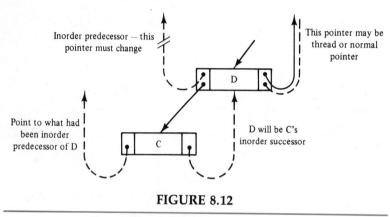

FIGURE 8.12

Insert C as left child of leaf node D

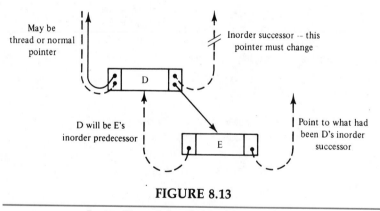

FIGURE 8.13

Insert E as right child of leaf node D

These pointer manipulations are achieved by the following procedure InsertThreaded. Notice that, as is essential to any efficient insertion algorithm, no actual data are moved within the tree.

{Global variables and data Types}

```
TYPE
  Pointer = ^TreeNode;
  TreeNode =
    RECORD
      LeftThread : boolean;
      LeftChild : Pointer;
      Data : char; {Or other appropriate type}
      RightChild : Pointer;
      RightThread : boolean
    END;

PROCEDURE InsertThreaded(Root : Pointer;
                         Item : char);
  {Procedure to insert Item into a threaded tree pointed to by Root.}

  {Local variables}

  VAR
    q, p, Parentq : Pointer;
    Left : boolean;

  BEGIN
    new(p);
    p^.Data := Item;
```

{Next allow this pointer to travel down appropriate branch of the tree until an insertion spot is found.}

```
    q:= Root;
    Parentq := NIL;
    REPEAT
      IF Item < q^.Data THEN
        BEGIN
        Parentq := q;
        q := q^.LeftChild;
        Left := true
        END
      ELSE
        BEGIN
        Parentq := q;
        q := q^.RightChild;
        Left := false
        END
```

UNTIL conditional controlling REPEAT

Parentq

Leaf node may be reached with
Left AND Parentq^.LeftThread
OR
Leaf node may be reached with
NOT Left AND Parentq^.RightThread

Parentq

```
    UNTIL (Left AND Parentq^.LeftThread) OR (NOT Left AND
                                  Parentq^.RightThread);
```

```
{Now insert p as the left or right child of Parentq.}

p^.LeftThread := true;
p^.RightThread := true;
IF Left THEN
  BEGIN
  p^.LeftChild := Parentq^.LeftChild;
  p^.RightChild := Parentq;
  Parentq^.LeftChild := p;
  Parentq^.LeftThread := false
  END

ELSE
  BEGIN
  p^.RightChild := Parentq^.RightChild;
  p^.LeftChild := Parentq;
  Parentq^.RightChild := p;
  Parentq^.RightThread := false
  END
END; {End InsertThreaded}
```

Efficiency Considerations for Threading a Tree. Deletion of a node from a threaded tree may be handled by considering the same cases that we discussed in Section 7.5. The only additional consideration to our previous discussion is the maintenance of the Boolean thread indicators. Hence, a threaded tree is a structure with very little overhead. The only new fields required are the threads. Moreover, in practice, if space limitations are severe, they may be incorporated into a bit of the left and right child pointers (though methods for doing this will be highly system-dependent). Threading thus represents a true bargain. By spending very little, one regains both the time and stack space that were required for recursion.

DESIGNER'S WORKBENCH

Planning for Problems, Change, and Debugging

Though all of us would like to claim that our programs always work correctly the first time and that there is never a need to apply fixes to our coding efforts, the reality of the system life cycle as described in Chapter 3 makes that an unrealizable goal. The complexity of problems posed by end users and the changing world in which those problems exist make it imperative for the software designer to think ahead and build debugging aids into the system. One such debugging aid which is particularly valuable is tracer output. Tracer output for a module is gathered by the placement of **write** statements at the beginning and end of a module. The purpose of these **write** statements is not to produce output which will be seen by the end users. Rather they are to trace the values of the data received by and information returned from a module.

For instance, consider the following version of the CurrentPathStillViable function from the VersatilePermutations program of this chapter.

```
FUNCTION CurrentPathStillViable(Level : integer) : boolean;

  { Return true if CurrentPermutation still contains a viable
    beginning for a permutation. }

  CONST
    DebugMode = true; { Switch to trigger tracer output. }

  VAR
    Viable : boolean;
    i : integer;

  BEGIN
    IF DebugMode THEN { BeginTracer output. }
      BEGIN
      writeln('Entering CurrentPathStillViable with Level = ', Level);
      writeln('and CurrentPermutation array');
      FOR i := 1 TO Level DO
         write(CurrentPermutation[i]);
      writeln
      END;    { End Tracer output. }
    Viable := true;
    i := 1;
    WHILE (i <= Level) AND Viable DO
      BEGIN
      Viable := (CurrentPermutation[i] <> CurrentPermutation[Level]);
      i := i + 1
      END;
    IF DebugMode THEN { Begin Tracer output. }
      writeln('Returning value ',Viable,' in CurrentPathStillViable');
                        { End Tracer output. }
    CurrentPathStillViable := Viable
  END;
```

This function differs in two respects from that which appears in the chapter. First, it contains an obscure bug (which you are asked to find in the Designer's Workbench Exercises). Second, it contains tracer output **write** statements which are executed upon entering and leaving the function. Notice that the execution of these tracers is dependent upon whether or not the constant DebugMode is set to **true** or **false**. With the current setting of DebugMode to **true**, we would see tracer output such as

```
Entering Current Permutation Still Viable with Level = 4
and CurrentPermutation array
1  2  3  4
Returning value false in CurrentPathStillViable
```

Clearly, this is not what we would expect if the module were working correctly. The tracer output has informed us that there is faulty logic somewhere inside this module.

From the perspective of working on an entire system, the use of such tracers upon entering and leaving each module in the system can help us quickly narrow the range of where we must look for the source of an error. That is, by examining the output of such tracers in the overall calling sequence of the system, we can determine exactly which module is the first to receive valid data but return erroneous information. With that knowledge, the task of debugging can be completed much more quickly.

We strongly recommend that the execution of such tracers be controlled by a DebugMode constant which can be set to **false** once the system is apparently working correctly. This is a much better approach than physically removing the **write** statements once the program is perfected. Why? Because the very nature of the system life cycle dictates that a program is never perfected. Future changes in the needs of the end users will necessitate modifications in the best of programs. The presence of tracer output controlled by the simple setting of a Boolean flag will greatly facilitate making those future modifications.

Designer's Workbench Exercises

1. Use the tracer output to determine the bug in the version of Current-PathStillViable which appears in this Designer's Workbench.
2. A bubble sort procedure with an obscure bug follows. Insert tracer output instructions at strategic points and use them to help in finding the bug.

```
PROCEDURE BubbleSort (n : integer; VAR KeyList : SortArray);
    {Given array KeyList containing entries in locations 1 through n,
     use bubble sort algorithm to return KeyList with these n
     entries arranged in ascending order.}

VAR i,j : integer;
    Temp : SortType;

BEGIN
    FOR i:=1 TO n-1 DO {Number of passes}
      FOR j:=i TO n-i DO {Number of comparisons on ith pass}
        IF KeyList[j] > KeyList[j+1] THEN {Must interchange}
          BEGIN
          Temp := KeyList[j];
          KeyList[j] := KeyList[j+1];
          KeyList[j+1] := Temp
          END
END; {BubbleSort}
```

3. An insertion sort procedure with an obscure bug follows. Add tracer output instructions at strategic points and use them to help in finding the bug.

```
PROCEDURE  InsertionSort (n : integer; VAR KeyList : SortArray);

{Given array KeyList containing entries in locations 1 through n, use
  insertion sort algorithm to return KeyList with these n entries
  arranged in ascending order. }

VAR  i,j : integer;
     Done : boolean;
     Temp: SortType;
```

```
BEGIN
  FOR i:=2 TO n DO {On pass i, the ith element must be positioned.}
    BEGIN
    j:=i;
    DONE:=false;   {As soon as the jth element > (j-1)th element,
                    we know it is appropriately positioned.}
    WHILE (j>=3) AND NOT Done DO
      IF Keylist [j] < Keylist [j-1] THEN
                {Move jth entry to position j-1.}
        BEGIN
        Temp := Keylist[j];
        KeyList[j] := KeyList[j-1];
        KeyList[j-1] := Temp;
        j:=j-1
        END
      ELSE    {We know array is now sorted in first i positions.}
        Done:=true  {So shut off the inner loop.}
    END {FOR loop}
END; {InsertionSort}
```

4. A selection sort procedure with an obscure bug follows. Insert tracer
   output instructions at strategic points and use them to help in locating
   and correcting the bug.

```
PROCEDURE SelectionSort (n : integer; VAR KeyList : SortArray);

    {Given array KeyList containing entries in locations 1 through n,
    use selection sort algorithm to return KeyList with those n
    entries arranged in ascending order.}

VAR  i, j, MaxPosition, Last : integer;
     Temp, MaxValue : SortType;

BEGIN
    FOR i:=1 TO n-1 DO {number of passes}
      BEGIN
      Last:=n-i;
      MaxPosition:=1; {Initially assume first is largest.}
      FOR j:=2 TO Last DO  {Test previous largest.}
        IF KeyList[j] > KeyList[MaxPosition]
            THEN MaxPosition := j;
                {Must change our view of largest.}
      Temp := KeyList[Last];   {Now swap largest outside the inner
            loop.}
      KeyList[Last] := KeyList[MaxPosition];
      KeyList[MaxPosition] := Temp
      END
END;  {SelectionSort}
```

5. Many Pascal compilers have sophisticated debuggers which allow you
   to momentarily halt program execution and examine the contents of key
   variables without having to actually insert **write** statements in your
   program. Explore the documentation for your Pascal compiler to find
   out what kind of debugging aids are provided. Use these aids to assist

you in debugging the procedures in Designer's Workbench Exercises 2, 3, and 4. ∎

Summary

Our closer look at recursion has explored both the high and low points of this technique. On the plus side, we have seen that recursion can be used to solve a complex class of problems by using trial-and-error, backtracking logic. This was illustrated in our discussion of the permutation problem and the Eight Queens Problem.

On the negative side, we have analyzed in greater depth the efficiency of recursion as a programming technique. This analysis demonstrated that recursion can consume a tremendous amount of resources, particularly in terms of its run-time efficiency. For instance, the run-time of the Towers of Hanoi algorithm was shown to be exponential in n; that is, an $O(2^n)$ algorithm.

To enhance the efficiency of implementations of recursive algorithms, we studied three methods of eliminating recursion. Tail recursive algorithms may be easily rewritten in nonrecursive fashion using an appropriate iterative control structure. Recursion may be eliminated from tree traversals by threading the tree. Finally, recursion may always be eliminated by simulating the system stack. The following table summarizes the advantages and disadvantages of each of these methods:

Method	Advantages	Disadvantages
Elimination of tail recursion via iterative control structures.	Will always be more space efficient because system stack not needed.	May not express the algorithm in as natural a fashion as recursion does.
Elimination of recursion from tree traversals by threading.	By allowing us to skip levels of a tree that would otherwise be encountered when returning from a recursive call, will generally be more time efficient. Allows recursive tree traversals in languages which do not support recursion.	Slight amount of space is expanded in storing Boolean thread indicators.
Elimination of recursion by simulating system stack.	Allows implementation of recursive methods in languages which do not support recursion. Fosters greater understanding of recursion.	Never achieves order of magnitude improvements in time or space efficiency.

Key Terms

binding time problem	LISP
Eight Queens Problem	permutation problem
eliminating tail recursion	simulation of system stack
generalized nested loops	threaded trees
inorder predecessor	tracer output
inorder successor	trial-and-error backtracking
inorder threads	

Exercises

1. Consider the following function to compute $n!$

```
FUNCTION Factorial (n : integer) : integer;

VAR i : integer;

BEGIN
  Factorial := 1;
  FOR i := 2 TO n DO
    Factorial := Factorial*i
END; {Factorial}
```

   Is this recursive or nonrecursive? Will it work? Explain why or why not.

2. Consider the VersatilePermutations program discussed in Section 8.2. Suppose that $n = 3$ in a particular run of this program and that we printed out the contents of the CurrentPermutation array each time the Try procedure was invoked in this run. How many times would the array be printed? What would be the overall output?

3. Consider the following representation of a binary tree via parallel arrays (with zero indicating a **NIL** pointer).

Tree

Location	LeftChild	Data	RightChild	
1	3	A	5	
2	7	B	11	
3	6	C	0	
4	0	D	0	**Root**
5	8	E	10	**1**
6	4	F	2	
7	0	G	0	
8	0	H	0	
9	0	K	0	
10	0	L	9	
11	0	I	0	

a. Draw the binary tree represented by this implementation.
b. By filling in the spaces in the following table, show the full memory representation for this tree with a header node and right threads (for an inorder traversal) added. Also indicate a new value for the root pointer.

Location	LeftChild	Data	RightChild	RightThread
1		A		
2		B		
3		C		
4		D		
5		E		
6		F		
7		G		
8		H		
9		K		
10		L		
11		I		
12				

Root

4. Consider the following tree:

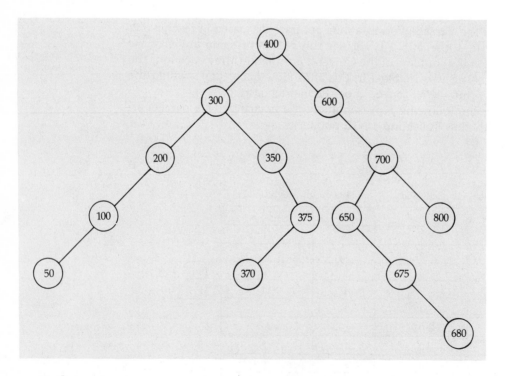

Redraw it as a threaded binary tree. Show the dummy header, inorder predecessor threads, and inorder successor threads in your drawing.

5. Consider the following program:

```
PROGRAM RecursiveTest(input,output);

   VAR    n : integer;
          a : ARRAY [1..16] OF integer;

   FUNCTION WhyMe(t,b,h : integer) : integer;

     VAR   m : integer;

     BEGIN
     writeln(b,h);               { <-- Note the output here.}
     m := (b + h) DIV 2;
     IF t < a[m] THEN
         WhyMe := WhyMe(t,b,m-1)
     ELSE IF t > a[m] THEN
         WhyMe := WhyMe(t,m+1,h)
     ELSE
         WhyMe := m
     END;   { WhyMe }

BEGIN
FOR n := 1 TO 16 DO
  read(a[n]);
readln;
read(n);
writeln( WhyMe(n,1,16) )    { <-- Note the output here. }
END.
```

Suppose that the following 16 numbers are entered in response to the first 16 **read**s.

12 18 20 34 45 47 50 51 57 60 68 69 70 80 82 84

Suppose also that 57 is entered in response to the **read**(n) instruction. What then will be the output of this program?

6. Suppose you used the permutations procedure of this chapter to compute all permutations of 1, 2, 3, and 4. What would the complete tree diagram of procedure calls look like for such a run? Can you generalize from this tree of procedure calls the efficiency of the permutations procedure? State your answer in big-O terms with respect to both stack size and number of stack operations.

7. Ackermann's function is defined recursively for two nonnegative integers m and n as follows:

$$\text{Ackermann}\,(m,n) = \begin{cases} n + 1 \text{ if } m = 0 \\ \text{Ackermann}\,(m - 1, 1) \text{ if } n = 0 \\ \text{Ackermann}\,(m - 1, \text{Ackermann}\,(m, n - 1)) \text{ otherwise} \end{cases}$$

Write recursive and nonrecursive versions of this function. Develop a tree of procedure calls for the recursive version when $m = 2$ and $n = 3$.

Attempt to deduce the big-O efficiency of the recursive version with respect to stack size and stacking operations.

8. Can any of the push operations in the NonrecursiveHanoi procedure of this chapter be eliminated in the interest of minimizing stack space and operations?

9. Explain why it is not possible to thread a tree for a postorder traversal.

10. Write a recursive procedure to process in reverse order the nodes on a singly linked list. Then rewrite this procedure in a nonrecursive fashion.

11. Consider the recursive description of Euclid's algorithm for computing greatest common divisors given in the Programming Problems for Chapter 6. Implement this algorithm as a nonrecursive procedure.

12. Rewrite PROGRAM VersatilePermutations in a fashion which takes into account the economies discussed in Section 8.2.

13. Write a procedure that uses a stack to achieve a nonrecursive postorder traversal of a binary tree.

14. Write a procedure that uses a stack to achieve a nonrecursive inorder traversal of a binary tree.

15. Write a procedure which uses the predecessor pointers in a threaded binary tree to generate a reverse inorder traversal.

16. Write a procedure to delete a node from a threaded binary tree which has the ordering property.

17. If the inorder predecessor pointers appearing in Figure 8.13 were not maintained, that is, if **NIL** pointers were stored in their place, it would still be possible to complete a threaded inorder traversal. Indeed we would only lose the ability to complete a threaded reverse inorder traversal. How would the procedure ThreadedInorder of this chapter need to be modified if no predecessor threads were maintained?

18. Redraw the threads in Figure 8.13 to indicate preorder traversals of the tree.

19. Write a Pascal procedure for the preorder traversal diagram suggested in exercise 18.

Programming Problems

1. Implement the registrar's system using a threaded binary tree implementation of a general list.

2. Write a program to complete the Eight Queens Problem.

3. There are five other teams in the same league as the Bay Area Brawlers. Over a given five-week period, the Brawlers must play each of the other teams exactly once. Using a recursion, write a program to determine the ways in which such a five-week schedule could be accomplished. For an added challenge, introduce more realistic scheduling considerations into this problem. For instance, have your program determine the ways in which a fifteen-game schedule could be constructed such that the Brawlers play each of the other teams exactly three times.

4. Write a procedure which uses a random number generator to produce mazes. One way of viewing a maze is as a two-dimensional array of records.

```
RECORD
  NorthBlocked,
  EastBlocked,
  SouthBlocked,
  WestBlocked  : boolean
END
```

At each square in the array, the Boolean fields are set to indicate whether or not we can proceed in the indicated direction. After your maze-generating procedure is working, develop a procedure which uses trial-and-error backtracking to solve the maze.

5. A transportation network such as the following can be represented as a two-dimensional integer array with rows and columns indexed by the cities in the network. The number stored at position (i, j) of such an array represents the distance of the link between two cities, with zero indicating that two cities are not directly linked.

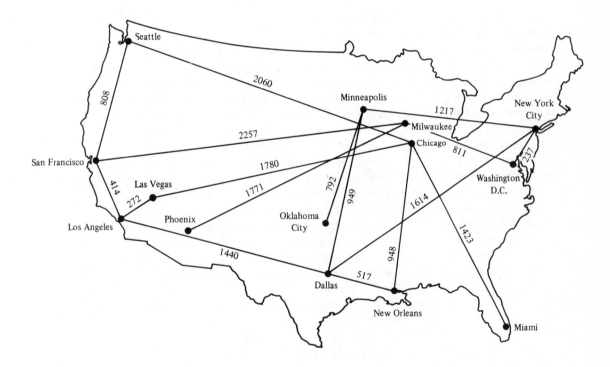

Write a program which, for input of two cities, will output all possible paths connecting the two cities. Then modify the program so that it only outputs the shortest path linking the two cities. (Achieve this latter modification using only the recursive techniques of this chapter, not Dijkstra's shortest-path algorithm described in Chapter 7.)

6. Another classic chess problem which can be solved by trial-and-error backtracking is known as the Knight's Tour. Given a chessboard with a knight initially placed at coordinates x_0, y_0, the problem is to specify a series of moves for the knight that will result in each board location being visited exactly once. From a given square on the chessboard, a

knight may move to any of the eight numbered squares in the following diagram:

	3		2	
4				1
		*		
5				8
	6		7	

* — Current Position

Write a program to find a valid Knight's Tour.

7. There is a famous theorem in mathematics which states that four colors are enough to color any map in a fashion which allows each region on the map to be a different color from any of its adjacent neighbors. Write a program which initially allows input of a map. One way of doing this is to input each region followed by a list of its adjacent neighbors. This information can then be stored in a two-dimensional Boolean array with rows and columns indexed by region names. Store **true** at row i, column j if region i and region j are neighbors; otherwise store **false**. Once your program has appropriately stored the information associated with the input map, it should use trial-and-error backtracking to find a pattern for coloring the map with four colors. Note that the Four-Color Theorem from mathematics guarantees that such a pattern can be found.

8. Write a program to find a solution to the following stable marriage problem (or indicate that no solution exists for the input data). According to this problem, we have n men and n women, each of whom has stated distinct preferences for their possible partners. The data regarding these preferences is the input for this problem. It can be stored in two two-dimensional arrays: one in which each woman has rated each of the men as 1st choice, 2nd choice, . . . , nth choice and another in which each man has similarly rated each of the women. Given this input, a solution to the stable marriage problem is to find n couples (marriages) such that

1. Each man is part of exactly one couple (marriage).

2. Each woman is part of exactly one couple (marriage).

3. There does not exist a man and a woman who are not married but who would prefer each other to their spouses.

If a pair as specified in requirement 3 does exist, then the assignment of n couples is said to be unstable and should be avoided. Note that the stable marriage problem is representative of many real-life problems in which assignments have to be made according to preferences.

9. Write a program to analyze football team scores by computing the point spread for any team A playing any team B. Your program should compute the point spreads for

Level I Analysis: Team A played B in past
Level II Analysis: Average point spreads for situations such as
                          A played C—point spread 3
                          C played B—point spread 7
                          Total point spread 10
Level III Analysis: Average point spread for situations such as
                          A played C—point spread 3
                          C played D—point spread −14 (C lost)
                          D played B—point spread 7
                          Total point spread −4
Level IV Analysis: Average point spreads for situations such as
                          A played C—point spread 3
                          C played D—point spread −14
                          D played E—point spread 21
                          E played B—point spread 4
                          Total point spread 14

All level II point spreads are then averaged for a final level II point spread figure. Point spreads are similarly averaged for levels III and IV. Items that potentially need to be stacked in this program include

- ☐ Accumulated point spread at current position.

- ☐ Number of scores reflected in the accumulated point spread at current position.

- ☐ Current position, that is, team A playing team B.

- ☐ Path to the current position, that is, teams played to get to the current position.

9

More Powerful Sorting Methods

Hadley's Law: Don't ever confuse motion with progress.

9.1

Introductory Considerations

In Chapter 2 we analyzed three simple sorting algorithms: bubble sort, insertion sort, and selection sort. We also discussed a technique called a pointer sort which can be combined with any of these three algorithms to minimize data movement when large records are being sorted by a particular key field. The essence of the pointer sort is to maintain an array of pointers which dictates the logical order of the records in an array of records. When the sorting algorithm dictates a swap, only the pointers must be interchanged, not the actual records.

With all three of our sorting algorithms, however, we ran into a barrier. This barrier was a run-time efficiency of $O(n^2)$ comparisons. Since the pointer sort technique reduces data movement but not the number of comparisons, this barrier exists whether or not we incorporate the pointer sort idea into the sorting algorithm. Our goal in this chapter is to study sorting algorithms that break the $O(n^2)$ comparisons barrier. These new algorithms will make use of what we have learned since Chapter 2. In particular, both recursion and a conceptual understanding of trees are essential prerequisites to analyzing these more powerful methods.

Before we begin a systematic presentation of these new algorithms, recall the general setup for sort algorithms which was presented in Chapter 2; this included the following Pascal declarations:

```
CONST MaxIndex = {Appropriate size for array to be sorted};

TYPE SortType = {Any type with a well-defined ordering};
     SortArray = ARRAY [1..MaxIndex] OF SortType;
```

Our algorithms for this chapter will be presented in the context of sorting arrays in ascending order. However, the algorithms apply more generally to any list whose elements can be directly accessed (for example, random access files) and they can be easily modified to sort in descending order. Moreover, one of the methods we will discuss (merge sort) actually does not require direct access into the list. Hence it could be applied to lists which are just sequentially accessible such as sequential files and linked lists.

—— **9.2**

The Shell Sort Algorithm

The shell sort, named after its inventor D. L. Shell, incorporates the logic of the insertion sort to a certain extent. However, instead of sorting the entire array at once, it first divides the array into smaller, noncontiguous segments which are then separately sorted using the insertion sort. The advantage of doing this is twofold. First, where a comparison dictates a swap of two data items in a segment, this swap within a noncontiguous segment of the array moves an item a greater distance within the overall array than the swap of adjacent array entries in the usual insertion sort. This means that one swap is more likely to place an element closer to its final location in the array when using shell sort than when using the simple insertion sort. For instance, a large-valued entry which appears near the front of the array will more quickly move to the tail end of the array because each swap moves it a greater distance in the array. The second advantage of dividing the array into segments is tied to the first. That is, because early passes tend to move elements closer to their final destination than early passes would in a straight insertion sort, the array becomes partially sorted quite fast. The fact that the array is likely to become partially sorted relatively early then allows the embedded insertion sort logic to make more frequent use of its loop shutoff check. (Recall that this check is what makes the insertion sort particularly efficient for arrays that are partially sorted.)

An example will help clarify the shell sort rationale discussed in the previous paragraph. Suppose we have an array Key containing nine integers which appears originally as

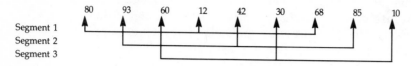

We first divide this into three segments of three elements each.

$$
\begin{array}{ccc}
80 & 12 & 68 \longrightarrow \quad \text{Segment 1} \\
93 & 42 & 85 \longrightarrow \quad \text{Segment 2} \\
60 & 30 & 10 \longrightarrow \quad \text{Segment 3}
\end{array}
$$

and sort each of the segments.

$$
\begin{array}{ccc}
12 & 68 & 80 \\
42 & 85 & 93 \\
10 & 30 & 60
\end{array}
$$

The original array, partially sorted, now appears as

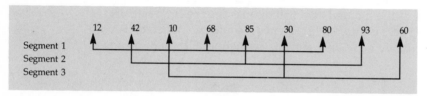

We divide this partially sorted array as

$$
\begin{array}{ccccc}
12 & 10 & 85 & 80 & 60 \longrightarrow \text{Segment 1} \\
42 & 68 & 30 & 93 & \longrightarrow \text{Segment 2}
\end{array}
$$

These segments are then sorted and the array Key takes the form

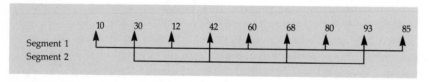

Finally, this array is sorted as one segment; 12 and 30, and 93 and 85 are swapped to give us the sorted array

$$10 \quad 12 \quad 30 \quad 42 \quad 60 \quad 68 \quad 80 \quad 85 \quad 93$$

The key to the shell sort algorithm is that the whole array is first fragmented into k segments for some number k, where k is preferably a prime number. If the size of the array Key is n, then the segments are

```
Key[1], Key[k+1], Key[2*k+1], ...
Key[2], Key[k+2], Key[2*k+2], ...
    .
    .
    .
Key[k], Key[2*k], Key[3*k], ...
```

Because each segment is sorted, the whole array is partially sorted after the first pass. For the next pass, the value of k is reduced, which increases the size of each segment, hence reducing the number of segments. Preferably, the next value of k is also chosen so that it is prime relative to its previous value, or relatively prime. (Two integers are said to be relatively prime to each other if they have no common factor greater than 1.) The process is repeated until $k = 1$, at which point the array is sorted. The insertion sort is applied to each segment, so each successive segment is partially sorted. Consequently, the later applications of the insertion sort become very efficient, dramatically increasing the overall efficiency of the shell sort.

To emphasize the fashion in which the shell sort algorithm relies on the logic of insertion sort, we first present a SegmentedInsertionSort procedure which arranges each of k segments in an n–element array into ascending order.

```
PROCEDURE SegmentedInsertionSort (VAR Key : SortArray;
                                  n,k : integer);

   { View n-element array Key as divided into k segments. Arrange each
     segment into order using insertion sort logic. }

VAR i,j : integer;
    Temp : SortType;

BEGIN

FOR i := k+1 TO n DO
   BEGIN
   j := i-k; {j counts down through current segment}
   WHILE j > 0 DO
      IF key[j] > Key[j+k] THEN
         {Adjacent entries in current segment compared.}

         BEGIN  {Interchange if out of order}
         Temp := Key [j];
         Key [j] := Key [j+k];
         Key [j+k] := Temp;
         j := j-k
         END
      ELSE
         j := 0  {To shut off j loop}
   END  {FOR}
END; {SegmentedInsertionSort}
```

With n=6 and k=3, array is divided into 3 segments of 2 elements each.

80	12	Segment 1
93	42	Segment 2
60	30	Segment 3

Sort each of the segments:

12	80
42	93
30	60

Given the SegmentedInsertionSort procedure, we now merely call on this with values of *k* that become successively smaller. Eventually, SegmentedInsertionSort must be called with *k* = 1 to guarantee that the array, viewed as one segment, is completely sorted. The procedure ShellSort that follows illustrates these successive calls to SegmentedInsertionSort for values of *k* which are repeatedly halved.

```
PROCEDURE ShellSort (VAR Key : SortArray; n : integer);

  {Sort first n elements of Key into ascending order.}

VAR k : integer;

  PROCEDURE SegmentedInsertionSort (VAR Key : SortArray;
                                    n,k : integer);

      {As discussed earlier, this procedure would be local to ShellSort.}

BEGIN
k := n DIV 2;    {k represents current number of segments.}
WHILE k > 0 DO
  BEGIN
  SegmentedInsertionSort (Key, n, k);
  k := k DIV 2    {Reduce number of segments}
  END
END;  {ShellSort}
```

Efficiency of the Shell Sort

The shell sort is also called the diminishing increment sort because the value of *k* (the number of segments) continually decreases. The method is more efficient if the successive values of *k* are kept relatively prime to each other. D. E. Knuth has mathematically estimated that, with relatively prime values of *k*, the shell sort will execute in an average time proportional to $O(n(\log_2 n)^2)$. (See Donald E. Knuth, *Searching and Sorting*. Vol 3 of *The Art of Computer Programming*. (Menlo Park, Calif.: Addison-Wesley, 1973).) However, the sort will work for any values of *k*, as long as the last value of *k* is 1. For instance, note that in the version of ShellSort we have given, the successive values of *k* will not be relatively prime for many possible values of the parameter *n*. When the values of *k* are not relatively prime, then the efficiency of the shell sort is of the order $O(n^r)$, where $1 < r < 2$. The particular value of *r* makes the sort less efficient than $O(n(\log_2 n)^2)$ for large values of *n*, but better than the $O(n^2)$ methods of Chapter 2.

The shell sort is most efficient on arrays that are nearly sorted. In fact, the first chosen value of *k* is large to insure that the whole array is fragmented into small individual arrays, for which the insertion sort is highly effective. Each subsequent sort causes the entire array to be more nearly sorted, so that the efficiency of the insertion sort as applied to larger partially sorted arrays is increased. Trace through a few examples to convince yourself that the partially ordered status of the array for one value of *k* is not affected by subsequent partial sorts for a different value of *k*.

It is not known with what value of k the shell sort should start, but Knuth suggests a sequence of values such as 1, 3, 7, 15, . . . , for reverse values of k; that is, the $(j + 1)$th value is two times the jth value plus 1. There are other possible values of k suggested by Knuth, but generally the initial guess at the first value of k is all that you need. The initial guess will depend on the size of the array, and, to some extent, on the type of data being sorted.

_____ 9.3

The Quick Sort Algorithm

Even though the shell sort provides a significant advantage in run-time over its $O(n^2)$ predecessors, its average efficiency of $O(n(\log_2 n)^2)$ may still not be good enough for large arrays. The next group of methods, including the quick sort, have an average execution time of $O(n(\log_2 n))$, which is the best that can be achieved. Compared to $O(n(\log_2 n)^2)$ or $O(n^r)$ for $1 < r < 2$, an $O(n(\log_2 n))$ sort is often a good choice as the main vehicle for large sorting jobs.

The essence of the quick sort algorithm is to rely on a subordinate algorithm to partition the array. The process of partitioning involves moving a data item, called the pivot, in the correct direction just enough for it to reach its final place in the array. The partitioning process, therefore, reduces unnecessary interchanges and potentially moves the pivot a great distance in the array without forcing it to be swapped into intermediate locations. Once the pivot item is chosen, moves are made so that data items to the left of the pivot are less than (or equal to) it, whereas those to the right are greater (or equal). The pivot item is thus in its correct position. The quick sort algorithm then recursively applies the partitioning process to the two parts of the array on either side of the pivot until the entire array is sorted.

We shall illustrate the mechanics of this partitioning logic by applying it to an array of numbers. Suppose the array Key contains integers initially arranged as

15   20   5   8   95   12   80   17   9   55

Figure 9.1 shows a partitioning pass applied to this array. The following steps are involved:

1. Remove the first data item, 15, as the pivot, mark its position, and scan the array from right to left, comparing data item values with 15. When you find the first smaller value, remove it from its current position and put in position Key[1]. (This is shown in line 2.)

2. Scan line 2 from left to right beginning with position Key[2], comparing data item values with 15. When you find the first value greater than 15, extract it and store it in the position marked by parentheses in line 2. (This is shown in line 3.)

3. Begin the right to left scan of line 3 with position Key[8] looking for a value smaller than 15. When you find it, extract it and store it in

Line Number	Key[1]	Key[2]	Key[3]	Key[4]	Key[5]	Key[6]	Key[7]	Key[8]	Key[9]	Key[10]
1	15*	20	5	8	95	12	80	17	9	←55
2	9	→20	5	8	95	12	80	17	( )	55
3	9	( )	5	8	95	12	80	←17	20	55
4	9	12	→5	8	95	( )	80	17	20	55
5	9	12	5	8	( )	95	←80	17	20	55
6	9	12	5	8	15	95	80	17	20	55

FIGURE 9.1

Each call to QuickSort partitions an array segment

the position marked by the parentheses in line 3. (This is shown in line 4.)

4. Begin scanning line 4 from left to right at position Key[3]. Find a value greater than 15, remove it, mark its position, and store it inside the parentheses in line 4. (This is shown in line 5.)

5. Now, when you scan line 5 from right to left beginning at position Key[7], you find no value smaller than 15 before you come to a parenthesized position, position Key[5]. This is the location to put the first data item, 15. (This is shown in line 6.) At this stage, 15 is in its correct place relative to the final sorted array.

Notice that all values to the left of 15 are less than 15, and all values to the right of 15 are greater than 15. The method will still work if two values are the same. The process can now be applied recursively to the two segments of the array on the left and right of 15. Notice that it is these recursive calls which eventually result in the entire array's being sorted. The result of any one call to **PROCEDURE** QuickSort is merely to partition a segment of the array so that the pivotal item is positioned with everything to its left being less than or equal to it and everything to its right being greater than or equal.

The procedure Partition that follows achieves one such partitioning pass in the overall QuickSort algorithm. The indices i and j represent the pointers that move from the left and right respectively until they meet at the appropriate location for the Pivot. The pivotal value is initially chosen to be Key[i]. We will later discuss the possible implications of choosing a different pivotal value. Note that it is crucial for Partition to return in PivotPoint the position where the pivotal value was finally inserted. As we shall see, this information will allow the QuickSort procedure which calls upon Partition to determine whether or not a recursive out has been reached.

```
PROCEDURE Partition (VAR Key : SortArray;
                     i,j : integer;
                     VAR PivotPoint : integer);
```

```
{Using Key[i] as pivotal value, partition the Key array between indices
 i and j.  Return final position of pivotal value in PivotPoint.}

VAR Pivot : Sorttype;

BEGIN
Pivot := Key[i];
WHILE i < j DO
  BEGIN
  {Begin right-to-left scan}
  WHILE (Pivot < Key[j]) AND (i < j) DO
    j := j-1;
  IF j <> i THEN
    {Move jth entry to left side of partition.}
    BEGIN
    Key [i] := Key [j];
    i := i+1
    END;
```

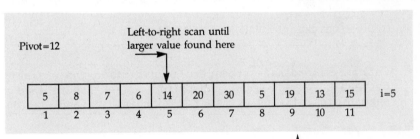

```
  {Begin left-to-right scan.}
  WHILE (Pivot > Key[i]) AND (i < j) DO
    i := i+1;
  IF j <> i THEN
    {Move ith entry to right side of partition.}
    BEGIN
    Key [j] := Key [i];
    j := j-1
    END
  END; {WHILE i < j}
```

```
{i and j met somewhere between
  their initial settings.}
Key[j] := Pivot;
PivotPoint := j
END; {Partition}
```

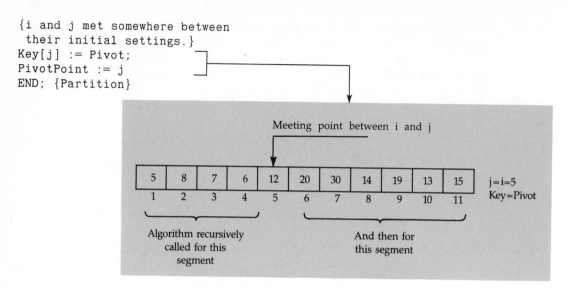

Given the previous Partition procedure, QuickSort itself must call on Partition and then use the returned value of PivotPoint to decide whether or not recursive calls are necessary to perform more refined partitioning of the segments to the left and right of PivotPoint. The recursive logic for this decision is given in the following **PROCEDURE** QuickSort. Partition would be incorporated as a subordinate local procedure within QuickSort.

```
PROCEDURE QuickSort (VAR Key : SortArray;
                     Lower, Upper : integer);

  {Call on subordinate procedure to partition the segment of Key array
   between Lower and Upper subscripts.  Then recursively partition
   segment to left and right of PivotPoint to complete the sort.}

VAR  PivotPoint : integer;

  PROCEDURE Partition (VAR Key : SortArray;
                       i,j : integer;
                       VAR PivotPoint : integer);
    {Previously discussed Partition procedure would appear here,
     subordinate to QuickSort.}

BEGIN
Partition (Key, Lower, Upper, PivotPoint);

{Recursive calls partition left and right segments.}
IF Lower < PivotPoint THEN
    QuickSort(Key, Lower, PivotPoint-1);
IF Upper > PivotPoint THEN
    QuickSort(Key, PivotPoint + 1, Upper)
END; {QuickSort}
```

For instance, after the first call to QuickSort for a partitioning pass on the data in Fig. 9.1, we would then recursively call on QuickSort with Lower = 1 and Upper = 4. This would trigger deeper-level recursive calls from which we would ultimately return, knowing that the segment of the array between indices 1 and 5 is now sorted. This return would be followed by a recursive call to QuickSort with Lower = 6 and Upper = 10. The entire tree of recursive calls to QuickSort for the data of Figure 9.1 is given in Figure 9.2. You should trace through the procedure to verify this call-return pattern.

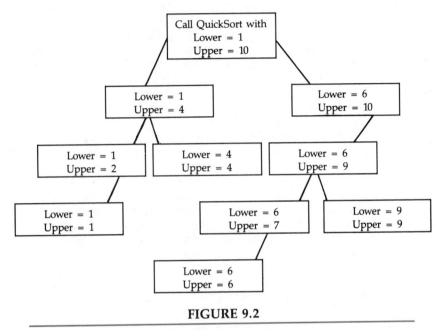

FIGURE 9.2

Tree of (recursive) calls to QuickSort for data in
Figure 9.1

Efficiency of the Quick Sort

As mentioned earlier, the average run-time efficiency of the quick sort is $O(n\log_2 n)$, which is the best that has been achieved for a large array of size n. In the best case, it is quite easy to provide a rationale for this $O(n\log_2 n)$ figure. This best case occurs when each array segment recursively passed to QuickSort partitions at its midpoint; that is, the appropriate location for each pivotal value in the series of recursive calls is the midpoint of the segment being partitioned. In this case,

> 1 call to QuickSort (the first) is made with a segment of size n.
> 2 calls to QuickSort are made with segments of size n **DIV** 2.
> 4 calls to QuickSort are made with segments of size n **DIV** 4.
> 8 calls to QuickSort are made with segments of size n **DIV** 8.
>
> .   .
>   .   .
> .   .
>
> n calls to QuickSort are made with segments of size 1.

Since each call with a segment of size m requires $O(m)$ comparisons, it is clear that k calls with segments of size n **DIV** k will require $O(n)$ compari-

A Relevant Issue . . .

Fourth Generation Languages: Getting Users More Involved

Two trends have marked the development of computer languages: the ease with which they can be used and the number of fundamental machine operations associated with a single command in the language. The first generation of computer languages resembled what we typically call assembler languages. Such languages are not standard across machines, and usually one instruction in such a language corresponds to one fundamental machine operation. For instance, to achieve the equivalent of Pascal's

```
A := B + C
```

instruction in assembler, we may have to code

```
LDA B {Load contents of B into
accumulation.}
ADD C {Add contents of C to
accumulator.}
STA A {Store accumulator in memory
location A}
```

Such first generation languages are certainly not convenient for general users and for most programmers. However, learning them is appropriate for computer science majors since the development of certain software (for example, operating systems and compilers) may still be tied to these languages and an understanding of them provides a basis for certain efficiency considerations even when working in a high-level language like Pascal.

The second generation of computer languages was marked by a more powerful ratio of fundamental machine operations to each instruction in the language. In languages such as FORTRAN and BASIC, one instruction such as

```
DISCRIMINANT = B*B - 4*A*C
```

could generate all the appropriate machine-level instructions with the programmer never having to worry about such details. To use the abstraction terminology that has appeared throughout this book, second generation languages raised the programmer's level of abstraction in a way which focused attention on the problem to be solved instead of on an intricate knowledge about how a particular computer worked. The obvious benefit of this higher level of abstraction was that solutions to more complex problems could be developed.

The missing ingredient in second generation languages was the ability to program in a structured way. Typically **GOTO**s were required to implement a logical construct, and methods of parameter passing between procedures were often quite limited. These problems were alleviated by third generation languages such as Pascal, Modula-2, and Ada. These are the languages that are frequently the cornerstones of modern computer science curricula. Notice that these third generation languages are still

sons. Hence the total number of comparisons resulting from the preceding sequence of calls will be $O(n\log_2 n)$.

If segments partition away from the midpoint, the efficiency of quick sort begins to deteriorate. In the worst case situation, when the array is already sorted, the efficiency of the quick sort may drop down to $O(n^2)$ due to the continuous right-to-left scan all the way to the last left boundary. In the Exercises at the end of the chapter, you will explore how the worst case situation is affected by your choice of the pivotal element.

You may wonder how large a stack is needed to sort an array of size n. (Remember that this stack is implicitly created even when you use a lan-

geared to a programmer's mind-set. A typical "computer literate" user finds them difficult to use and hence relies on systems analysts and programmers to develop applications in them.

What are fourth generation languages? This is difficult to pinpoint because they are just beginning to emerge. Hence, no universal standards for them have been developed. However, it is evident that they offer continued evolution along the two trend lines we have already cited. They are easier to use, allowing statements with near-English syntax. For example,

```
SORT REGISTRAR-LIST IN ASCENDING
ORDER USING STUDENT-NAME
```

is typical of a command in such a fourth generation language (sometimes referred to as 4GL). It is also evident from this example that the issuer of such a 4GL command gets significantly more work from the computer per command than a programmer in a third generation language. Again we are witnessing an elevation in the level of abstraction at which the user may work. Sorting is a particularly good example of this. Users of a 4GL will not have to understand sorting algorithms because all they have to do is issue the command SORT. By contrast, developers of software in third generation languages often had to develop and implement their own sorting algorithms.

The prediction often made is that 4GLs will become so easy to use and so powerful in their commands that users will be able to perform an increasing number of applications for themselves. What does this portend for those of us in the computer profession? There may well be less demand for applications programmers in the future. Such programmers typically write code specifically for one user's application, and 4GLs may well allow users to take over many such applications. This is good from the users' perspective because users will become more involved in the software systems as they are developed; hence such a system should better meet users' needs. The computer specialist, instead of turning out code in a third generation language, may well have to become an expert at the use of various 4GLs and act on a consulting basis to users who are running into problems with particularly complex applications.

What about the need for computer science majors to study sorting algorithms? Will 4GLs make this a necessity of the past? Hardly. When a user issues the SORT command in a 4GL, that command must somehow translate into an appropriate sorting algorithm at a level from which the user is shielded. Moreover, that user will expect a quick response to the SORT command. Hence the need to understand sorting algorithms will shift from the developers of particular applications to the developers of the 4GLs themselves. At this level, the efficiency of the sort algorithm used by the 4GL will be critical to its survival in what promises to be a very competitive market.

guage that permits recursion.) Knuth has mathematically estimated that the size of the stack cannot exceed $(1+\log_2((1/3)(n+1)))$. (See D. E. Knuth's text, *Searching and Sorting,* cited toward the end of Section 9.2.)

9.4

The Heap Sort Algorithm

The heap sort is a sorting algorithm which is roughly equivalent to the quick sort; its average efficiency is $O(n\log_2 n)$ for an array of size n. The method, originally described by R. W. Floyd, has two phases. In the first phase, the array containing the n data items is viewed as equivalent to a full binary tree. That is, the array to be sorted is viewed as the linear representation of a full binary tree containing n items (see Chapter 7). (If you want to read Floyd's description of this method, see his article, entitled "Algorithm 245: Tree Sort3" found in *Communications of the ACM 7* (1964):701.)

As an example, suppose we wish to sort the following array:

| 11 | 1 | 5 | 7 | 6 | 12 | 17 | 8 | 4 | 10 | 2 |

The first-phase tree appears as shown in Figure 9.3.

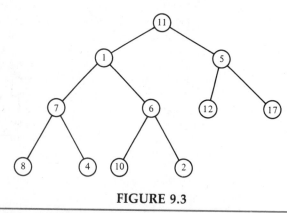

FIGURE 9.3

Full binary tree corresponding to array

The goal of phase 1 is now to sort the data elements along each path from leaf node level to the root node. If we wish to sort in ascending order, then the numbers along any path from leaf node to root should be in increasing order. Eventually, after phase 1, the tree will be a heap as described in Chapter 7. That is, the data item at each node will be greater than or equal to both of its children. To achieve this, we take the following steps:

1. Process the node which is the parent of the rightmost node on the lowest level. If its value is less than the value of its largest child, swap these values; otherwise do nothing.

2. Move left on the same level. Compare the value of the parent node with the values of the children. If the parent is smaller than the largest child, swap them.

3. When the left end of this level is reached, move up a level, and, beginning with the rightmost parent node, repeat step 2. Continue swapping the original parent with the larger of its children until it is larger than its children. In effect, the original parent is being walked down the tree in a fashion which insures that numbers will be in increasing order along the path.

4. Repeat step 3 until the root node has been processed.

Figure 9.4 shows these steps applied to Figure 9.3.

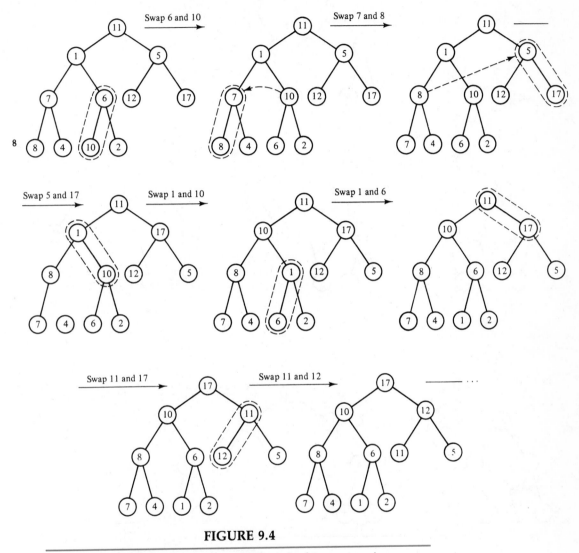

FIGURE 9.4

Phase 1 of heap sort applied to the binary tree in
Figure 9.3

Phase 2 of the heap sort finds the node with the largest value in the tree
and cuts it from the tree. This is then repeated to find the second largest
value, which is also removed from the tree. The process continues until
only two nodes are left in the tree; they are then exchanged if necessary.
The precise steps for phase 2 are as follows:

1. Swap the root node with the bottom rightmost child, and sever this
   new bottom rightmost child from the tree. This is the largest value.

2. Continue swapping the new root value with the larger of its children until it is not exceeded by either child. In effect, this new root

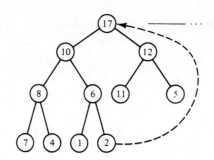

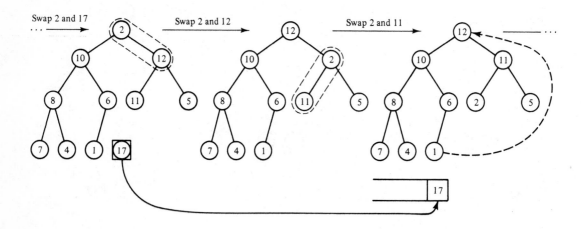

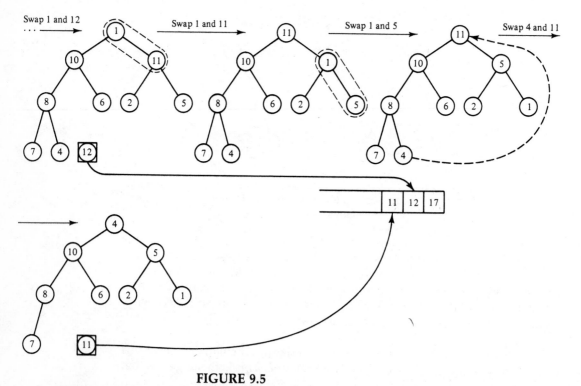

FIGURE 9.5

Phase 2 of the heap sort for three values

value is now being walked down a path in the tree to insure that all paths retain values arranged in ascending order from leaf node to root node. That is, the tree is being restored to a heap.

3. Repeat steps 1 and 2 until only one element is left.

Phase 2 of the heap sort begun in Figure 9.4 is shown in Figure 9.5 for the three highest values.

Both phase 1 and phase 2 use the same strategy of walking a parent down a path of the tree via a series of swaps with its children. The following procedure WalkDown isolates this crucial subordinate algorithm. In the linear representation of a tree assumed by WalkDown, the assignment statement $k := 2 * i$ will make k reference the left child of the node indicated by i. That is, this statement will allow us to descend a level deeper into the tree.

```
PROCEDURE WalkDown (VAR Key : SortArray; j, n : integer);

  {This procedure repeatedly exchanges a parent with the child of greatest
   value until the parent is larger than both children.  j is the index of
   original parent and n is the logical size of array.}
```

*The miracle is that all 4 billion 83 million of us fit somewhere into a
computer*

```
VAR  i,k : integer;
     Ref : SortType;
     FoundSpot : boolean;

BEGIN {WalkDown}
  FoundSpot := false;
  i := j;
  Ref := Key[i];
  {Key [i] will move along the appropriate path in tree.}
  k := 2*i; {Initially k references left child.}

  WHILE (k <= n) AND NOT FoundSpot DO
  BEGIN
    IF k < n THEN {Have k reference largest child.}
       IF Key[k+1] > Key[k] THEN
          k := k+1;
    IF Key[k] > Ref THEN {Child must move up.}
       BEGIN
       Key[i] := Key[k];
       i := k;
       k := 2*i
       END
    ELSE  {Appropriate spot has been found.}
       FoundSpot := true
  END;
  Key[i] := Ref
END;  {WalkDown}
```

Key[k] larger of

IF Key[k] is larger than Ref then it moves up

With the essential WalkDown logic isolated in a separate procedure, Phases 1 and 2 of HeapSort may now be easily developed. The loop for phase 1 repeatedly calls on WalkDown to form the tree into a heap. Then a loop for phase 2 repeatedly swaps the root of the tree with the last child and calls on WalkDown to allow this new root to find an appropriate position in the heap.

```
PROCEDURE  HeapSort (VAR Key : SortArray; n : integer);

  {Apply HeapSort algorithm to n elements of array Key.  Use internal
   procedure WalkDown to move item down path in tree.}

VAR  y : integer
     Temp : SortType;
```

```
{Here WalkDown would be located as a procedure local to HeapSort.}

   PROCEDURE WalkDown (VAR Key : SortArray; j,n : integer);

BEGIN  {HeapSort}

{First phase 1 arranges the tree into a heap.}

y := n DIV 2   {y starts at the last node to have child.}
WHILE  y > 0 DO
   BEGIN
   WalkDown (Key, y, n);
   y := y-1
   END;

{Phase 1 done.  Now begin phase 2.}

{In phase 2, y is used to point at the current last array slot.}

y := n;
WHILE y > 1 DO
   BEGIN
   {Interchange root with bottom right leaf node.} ───────────┐
   Temp := Key[1];                                            │
   Key[1] := Key[y];                                          ↓
   Key[y] := Temp;
   y := y-1;
   WalkDown (Key,1,y)
   END  (While)
END;  {HeapSort}
```

Swap these two and then remove leaf node from further consideration.

Efficiency of the Heap Sort

It is relatively easy to deduce that the heap sort requires $O(n\log_2 n)$ comparisons. To see this, note that the phase 1 loop in the preceding Pascal procedure will execute $n/2$ times. Inside this loop we call WalkDown, which in turn has a loop that will execute at most $\log_2 n$ times (because it merely follows a path down a binary tree). Hence phase 1 requires at most $(n/2) * \log_2 n$ iterations at its deepest level. Phase 2 may be similarly analyzed. The phase 2 loop iterates n times. Within each iteration, WalkDown is called, resulting in at most $\log_2 n$ nested iterations. Thus phase 2 requires at most $n * \log_2 n$ iterations at its deepest level. Overall, we get

$$1.5 \, n * \log_2 n$$

as an upper bound for the number of iterations required by the combination of phases 1 and 2.

Thus, both quick sort and heap sort yield $O(n\log_2 n)$ efficiencies. In *Searching and Sorting*, referenced in Sections 9.2 and 9.3, Knuth has shown that, on the average, quick sort will be slightly faster since its big-O constant of proportionality will be smaller than that for heap sort. However, heap sort offers the advantage of guaranteeing an $O(n\log_2 n)$ efficiency regardless of the data being sorted. As we have already noted for quick sort, worst case data can cause its performance to deteriorate to $O(n^2)$.

_____ **9.5**

The Merge Sort Algorithm

The essential idea behind merge sort is to make repeated use of a procedure which merges two lists, each already in ascending order, into a third list, also arranged in ascending order. The merge procedure itself only requires sequential access to the lists. Its logic is similar to the method you would use if you were merging two sorted piles of index cards into a third pile. That is, start with the first card from each pile. Compare them to see which one comes first, transfer that one over to the third pile, and advance to the next card in that pile. Repeat the comparison, transfer, and advance operations until one of the piles runs out of cards. At that point, merely move what is left of the remaining pile over to the third merged pile. This logic is reflected in the generalized Merge procedure which follows. For reasons that will become apparent when we incorporate it into a full sorting procedure, this version of Merge begins with the two sorted lists stored in one array. The first list runs from subscript Lower to Mid of array Source. The second runs from subscript Mid + 1 to Upper of the same array. The merging of the two lists is generated in a second array Destination.

```
PROCEDURE Merge (VAR Source, Destination : SortArray;
                      Lower, Mid, Upper      : integer);

   {Assuming Source [Lower..Mid] and Source [Mid+1..Upper] are
     arranged in ascending order, merge them into Destination [Lower..Upper].}

VAR  s1, s2, d: integer; {Pointers into two Source lists and Destination}

BEGIN
{Initialize pointers}
s1 := Lower;
s2 := Mid+1;
d := Lower;

{Repeat comparison of current item from each list.}

REPEAT
  IF Source[s1] < Source[s2] THEN
    BEGIN
      Destination[d] := Source[s1];
      s1 := s1+1
    END
```

```
    ELSE
       BEGIN
        Destination[d] := Source[s2];
        s2 := s2+1
       END;
     d := d+1
UNTIL (s1 > Mid) OR (s2 > Upper);
{Move what is left of remaining list.}
IF (s1 > Mid) THEN
   REPEAT
     Destination[d] := Source[s2];
     s2 := s2+1;
     d := d+1
   UNTIL s2 > Upper
ELSE
   REPEAT
     Destination[d] := Source[s1];
     s1 := s1+1;
     d := d+1
   UNTIL s1 > Mid
END; {Merge}
```

Clearly Merge is an $O(n)$ algorithm where n is the number of items in the two lists to be merged. The question which remains to be answered is how Merge can be used to actually sort an entire array. To answer this we need another procedure called Order which will take the values in indices Lower through Upper of an array Source and arrange them in ascending order in subscripts Lower through Upper of another array called Destination. Notice that Order is itself almost a sorting procedure except that it produces a sorted list in a second array instead of actually transforming the array it originally receives. Our use of Order will be to obtain two sorted half-length sequences from our original array. Then we will use the Merge procedure we have already developed to merge the two sorted half-length sequences back into the original array. Of course, this merely defers our original question of how to use Merge to sort because now we are faced with the question of how Order will be able to produce two sorted half-length sequences. Here is where recursion enters the picture. To produce a sorted half-length sequence, we use Order to produce two quarter-length sequences and apply Merge to the results. Similarly, the quarter-length sequences are produced by calling on Order to produce eighth-length sequences and apply Merge to the results. The recursive out for this descent into shorter and shorter ordered sequences is when Order receives a sequence of length 1.

Given the crucial Order procedure, the MergeSort procedure itself is almost trivial. It need merely create a copy of the array to be sorted and then call on Order to sort the elements of the copy into the original. Note that, because Order continually calls on Merge and Merge cannot do its work within one array, the need to create a copy of the original array is unavoidable. Complete Pascal versions of MergeSort and Order follow:

```
PROCEDURE MergeSort (VAR Key : SortArray; n : integer);

    {MergeSort first n entries in array Key by making a copy of it and
     calling on Order to sort the copy back into Key.}
```

```
VAR    CopyKey : SortArray;
       i : integer;

   PROCEDURE Merge (VAR Source, Destination : SortArray;
                         Lower, Mid, Upper :      integer);

      {The previously developed Merge procedure would be inserted as a
       local procedure here.}

   PROCEDURE Order (VAR Source, Destination : SortArray;
                         Lower, Upper : integer);

    {Transfer Source [Lower..Upper] in ascending order to
     Destination [Lower..Upper].  Assume Destination passed in as copy
     of Source.}

   VAR Mid : integer;

   BEGIN {Order}

   IF Lower <> Upper THEN {Recursively call to get smaller pieces which are
                          then ordered.}

      BEGIN
        Mid := (Lower + Upper) DIV 2;
        Order (Destination, Source, Lower, Mid);
        Order (Destination, Source, Mid + 1, Upper);
        Merge (Source, Destination, Lower, Mid, Upper)
        END

   END; {Order}

BEGIN   {MergeSort}
{Make copy for call to Order.}
FOR i := 1 TO n DO
  CopyKey[i] := Key[i];
Order (CopyKey, Key, 1, n)

END; {MergeSort}
```

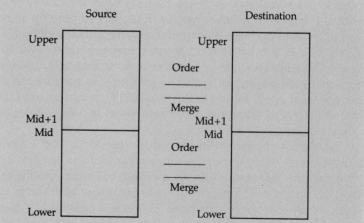

Recursively call Order to get two sorted segments in Source which are then merged into Destination. This requires that Destination originally be a copy of Source.

The tree of procedure calls in Figure 9.6 highlights the interaction between Order and Merge triggered by calling MergeSort with a sample array of size $n = 11$.

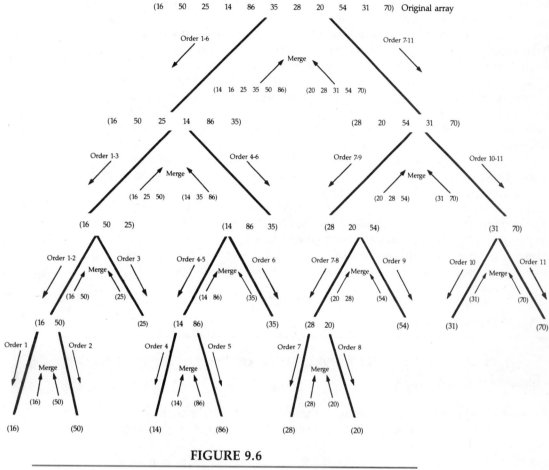

FIGURE 9.6

Tree of procedure calls to order and merge

Analysis of Merge Sort

From a tree of procedure calls such as that appearing in Figure 9.6, it is quite easy to deduce that merge sort requires $O(n\log_2 n)$ comparisons. The reasoning required for this deduction is as follows. All the merge operations across any given level of the tree will require $O(n)$ comparisons. There are $O(\log_2 n)$ levels to the full binary tree of procedure calls. Hence, the overall efficiency is the product $O(n\log_2 n)$. Notice that, like the heap sort, the merge sort can guarantee this efficiency regardless of the original data. That is, there is no worst case which can cause its efficiency to deteriorate (as there is for quick sort).

The price paid for using merge sort is in the memory space it requires. Of course, there is the stack space associated with recursion. More important, however, is the need for a duplicate copy of the array being sorted. In applications where the original array barely fits in memory, this space requirement will make merge sort totally impractical.

As steep as the memory price is, there is an added benefit to merge sort which makes it the only possible choice for certain applications. This benefit is that merge sort may be written in a way which necessitates only sequential access to the lists being manipulated. As we have presented it here, random access is required at only one point in the algorithm, namely, in the Merge procedure to access the second list beginning at subscript (Mid + 1) of Source. The need for this could have been eliminated by having Merge work with two separate source arrays. That is, we would merge ordered arrays Source1 and Source2 into Destination. This would be very costly with arrays since it would necessitate using three arrays to sort one array. However, it is less costly when the lists being manipulated are being implemented not by arrays but rather by dynamically allocated linked lists or sequential files. In both of these latter situations, the need to use sequential access would make the merge sort strategy the only appropriate sorting method. In the Exercises and Programming Problems at the end of the chapter, you will be asked to adapt MergeSort to such sequential implementations of a list. In particular, when the list exists in a file instead of main memory, the sorting method employed is said to be an external sort (as opposed to the internal sorts we have studied in this chapter).

DESIGNER'S WORKBENCH

Stepwise Refinement, Description of Algorithms, and Run-time Efficiency

For each of the more complex sort algorithms discussed in this chapter, we have found it convenient to initially focus on a subalgorithm. For ShellSort, this subalgorithm was the SegmentedInsertionSort; for QuickSort, it was Partition; for HeapSort, it was WalkDown; and for MergeSort, it was Merge. This parceling out of subordinate responsibilities to a well-defined, focused subalgorithm is consistent with the qualities of software design introduced in Chapters 1–3. In particular, it is illustrative of the stepwise refinement approach to problem solving. That is, break a complex problem down into smaller problems, solve these smaller problems, and then tie these solutions together to solve the original large problem. To that extent, presenting these more powerful sorting methods via subordinate algorithms and stepwise refinement has helped us considerably in describing and understanding the algorithms.

It is also important to note that describing and understanding algorithms is an issue which is separate from their actual implementation in a specific programming language and on a real machine. What are the implications of this separation of algorithm description and algorithm implementation? One such implication is the run-time cost associated with a procedure call. For instance, in specifying a sorting algorithm, it may be appropriate to call on a procedure to interchange two data items as in the following segment:

```
IF Key[j] > Key[j+1] THEN
  Swap (Key[j], Key[j+1])
```

However, do we really want to implement this segment by making an actual call to a procedure Swap or do we merely want to insert the three lines of code that will achieve the swap for us? The answer to this implementation question must consider the following:

□ The hidden costs of making a procedure call: pushing the return address on the system stack, allocating parameters and local variables on the system stack, and transferring control to and from the procedure.

□ How deeply embedded is the procedure call in the iterative structure of the calling module?

For instance, if the call to Swap in our previous example is contained within the inner loop of a BubbleSort procedure, then the hidden costs of making a procedure call to Swap will be compounded $O(n^2)$ times. This could be a considerable run-time expense. Depending upon the machine you are using, calling procedure Swap instead of directly inserting the code necessary to interchange may mean that your program spends more run-time handling the hidden cost of procedure calls than it does in actually interchanging data items.

In an example such as this, it is thus evident that, if large data sets are being sorted and if run-time efficiency is of primary importance, then we should implement our algorithm without actually calling on a procedure Swap to exchange items. It is important to keep in mind the distinction between algorithm description and algorithm implementation when making decisions about whether or not to proceduralize a given sequence of instructions. What may be appropriately isolated as a trivial subalgorithm at the time when a designer is concerned with describing an algorithm may carry with it a steep price if implemented as a trivial procedure which is called upon many times when the resulting program is put into use. In making the decision as to whether to use procedures or use in-line code when implementing an algorithm, the designer must carefully weigh run-time considerations with respect to the clarity and readability of code. One useful rule of thumb to apply in this regard is that, only in exceptional circumstances, should the code associated with a module exceed one printed page in length. This guideline allows in-line insertion of code for simple algorithmic units while at the same time assuring that the overall software system does not become unwieldy.

Designer's Workbench Exercises

1. For each of the sort algorithms we have studied in Chapters 3 and 9, estimate the overall hidden costs of making procedure calls if a Swap procedure were called to exchange two data items. Express your answer

COMPARISON OF SORTING ALGORITHMS

Sorting Method	Chapter	Number of Comparisons Proportional to the Number of Data Items Being Sorted (n)	Space Requirement	Additional Comments
Bubble	2	n^2	No additional overhead	Loop check allows early exit as soon as array is ordered.
Selection	2	n^2	No additional overhead	
Insertion	2	n^2	No additional overhead	Loop check allows early exit as soon as array is ordered.
Binary tree	7	Between $O(n^2)$ and $O(n \log_2 n)$ depending on original data and whether tree height-balanced	Pointers for tree and possible stack space for recursive traversals	
Shell	9	Between $O(n(\log_2 n)^2)$ and $O(n^{1.5})^2$ depending on increments used	No overhead	
Quick	9	$O(n \log_2 n)$ on the average but $O(n^2)$ for worst cases	Stack space for recursion	
Heap	9	$O(n \log_2 n)$	No overhead	
Merge	9	$O(n \log_2 n)$	Requires duplicate array and stack space for recursion	Since only requires sequential access, can be used for linked lists and sequential files.
Pointer	2	Depends on method with which it is combined	Requires list of pointers to maintain logical order	Can be combined with any method to substantially reduce size of data items being interchanged.

in big-O terms. For Designer's Workbench Exercises 2–5, implement the indicated procedure. Then determine whether the resulting procedure violates the one-page rule. Estimate in big-O terms the run-time savings achieved by this alternative implementation.

2. Implement the ShellSort procedure of this chapter using in-line code instead of calling the procedure SegmentedInsertionSort.

3. Implement the QuickSort procedure of this chapter using in-line code instead of calling the procedure Partition.

4. Implement the MergeSort procedure of this chapter using in-line code instead of calling the procedure Merge.

5. Implement the HeapSort procedure of this chapter using in-line code instead of calling the procedure WalkDown. What is the argument against inserting in-line code for WalkDown in HeapSort that does not apply in the previous three exercises?

Summary

This chapter has added four sorting algorithms to those already presented in Chapter 2. This give us a large variety of tools to choose from when there is a sorting job to be done. The comparison table on page 360 summarizes the pros and cons of each method.

Key Terms

assembler language
diminishing increment sort
external sort
fourth generation language (4GL)
heap sort
internal sort
merge sort

partition
pivot
quick sort
relatively prime
shell sort
stepwise refinement

Exercises

For Exercises 1–4, assume a seven-element array initially containing

60 12 90 30 64 8 6

1. Consider the MergeSort procedure given in this chapter. Note that this procedure contains a subordinate procedure called Order. Suppose that we were to insert the following tracer output immediately after the initial **BEGIN** for this procedure.

```
writeln(Lower,Upper);
FOR i := Lower to Upper {i declared as scratch variable.}
    write(Source[i]);
writeln;
```

What would we see as output from these tracers if we were to call on MergeSort?

2. Consider the QuickSort procedure given in this chapter. Suppose that we were to insert the following tracer output immediately after the initial **BEGIN** for this procedure.

```
writeln(Lower,Upper);
FOR i :=Lower TO Upper DO
   write(Key[i]);
writeln;
```

What would we see as output from these tracers if we were to call on QuickSort?

3. Consider the HeapSort procedure given in this chapter. Note that WalkDown is called at two points in the procedure: once in phase 1 and again in phase 2. Suppose that we were to trace the contents of the array being sorted after each call to WalkDown. What would we see as output if we called HeapSort?

4. Consider the ShellSort procedure given in this chapter. Suppose that we were to trace the contents of the array being sorted after each call to the procedure SegmentedInsertionSort. What would we see as output if we called ShellSort?

5. Repeat Exercise 1 for a six-element array which initially contains

   1 8 2 7 3 6

6. Repeat Exercise 2 for a six-element array which initially contains

   1 8 2 7 3 6

7. Repeat Exercise 3 for a six-element array which initially contains

   1 8 2 7 3 6

8. Repeat Exercise 4 for a six-element array which initially contains

   1 8 2 7 3 6

9. Why is the heap sort called by that name?
10. What is a heap?
11. Why is the shell sort called by that name?
12. Is a heap sort always better than a quick sort? When is it? When isn't it?
13. When is a bubble sort better than a quick sort?
14. Why is the shell sort most efficient when the original data are in almost sorted order?
15. What advantage do the relatively prime values of the increments have over other values in a shell sort?

16. Under what circumstances would you not use a quick sort?

17. What is the worst case and average case efficiency of the heap sort?

18. A sorting method is said to be stable if two data items of matching value are guaranteed not to be rearranged with respect to each other as the algorithm progresses. For example, in the four-element array

60 42_1 80 42_2

a stable sorting method would guarantee a final ordering

42_1 42_2 60 80

Classify each of the sorting algorithms studied in this chapter and Chapter 2 as to their stability. (To see why stability may be important, consider Programming Problems 2 and 6.)

19. What is the property that the sequence of diminishing increments in the shell sort must have to insure that the method will work?

20. Identify and give an example of best case and worst case data sets for each of the sorting algorithms studied in this chapter.

21. How does the choice of the pivotal value affect the efficiency of the quick sort algorithm? Suppose that the middle value or the last value in a segment to be partitioned were chosen as the pivotal value. How would this alter the nature of best case and worst case data sets? Give examples to illustrate your answer.

22. Develop trees of procedure calls to QuickSort for a variety of test data sets (analogous to what was done in Figure 9.2). Use these trees to analyze the efficiency of QuickSort. What types of data sets yield $O(n\log_2 n)$ efficiency? What types yield $O(n^2)$ efficiency?

23. Provide examples of best case and worst case data sets for the shell sort algorithm presented in this chapter.

24. You are to sort an array in a program in which the following considerations are to be taken into account. First, there is a large amount of data to be sorted. The amount of data to be sorted is so large that frequent $O(n^2)$ run-times will prove unsatisfactory. The amount of data will also make it impossible for your program to use a large amount of "overhead data" (for example, stack space) to make the sort efficient in its run-time. This is because the space required by the overhead data would potentially take up space needed by the array to be sorted. Second, you are told that the array to be sorted is often nearly in order to start with. For each of the six sorting methods indicated, specify whether or not that method would be appropriate for this application and, in a brief statement, explain why your answer is correct.
    a. Bubble sort
    b. Insertion sort
    c. Selection sort
    d. Quick sort
    e. Heap sort
    f. Merge sort

25. In Chapter 2, PointerSort uses an index of pointers to sort data logically without rearranging it. Identify the sort algorithm that was behind the Pascal PointerSort procedure. Adapt the pointer sort procedure to each of the other algorithms presented in this chapter.

26. Implement QuickSort in a nonrecursive fashion.
27. Implement MergeSort in a nonrecursive fashion.

Programming Problems

1. Given a sequential file containing an unordered list of passengers and their flight numbers for Wing-and-a-Prayer Airlines, produce a listing arranged in flight-number order. Passengers on the same flight should be ordered by last name. The easy version of this program assumes that all information will fit in the memory, allowing the use of an internal sort. For an added challenge, write the program using an external sort algorithm. (*Hint*: Adapt MergeSort along the lines discussed in the text.)
2. The Bay Area Brawlers professional football team has stored the records of all the players who have played on the team during the history of the team. One player's record consists of

   Name
   Total points scored
   Number of touchdowns
   Number of field goals
   Number of safeties
   Number of extra points

   Write a program which will list players in order from the highest scorer in the team's history down to the lowest. Those players who have scored the same number of points should then be arranged in alphabetical order.
3. Take N randomly generated integers. Now apply a bubble sort, a shell sort, a quick sort, a heap sort, and a merge sort. Observe, compare, and plot their execution time for N = 100; N = 1,000; N = 10,000; N = 100,000, ...
4. Put some hypothetical data on an external file and apply a modified merge sort to them.
5. Write a Pascal program to complete the following steps. Artificially create a file with a large number of randomly chosen names. Read into an array all those names which begin with *A* through some letter, say *G*, chosen so that all the names will fit in the array. Sort this array with one of the sorting algorithms from this chapter and store this sorted array into another file. Now read into the array all those names from the file which begin with *H* through another appropriate letter. Sort the array and append it to the end of the new file. Repeat this process until all names from the original file have been processed. The new file will be the sorted version of the original. Observe the execution time of your program. Analyze its efficiency in big-O terms.
6. Consider a list of records, each containing four fields.

   Name
   Month of birth
   Day of birth
   Year of birth

Write a program to sort this list in oldest-to-youngest order. People with the same birth date should be arranged alphabetically. One strategy you could employ would be to concatenate strategically the four fields into one, and then just sort that one field. Another strategy would be to sort the list four times, each time by a different field. (Think carefully about which field to sort first.) Which of the strategies would require that you choose a stable sorting algorithm? (See Exercise 18.)

7. Modify MergeSort so that it will sort a linked list instead of an array.

8. Modify the shell sort procedure so that it uses a sequence of diminishing increments which are relatively prime. Observe, compare, and plot the execution time of this procedure versus the version presented in this chapter for a varied collection of data sets.

9. Modify the shell sort procedure so that it employs bubble sort logic on segments instead of insertion sort. Observe, compare, and plot the execution time of this procedure versus the version presented in this chapter for a varied collection of data sets.

More Powerful Search Methods

Information is where you find it.

Librarian's Motto

Introductory Considerations

In earlier chapters, three methods of searching for items within a list have been analyzed: sequential search, binary search, and binary tree search. The sequential search, though easy to implement and applicable to short lists, is limited in many practical situations by its $O(n)$ search efficiency. The binary search offers a much faster $O(\log_2 n)$ search efficiency but also has limitations. Foremost among these limitations are the need to maintain the list in physically contiguous order and the need to maintain a count of the number of records in the list. Both of these limitations are particularly restrictive for volatile lists; that is, lists in which insertions and deletions are frequently made. In Chapter 6, a binary tree search emerged as offering the best of both worlds. Insertions and deletions can be done on an ordered binary tree by merely manipulating pointers instead of moving data, and an $O(\log_2 n)$ search efficiency can be achieved if the tree remains close to full. Unfortunately, to guarantee that the tree remains nearly full and hence insure the $O(\log_2 n)$ efficiency, a sophisticated technique known as height balancing (see Chapter 7, Section 7.5) is required. The complications involved in implementing this technique frequently dictate that it not be used. Essentially you must weigh the significant cost in development time to implement a height-balanced tree against the risk that the order in which data arrive for insertion may cause search efficiency to deteriorate from $O(\log_2 n)$ to $O(n)$. If data items arrive in a relatively random order, then taking that risk may well be the prudent choice.

The efficiency of all three of these techniques is dependent on the number of items in the list being searched. In this chapter, we shall study another alternative called hashing whose efficiency is measurable in terms of the amount of storage you are willing to waste. In this sense, hashing can achieve phenomenally fast search times regardless of how much data you have, provided that you can afford to keep a large amount of unused list space available.

We shall also explore in this chapter some of the special considerations that enter into searching for data stored in a disk file instead of main memory. These considerations lead to a variety of search schemes, all of which employ some variation of a data structure known as an index.

_____ **10.2**

Density-Dependent Search Techniques

In an ideal data processing world, all identifying keys such as product codes, Social Security numbers, and so on, would start at 1 and follow in sequence thereafter. Then, in any given list, we would merely store the key and its associated data at the position which matched the key. The search efficiency for any key in such a list would be one access to the list, and all data processors could live happily ever after! Unfortunately, in the real world, users (not being concerned with the happiness of data processing personnel) desire keys that consist of more meaningful characters, such as names, addresses, region codes, and so on. For instance, it may be that in a given inventory-control application, product codes are numbered in sequence beginning with 10,000 instead of 1. A moment's reflection should indicate that this is still a highly desirable situation since, given a key, we need merely locate the key at position

$$\text{KeyValue} - 9999$$

in the list, and we still have a search efficiency of 1. What we have done here is to define what is known as a key-to-address transformation, or hashing function. The idea behind a hashing function is that it acts upon a given key in such a way as to return the relative position in the list where we expect to find the key.

Most hashing functions are not as straightforward as the preceding one and present some additional complications which we can quickly illustrate. Suppose we use the following hashing function:

$$\text{Hash(KeyValue)} = (\text{KeyValue MOD 4}) + 1$$

Then the set of keys 3, 5, 8, and 10 will be scattered as illustrated here.

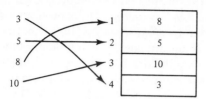

However, if we happen to have 3, 4, 8, and 10 as keys instead of 3, 5, 8, and 10, a problem arises: namely, 4 and 8 hash to the same position. They are said to be synonyms, and the result is termed a collision. This situation, here a collision at position 1, is shown in the following illustration.

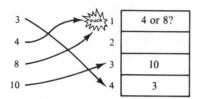

Clearly, one of the goals of the hashing functions we develop should be to reduce the number of collisions as much as possible.

The Construction of Hashing Functions

The business of developing hashing functions can be quite intriguing. The essential idea is to build a mathematical black box which will take a key value as input and issue as output the position in the list where that key value should be located. The position emitted should have a minimal probability of colliding with the position that would be produced for a different key. In addition, the black box we create must insure that a given key will always produce the same position as output. You should begin to note a similarity between some of the properties possessed by a good hashing function and a good random number generator such as that used in our simulation case study in Chapter 5. Indeed, list access via a hashing function is sometimes called randomized storage, and the first type of hashing function we discuss makes direct use of a random number generator.

Method 1: Use of a Random Number Generator. Many high-level languages provide a random number generator to produce random sequences of real values between 0 and 1. If one is not provided by the language, you may easily write one using a method such as that employed in the case study of Chapter 5. (For readable discussions of other methods of random number generation, see Chapter 7 of *Numerical Recipes* by William H. Press, Brian P. Flannery, Saul A. Teukolsky, and William T. Vetterling (Cambridge, England: Cambridge University Press, 1986).) Typically, all of these methods rely on having a global seed to start the process of generating random numbers. Computations done on this seed produce the random number. At the same time, the computations alter the value of the seed so that the next time the random number generator is called, a different random number will almost surely be produced. You should refer back to the case study of Chapter 5 to review how this process worked. In typical applications of random number generation, you need merely initialize the seed to some arbitrary value to start the random sequence. Notice that, once the seed is supplied, the random sequence is completely determined. If you have access to a system procedure which returns the current time, day, month, and year, this can be called to initialize the seed in a fashion which insures there is only a very small likelihood of generating the same random sequence twice.

How does all of this relate to hashing? For a hashing application, we must slightly alter the definition of our random number generator so that the seed is supplied as a value parameter. Then we will supply the values of search keys as the seeds. The nature of the random number algorithm insures that

- ☐ Each time the same key is passed to the function, the same random value will be returned.

- ☐ It is unlikely that two different keys will yield the same random value.

The random number between 0 and 1 which is correspondingly produced can then be appropriately multiplied, truncated, and shifted to produce a hash value within the range of valid positions.

Method 2: Folding. In situations where the key to be positioned is not a pure integer, some preliminary work may be required to translate it into a usable form. Take, for instance, the case of a Social Security number such as

387-58-1505

Viewed as one integer, this would cause overflow on many machines. By a method known as shift folding, this Social Security number would be viewed as three separate numbers to be added

$$
\begin{array}{r}
387 \\
58 \\
+1505 \\
\hline
\end{array}
$$

producing the result 1,950. This result could either be regarded as the hash position itself or, more likely, as a pure integer which now could be further acted upon by Method 1 or 4 to produce a final hash position in the desired range.

Another often-used folding technique is called boundary folding. The idea behind boundary folding is that, at the boundaries between the numbers making up the key under consideration, every other number is reversed before being added to the accumulated total. Applying this method to our Social Security number example, we would have

$$
\begin{array}{r}
387 \\
85 \text{ (this number reversed)} \\
+1505 \\
\hline
\end{array}
$$

yielding a result of 1,977. Clearly, the two methods do not differ by much, and a choice between them must often be made on the basis of some experimentation to determine which will produce more scattered results for a given application.

Regardless of whether shift or boundary folding is used, one of the great advantages of the folding method is its ability to transform noninteger keys into an integer suitable for further hashing action. For keys such as names which contain alphabetic characters, the type of folding just illustrated may be done by translating characters into their ASCII (or other appropriate) codes.

Method 3: Digit or Character Extraction. In certain situations, a given key value may contain specific characters which are likely to bias any hash value arising from the key. The idea in extraction is to remove such digits or characters before using the result as a final hash value or passing it on to be further transformed by another method. For instance, a company may choose to identify the various products it manufactures by using a nine-character code which always contains either an A or B in the first position and either a 1 or 0 in the fourth position. The rest of the characters in the code tend to occur in less predictable fashion. Character extraction would remove the biased first and fourth characters, leaving a seven-character result to pass on to further processing.

Method 4: Division Remainder Technique. All hashing presupposes a given range of positions which can be valid outputs of the hash function. In the remainder of this section, we shall assume the existence of a global constant RecordSpace which represents the upper limit of our hashing function. That is, the function should produce values between 1 and RecordSpace. It should than be evident that

$$\text{Hash(KeyValue)} = (\text{KeyValue MOD RecordSpace}) + 1$$

Position	Key
1	0
2	91
3	92
4	0
5	0
6	50
7	0
8	0
9	0
10	0
11	0
12	41
13	12
14	58
15	0

TABLE 10.1

Array with RecordSpace 15 loaded using a division
remainder hashing function

is a valid hashing function for integer KeyValue. To begin examining criteria for choosing an appropriate RecordSpace, let us load the keys 41, 58, 12, 92, 50, and 91 into a list with RecordSpace 15. Table 10.1 shows the results. In this table, zeros are used to denote empty positions.

However, if we keep RecordSpace the same and try to load the keys 10, 20, 30, 40, 50, 60, and 70, we have many collisions, as shown in Table 10.2.

Position	Key			
1	30	60	(collision)	
2	0			
3	0			
4	0			
5	0			
6	20	50	(collision)	
7	0			
8	0			
9	0			
10	0			
11	10	40	70	(collision)
12	0			
13	0			
14	0			
15	0			

TABLE 10.2

Array from Table 10.1, loaded differently, with
several collisions

Hence, with this choice of RecordSpace, a different set of keys causes disastrous results even though the list seemingly has plenty of room available. On the other hand, if we choose RecordSpace to be 11, we have a list with considerably less room but no collisions. Table 10.3 indicates the hashing positions when the same set of keys is acted upon by 11 instead of by 15.

Position	Key
1	0
2	0
3	0
4	0
5	70
6	60
7	50
8	40
9	30
10	20
11	10

TABLE 10.3

Array with the same set of keys as Table 10.2, but with
RecordSpace 11: no collision results

Although these examples are far from conclusive, they suggest that choosing a prime number for RecordSpace may produce a more desirable hashing function. The Exercises at the end of the chapter will have you explore this question more deeply. Apart from considerations of whether or not RecordSpace should be prime, it is clear that the nature of a particular application may dictate against the choice of certain RecordSpace values. For instance, in a situation where the rightmost digits of key values happen to follow certain recurring patterns, it would be unwise to choose a power of 10 for RecordSpace. (Why?)

Despite such considerations, no hashing function can rule out the possibility of collisions; it can only make them less likely. You should quickly be able to imagine a key value which will produce a collision for the hashing function used in determining the list of Table 10.3. Notice that, as the list becomes fuller, the probability that collisions will occur increases. Hence, when using hashing as a search strategy, one must be willing to waste some positions in the list; otherwise search efficiency will drastically deteriorate. How much space to waste is an interesting question that we will soon discuss. Another conclusion that emerges from the previous discussion is that, since no hashing function can eliminate collisions, we must be prepared to handle them when they occur.

Collision Processing

The essential problem in collision processing is to develop an algorithm that will position a key in a list when the position dictated by the hashing function itself is already occupied. Ideally, this algorithm should minimize the possibility of future collisions; that is, the problem key should be located at a position that is not likely to be the hashed position of a future key.

However, the nature of hashing makes this latter criterion difficult to meet with any degree of certainty, since a good hashing function does not allow prediction of where future keys are likely to be placed. We will discuss five methods of collision processing: linear, quadratic, rehashing, linked, and buckets. In all of the methods, it will be necessary to detect when a given list position is not occupied. To signify this, we use a global constant Empty to distinguish unoccupied positions. As the methods are being discussed, you should give some thought to the question of how deletions could be processed from a list accessed via one of these hashing methods. In particular, will the Empty flag suffice to denote both positions which have never been occupied and positions which were previously occupied but are now vacant? This question is explored in the Exercises and Programming Problems at the end of the chapter.

Linear Collision Processing

The linear method of resolving collisions is the simplest to implement (and, unfortunately, the least efficient). It requires that, when a collision occurs, we proceed down the list in sequential order until a vacant position is found. The key causing the collision is then placed at this first vacant position. If we come to the physical end of our list in the attempt to place the problem key, we merely wrap around to the top of the list and continue looking for a vacant position. For instance, suppose we use a hashing function of

$$\text{Hash(KeyValue)} = (\text{KeyValue MOD RecordSpace}) + 1$$

with RecordSpace equal to 7, and attempt to insert the keys 18, 31, 67, 36, 19, and 34. The sequence of lists in Figure 10.1 shows the results of these insertions. When a collision occurs at the third insert, it is processed by the linear method; 67 is thus loaded into position 6.

Pos	1st insert	2nd insert	3rd insert	4th insert	5th insert	6th insert
1	0	0	0	0	0	34
2	0	0	0	36	36	36
3	0	0	0	0	0	0
4	0	31	31	31	31	31
5	18	18	18	18	18	18
6	0	0	67	67	67	67
7	0	0	0	0	19	19
	Hash(18) = 5	Hash(31) = 4	Hash(67) = 5	Hash(36) = 2	Hash(19) = 6	Hash(34) = 7

FIGURE 10.1

Insertion with linear collision processing

The Pascal algorithm to seek a Target loaded by the linear method follows:

```
{Global declarations}

CONST RecordSpace = {Appropriate size};
      Empty       = {Appropriate flagging value};

TYPE  KeyType = {Appropriate data type for key field in record};
      DataRec = RECORD
                    Key : KeyType;
                    OtherData : {Appropriate Type}
                END;
      DataArray = ARRAY [1..RecordSpace] OF DataRec;
```

```
{------------------------------------------------------------------}

PROCEDURE    LinearHash (Target : KeyType;
                        VAR SearchList : DataArray;
                        VAR InfoWanted : DataRec;
                        VAR Found : boolean);

{Given collection of records in SearchList loaded by linear collision
 processing and Target storing the key value of record being sought, return
 in InfoWanted all data associated with Target key.  In case Target cannot
 be located, return Found as false.}

    VAR  i, j : integer;
         Traversed : boolean;
```

```
BEGIN
  Found := false; {Assume failure}
  Traversed := false; {Toggled to true if entire list is traversed}
  i := Hash(Target); {Call on hashing function}
  j := i;
  WHILE (SearchList[j].Key <> Empty) AND NOT (Traversed OR Found) DO
    IF Target = SearchList[j].Key THEN
      BEGIN
      InfoWanted := SearchList[j];
      Found := true
      END
    ELSE
      BEGIN
      j := (j MOD RecordSpace) + 1;   {MOD insures wraparound}
      Traversed := (j=i)
      END
END; {LinearHash}
```

	1	419	Target = 419

Hash(419) = RecordSpace−2

		:	

RecordSpace−2	511	
RecordSpace−1	312	Repeated applications of ELSE
RecordSpace	705	clause insure eventual wraparound to 1st slot

Several remarks are in order concerning this procedure. First, note that the procedure as it stands would not handle list processing in which it was necessary to process deletions. In such a situation, an additional flagging value would be needed to indicate a list position that had once been occupied and is now vacant because of a deletion. Without this distinction, we would not know whether or not to exit the search loop upon encountering an empty slot. You will explore the problem of deletions from a list maintained by hashing in greater detail in the Exercises and Programming Problems at the end of the chapter. Second, note that the linear method is not without its flaws. In particular, it is prone to a problem known as clustering. Clustering occurs when a hashing function is biased toward the placement of keys into a given region within the storage space. When the linear method is used to resolve collisions, this clustering problem is compounded. This is because the linear method locates keys which collide with an already existing key relatively close to the initial collision point. Hence, linear hashing is more likely to result in the clustering type of situation pictured in Figure 10.2 than the other methods we will discuss.

Efficiency Considerations for Linear Hashing. A final point to note about the linear hashing method is its search efficiency. Knuth has shown that the average number of list accesses for a successful search using the linear method is

$$(1/2) * (1+1/(1-D))$$

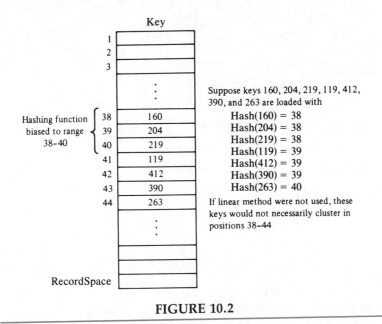

Key

Suppose keys 160, 204, 219, 119, 412, 390, and 263 are loaded with

Hashing function biased to range 38-40

38	160
39	204
40	219
41	119
42	412
43	390
44	263

Hash(160) = 38
Hash(204) = 38
Hash(219) = 38
Hash(119) = 39
Hash(412) = 39
Hash(390) = 39
Hash(263) = 40

If linear method were not used, these keys would not necessarily cluster in positions 38–44

RecordSpace

FIGURE 10.2

Clustering due to biased hashing function and
linear processing

where

$$D = (\text{Number of currently active records})/\text{RecordSpace}$$

(See Donald E. Knuth, *Searching and Sorting*. Vol. 3 of *The Art of Computer Programming*. (Menlo Park, Calif.: Addison-Wesley, 1973).) An interesting fact about this search efficiency is that it is not solely dependent upon the number of records in the list but rather upon the density ratio of the number of records currently in the list divided by the total record space available. In other words, no matter how many records there are, a highly efficient result can be obtained if one is willing to waste enough vacant records. This is what is meant by a density-dependent search technique. In the case of searching for a key which cannot be found, Knuth's results indicate that the average search efficiency will be

$$(1/2) * (1+1/(1-D)^2)$$

Table 10.4 illustrates the effectiveness of linear collision resolution by showing the computed efficiencies for a few strategic values of D.

Quadratic and Rehashing Methods of Collision Processing

Both the quadratic and rehashing methods attempt to correct the problem of clustering which occurs with the linear method. They force the problem-causing key to immediately move a considerable distance from the initial collision. By the rehashing method, an entire sequence of hashing functions may be applied to a given key. If a collision results from the first

D	Efficiency for Successful Search (number of accesses)	Efficiency for Unsuccessful Search (number of accesses)
0.10	1.06	1.18
0.50	1.50	2.50
0.75	2.50	8.50
0.90	5.50	50.50

TABLE 10.4

Average search efficiency for linear collision processing

hashing function, a second is applied, then a third, and so on, until the key can be successfully placed.

The quadratic method has the advantage of not requiring numerous hashing functions for its implementation. Suppose that a key value initially hashes to position K and a collision results. Then, on its first attempt to resolve the collision, the quadratic algorithm attempts to place the key at position

$$K + 1^2$$

Then, if a second attempt is necessary to resolve the collision, position

$$K + 2^2$$

is probed. In general, the Rth attempt to resolve the collision probes position

$$K + R^2$$

(with wraparound taken into account). Figure 10.3 highlights this scattering pattern. At this point you should verify that, if the hashing function

$$Hash(KeyValue) = (KeyValue\ MOD\ RecordSpace) + 1$$

is used with RecordSpace equal to 7, the keys 17, 73, 32, and 80 will be located in positions 4, 5, 6, and 1 respectively.

Efficiency Considerations for the Quadratic and Rehashing Methods.
Knuth's results (see *Searching and Sorting*, cited earlier in this section) demonstrate the effectiveness of the rehashing and quadratic methods versus the linear method. Average search efficiencies improve to

$$-(1/D) * \log_e(1-D)$$

for the successful case and

$$1/(1-D)$$

for an unsuccessful search. Compare the numbers presented in Table 10.5 to those for the linear method given in Table 10.4.

You may have surmised that the increased efficiency of the quadratic method entails at least some drawbacks. First, the computation of a posi-

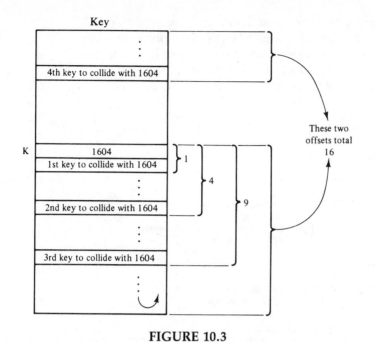

FIGURE 10.3

Quadratic collision processing

D	Efficiency for Successful Search (number of accesses)	Efficiency for Unsuccessful Search (number of accesses)
0.10	1.05	1.11
0.50	1.39	2.00
0.75	1.84	4.00
0.90	2.56	10.00

TABLE 10.5

Average search efficiency for quadratic collision processing

tion to be probed when a collision occurs is somewhat more obscure than it was with the linear method. We leave it for you to verify that the position for the Rth probe after an initial unsuccessful hash to position K is given by

$$(K+R^2-1) \text{ MOD RecordSpace} + 1$$

A more significant problem, however, is that the quadratic method seemingly offers no guarantee that we will try every position in the list before concluding that a given key cannot be inserted. With the linear method, as the list became relatively dense when keys and insertions were attempted, the only way that the insertion could fail would be for every position in the list to be occupied. The linear nature of the search, although inefficient, insured that every position would be checked. However, with the quadratic method applied to the RecordSpace of Figure 10.4, you can confirm that an initial hash to position 4 will lead to future probing of positions 4, 5, and 8 only; it will never check positions 1, 2, 3, 6, or 7.

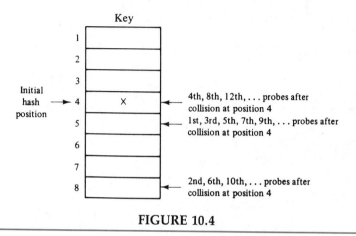

FIGURE 10.4

Quadratic probing after initial hash to 4

A satisfactory answer to the question of what portion of a list will be probed by the quadratic algorithm was fortunately provided by Radke for values of RecordSpace that are prime numbers which satisfy certain conditions. Radke's results and their application to the quadratic algorithm are explored in the Exercises at the end of the chapter. (If you wish to read Radke's results, see C. E. Radke, "The Use of Quadratic Residue Research." *Communications of the ACM* 13(1970): 103–105.)

Linked Method of Collision Processing

The logic of this method completely eliminates the possibility that one collision begets another. It requires a storage area divided horizontally into two regions: a prime hash area and an overflow area. Each record requires a Link field in addition to the Key and OtherData fields. The global constant RecordSpace is applicable to the prime hash area only. This storage concept is illustrated in Figure 10.5.

Initially, the hashing translates function keys into the prime hashing area. If a collision occurs, the key is inserted into a linked list with its initial node in the prime area and all following nodes in the overflow area (no dummy header is used). Figure 10.6 shows how this method would load the keys 22, 31, 67, 36, 29, and 60 for a RecordSpace equal to 7 and hashing function

$$\text{Hash(KeyValue)} = (\text{KeyValue MOD RecordSpace}) + 1$$

The Pascal procedure to implement the linked method of collision processing follows. We have made the Link fields integer pointers to other

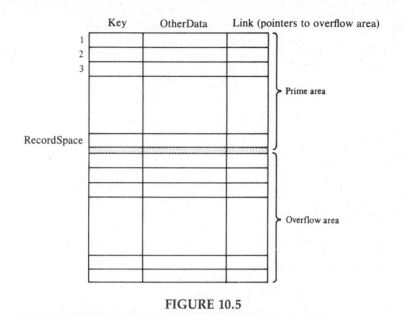

FIGURE 10.5

Storage allocation for linked collision processing

	Key	Link
1	0	NULL
2	22	8
3	0	NULL
4	31	NULL
5	67	10
6	0	NULL
7	0	NULL
8	36	9
9	29	NULL
10	60	NULL
11	0	NULL
12	0	NULL
13	0	NULL
14	0	NULL
15	0	NULL
16	0	NULL
17	0	NULL

FIGURE 10.6

Loading keys with KeyValue **MOD** 7 + 1 and linked
collision processing

array locations instead of Pascal dynamic memory pointers to facilitate using the algorithm with a random access file. As written, the procedure assumes that all key locations in the prime area have had their corresponding Key and Link fields initialized to appropriate constant flags for Empty and Null respectively. The assumption is also made that no keys will be deleted.

```
{Global declarations}

CONST   RecordSpace = {Appropriate size for prime area};
        PrimePlusOverflow = {Actual array size};
        Empty = {Appropriate flag for key field of empty record};
        Null = {Appropriate flag for end-of-list pointer};

TYPE    KeyType = {Appropriate type for key field in record};
        DataRec = RECORD
                    Key : KeyType;
                    OtherData : {Appropriate Type};
                    Link : integer {or Pascal pointer variable if desired}
                  END;

        DataArray = ARRAY [1..PrimePlusOverflow] OF DataRec;

{---------------------------------------------------------------------------}

PROCEDURE  LinkedHash (Target : Keytype;
                            VAR SearchList : DataArray;
                            VAR InfoWanted : DataRec;
                            VAR Found : boolean);

  {Given collection of records in SearchList loaded by linked collision
   processing and Target storing the key value of record being sought,
   return in InfoWanted all data associated with Target key.  In case Target
   cannot be located, return Found as false.}

VAR i : integer;

BEGIN
    Found := false; {Assume failure}
    i := Hash(Target); {Call on hashing function}
    REPEAT
      IF Target = SearchList[i].Key THEN
        BEGIN
        InfoWanted := SearchList[i];
        Found := true
        END
      ELSE
        i := SearchList[i].Link

    UNTIL Found OR (i = Null)
END; {LinkedHash}
```

Efficiency Considerations for Linked Hashing. Knuth's efficiency results for the linked hashing method depend on a density factor (D) which is computed using the RecordSpace in the prime hashing area only. Hence, unlike the other hashing methods we have discussed, the linked method allows a density factor greater than 1. For example, if the RecordSpace for the primary hash area were 200 and the overflow area contained space for 300 additional records, then 400 active records would yield a density factor of 2. Given this variation, average search efficiencies for the successful and unsuccessful cases are $1 + D/2$ and D respectively. Table 10.6 shows computations of this search efficiency for selected values of D, and should be compared to the corresponding results for the linear and quadratic methods, which were presented in Table 10.4 and Table 10.5, respectively.

D	Efficiency for Successful Search (number of accesses)	Efficiency for Unsuccessful Search (number of accesses)
2	2	2
5	3.5	5
10	6	10
20	11	20

TABLE 10.6

Average search efficiencies for the linked method

Bucket Hashing

In the bucket hashing strategy of collision processing, the hashing function transforms a given key to a physically contiguous region of locations within the list to be searched. This contiguous region is called a bucket. Thus, instead of hashing to the ith location, a key would hash to the ith bucket of locations. The number of locations contained in this bucket would depend upon the bucket size. (We assume that all buckets in a given list are the same size.) Figure 10.7 illustrates this concept for a list with seven buckets and a bucket size of 3.

Having hashed to a bucket, the Target must then be compared in sequential order to all of the keys in that bucket. On the surface, it would seem that this strategy could do no better than duplicate the efficiency of the linked hash method discussed earlier. Indeed, because a sequential search is conducted in both cases after the initial hash is made, the average number of list accesses for a successful or unsuccessful search cannot be improved by using buckets. Moreover, provisions for linking to some sort of overflow area must still be made in case a series of collisions consumes all of the space in a given bucket.

What then could be a possible advantage of using buckets? If the list to be searched resides entirely in main memory, there is no advantage. How-

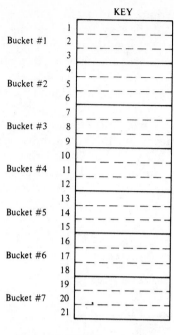

FIGURE 10.7

Storage allocation for bucket hashing

ever, if the list resides in a disk file, the bucket method will allow us to take advantage of some of the physical characteristics of the storage medium itself. To see this, let us assume a one-surface disk divided into concentric tracks and pie-shaped sectors as indicated in Figure 10.8.

There are two ways in which the bucket hashing strategy may take advantage of the organization of the data on the disk. First, when records in a contiguous random access file are stored on a disk, they are generally located in relative record number order along one track, then along an adjacent track, and so on. The movement of the read-write head between tracks is generally the cause of the most significant delays in obtaining data from a disk. The farther the movement, the greater the delay will be. Hence, if our knowledge of the machine in question allows us to make a bucket coincide with a track on the disk, then hashing to the beginning of a bucket and proceeding from there using a sequential search within the bucket (that is, the track) will greatly reduce head movement. A linked hashing strategy, on the other hand, could cause considerable movement of the read-write head between tracks on the disk, thereby slowing program execution. This consideration is an excellent example of how one must examine more than just the number of list accesses when measuring the efficiency of a program involving disk files.

A second advantage in using the bucket hashing algorithm when disk files are being searched is related to the way in which records are transferred between the disk and main memory. Frequently, programming languages create the illusion that each record accessed requires a separate disk access. However, records are frequently blocked, that is, positioned in

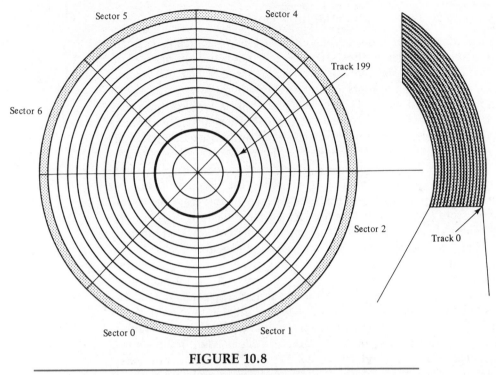

FIGURE 10.8

A one-surface disk

contiguous regions on a track of the disk, so that a fixed number of them are brought into main memory when a record in that block is requested. This means that, if the record requested happens to be part of the block presently in main memory, a program statement which requests a record may not even require a disk access but only a different viewing window applied to the block already in main memory. Since main memory manipulations are orders of magnitude faster than the rate of data transfer to and from a disk, this means that positioning our buckets to coincide with a disk block will necessitate only one disk access each time an entire bucket is sequentially searched. Here again, the more scattered nature of a purely linked hashing algorithm would not allow this disk-oriented efficiency consideration to be taken into account.

_____ **10.3**

Two Case Studies Revisited

We can analyze hashing from a pragmatic perspective by considering how it might be used to implement solutions to the two case studies introduced in Chapter 1: the list maintenance problems of the registrar's system and the sparse table problem of the Wing-and-a-Prayer flight/pilot data base. You will then be asked to carry out these implementations in the Programming Problems at the end of the chapter.

The Registrar's System Implemented by Hashing

In this context, hashing emerges as yet another list maintenance strategy to be evaluated and compared to those strategies we have already discussed: array (or random access file) with binary search, linked list, and binary tree. Hence we must examine its performance with respect to the same ACIDS (Add, Change, Inspect, Delete, and Sort) criteria for lists that were introduced in Chapter 1 and then used to evaluate these other list implementation techniques. Assuming the existence of an appropriate hashing function to act on the student name key of the registrar's system and a willingness to waste enough storage to allow for fast searching, hashing will clearly perform very well in all of these areas with the possible exception of sorting and ordering data. Here is where we have to pay a price for the scattered storage of records that are located via a hashing function.

Nonetheless, there are strategies that can be used to allow hashing and ordering of data to coexist. One such strategy would simply be to use a pointer sort algorithm (see Chapters 2 and 9) to logically sort the data when an ordered list is needed. This strategy has the drawback of not maintaining the list in order but actually performing a potentially costly sort algorithm each time an ordering is requested. Clearly, this strategy would not be wise if such an ordering were requested frequently and unpredictably. However, this is not the case for the registrar's system. Here requests for ordered lists come only at a relatively few regularly scheduled intervals. Hence, the time required to perform a pointer sort would probably not be a negative factor from a user's perspective.

In situations where requests for ordering would come frequently enough to make maintaining the list in order (as opposed to sorting) a necessity, we could follow a strategy which would combine the search speed of hashing with the ordered list advantages offered by a linked list implementation. This combination would have us use hashing to search for an individual record but would add link fields to each record so that a linked list for each desired ordering could be woven through the collection of hashed records. Implementing this combination of hashing and linked list would entail the following considerations with respect to the ACIDS operations:

□ Add. In effect, the hashing/collision processing algorithm would provide us with an available node to store data. Each linked list involved would then have to be traversed to link the node into each ordering in the appropriate logical location.

□ Change. Hashing could be used to find the record to be altered. If the change was to occur in a field by which the record was ordered, the links would have to be appropriately adjusted. For this purpose, the use of a doubly linked list might offer a substantial advantage. (Why?)

□ Inspect. There is no problem here because the hash algorithm should find the desired record quickly.

□ Delete. This is similar to the change operation. Use hashing to find the record to be deleted, then adjust the link field appropriately.

Here again a doubly linked list could prove to be particularly valuable. (Why?)

☐ Sorting/Ordering. There is no problem here because the linked lists constantly maintain the appropriate orderings.

With respect to the registrar's system in particular, the low frequency with which ordered listings are requested could well mean that the added complications posed by the combined hashing/linked list strategy make it a nonproductive choice for this system. This is not to say that the complications cannot be overcome but rather that, from a practical viewpoint, the development time required to overcome them is not justified by the way the system will be used. Though such a utilitarian outlook may offend the purist in each of us, it is an outlook which cannot be overlooked given the backlog of projects and intense scheduling pressure often faced by system developers.

Wing-and-a-Prayer's Flight/Pilot Data Base Implemented by Hashing

Recall that the problem faced by Wing-and-a-Prayer Airlines was that of implementing a sparse table of Boolean values with rows indexed by pilot number and columns indexed by flight number. We have already suggested two implementation strategies for such tables.

1. In Chapter 3 we described a strategy that would simply create a list of the (pilot, flight) pairs corresponding to nontrivial (that is **true**) values in the table. Thus, determining the value of the data at a conceptual row/column location is simply a matter of searching this list.

2. In Chapter 4, we described a strategy that would form a linked list of the nontrivial columns in each row. Here, determining the value of the data at a conceptual row/column location is reduced to the problem of sequentially searching a relatively small linked list.

At the time we explored these two strategies, the first one appeared to be less attractive. Because the data in the list of **true**-valued row/column coordinates is likely to be volatile, physically ordering it for a binary search would not be practical. Yet, without a binary search, requests to inspect the value at any given location are met with the O(n) response time of a sequential search. Hashing allows us to search for a row/column coordinate in the list of the first strategy in a very efficient fashion, probably faster than the sequential search along the linked list representing a given row required by the second strategy. Moreover, since the order of the data in the list is not important for this application, the scattered nature of hashed storage does not present any obstacle at all.

The considerations we have discussed with respect to these two case studies make it evident that hashing is a very attractive list implementation technique. It will be extremely efficient in regard to the add, change, inspect, and delete list operations if we are willing to pay the price of wasting

A Relevant Issue . . .

Data Integrity, Concurrent Updates, and Deadlock

The problems of finding and allowing a user to access a particular record in a file are complicated somewhat in a system that allows several users to access that file simultaneously. To see why this is so, it is important to recall that when you actually manipulate a record or part of an index from a file, you really have a copy of that portion of the file in your main memory area. Now suppose that two users are not only accessing the same file simultaneously but also the same record in that file simultaneously. A scenario such as the following could emerge:

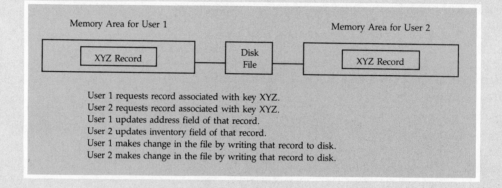

User 1 requests record associated with key XYZ.
User 2 requests record associated with key XYZ.
User 1 updates address field of that record.
User 2 updates inventory field of that record.
User 1 makes change in the file by writing that record to disk.
User 2 makes change in the file by writing that record to disk.

What will be wrong with the new record that exists in the disk file? Clearly, the address change made by User 1 will have been destroyed when User 2's copy of the record is written back to the disk. We have what is known as a data integrity problem caused by the concur-

enough storage to get a reasonably low density ratio. The only other drawback to hashing, in addition to this wasted storage, is the price that must be paid if various orderings of the data are frequently needed. However, even this can be overcome by the methods described in our discussion of the registrar's system.

_____ **10.4**

Indexed Search Techniques

As we indicated in our discussion of file processing in Chapter 3, all of the search strategies we have studied up to this point could be applied to lists implemented in main memory or on a random access disk. However, with the exception of bucket hashing, none of the methods we have studied actually take into account physical characteristics of disk storage in an attempt to enhance their efficiency. In practice, because retrieval of data from a disk file is orders of magnitude slower than retrieval from main memory, we often cannot afford to ignore these special characteristics of

rent updating of the same record by two users. The situation can become much worse than merely losing an address change. Imagine the havoc created if one of the users deleted the record while the other was processing it or if the portion of the file being simultaneously updated by two users was not a data record but instead part of the file index.

The concurrent update problem must be avoided in any multiuser system if data integrity is to be insured. The solution used in many systems is that of a record lock facility. With such a facility, the user who has a file record in main memory for updating is considered the owner of that record to the exclusion of any other users accessing that record. That lock on the record exists until the user writes the (perhaps altered) record back to the disk file. Hence, in our scenario, User 2 would not have been able immediately to obtain the record for key XYZ. Instead, that user would sit idle in a wait state until the record became available.

Although this record-locking approach guarantees data integrity, it is not without its own set of problems. For instance, consider the following scenario:

> User 1 requests and gets record for key XYZ.
> User 2 requests and gets record for key ABC.
> To process record XYZ, User 1 needs data associated with record ABC.
> > Because record is owned by User 2, User 1 must wait in idle state.
> To process record ABC, User 2 needs data associated with record XYZ.
> > Because record is owned by User 1, User 2 must wait in idle state.

Though data integrity has been maintained, we now have two users in an infinite wait state known as a deadlock or, more glamorously, fatal embrace. The avoidance and/or detection of deadlock situations in a multiuser environment is a nontrivial problem. If you are interested in exploring it more deeply, see Harvey M. Deitel's *An Introduction to Operating Systems*. rev. 1st ed. (Reading, Mass.: Addison-Wesley, 1984).

disk files if we want reasonable response time for our searching efforts. The indexing schemes that we are about to discuss in this section are primarily directed toward file-oriented applications and thus will take into account the operational properties of this storage medium. We encourage you to reread the discussion of bucket hashing at the end of Section 10.2 for a summary analysis of file storage considerations.

The idea behind the use of an index is analogous to the way in which we routinely use an address book to find a person whom we are seeking. That is, if we are looking for a person, we do not knock on the doors of numerous houses until we find the one where that person lives. Instead, we apply a search strategy to an address book. There we use the name of the person as a key to find a pointer—that is, an address—which swiftly leads us to where the person can be found. Only one actual "house access" must be made, although our search strategy may require numerous accesses into the address book index.

In a computer system, records (or more precisely blocks) could play the role of houses in the search scenario just described. Data records on disk are (when compared to main memory) terribly slow and awkward creatures to access. One of the reasons for this is that there is often so much data that must be moved from disk to main memory every time a record is accessed. Because of this, we must revise the conceptual picture we have for the general setup for an indexed search so that our list of keys is no longer parallel to the actual data they are logically associated with but rather is parallel to a list of pointers which will lead us to the actual data. The revised picture is presented in Figure 10-9.

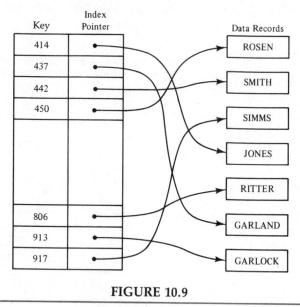

FIGURE 10.9

General setup for an indexed search

The general strategy of an indexed search is to use the key to efficiently search the index, find the relative record position of the associated data, and from there make only one access into the actual data. Because the parallel lists of keys and relative record positions require much less storage than the data itself, frequently the entire index can be loaded and permanently held in main memory, necessitating only one disk access for each record being sought. For larger indices, it still remains true that large blocks of keys and associated pointers may be manipulated in main memory, thereby still greatly enhancing search efficiency.

Indexed Sequential Search Technique

The indexed sequential search technique is also commonly recognized by the acronym ISAM, which stands for Indexed Sequential Access Method. Essentially it involves carefully weighing the disk-dependent factors of blocking and track size to build a partial index. The partial index, unlike some other index structures we will study, does not reduce to one the number of probes which must be made into the actual data. To continue the analogy between searching for data and searching for a person, the indexed sequential strategy is somewhat like an address book which would lead us to the street on which a person lives but leave it to us to check each of the houses on that street. The ISAM method correspondingly leads us to an appropriate region (often a track or a cylinder containing multiple tracks within a disk pack) and then leaves it to us to search sequentially within that region.

As an example, let us suppose that we can conveniently fit the partial index, or directory, pictured in Figure 10.10 into main memory and that the organization of our disk file allows six records per track.

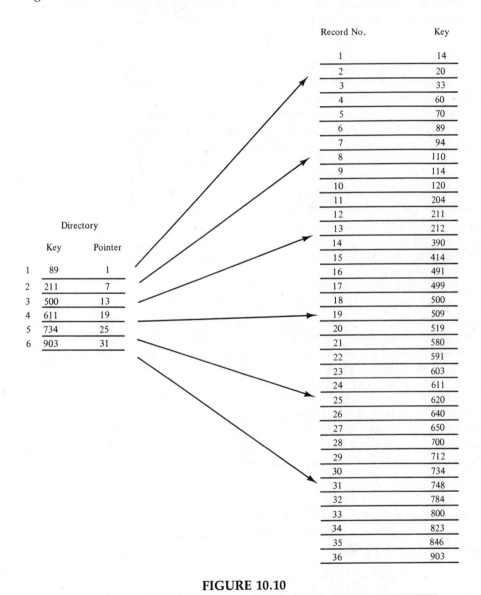

FIGURE 10.10

One-level indexed sequential file

This directory is formed by choosing the highest key value in each six-record track along with a pointer indicating where that track begins. Here our pointers are simply relative record numbers; in practice they could well be a more disk-dependent locator. The strategy to conduct an indexed sequential search is to

1. Search the main memory directory for a key which is greater than or equal to the Target.

2. Then follow the corresponding pointer out to the disk and there search sequentially until we find a match (success) or the key that the directory maintains as the high key within that particular region (failure).

For the data given in Figure 10.10, this technique would mean that the 36-record file would require no more than six main memory index accesses plus six disk accesses, all of which are located in the same track.

For larger files, it may be advantageous to have more than one level of these directory structures. Consider, for instance, the two-level directory structure for a file with 216 records as given in Figure 10.11. Here we might suppose that storage restrictions allow the entire primary directory to be kept in main memory, the secondary directory to be brought in from a disk file in blocks of six key-pointer pairs each, and the actual data records to be stored six per track. The primary directory divides the file into regions of 36 records each. The key in the primary directory represents the highest-valued key in a given 36-record region, but the pointer leads us into the subdirectory instead of the actual file. So, we search the primary directory for a key greater than or equal to the target we are seeking. Once this is done, we follow the primary directory pointer into the secondary directory. Beginning at the position indicated by the primary directory's pointer, we again search for a key greater than or equal to the target. Notice that fetching one block of six key-pointer pairs from the subdirectory has necessitated one disk access in our hypothetical situation. In return for this single disk access, we are able to subdivide the 36-record region determined by the primary directory into six 6-record regions, each of which will lie entirely on one track by the time we get out to the actual disk file. Following the subdirectory's pointer to the file, we end up with a relatively short sequential search on the storage medium itself. In this example, the maximum number of disk accesses required to find any record would be seven, and six of those would be isolated on one track of the disk.

Efficiency Considerations for the Indexed Sequential Search. It should be clear from the preceding discussion that the search efficiency of the indexed sequential technique depends on a variety of factors. Included among them are

☐ To what degree the directory structures are able to subdivide the actual file.

☐ To what degree the directory structures are able to reside in main memory.

☐ The relationship of data records to physical characteristics of the disk such as blocking factors, track size, cylinder size, and so on.

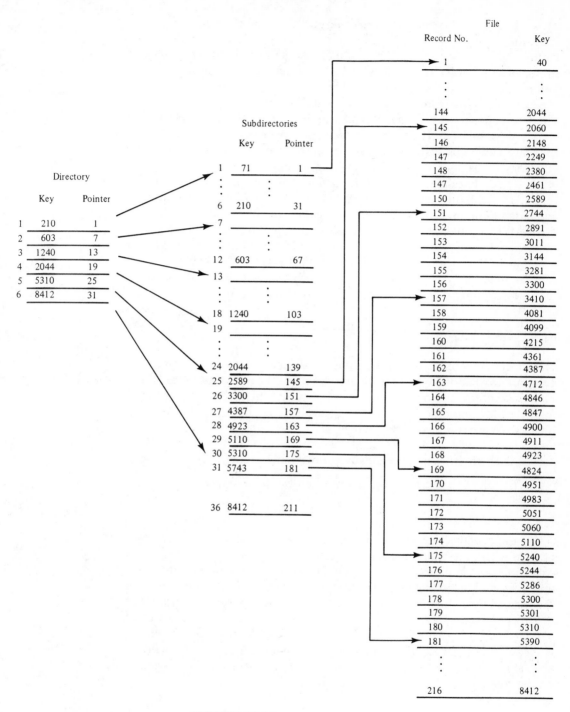

FIGURE 10.11

Two-level directory structure

It should also be clear that the indexed sequential method may not be ideal for a highly volatile file. This is because, as implicitly indicated in Figures 10.10 and 10.11, the actual data records must be physically stored in increasing (or decreasing) key order. The requirement for physical ordering is obviously not conducive to frequent insertions and deletions. In practice, the solution to this problem is that each file subregion which is ultimately the subject of a sequential search is equipped with a pointer to an overflow area. Insertions are located in this overflow area and linked to the main sequential search area. As the overflow area builds up, the search efficiency tends to deteriorate. In some applications, this deterioration can be so severe that data processing personnel have been known to refer to the ISAM technique as the Intrinsically Slow Access Method. The way to avoid deterioration is to periodically reorganize the file into a new file with no overflow. However, such reorganization cannot be done dynamically. It requires going through the file in key sequential order and copying it into a new one. Along the way, the indices must be rebuilt, of course. These types of maintenance problems involved with the ISAM structure have led to the development of several more dynamic indexing schemes.

Binary Tree Indexing

The concept of a binary tree search has already been covered in Chapter 7. The only twist added when the binary tree plays the role of an index is that each node of the tree contains a key and a pointer to the record associated with that key in some larger data aggregate. The advantages of using a binary tree as an index structure include:

□ A search efficiency potentially proportional to $\log_2 n$.

□ The ability to traverse the list indexed by the tree in key order.

□ Dynamic insertion and deletion capabilities.

These qualities make the binary tree the ideal index structure for situations in which the entire tree can fit in main memory. However, if the data collection is so large that the tree index must itself be stored on disk, the efficiency of the structure is less than optimal. This is because each node of the index may lie in a disk block separate from the other nodes and hence require a separate disk access. Using an example of 50,000 keys, a search of a binary tree index could require 16 disk accesses. To solve this problem, we would like to cluster those nodes along a given search path into one, or at least relatively few, disk blocks. The B-tree index structure is a variation on the tree index which accomplishes this goal.

B-Tree Indexing

We begin this discussion of B-trees by reminding you that one index entry requires nothing more than a key and a pointer. Moreover, we have been assuming that both the key and the pointer are integers, and we will continue to operate under this assumption during our discussion of B-trees. We emphasize this point here because, in a B-tree, a given tree node will in fact contain many such key-pointer pairs. This is because a given B-tree node will in fact coincide with one disk block. The idea behind a B-tree is that we will somehow group key-pointer pairs which are related in the search algorithm into a few strategic B-tree nodes, that is, disk blocks. At this point, we make the following formal definition. The definition will then be clarified via some examples.

B-Tree of Order n   A B-tree of order n is a structure with the following properties:

1. Every node in the B-tree has sufficient room to store $n - 1$ key-pointer pairs.

2. Additionally, every node has room for n pointers to other nodes in the B-tree (as distinguished from the pointers within key-pointer pairs, which point to the position of a key in the file).

3. Every nonterminal node except for the root must have at least $n/2$ non-null pointers to other nodes in the B-tree.

4. All terminal nodes are on the same level.

5. If a node has $m + 1$ non-null pointers to other B-tree nodes, then it must contain m key-pointer pairs for the index itself.

6. For each B-tree node, we require that the key value in key-pointer pair KP_{i-1} is less than the key value in key-pointer pair KP_i, that all key pointer pairs in the node pointed to by P_{i-1} contain keys which are less than the key in KP_i, and that all key-pointer pairs in the node pointed to by P_i contain key values which are greater than the key in KP_i.

Stipulation 5 says that we can think of a B-tree node as a list

$$P_0, \; KP_1, \; P_1, \; KP_2, \; P_2, \; KP_3, \; \ldots , \; P_{m-1}, \; KP_m, \; P_m$$

where P_i represents the ith pointer to another B-tree node and KP_i represents the ith key-pointer pair. Note that a B-tree node will always contain one more pointer to another B-tree node than it does key-pointer pairs. With this picture in mind, the sixth and final stipulation of our definition makes sense. Figure 10.12 illustrates how this rather involved definition applies to a B-tree node with three key-pointer pairs.

As a further illustration of this definition, a complete B-tree of order 6 serving as an index structure for the 36-record file of Figure 10.10 appears in Figure 10.13. (In this figure, the slash between numbers denotes a key-pointer pair; ⊢ denotes a null pointer.) The reader should carefully verify that all six defining properties are satisfied.

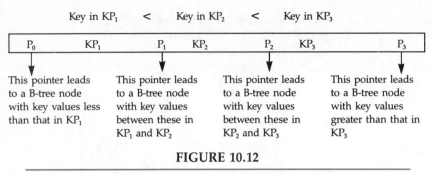

Key in KP₁   <   Key in KP₂   <   Key in KP₃

| P_0 | KP_1 | P_1 | KP_2 | P_2 | KP_3 | P_3 |

This pointer leads to a B-tree node with key values less than that in KP_1

This pointer leads to a B-tree node with key values between these in KP_1 and KP_2

This pointer leads to a B-tree node with key values between these in KP_2 and KP_3

This pointer leads to a B-tree node with key values greater than that in KP_3

FIGURE 10.12

Example of a B-tree node with three key-pointer pairs

The choice of order 6 for Figure 10.13 was made only for the purposes of making the figure fit on a page of text. In practice, the order chosen would be the maximum number of B-tree pointers and key-pointer pairs that we could fit into one disk block. That is, the choice should be made to force a disk block to coincide with a B-tree node. It is also worth noting that B-trees of order 3 have special application as a data structure apart from indexing considerations. This application will be covered in the Programming Problems at the end of the chapter.

Efficiency Considerations for B-Tree Indexing. Let us now consider what is involved in searching a B-tree for a given key. Within the current node (starting at the root), we must search sequentially through the key values in the node until we come to a match, a key value which is greater than the one being sought, or the end of the key values in that particular node. If a

"Hazel, help me! I can't find my cubbyhole."

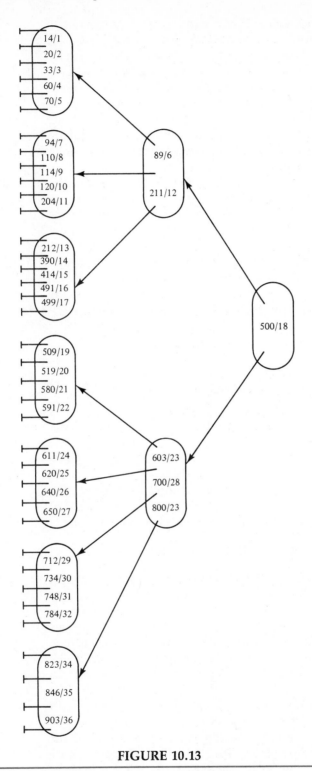

FIGURE 10.13

B-tree index of order 6 for file in Figure 10.10

match is not made within a particular B-tree node, we have a pointer to follow to an appropriate follow-up node. Again, you should verify this algorithm for several of the keys appearing at various levels of Figure 10.13. The sequential search on keys within a given node may at first seem unappealing. However, the key fact to remember here is that each B-tree node is a disk block which is loaded entirely into main memory. Hence, it may be possible to search sequentially on hundreds of keys within a node in the time it would take to load one new node from disk. Our main concern is to minimize disk accesses, and here we have achieved a worst case search for our 36-entry file in three disk accesses.

What in general is the search efficiency for a B-tree index? It should be clear from the nature of the structure that the maximum number of disk accesses for any particular key will simply be the number of levels in the tree. So the efficiency question really amounts to knowing the maximum number of levels that the six defining criteria would allow for a B-tree containing n key-pointer pairs. That is, this number would be the worst case search efficiency. To determine this number, we use the minimum number of nodes that must be present on any given level. Let L be the smallest integer greater than or equal to N/2 where N is the order of the B-tree in question. Then

> Level 1 contains at least 1 node.
> Level 2 contains at least 2 nodes.
> Level 3 contains at least 2*L nodes.
> Level 4 contains at least $2*L^2$ nodes.
>
> .   .
>   .   .
>   .   .
> Level m contains at least $2*L^{m-2}$ nodes.

An argument based on Knuth's research (see Searching and Sorting, cited in Section 10.2) uses this progression to show that the maximum number of levels (and thus the worst case search efficiency) for n key-pointer pairs is

$$\log_N((n + 1)/2)$$

Thus, a B-tree search has an $O(\log_N n)$ efficiency where n is the number of records and N is the order of the B-tree. Note that this can be considerably better than on $O(\log_2 n)$ search efficiency. As an example, the index for a file of 50,000 records which would require on the order of 16 disk accesses using a binary tree structure could be searched with 3 disk accesses using a B-tree of order 250. The reader should note here that, given typical block sizes for files, the choice of order 250 for this example is not at all un-realistic.

Unlike ISAM, the B-tree index can dynamically handle insertions and deletions without a resulting deterioration in search efficiency. We will next discuss how B-tree insertions are handled; making deletions is left for an exercise. The essential idea behind a B-tree insertion is that we must first determine which bottom-level node should contain the key-pointer pair to be inserted. For instance, suppose that we want to insert the key 742 into the B-tree of Figure 10.13. By allowing this key to walk down the B-tree from the root to the bottom level, we could quickly determine that this key belongs in the node presently containing

$$\boxed{712/29 \quad 734/30 \quad 748/31 \quad 784/32}$$

Since, by the definition of a B-tree of order 6, this node is not presently full, no further disk accesses would be necessary to perform the insertion. We would merely need to determine the next available record space in the actual data file (37 in this case) and then add the key-pointer pair 742/37 to this terminal node, resulting in

$$\boxed{712/29 \quad 734/30 \quad 742/37 \quad 748/31 \quad 784/32}$$

A slightly more difficult situation arises when we find that the key-pointer pair we wish to add should be inserted into a bottom-level node that is already full. For instance, this would occur if we attempted to add the key 112 to the B-tree of Figure 10.13. We would load the actual data for this key into file position 38 (given the addition already made in the preceding paragraph) and then determine that the key-pointer pair 112/38 belongs in the bottom-level node

$$\boxed{94/7 \quad 110/8 \quad 114/9 \quad 120/10 \quad 204/11}$$

The stipulation that any given B-tree node have minimally $6/2 = 3$ pointers to other B-tree nodes will now allow us to split this node, creating one new node with two key-pointer pairs, and one with three key-pointer pairs. We would also have to move one of the key-pointer pairs up to the parent of the present node. The resulting B-tree is given in Figure 10.14.

Although it does not happen in this particular example, note that it would be entirely possible that the moving of a key-pointer pair up to a parent node that is already full would necessitate a split of this parent node, using the same procedure. Indeed it is possible that key-pointer pairs could be passed all the way up to the root and cause a split of the root. This is in fact how a new level of the tree would be introduced. A split of the root would force the creation of a new root which would only have one key-pointer pair and two pointers to other B-tree nodes. However, at the root level this is still a sufficient number of pointers to retain the B-tree structure. Because the insertion algorithm for a B-tree requires checking whether a given node is full and potentially moving back up to a parent node, it is convenient to allow space within a node to store both of the following:

□ A count of the number of key-pointer pairs in the node.

□ A back pointer to the node's parent.

Trie Indexing

In all of the indexing applications we have discussed so far, the keys involved have been integers. In practice, however, we must be prepared to deal with keys of different types. Perhaps the worst case is that of keys which are variable length character strings. Trie indexing has developed as

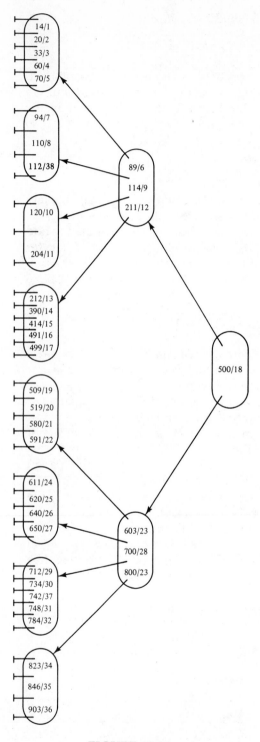

FIGURE 10.14

B-Tree of Figure 10.13 after insertion of 112/38 and
742/37

a means of retrieving keys in this worst case. (The term itself is derived from the four middle letters of "retrieve," though it is usually pronounced "try.") Let us suppose, for instance, that the strings in the following list represent a set of keys. Each string may be thought of as a last name followed by initials and a delimiting $.

        ADAMS BT$
        COOPER CC$
        COOPER PJ$
        COWANS DC$
        MAGUIRE WH$
        MCGUIRE AL$
        MEMINGER DD$
        SEFTON SD$
        SPAN KD$
        SPAN LA$
        SPANNER DW$
        ZARDA JM$
        ZARDA PW$

An individual node in a trie structure for these keys follows:

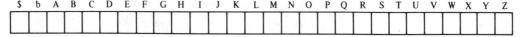

$	b	A	B	C	D	E	F	G	H	I	J	K	L	M	N	O	P	Q	R	S	T	U	V	W	X	Y	Z

Trie Node

It is essentially a fixed length array of 28 pointers: one for each letter of the alphabet, one for a blank, and one for the delimiter. Each pointer within one of these nodes can lead to one of two entities—either another node within the trie or the actual data record for a given key. Hence it may be convenient to embed a Boolean flag in each pointer indicating the type of entity to which it is pointing. The trie structure for the preceding list of keys is given in Figure 10.15. In this figure, pointers to nodes labeled as data records lead us outside of the trie structure itself.

The logic behind a trie structure may best be seen by tracing through an example. This search algorithm involves examining the target key on a character-by-character basis. Let us begin by considering the easy case of finding the data record for ADAMS BT$. In this case, we look at A, the first character in the key, and follow the A pointer in the root node to its destination. From what we have previously said, we know that its destination will be either another node within the trie structure or an actual data record. If it were a node within the trie, it would be a node on the search path for all keys which begin with A. In this case, there is only one key in our list which begins with A, so the A pointer in the root node leads us directly to the actual data record for ADAMS BT$. On the other hand, the search path to find the key COOPER CC$ in the trie is somewhat longer. We follow the C pointer from the root node down a level to a node shared by all keys starting with C. From there, the O pointer is followed to a trie node shared by all keys which start with CO. The process continues down level by level, following the O pointer to a trie node shared by all keys starting with COO, then the P pointer to a node for all keys starting with

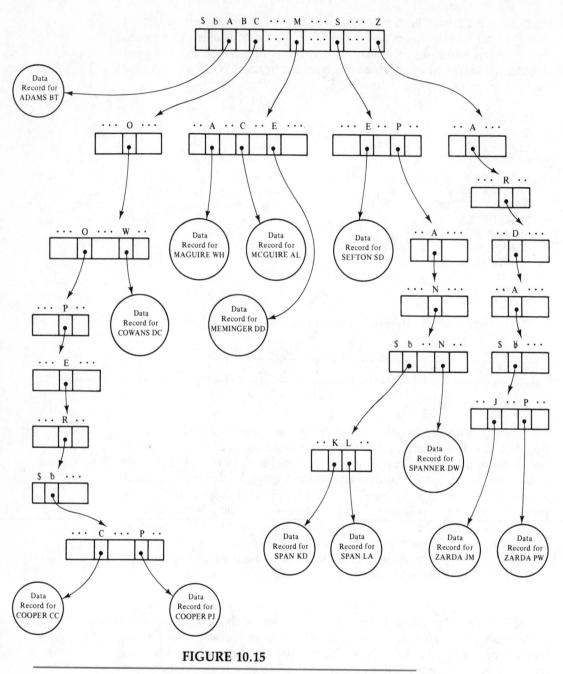

FIGURE 10.15

Trie index structure

COOP, the E pointer to a node for all keys starting with COOPE, the R pointer to a node for all keys starting with COOPER, and the blank pointer to a node shared by all keys starting with COOPER followed by a blank. Notice that, as each character is read in, we must continue following these pointers from trie node to trie node (instead of from trie node to actual data record) until we finally reach a point where the next character to be read will uniquely define the key. At this point, the key in question need no longer share its pointer with other keys which match it on an initial sub-string. Hence the pointer may now lead to an actual data record. This is what happens in our example when we read in the next C to form the uniquely defining substring COOPER C.

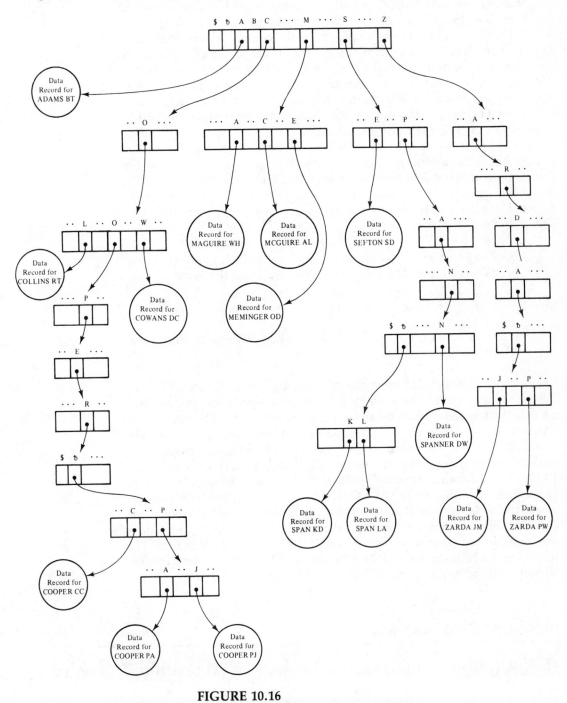

FIGURE 10.16

Trie of Figure 10.15 after inserting COLLINS RT$ and
COOPER PA$

Efficiency Considerations for Trie Indexing. The search efficiency for the trie index is quite easily determined. The worst case occurs when a key is not uniquely defined until its last character is read in. In this case, we may have as many disk accesses as there are characters in the key before we finally locate the actual data record. The astute reader should observe, however, that there is another efficiency consideration to be taken into account when using the trie method. This is the amount of wasted storage in the trie nodes. In our example using a short list of keys, only a small percentage of the available pointers are ever used. In practice, however, a trie would only be used for an extremely large file, such as the list represented by a phone book with names as keys. In such a situation, a much larger number of character combinations occurs and the resulting trie structure is correspondingly much less sparse.

A final point to consider relative to trie indexes is their ability to dynamically handle insertions and deletions. We will discuss the case for insertions and leave deletions as an exercise. Insertions may be broken down into two cases. For both we must begin by reading the key to be inserted, character by character, and following the appropriate search path in the trie until

☐ We come to a trie node which has a vacant pointer in the character position corresponding to the current character of the insertion key.

or

☐ We come to an actual data record for a key different from the one which is being inserted.

The first case is illustrated by trying to insert the key COLLINS RT$ into the trie of Figure 10.15. We would follow the search path pointers until we came to the trie node shared by all keys starting with CO. At this point, the L pointer is null. The insertion is completed by merely aiming the presently null L pointer to a data record for the key COLLINS RT$. The second case is illustrated by trying to insert the key COOPER PA$ into the trie of Figure 10.15. Here, following the search path of the trie would eventually lead us to the data record for the key COOPER PJ$. The dynamic solution is to get a new trie node, aim the P pointer presently leading to the data record for COOPER PJ$ to this new trie node, and use the A and J pointers in the new trie node to lead us to data records for COOPER PA$ and COOPER PJ$ respectively. Both the COLLINS RT$ and COOPER PA$ insertions are shown with the resulting trie of Figure 10.16 on page 401.

DESIGNER'S WORKBENCH

Empirically Measuring and Evaluating Algorithm Efficiency

Throughout this text we have emphasized the importance of big-O algorithm analysis as a means of predicting beforehand the practicality of an algorithm in a given application. In this regard, big-O notation and analy-

sis serves a vital purpose—the estimation of the time and space requirements of an algorithm in order of magnitude terms. However, when designing software systems in the very competitive and demanding real
world, we often require a more detailed measurement of an algorithm's
performance than that which can be achieved simply with a big-O analysis.
One reason for this is the variety of complications which cannot be conveniently plugged into a big-O formula. Included among these complications
are

☐ The variety of hardware on which an algorithm must ultimately be
executed. There will be vast differences in both the time and space
limitations of such hardware. Moreover, the details of such limitations are often buried deep in system reference manuals and can be
exceedingly hard to find.

☐ Discrepancies which frequently arise between a user's projection of
his or her computer needs and the unforeseen demands which mate-
rialize once the software system is put into use. A good systems
analyst can hold those discrepancies to a minimum but not totally
eliminate them.

☐ The elements of chance and probability that are inherent in many
algorithms.

Examples of this final point are order of arrivals for insertion into a
binary tree, the original order of data serving as input to a sorting algorithm, and the distribution of keys which are thrown at a hashing function.
Consider some of the questions which big-O analysis leaves unanswered
for these techniques.

☐ We can guarantee that search efficiency in an ordered binary tree
will be between $O(n)$ and $O(\log_2 n)$. We can specify best and worst
cases. But what happens in between? When do we crossover from
response times that are acceptable to those that are not? Real-life
data are rarely best case or worst case. Hence the "in between"
question is often of vital importance. Yet it is also the one which a
pure big-O analysis leaves relatively unanswered.

☐ Sorting algorithms such as the quick sort pose similarly vexing questions. We know quick sort has an $O(n\log_2 n)$ best case time and an
$O(n^2)$ worst case time, but, again, what about the in between cases?
When do we crossover from acceptable to unacceptable? What percentage of cases fall into each of these categories?

☐ We have estimates for search efficiencies for various hashing techniques based upon the amount of storage we are willing to waste.
But how accurately will these estimates reflect what happens when
our systems are in daily use? Many of these estimates rely on sophisticated statistical analyses which assume the existence of a perfectly
random distribution of keys. What if our hashing function is not
perfectly random? What if the distribution of keys is such as to cause
unforeseen clustering?

The goal of this discussion is not to make you doubt the validity of big-O analysis when applied to real-world problems. Rather, we want to emphasize that big-O analysis *alone* is often not a sufficient predictor of how an algorithm will react to live data on an actual machine. Software developers must also empirically test the performance of their algorithms when faced with a variety of test situations. The results of such empirical testing can be used to fill in the gaps that a big-O analysis might leave.

What are some of the ways in which the implementation of an algorithm may be empirically tested? One frequently used technique is to profile the execution of an algorithm. Profiling an algorithm involves the insertion of counters into a program which keep track of how many times certain instructions are executed during a run of the program. For instance, if we wanted to empirically measure the average number of data interchanges in a sort algorithm, we could include the incrementation of a profiling counter before each data swap as in the following segment of code:

```
If Key[j] < Key[j+1] THEN
   BEGIN
     ProfileSwapCount := ProfileSwapCount + 1; {For profiling}
     Temp := Key [i];
     Key[i] := Key [i+1];
     Key[i+1] := Temp
   END;
```

By generating numerous random sequences of test data and determining the average of the resulting profile counts, we could in effect simulate the performance of our algorithm under the same type of unpredictable conditions that it will encounter when released to users.

Another technique that can be used to empirically measure an algorithm is to time the duration of its execution. On a single-user computer, this is relatively easy to do. Merely insert "Entering algorithm" and "Leaving algorithm" tracers at the beginning and end of an algorithm and manually time the span between the appearance of these tracers. On a larger time-sharing system, timing an algorithm becomes slightly more complex. Because we want to time only our algorithm and not be charged for the time another user's program is executing, manual timing will not suffice. However, most versions of Pascal offer nonstandard ways of accessing operating system timing utilities. For instance, in the VAX Pascal dialect used by one of the authors, there is a supplied library function CLOCK which takes no parameters and returns the amount of CPU time in milliseconds that has been logged by an individual user's job. Hence to determine the execution time in milliseconds of PROCEDURE X, we need merely generate the following code sequence:

```
t := clock; {t an integer variable}
X;   {Call procedure X}
writeln (clock-t);
       {Write the difference between the current amount of CPU
        time used and the amount used before X was called.}
```

Until the mathematical analysis of algorithms via big-O or similar techniques reaches a level of maturity where it can accurately predict the complexities of the real world (and that may never happen), empirical comparisons of different implementation strategies for an algorithm or data structure will continue to be a valuable aid in the fine-tuning of software systems

---

Designer's Workbench Exercises

1. Add a profiling counter to keep track of the number of comparisons made in each of the following sort procedures:
   a. Bubble sort.
   b. Insertion sort.
   c. Selection sort.
   d. Quick sort.
   e. Shell sort.
   f. Heap sort.
   g. Merge sort.
2. Add a profiling counter to keep track of the number of data interchanges made in each sort algorithm cited in the previous exercise.
3. Add a profiling counter to keep track of the number of list accesses for successful and unsuccessful searches in each of the following algorithms:
   a. Binary search.
   b. Binary tree search.
   c. Hashing with linear collision resolution.
   d. Hashing with quadratic collision resolution.
   e. Hashing with linked collision resolution.
4. Consult your local system documentation for timing tools which may be provided with your version of Pascal. Use them to conduct a comparison timing analysis for several algorithms.
5. Some Pascal systems provide profiling utilities to monitor program execution and thus make it unnecessary for the Pascal programmer to actually insert profiling counter instructions. Consult your local system documentation for the availability of such utilities with your version of Pascal. If available, learn how to use them and apply them in making execution time comparisons of several algorithms.
6. Explain how the empirical testing of a variety of strategies is facilitated by a system development philosophy which emphasizes data abstraction. ∎

Summary

The following table gives a concise synopsis of the search strategies that have been discussed in this and earlier chapters. Additional comments emphasize particular strengths or weaknesses of the strategy in terms of the ACIDS criteria we have considered throughout the text.

Method	Efficiency (n = Number of Records)	Other Comments Regarding ACIDS Criteria
Sequential	$O(n)$	
Binary	$O(\log_2 n)$	Data must be maintained in physical order, hence making insertions and deletions inefficient.
Linear hashing	Average successful: $(1/2) * (1+1/(1-D))$ Average unsuccessful: $(1/2)(1+1/(1-D)^2)$ where density D = n/RecordSpace	Data not maintained in any order.
Quadratic hashing	Average successful: $-(1/D) * \log_e(1-D)$ Average unsuccessful: $1/(1-D)$	Data not maintained in any order.
Linked hashing	Average successful: $1+D/2$ Average unsuccessful: D (where RecordSpace used in computation of D is that in primary hash area)	Data not maintained in any order.
Indexed sequential	O(size of index) index probes, $O(n/$(size of index)) file probes	Index and file require physical ordering to maintain efficiency.
Binary tree index	$O(\log_2 n)$ index probes, 1 file probe	Guaranteeing this efficiency requires height balancing.
B-tree index order N	Worst case requires $1 + \log_N((n+1)/2)$ disk accesses for index	Choose N so that index node coincides with disk block.
Trie index	O(number of characters in Target)	Specifically suited for character strings.

In addition to hashing, we have described other search strategies specifically oriented toward file structures. These strategies include indexed sequential search, B-trees, and tries.

In this chapter, hashing has been presented as yet another implementation strategy for general lists. In this regard, it fares very well in all of the ACIDS criteria except sorting/ordering. It thus represents a very viable addition to the list implementation strategies discussed in earlier chapters: array or random files with binary search, linked lists, and binary trees.

Key Terms

binary search
binary tree index

binary tree search
boundary folding

B-tree
buckets
clustering
collision
concurrent updating
cylinder
data integrity
deadlock
density-dependent search tech-
    niques
digit/character extraction
directory
division remainder technique
fatal embrace
folding
hashing
hashing function
index
Indexed Sequential Access
    Method (ISAM)
indexed sequential search

key-to-address transformation
linear collision processing
linked collision processing
overflow area
prime hash area
profile an algorithm
quadratic collision processing
random access disk file
randomized storage
random number generator
record lock facility
rehashing
sectors
seed
sequential search
shift folding
subdirectory
synonyms
tracks
trie index

Exercises

1. Assume a hashing function has the following characteristics:

   Keys 459 and 333 hash to 1.
   Key 632 hashes to 2.
   Key 1090 hashes to 3.
   Keys 1982, 379, 238, and 3411 hash to 10.

   Assume that insertions into a hashed file are performed in the order
   1982, 3411, 333, 632, 1090, 459, 379, and 238.
   a. Indicate the position of the keys if the linear method is used to
      resolve collisions.

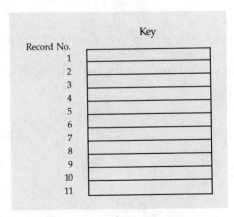

b. Indicate the position of the keys if the quadratic method is used to resolve collisions.

	Key
Record No.	
1	
2	
3	
4	
5	
6	
7	
8	
9	
10	
11	

c. Indicate the position of the keys and the contents of the link fields if the chaining (that is, linked lists) method is used to resolve collisions. Use zeros to represent **NIL** links and assume that the first record used in the overflow area is 12, then 13, then 14, and so on.

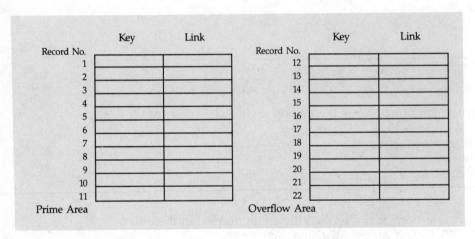

Record No.	Key	Link		Record No.	Key	Link
1				12		
2				13		
3				14		
4				15		
5				16		
6				17		
7				18		
8				19		
9				20		
10				21		
11				22		
Prime Area				Overflow Area		

2. Repeat Exercise 1 with the order of insertion of keys reversed.
3. a. Suppose that the records associated with keys 810, 430, 602, 946, 289, 106, and 732 are stored in positions 1, 2, 3, 4, 5, 6, and 7 respectively of a file. Draw a B-tree index of order 8 for this file.
   b. Suppose the key 538 then arrives for insertion in position 8. Redraw your B-tree of order 8 after this insertion.
4. Suppose that the following strings arrive for insertion into a trie index.

CARTER
HERNANDEZ
HERMAN
HERMANSKI
HERSCHEL
HALL
CARSON
CARSWELL
CARSEN

   a. Draw the trie index.

   b. Draw the index after CARSWELL and HERMANSKI have been deleted.

5. Suppose that we combine hashing with a linked list in the fashion described in Section 10.3 so that all five ACIDS list operations can be efficiently performed. Which of the variations on a linked list structure would be most effective in this context? Why? (*Hint:* Think about the change and delete operations.)

6. Discuss a key deletion strategy for B-trees. Write a procedure which implements your strategy.

7. Discuss a key deletion strategy for trie indexes. Write a procedure to implement your strategy.

8. Carefully read your system reference material concerning the specifics of how disk file records are blocked. Then explain how this knowledge would influence your decisions in the construction of

   a. An ISAM index structure.

   b. A B-tree index structure.

   c. A trie index structure.

   d. A bucket hashing structure.

9. All of the search strategies we have discussed assume a key which is uniquely valued. That is, no two records have the same value for their key field. In practice this will not always be the case. We may have duplicate keys. For instance, a list of personnel records may contain two records for different people with the same name. Discuss how each of the search strategies we have covered would have to be modified to perform a duplicate key search. What effect would these modifications have on the performance of the algorithm?

10. We have covered binary search, linked lists, binary trees, and hashing as methods of implementing a general list to be acted upon by ACIDS operations. Choose the method you would use to implement the data list involved for each of the following three real-world applications. In each case you should choose the most appropriate implementation technique. "Most appropriate" here means efficiently handling all of the required operations while not being too powerful; that is, not doing something that should be easy in an overly complicated way. Then provide a rationale as to why yours would be the appropriate method.

   a. The list to be maintained is the card catalog of a library. Frequent additions to and deletions from this catalog are made by the library. Additionally, users are frequently searching for the data associated with a given book's key. However, the library rarely prints out an ordered list of all its holdings. Hence ordering the list is not to be considered a high priority.

   b. You are writing a program that maintains the lists of passengers on flights for an airline company. Passengers are frequently being added to these lists. Moreover, quite often passengers cancel flight plans and must be removed from a list. You are also told that the airline frequently wants alphabetized listings of the passengers on a given flight and often needs to search out a particular passenger by name when inquiries are received from individuals.

   c. You are writing a program which will access a large customer data base and build up counts for the numbers of customers from each of the 50 states (plus the District of Columbia). To do this you will use a list of records consisting of the two-character state abbreviation and an integer representing the count of customers from that state. For each customer you read in from the data base, you must find the customer's home state in your list and increase the corresponding count field. At the end, print out the counts in order alphabetized by the two-character state abbreviation.

11. Write procedures to insert a key into a list to be searched by
    a. Linear hashing.
    b. Quadratic hashing.
    c. Linked hashing
    d. Bucket hashing.

12. Write procedures to search for a key via
    a. Quadratic hashing.
    b. Bucket hashing.

13. Devise strategies to delete keys from a list being maintained by each of the four hashing strategies in Exercise 11. Write Pascal versions for each of these algorithms. Given your deletion strategy, what modifications must be made in the various search and insertion procedures of Exercises 11 and 12?

14. In Section 10.2 we mentioned a result by Radke that answered the question of how many array slots would be probed by the quadratic hashing algorithm for certain values of RecordSpace. In particular, Radke showed that if RecordSpace is a prime number of the form $4m + 3$ for some integer m, then half of the array slots would be probed by the sequence of probes

    $$K, K+1^2, K+2^2, K+3^2, \ldots$$

    where K is the original hash position. Radke also showed that the other half would be probed by the sequence

    $$K-1^2, K-2^2, K-3^2, \ldots$$

    Rewrite your insertion and search procedures for the quadratic method in Exercises 11 and 12 to take into account Radke's result.

15. Develop a procedure to search a list via ISAM. Initially assume just one directory. Then alter the procedure so that it would work with one subdirectory.

16. Devise procedures to handle insertions into and deletions from a list maintained by the indexed sequential method. Do the strategies reflected by these procedures require any modifications in your answers to Exercise 15?

17. Write the algorithm to insert a key into a B-tree.

18. Write an algorithm to insert a key and its data record into a trie.

Programming Problems

1. Implement the registrar's system described in Chapter 1 using hashing as a list maintenance technique. Be sure that you devise an appropriate strategy to output the ordered listings that the registrar must produce.

2. Implement the Wing-and-a-Prayer flight/pilot data base using the implementation technique described in Section 10.3. For an added challenge, assume that the rows of the flight/pilot table are indexed by pilot name instead of pilot number. How could this complication be handled in a way which minimizes the memory needed to store the implementation of a sparse table?

3. A B-tree of order 3 is often called a 2-3 tree since each node has 2 or 3 children. Because of its low order, a 2-3 tree is not particularly applicable as a file index. However, if we store up to two actual data records in each node instead of up to two key-pointer pairs, then a 2-3 tree becomes an alternative to an ordered binary tree for implementing a list. Develop search, insertion, and deletion algorithms for such a 2-3 tree structure. Compare its performance characteristics with those of an ordered binary tree.

4. Implement the registrar's system using a 2-3 tree representation of a list. (See Programming Problem 3.)

5. Wing-and-a-Prayer Airlines has the records of all its customers stored in the following form:

   □ Last name.

   □ First name.

   □ Address.

   □ Arbitrarily long list of flights on which reservations have been booked.

   Using a trie index, write a search-and-retrieval program that will allow input of a customer's last name (and, if necessary, the first name and address to resolve conflicts created by matching last names) and then output all flights on which that customer has booked reservations.

6. SuperScout Inc. is a nationwide scouting service for college football talent to which the Bay Area Brawlers professional team subscribes. As the pool of college talent increases in size, SuperScout has found that its old recordkeeping system has deteriorated considerably in its ability to quickly locate the scouting record associated with a given player in its file. Rewrite their scouting record system using a trie to look up the record location of the data associated with a given player's name.

7. Using a large collection of randomly generated keys, write a series of programs which will test various hashing functions you develop. In particular, your programs should report statistics on the number of collisions generated by each hashing function. This information could be valuable in guiding future decisions about which hashing functions and techniques are most effective for your particular system.

8. Consider a student data record which consists of

   □ Student identification number.

   □ Student name.

   □ State of residence.

   □ Sex.

Choose an index structure to process a file of such records. Then write an ACIDS program to maintain such a file.

9. Suppose that data records for a phone book file consist of a key field containing both name and address, and a field containing the phone number for that key. Devise an appropriate index for such a file. Then write a program which calls for input of

a. A complete key.

b. If a complete key's not available, as much of the initial portion of a key as the inquirer is able to provide.

In the case of a, your program should output the phone number corresponding to the unique key. In the case of b, have your program output all keys (and their phone numbers) which match the provided initial portion.

10. Consider the following problem faced in the development of a compiler. The source program contains many character-string symbols such as variable names, procedure names, and so on. Each of these character-string symbols has associated with it various attributes such as memory location, data type, and so on. However, it would be too time-consuming and awkward for a compiler to actually manipulate character strings. Instead, each string should be identified with an integer which is viewed as an equivalent to the string for the purpose of compiler manipulation. In addition to serving as a compact equivalent form of a string symbol within the source program, this integer can also serve as a direct pointer into a table of attributes for that symbol. Devise such a transformation which associates a string with an integer, which in turn serves as a pointer into a table of attributes. Test the structure(s) you develop by using them in a program which scans a source program written in a language such as Pascal. You will in effect have written the symbol table modules for a compiler.

11. Write a spelling checker program. Such a program must scan a file of text, looking up each word it finds in a dictionary of correctly spelled words. When a word cannot be found in the dictionary, the spelling checker should convey this fact to its user, giving the user the opportunity to take one of the following steps:

a. Change the spelling of the word in the text file.

b. Add the word to the dictionary so it will not be reported as incorrectly spelled in the future.

Since the dictionary for such a program will be frequently searched and is likely to become quite large, an efficient search algorithm is an absolute necessity. One possibility in this regard is to use a trie index with pointers into a large string workspace instead of the pointers to data records described in Section 10.4. Test your program with a text file and dictionary large enough to handle all of the possibilities your algorithm and data structure may encounter.

Computer Science: Theory Meeting Practice

I find that a great part of the information I have was acquired by looking up something and finding something else on the way.

Franklin P. Adams

Introductory Considerations

The Relevant Issues in the preceding chapters have provided brief glimpses into some of the ways the topics we have studied find application in more specialized areas of computer science. Collectively, these glimpses offer a great deal of information about the emerging discipline of computer science. Our goal in this chapter is to take a retrospective look at those Relevant Issues and use them as a starting point in presenting an overview of computer science. This overview is not intended to be comprehensive, but rather to provide you with a better idea of where your future studies in computer science may lead. Perhaps more than anything else, this overview will emphasize what we find to be one of the most exciting aspects of computer science: the opportunity it offers to merge the theoretical results of logic and mathematics with the problem-solving strategies required to develop practical, effective software.

In particular, we will examine this blend of theory and practice in four areas of computer science:

1. Language compilers.

2. Operating systems.

3. Software reliability and formal verification.

4. Artificial intelligence and the Halting Problem.

Since the Relevant Issues will play a central role in our discussion, we encourage you to review them. For your convenience, a summary of the issues we have covered in these sections is presented in Table 11.1. We suggest that you review these sections before going on to the indicated section of this chapter.

Chapter	Relevant Issue Section	Section
1	Sparse Tables and Language Compilers	Language Compilers (11.2)
2	Artificial Intelligence, the Complexity of Algorithms, and Parallel Processing	Artificial Intelligence and the Halting Problem (11.5)
3	Software Reliability and Defense Systems	Software Reliability and Formal Verification (11.4)
4	Storage of Disk Files and Computer Security	Operating Systems (11.3)
5	Operating Systems and Scheduling Resource Use in a Time-Sharing Environment	Operating Systems (11.3)
6	Language Definition	Language Compilers (11.2)
7	Computer Security and Tree-Structured File Systems	Operating Systems (11.3)
8	Recursion, LISP, and the Practicality of Artificial Intelligence	Artificial Intelligence and the Halting Problem (11.5)
9	Fourth Generation Languages: Getting Users More Involved	Software Reliability and Formal Verification (11.4)
10	Data Integrity, Concurrent Updates, and Deadlock	Operating Systems (11.3)

TABLE 11.1

Summary of Relevant Issues

_____ **11.2**

Language Compilers

The essential task of a language compiler is to translate. This translation is from a high-level programming language such as Pascal into the binary code of the particular machine you are using. This binary machine language is a sequence of 1s and 0s (actually ONs and OFFs in the internal circuitry of the computer) which represent your program in the form that can ultimately be executed by the computer. Some compilers translate into assembly code instead of this binary machine code. Assembly code is a mnemonic version of machine code in which the names of operations are used in place of binary codes for essential machine operations and in which symbolic label references are used in place of actual memory addresses. Unlike the situation for a high-level language, in assembly code there is a one-to-one correspondence between mnemonic instructions and the fundamental operations which can be performed by the computer. Another simpler translating program called the assembler then completes the translation by transforming the assembly code into binary code. These two possibilities for the entire translation process are highlighted in Figure 11.1.

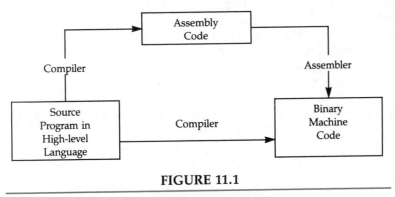

FIGURE 11.1

The two possible paths from source program to binary code

As an example of the compilation process, consider a simple Pascal assignment statement such as

$$A := B + C$$

On a simple computer with a single accumulating register in which to perform arithmetic, this may translate into assembly code which resembles

```
LDA    B
ADD    C
STO    A
```

Here the first assembly instruction is to load the accumulator (mnemonic LDA) with the data stored at memory location B. This is followed by the instruction to add the contents of C (mnemonic ADD) to the current contents of the accumulator. Finally, the contents of the accumulator are stored (mnemonic STO) at memory location C. If a compiler translated Pascal instructions into assembly code such as this, the assembler would then transform these mnemonics into the appropriate strings of 1s and 0s to be actually executed by the computer.

Our intent here is not to focus on the assembly code or the assembler software. The one-to-one correspondence between assembly code and fundamental operations available on the computer makes programming in assembly code rather laborious. It also makes the algorithm which drives the assembler relatively easy. The assembler must only look up mnemonics in a table where it finds the binary strings to associate with them. Rather we want to examine more closely what the compiler must do to successfully translate one high-level instruction into potentially *many* assembler instructions (or machine operations). Simply described, the compiler process may be broken down into three phases: lexical analysis, parsing (syntactic analysis), and code generation.

Lexical Analysis and Parsing

The lexical analysis phase is subordinate to parsing in the following sense. The parser determines whether an incoming stream of tokens constitutes a valid program in the source program's language. Thus, the task of the parser is analogous to determining whether a sequence of words comprise a valid English sentence. The parser itself processes words (that is, tokens) and is therefore not directly concerned with the rules for determining what constitutes a valid token in the language. This latter responsibility is assigned to the lexical analyzer. We saw this relationship illustrated in the case study for Chapter 6. However, a full-fledged compiler must be concerned with these lexical and parsing issues in a much broader sense than our integral evaluation case study from that chapter.

As the parser checks the syntax of an incoming source program, it may also build an internal data structure to represent the program in a form more convenient for further processing. This parallels what we did in transforming arithmetic expressions into postfix representation in Chapter 6. Again, a compiler has a substantially more difficult stream of tokens to transform than a mere arithmetic expression. However, a strategy taken by many compilers is to actually view the incoming source program as one large formal expression. Because the syntax of a programming language is considerably more complex than the syntax of algebraic expressions, a general tree is required to store the representation of the entire program that is constructed by the parsing phase of the compiler. For instance, a Pascal program as simple as the following:

```
PROGRAM Nothing(input, output);

VAR
  a,b : integer;

BEGIN
read(a,b);
IF a < b THEN
  BEGIN
    write (a);
    write (b)
  END
```

```
ELSE
  BEGIN
    write(b);
    write(a)
  END
END.
```

could possibly generate the tree representation pictured in Figure 11.2.

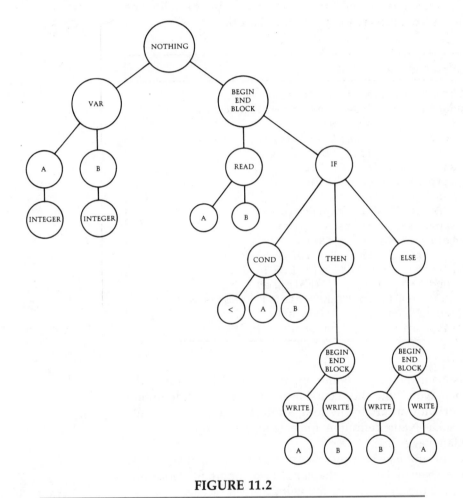

FIGURE 11.2

Tree representation of Pascal program

This tree representation of the incoming source program would vary slightly from compiler to compiler. Indeed, decisions about how to make such representations are often crucial in determining the efficiency of the resulting compiler. In general, trees representing the syntactical structure of a source program are called parse trees or abstract syntax trees. Once such a tree is constructed, the next phase of the compiler will then traverse it, generating assembly or binary code for the native machine along the way.

Obviously, the parsing phase of a compiler is not a simple task. Yet it also provides an excellent example of how the application of formal theory in software engineering has decreased the time required to develop the software while simultaneously improving its reliability. In developing a parser, a key first step is to formally define the syntax of the language being parsed. Such a definition inevitably involves recursive techniques (as we have already indicated in the Relevant Issue of Chapter 6). The form taken by such a recursive definition may be a graphical syntax diagram as illustrated in Chapter 6 or a textual form as illustrated by the following Backus-Naur language definitions for a subset of Pascal:

Text	Backus-Naur Definition
program	"VAR" decllist ";" cmpdstmt".".
decllist	declaration ¦ declaration ";" decllist.
declaration	IDENTIFIER ":" type.
type	"boolean" ¦ "char" ¦ "integer" ¦ "real".
cmpdstmt	"BEGIN" stmtlist "END".
stmtlist	stmt ¦ stmt ";" stmtlist.
stmt	simplstmt ¦ structstmt.
simplstmt	assingmstmt ¦ iostmt.
assignstmt	IDENTIFIER ":=" expression.
expression	expression "+" term ¦ term.
term	term "*" factor ¦ factor.
factor	"(" expression ")" ¦ IDENTIFIER.
iostmt	("read" ¦ "write") "(" IDENTIFIER ")".
structstmt	cmpdstmt ¦ ifstmt ¦ whilestmt.
ifstmt	"IF" condition "THEN" stmt ["ELSE" stmt].
whilestmt	"WHILE" condition "DO" stmt.
condition	expression Relation expression.

In such a Backus-Naur language definition, the vertical line (¦) is to be interpreted as "or." Note how the recursion in such a formal definition allows a cmpdstmt with an arbitrarily long stmtlist. In formal language theory, such a Backus-Naur definition for a language is often called a grammar for the language.

One technique of language parsing relies on a state table similar to that we described in the Relevant Issue of Chapter 1. Two important algorithms from formal language theory allow the following:

1. The construction of such a parsing table from the grammar specifying the language.

2. The construction of a parser program driven by the previously constructed table.

What are the implications of a theory which encompasses two such algorithms? Essentially it tells us that the process of building a parser for a language is so well understood that it can be algorithmically automated. That is, we can write a program which takes as input the grammar for a language in Backus-Naur form and produces as output another program which is a parser for the language under consideration. Such a parser-producing program is often called a parser generator. The input/output sequence of a parser generator is depicted in Figure 11.3.

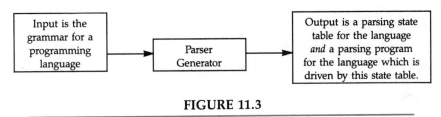

FIGURE 11.3

Input/output for a parser generator

The availability of parser generators has, in many cases, made it completely unnecessary for compiler developers to write their own parsing procedure. Instead, a grammar for the language is fed into a parser generator, and, by the magic of formal language theory, a parser for the language is automatically and immediately produced. Not only has the writing of a difficult procedure been transformed into an instantaneous process, but, because it is automated, it is also a virtually error-free process. Hence compiler writers may concentrate their efforts upon the code-generation phase which follows parsing.

Code Generation

The code-generation phase of a compiler takes the result of parsing (for example, a tree such as that in Figure 11.2) and uses it to produce assembly or binary code. From a theoretical perspective, the code-generation phase is not understood as well as the parsing phase. By this we mean that researchers in the area of compiler development have not yet developed a suitable formal theory to automate code generation in the way that parsing can be automated. Hence this phase is where much of the research effort in compiler theory is being directed. As this theory evolves, it is hoped that the development of code-generation procedures can be made as easy and painless as those for parsing. If and when that day comes, the whole process of writing a compiler may reduce to running a compiler-generator program which takes as input a grammar for your language and specifications of the operations which your particular computer can perform and then produces as output a complete, ready-to-use compiler. Clearly such a prospect presents some exciting possibilities. In the future, it may well be the case that new and more powerful languages can be defined and then implemented in a fraction of the time that it took to implement their more limited predecessors.

_____ **11.3**

Operating Systems

The keywords in any discussion of operating systems are scheduling and resource allocation. The operating system is comprised of the large collection of software that underlies any task done by a user of the computer. On a multiuser computer system, these scheduling and resource allocation issues become particularly complex. Consider some of these problems to which we have already been introduced via Relevant Issues.

1. Allocation of space for disk files in a fashion which allows users to conveniently extend them. (Chapter 4.)

2. Scheduling the use of resources, such as a printer, which may be needed by several users and yet cannot be allocated to a new user until the old owner of that resource is completely finished with it. (Chapter 5.)

3. Structuring an index (directory) for disk files in a way which assures the security of any given user's data. Ultimately, it is the operating system that is responsible for protecting the computer from a variety of abuses ranging from unintentional user errors and mischievous pranks to outright computer crime. (Chapter 7.)

4. Controlling access to records in a disk file by not allowing two users to concurrently update an individual record. This type of control guarantees the integrity of the data in the file but may lead to a deadlock situation. (Chapter 10.)

Memory Allocation and the Fragmentation Problem

Designers and implementors of operating systems must be Marxists at heart. That is, the algorithms which dole out system resources must have as their overriding goal a distribution scheme which assures that each user gets what he or she needs but not more. Additionally, as users finish with a resource, it must be immediately reclaimed by the operating system in its "big brother" role so that it may be reallocated to other needy users. As an example of the complications that arise in this allocate-reclaim-reallocate cycle, consider the problem faced by a multiuser operating system which must grant users the memory required to run their respective applications. A possible scenario for such a sequence of user requests is presented in Figure 11.4. This figure illustrates what is known as the fragmentation problem. That is, as memory is allocated to users and then returned, the resulting overall pattern of available memory contains relatively small, disconnected fragments of available space. The problem with this fragmented pattern is that we cannot honor a user request for a contiguous memory area which exceeds the size of the largest available memory block even though overall we may have more than enough memory to grant the request. This dilemma is illustrated by the 10K request in the final memory snapshot of Figure 11.4.

One solution to this fragmentation problem would be to move all used memory blocks down in memory, hence resulting in just one large free block whose size is equal to the sum of the sizes of all the original smaller free blocks. This strategy is called compaction and is not acceptable from an operating system perspective. Why? Operating systems must be extremely time efficient in their responses to users. The compaction process would require a stoppage of all user activity while memory is reorganized by

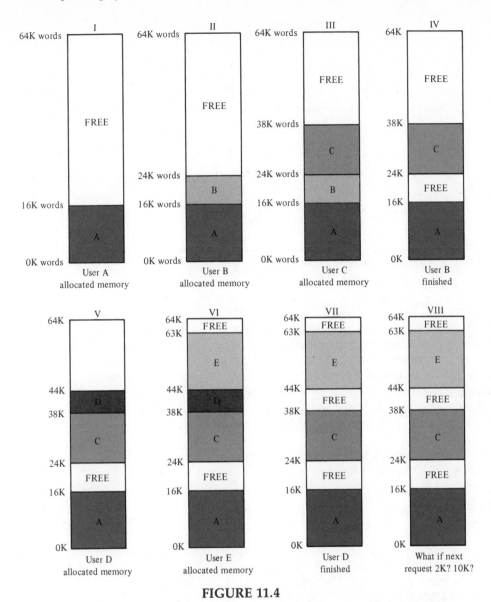

FIGURE 11.4

Fragmentation problem on a multiuser system

moving large amounts of data. Hence compaction would inevitably result in periodic and time-consuming interruptions in service that would be sure to annoy system users.

Another attempt at solving this problem is to generalize the algorithm behind the GetNode and ReturnNode procedures of Chapter 4, enabling them to handle variable length records. For instance, the free blocks pictured in the last memory snapshot of Figure 11.4 could be linked into an available list by allocating two words in each block to store the size of the block and a pointer to the next available block. (See Figure 11.5.) When a new user request is made of the list in Figure 11.5, the list could be

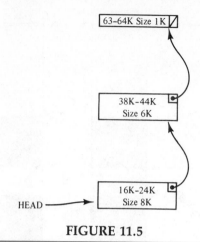

FIGURE 11.5

Available block list derived from snapshot VIII of
Figure 11.4

searched for the first block whose size meets the request (or for the block whose size comes closest to meeting the request). Having determined the block to allocate to the user, it would be wise to check next whether or not the user actually requires the entire block. If not, it could be split, giving the user what is requested and keeping what remains of the block in the available block list. This strategy, applied to the available block list of Figure 11.5 for a request of 2K memory, yields the result displayed in Figure 11.6.

Unfortunately, this scheme will only lead to another problem when it comes time to collect the memory blocks no longer needed by users. Con-

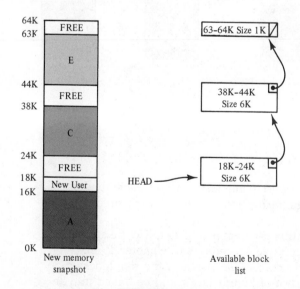

FIGURE 11.6

Honoring a 2K request from the available block list of
Figure 11.5

sider, for instance, what happens if the 2K memory block allocated in Figure 11.6 is returned by its user before any other changes are made in the available space structure. The new available space list now contains one additional 2K block as indicated in Figure 11.7.

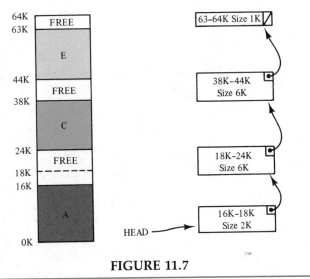

FIGURE 11.7

Available block list after returning the 2K block

Clearly what will happen as more and more of these relatively small blocks are returned is that the available list will have an inordinate number of very small blocks. This is not desirable because it will eventually make it impossible to fill the legitimate request of a user needing one large memory block. We will have small neighboring blocks, the sum of whose sizes may collectively surpass the total memory needed by the large request. However, their being partitioned into many small blocks instead of relatively few large blocks will make it impossible to fill the request. To remedy this problem, we must devise a method which will allow a block being returned to the available list to be coalesced with any other block(s) in the list which are the physical neighbor(s) of the returning block. Interestingly, one of the solutions we are about to describe makes use of a theoretical sequence of numbers from mathematics known as the Fibonacci sequence. Hence we again see the theme of theory meeting practice; this time it occurs in the area of operating systems.

Buddy Systems

A common method for insuring that a returning block coalesces with neighboring available memory is to designate for each block one or two buddy blocks. A buddy block must reside next to its corresponding block in memory. When a block is ready to be returned, we check the available space list for its buddy. If the buddy is also available, we coalesce the two before returning them as one block to available space. This is not quite as easy as it sounds, however. To determine the buddy of a given block, it will be necessary to impose certain restrictions upon block sizes and/or to store a fair amount of bookkeeping data in each block. We shall examine three buddy schemes.

1. Binary buddies.

2. Fibonacci buddies.

3. Boundary tag buddies.

These schemes differ in the data structures used for their implementation. After stating the general algorithms in pseudocode, we shall give a more detailed discussion of these data structures.

```
PROCEDURE Allocate(S,P)

{ Given a request for a memory block of size S, return a pointer P to a
  memory block which meets the request with a minimum amount of waste. }

  Call a search procedure to search the available block list(s)
    and find a block which surpasses the size requested with the
    least possible amount of excess.

  IF no such block can be found
    THEN Call InsufficientMemory

  ELSE IF the block found cannot be split into buddies (one of which
         would satisfy the size requested)
    THEN return the pointer from the search procedure as P

  ELSE { The buddy system being used allows splitting. }
         Split the block into two buddies
         Return one buddy appropriately to available block list(s)
         Return P as the pointer to the other buddy

  ENDIF

  END Allocate
```

The search procedure called upon to find a block in this procedure would be dependent upon the data structure used by a particular buddy system to store available blocks. Whether a block, once found, can be further split is determined by the restrictions the given buddy system imposes on block sizes.

A similar generic pseudocode algorithm to restore a returning memory block to available space is presented here in recursive form. The recursion expresses the fact that, once a returning block has been coalesced with its buddy on the left or right, we have a larger block that may itself be a candidate for coalescing with another buddy.

```
PROCEDURE ReturnBlock (P,Avail)

{ Return to available space the memory block being pointed to by P.
  Avail represents the available space structure used by the buddy
  system in question. }
```

{ Begin by recursively coalescing P with its buddies. }

Call Coalesce(P,Avail)   { See procedure Coalesce following. }

{ Upon return from Coalesce, P may well be pointing to a much larger block
  than it was before. The final step is now to attach this potentially
  larger block to the available space structure. }

Call Attach (P,Avail)

END ReturnBlock

PROCEDURE Coalesce (P,Avail)

  { This procedure will coalesce block pointed to by P with a buddy on its
    left or right. Avail represents the available block structure used
    by this particular buddy method. }

  { The call to CheckBuddies represents a call to a procedure
    which will determine whether buddies of P exist in the available
    space structure. If a left buddy of P is available, then a pointer
    to it is returned in LBuddy. Otherwise LBuddy is returned as Null.
    A similar process is followed for the pointer RBuddy. }

Call CheckBuddies (P,Avail,LBuddy,RBuddy)

  { If both LBuddy and RBuddy come back as Null, both of the conditional
    tests which follow will fail and an immediate return will result.
    Otherwise coalescing must occur on left and/or right. }

IF RBuddy <> Null THEN
    Remove RBuddy from Avail structure
    Change appropriate fields in P to coalesce P with RBuddy
        { Fields dependent upon buddy system being used. }
    Call Coalesce(P,Avail)
        { Recursively attempt to coalesce the new, larger P with
          its buddies }

ENDIF

IF LBuddy <> Null THEN
    Remove LBuddy from Avail structure
    Change appropriate fields in LBuddy to coalesce P with LBuddy
        { Fields dependent upon buddy system being used }
    Set P to LBuddy { P points to new, larger block }
    Call Coalesce(P,Avail)
        { Recursively attempt to coalesce the new, larger P with its
          buddies }

ENDIF

END Coalesce

We will now explain in more detail the methodology of each of the three previously cited buddy systems. From the generic procedures Allocate and ReturnBlock given, it is clear that a detailed exposition must describe both the data structure used to store available blocks and the bookkeeping type of data that must be stored within and about each memory block.

Binary Buddy System. The logic of this method requires that all blocks be of size 2^i for some i. Whenever a block is split, the resulting two buddies must be of equal size. That is, if a block of size 2^i is split, then the resulting buddies will each be of size $2^{(i-1)}$. As an example, let us suppose that we have 2^{16} (64K) words of memory to manage and that we wish to allocate no blocks smaller than 2^{10} (1K) words. Then, at any given time, we could potentially have free blocks of size 2 raised to the 10th, 11th, 12th, 13th, 14th, 15th, and 16th power. The available space structure in this case will consist of a doubly linked list of free blocks for each of the seven potential block sizes. Hence we would need head pointers as follows:

Avail(1)→Head of list for blocks of size 2^{10}
Avail(2)→Head of list for blocks of size 2^{11}
Avail(3)→Head of list for blocks of size 2^{12}
.
.
.
Avail(7)→Head of list for blocks of size 2^{16}

Each block would need to contain the following bookkeeping information:

☐ A Boolean flag to indicate whether or not it is free.

☐ An integer field to store its size.

☐ Left and right links used when it is a node in an Avail list.

A graphic illustration of such a node is given in Figure 11.8.

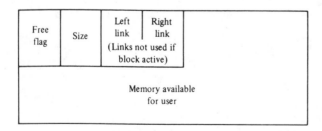

FIGURE 11.8

Bookkeeping information in block for binary
buddy system

Initially, all 2^{16} words of memory would be viewed as one free block; that is, Avail(7) would point to the beginning of memory and all other

Avail pointers would be Null. Now let us suppose that a sequence of user requests came in the following order:

   a. Request for memory block of size 2^{14}.

   b. Request for memory block of size 2^{13}.

   c. Request for memory block of size 2^{14}.

   d. Request for memory block of size 2^{14}.

   e. Block from request a no longer needed.

   f. Block from request b no longer needed.

The dynamic processing of these requests can best be described pictorially. In Figure 11.9, we have used tree diagrams to represent the splitting and coalescing that would occur as requests a through f are processed. Memory addresses in this figure are given as 0, 1, 2, . . . , 62, and 63; i represents the beginning of the $(i + 1)$st 1K memory block (of which there are 64 in all).

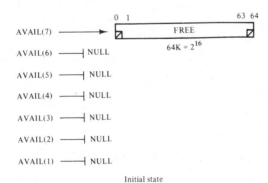

Initial state

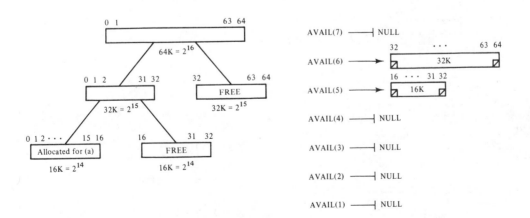

Request (a) processed

FIGURE 11.9

Processing requests using the binary buddy system

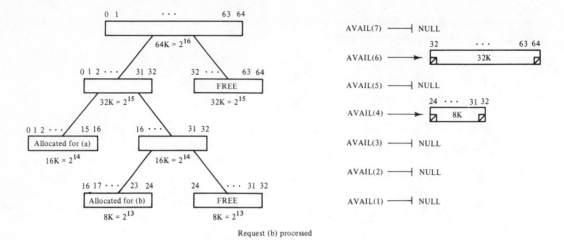

Request (b) processed

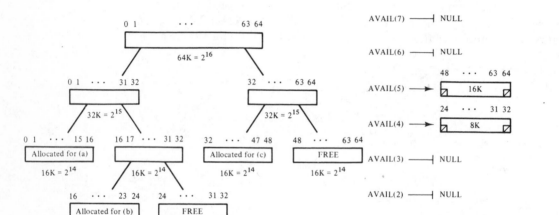

Request (c) processed – allocate block of size 2^{14}

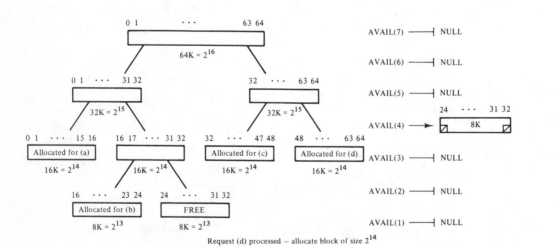

Request (d) processed – allocate block of size 2^{14}

FIGURE 11.9 Continued

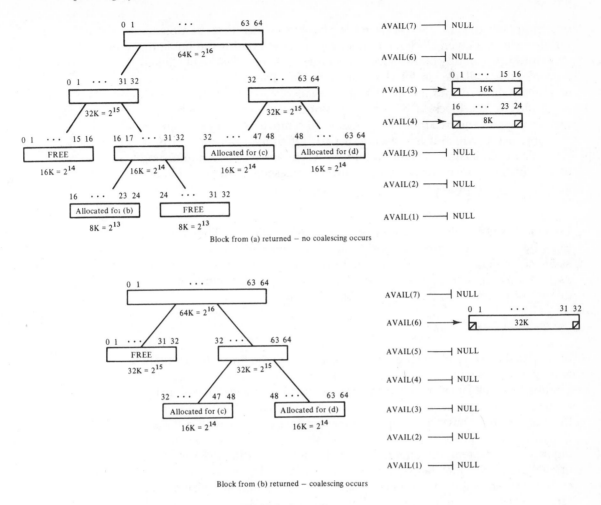

Block from (a) returned – no coalescing occurs

Block from (b) returned – coalescing occurs

FIGURE 11.9 Continued

Three comments are needed to explain more fully the actions highlighted in Figure 11.9. First, the point of coalescing is that one available block of size 2N is always preferred to two available blocks of size N. The whole is greater than the sum of its parts. This is why, in returning the block from request b in Figure 11.9, we coalesce two 8K blocks into a 16K block and then immediately take advantage of an available 16K left buddy to coalesce further into a 32K block.

Second, the binary splitting scheme means that, when a block is to be returned, the address of its buddy can be immediately determined. For instance, the block of size 2^{14} which begins at address 0 (relative to 1K blocks) has a right buddy of the same size which begins at address 16 (relative to 1K blocks). The location of this block's buddy is purely a function of the block's own size and location. In absolute terms, a block of size 2^i with starting address $n \times 2^i$ will have a right buddy with starting address $(n + 1) \times 2^i$ if n is even and a left buddy starting at address $(n - 1) \times 2^i$ if n is odd. This means that, as a block is being returned, a simple computation allows us to find its buddy, whose free flag would then be checked to determine whether or not coalescing is possible. Notice that, in a binary buddy system, a given block has either a left or a right buddy but not both.

Third, if the buddy of the block to be returned is free, the doubly linked nature of the available block lists becomes crucial. This is because we have essentially jumped into the middle of an available space list in accessing the buddy of the block to be returned. Without the double linking, we would not have the back pointer necessary to remove this buddy from the available list of which it is presently a part. Of course, once a returning block has been coalesced with its buddy, we now have a new returning block which may recursively undergo further coalescing as indicated in our generic Coalesce procedure.

Fibonacci Buddy System. Let us begin a consideration of Fibonacci systems by analyzing the binary buddy system. Contradictory as this may seem, the rationale is that we must define the relationships between block sizes that must exist in a buddy system of this type. Examining the sequence of possible block sizes in the binary system,

$$2^1, 2^2, 2^3, \ldots, 2^{10}, 2^{11}, \ldots$$

we notice that every member of the sequence except the first is the result of adding the previous member to itself. Since any block size (except the smallest possible) may result from coalescing two smaller blocks, it becomes clear that any sequence of possible block sizes for a buddy system of this variety must have the property that any size element within the sequence is the sum of two preceding members of the sequence. In the binary buddy system, this sum is always obtained by adding the size of the immediately prior member of the sequence to itself. However, the binary system is a special case; all that is really required is that any size can be represented as the sum of two smaller sizes.

Perhaps the most famous sequence of numbers having this property is the Fibonacci sequence. The ith member of the Fibonacci sequence can be recursively defined as

$$F_1 = 1$$
$$F_2 = 1$$
$$F_i = F_{(i-1)} + F_{(i-2)} \text{ for } i > 2$$

Hence, the initial members of the Fibonacci sequence are

1, 1, 2, 3, 5, 8, 13, 21, 34, . . .

Suppose, for instance, that we were managing 21K memory and were faced with the following requests for storage:

a. Request for 7K.

b. Request for 7K.

c. Request for 2K.

d. 7K from request b no longer needed.

e. 2K from request c no longer needed.

f. 7K from request a no longer needed.

Figure 11.10 illustrates the allocation, deallocation, and resulting coalescing that would occur as these requests were processed; circled digits are used to indicate left buddy counts.

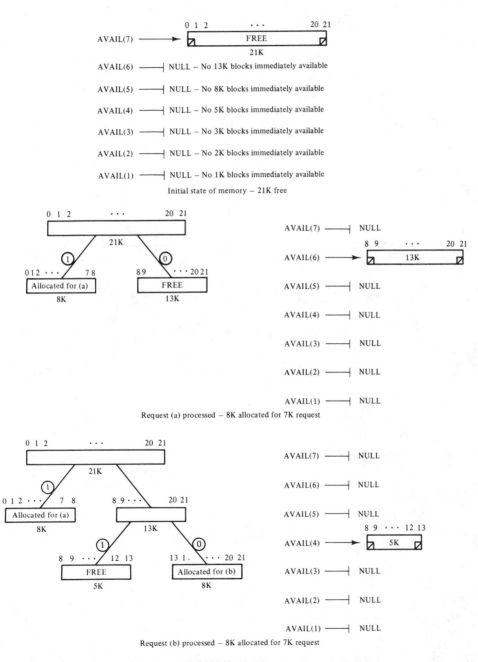

FIGURE 11.10

Processing requests using the Fibonacci buddy system

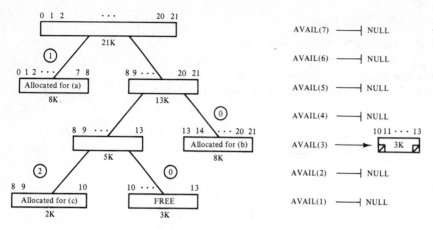

Request (c) processed – 2K allocated for 2K request

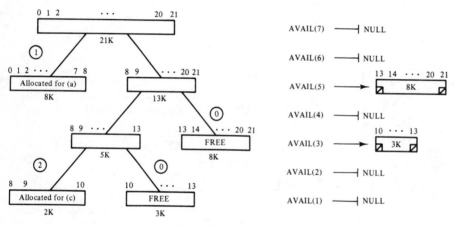

Request (d) processed – no coalescing

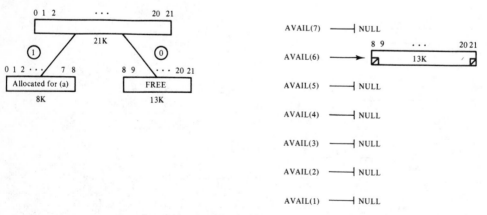

Request (e) processed – coalescing occurs up to 13K block

FIGURE 11.10 Continued

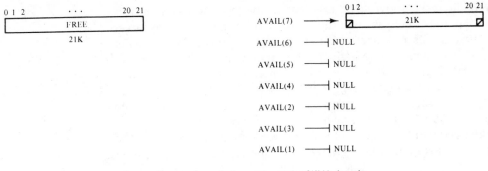

Request (f) processed – coalescing occurs – one free 21K block results

FIGURE 11.10 Continued

Naturally, some additional overhead (beyond that required for the binary buddy system) is required when the Fibonacci buddy system is used. First, depending upon the implementation scheme, it may be necessary to store the Fibonacci numbers themselves in an array to allow quick access to data necessary to allocate, split, and coalesce blocks. The alternative would be to recompute the sequence each time it is needed. Second, unlike the binary system, it is not clear from a block's size and location whether it is the left buddy or right buddy of another block. Consequently, it becomes necessary to store some additional bookkeeping data within each block, in the form of a left buddy count field as indicated in Figure 11.11. The left buddy count maintains a record of how deeply a given block is nested as the left buddy of other blocks. In Figure 11.10, the left buddy count is indicated by the circled digit appearing above each block. The algorithm for maintaining this left buddy count involves these steps.

1. As a block is split, the resulting left buddy has its left buddy count field increased by one. The resulting right buddy has its left buddy count field set to zero.

2. As coalescing occurs, the left buddy must always have its left buddy count field decreased by one.

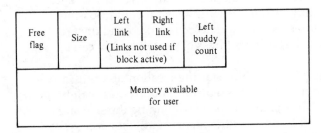

FIGURE 11.11

Bookkeeping information in block for Fibonacci buddy system

Given the increase in overhead involved in the Fibonacci system, it is certainly a valid question to ask whether or not it offers any advantage over the binary system. Its primary advantage is that it allows for a greater variety of possible block sizes in a given amount of memory than its binary counterpart. For instance, in 64K words of memory, the binary system would allow block sizes of 1K, 2K, 3K, 5K, 8K, 13K, 21K, 34K, and 55K; nine sizes in all. Clearly a greater variety of sizes will allow us to allocate memory in a fashion which minimizes the difference between what the user actually needs and what our block sizes force us to give.

In fact, if one uses a more generalized kth Fibonacci sequence defined by

$$F_j = 1 \text{ for } j = 1, 2, \ldots, k$$
$$F_j = F_{(j-1)} + F_{(j-k)}$$

then it can be readily seen that, the larger k becomes, the finer our partitioning of block sizes will be. (Notice that by this definition, the binary buddy system is in fact generated by the first Fibonacci sequence.) Of course, with each increase in k comes a corresponding increase in the overhead of bookkeeping information that must be balanced against the greater selection of block sizes. (For a more theoretical discussion of which k may be appropriate to choose in a given situation, see J. A. Hinds, *A Design for the Buddy System with Arbitrary Sequences of Buddy Sizes.* Technical Report, no. 74. (Buffalo, N.Y.: State University of New York at Buffalo, 1973).)

Boundary Tag Buddies. Both the binary and Fibonacci systems have the disadvantage of not allowing an arbitrary selection of block sizes, thereby forcing the waste of some memory each time a user's request does not precisely match one of the specified block sizes. The boundary tag method overcomes this drawback but only at the expense of requiring even more bookkeeping data than either of the other methods.

The reason that the binary and Fibonacci schemes limit us to a finite number of block sizes and splitting possibilities is that, without such a limitation, it would be impossible to determine where a block's buddy begins. For instance, suppose that we were using the Fibonacci buddy system and were about to return a block of size 13K whose left buddy count field was found to be zero. Because of the limitations on the sizes into which a block may be split under the Fibonacci method, we know that this block must have a left buddy of size 8K with which it could possibly coalesce. Using the starting address of the block to be returned and the fact that its left buddy has size 8K, the starting address of the left buddy can be obtained.

The problem of determining the size and starting location of a returning block's buddy is less complicated if the returning buddy has a right buddy instead of a left buddy. The distinction between finding the size and starting location of right and left buddies in the binary and Fibonacci systems can be seen in Figures 11.12 and 11.13. As highlighted in Figure 11.12, in a block with a right buddy, the starting location and size of the returning block would tell us the starting address of the right buddy. Then, provided we have stored the bookkeeping information for that right buddy precisely at its starting location, the size field and free flag are immediately available

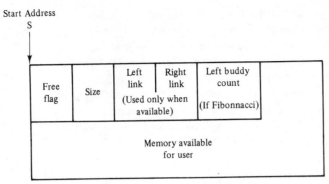

The bookkeeping information for this block's right buddy
can be accessed at memory address (S + size)

FIGURE 11.12

Determining size and start address of right Fibonacci or
binary buddy

for our inspection. Here, the bookkeeping information for the right buddy
can be accessed at memory address (S + Size).

As shown in Figure 11.13, the bookkeeping information for this block's
left buddy can be accessed at one of the following memory addresses:

□ (S − Size) if binary system.

□ (S − Fibonacci number preceding size) if Fibonacci system.

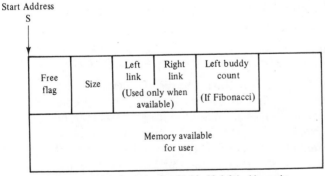

The bookkeeping information for this block's left buddy can be

accessed at memory address $\begin{cases} \text{(S − Size) if binary system} \\ \text{(S − Fibonacci number preceding size)} \\ \quad \text{if Fibonacci system} \end{cases}$

FIGURE 11.13

Determining size and start address of a left Fibonacci or
binary buddy

Figures 11.12 and 11.13 should make it apparent that, if we were willing to store duplicate copies of a block's size and free flag at its right

boundary as well as its left boundary, then the problem of determining the starting address of a left buddy would not require prior knowledge of what its size must be. Its size could be found by checking the bookkeeping information along the right boundary. The effect of this concept is that sizes can now be chosen arbitrarily to specifically meet a user's request. No longer would it be necessary to allocate 13K to meet an 11K request because the available choices of block sizes demanded it. This is the primary motivation behind the boundary tag buddy system. A block and the bookkeeping information within it would now appear as in Figure 11.14.

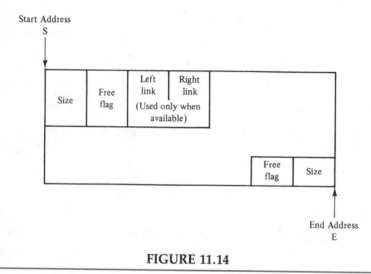

FIGURE 11.14

Block and bookkeeping information for boundary
tag method

The boundary tag technique has advantages and disadvantages which must be carefully considered before choosing it to use in a particular context. The major advantage, of course is that it allows a user's request to be granted precisely, with no excess memory being allocated and therefore wasted. The logic of the method also implies that a given block is not a left or right buddy per se. Rather any block except one starting or ending at a memory boundary has both a left and a right buddy with which it could coalesce. The primary disadvantages of the boundary tag method are the additional bookkeeping information that must be stored and maintained within each block, and the fact that the available space structure now must be sorted as one long doubly linked list instead of as a sequence of doubly linked lists for each of the respective block sizes allowed. This latter point means that, in determining whether a user's request can be met, the boundary tag method will require sequentially searching a single available space list, clearly a slower process than is required for either the binary or Fibonacci schemes. At this point, you are encouraged to trace through the actions diagrammed in Figure 11.15, highlighting the allocation and deallo-

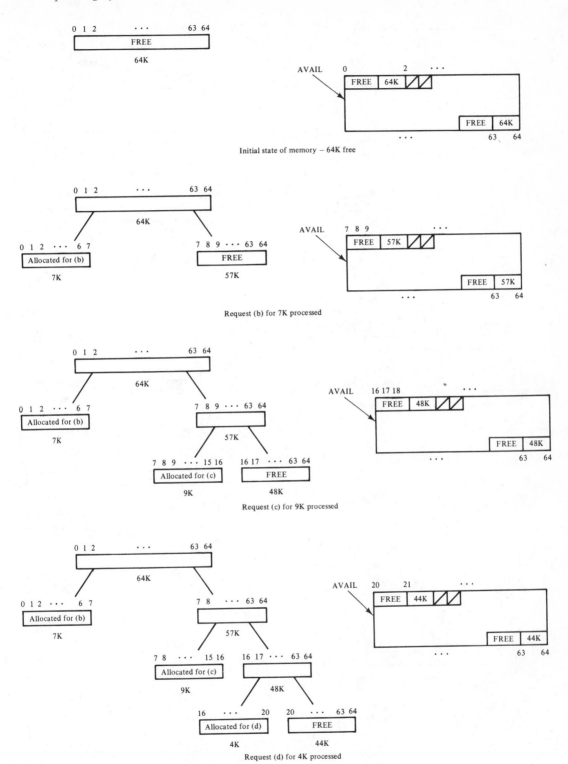

FIGURE 11.15

Processing requests using boundary tag buddy system

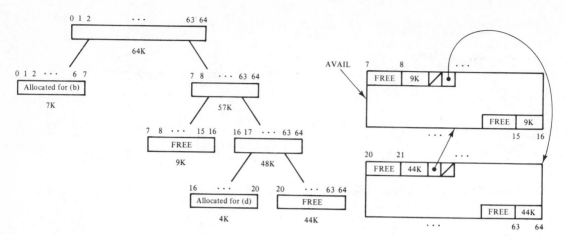

(e) Processed – no coalescing

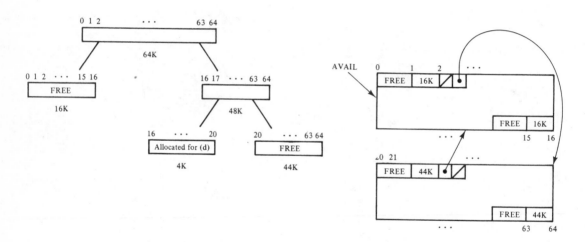

(f) Processed – returning block coalesces with right buddy

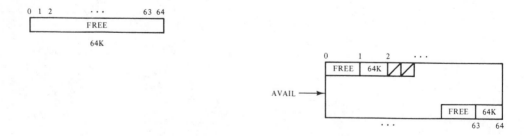

(g) Processed – coalescing occurs on both sides

FIGURE 11.15 Continued

cation of memory as the following requests are processed:

a. Initially all memory, 64K, is free.

b. User requests 7K.

c. User requests 9K.

d. User requests 4K.

e. Memory requested in c no longer needed.

f. Memory requested in b no longer needed.

g. Memory requested in d no longer needed.

Operating Systems: A Summary

The three memory management methods discussed in this section provide excellent illustrations of the application of data structures at the operating system level. Notice in particular that all three methods require the use of one or more doubly linked lists to store available memory blocks. The elegance of this relatively simple data structure allows us to delete a given block from the middle of an available list without having to traverse the entire list to find a back pointer as we would be forced to do with a singly linked list. This is yet another illustration of a principle we have emphasized throughout—knowing which data structure to choose for a particular application is one of the most important abilities a computer scientist must have.

The examples we have presented here and in the Relevant Issues clearly indicate the enormous complexity of the problems facing designers of operating systems. As computer systems continue to become more user-friendly, the burden put upon the operating system to do things for the user will become even greater. Compared to the design of language compilers (see Section 11.2), the area of operating systems is certainly more wide open. The problems are more complex and varied; the solutions are oftentimes less elegant. It is almost inconceivable to imagine a theory of operating systems so comprehensive that it could automate the process of producing an operating system (as we discussed doing with compilers in Section 11.2). This is not to say that theory does not have its place in operating systems but rather to say that operating systems theory must be balanced with an attitude of pragmatism. This difference between approaches in compiler design and operating systems design should not be a surprise. After all, operating systems deal with all the uncertainties that typify user activities on the computer. Compilers, on the other hand, are more directly focused on the simple elegance of formal languages.

_____ **11.4**

Software Reliability and Formal Verification

In the Relevant Issues for Chapters 3 and 9, we described two applications in which the reliability of software is certain to be of critical importance.

The first of these was computerized defense systems. Obviously, such systems *must* work correctly the first time they are used. The second area was fourth generation languages. Recall that the emphasis in a fourth generation language is to put more computing power into the hands of the end user. This computing power takes the form of languages with very powerful instructions, (for example, "SORT CUSTOMER FILE BY ZIP CODE"). In the Relevant Issue for Chapter 9, we described the positive side of these powerful new tools. They will get users much more involved in the software development process, even to the point of having many users write their own applications. People who know less (about the technical side of computing) will be able to do more than ever before. Is there a negative side of the "power to the people" direction? Yes, *if* the powerful software these people are using is not *completely* reliable. If the software backfires on these users, they will not necessarily be equipped with the technical know-how to be able to gracefully recover from the errors. The new power in their hands could become a software disaster, corrupting files and tying up systems.

For such problems to be avoided, we clearly must insist on reliable software. The approach we have taken in this text is to emphasize the construction of thorough and convincing test data as a means of verifying program/module correctness. However, this strategy of verification cannot be construed as a formal proof of the algorithm's correctness. We have attempted to show that an algorithm is correct by showing that it works for a comprehensive set of examples. But, from a mathematical perspective, a theorem cannot be proven by example. This is because there are infinitely many possibilities for such examples, hence making it in principle impossible to test every one. Instead of testing, a formal approach to algorithm verification demands an airtight proof using the basic axioms and principles of logic.

Formal Algorithm Verification by the Method of Inductive Assertions

Some work has been done in this area of formal algorithm verification. We shall attempt to summarize one of the more frequently used techniques, known as the the method of inductive assertions, by formally proving the correctness of the following algorithm. The algorithm is to compute n^m for n a real and m a nonnegative integer. Our correctness proof will use the principle of mathematical induction. (This principle is covered extensively in most discrete mathematics texts; be sure to review it before proceeding if you are not familiar with it.)

```
PROCEDURE Power (n : real;
                 m : integer;
                 VAR r : real);

{For nonnegative m, compute n raised to the power m and return
 result in r. }

BEGIN
  r := 1;
```

```
WHILE m > 0 DO
   BEGIN
      r := r * n;
      m := m - 1
   END
END;
```

A formal proof of such an algorithm involves appropriately identifying the input assertions, output assertions, and loop invariants of the algorithm. All three of these are statements about the algorithm expressed in formal mathematical terms. The input assertions represent all necessary input conditions to the algorithm. For our example, the input assertions would be

$$n \; \varepsilon \; \text{reals}$$
$$m \; \varepsilon \; \text{integers}$$
$$m \geq 0$$

The output assertions represent in formal terms the desired result. Here we would have

$$r = n^m$$

as the lone output assertion for our algorithm.

Finally, we must identify the loop invariants of our algorithm. A loop invariant may be thought of as a special type of assertion which expresses a relationship between variables which remains constant through all iterations of a loop. Note that it is not the variables which remain fixed but rather the relationship between them. This is a key distinction to make. As we shall see, correctly identifying loop invariants is often the most crucial and difficult step in setting the stage for a proof (by induction) of an algorithm's correctness. For the Power algorithm under consideration, let r_k and m_k be the respective values of r and m after k times through the **WHILE** loop. Both r and m change each time the loop is executed while n remains fixed throughout the algorithm. The loop invariant relationship we wish to prove is then given by

$$r_k \times n^{m_k} = n^m$$

If we can prove this loop invariant, then it follows immediately that the algorithm is correct. Why? If the looping ends after j times through the loop, m_j will be zero because of the conditional test in the **WHILE**. Hence, because of the loop invariant relationship, we will have

$$r_j \times n^{m_j} = n^m$$
$$\downarrow$$
$$r_j \times n^0 = n^m$$
$$\downarrow$$
$$r_j = n^m$$

Therefore, when the loop terminates after j iterations, r will contain the value n^m and thereby satisfy the output assertion. The entire problem of proving the algorithm's correctness has thus been reduced to achieving an inductive proof of the loop invariant relationship.

$$\text{Inductive proof of } r_k \times n^{m_k} = n^m$$

Basis Step with $k = 0$. Before looping begins, $r_0 = 1$ and $m_0 = m$ since these are then the values of the variable. Hence the loop invariant relationship for $k = 0$ becomes

$$1 \times n^m = n^m$$

which is trivially true.

Inductive Step. By the standard induction assumption, we assume

$$r_k \times n^{m_k} = n^m$$

and attempt to show

$$r_{k+1} \times n^{m_{k+1}} = n^m$$

In going from the kth pass through the **WHILE** loop to the $(k+1)$st pass through the loop we have

$$r_{k+1} = r_k \times n$$

and

$$m_{k+1} = m_k - 1$$

Hence

$$
\begin{aligned}
r_{k+1} &\times n^{m_{k+1}} \\
&= (r_k \times n) \times n^{(m_k - 1)} \\
&= r_k \times n^{m_k} \\
&= n^m
\end{aligned}
$$

by the induction assumption.

The inductive step thus completes the formal proof of the algorithm's correctness. Note how the pivotal point in the entire proof was the determination of the loop invariant. It is this determination which drives the rest of the proof. We can summarize the steps involved in the overall proof as follows:

1. Specification of input assertions.

2. Specification of output assertions.

3. Specification of loop invariants, from which the output assertions follow.

4. Proof (via induction) of the loop invariants.

What Do Proofs Really Prove?

One of the valid criticisms of our proof is that it proves correct an algorithm which is obviously correct to start with. This is a criticism which can often be made of formal correctness proofs as they presently stand. That is, the present state of the art in formal verification methods has not advanced to the point where they are of value in realistically complex situations. Other criticisms of the method include:

1. The proof method assumes the correctness of the input and output assertions. If they are wrong, a proof of the program could be done but the program could still contain errors.

2. The proof method says nothing about how the program will act when exceptional conditions occur which deviate from the input assertions.

3. The proof method focuses only on the logic within an individual module. It verifies nothing with respect to how the modules of a system will interact.

4. The proof method relies upon a completely accurate interpretation of the action dictated by a given algorithmic statement. This action is often called the semantics of the statement. If our interpretation of a statement's semantics does not match what actually happens when the program runs, the program may result in an error even though it has been proved correct.

5. Practical machine limitations such as round-off and overflow are usually not considered in formal correctness proofs.

6. Proof techniques ignore the problem of unwanted side effects caused by an algorithm. Such side effects may result in an error in the overall system even though each module has been proved correct.

7. Proofs of nonnumerical algorithms such as searching and sorting are much more difficult than proofs of numerical algorithms.

(These criticisms are set forth in more expanded form in Glenford Myer, *Software Reliability* (New York: John Wiley and Sons, 1976), 319–320.)

Formal correctness proofs must currently be considered as a technique of theoretical importance only. They simply are not sophisticated enough to find practical application in programs which solve realistically complex programs. However, a technique should not be rejected because it presently has little practical value. Many useful methods in computer science had their roots in pure theory. This fact has been one of the underlying themes of this chapter. Perhaps the ultimate hope for the formal correctness methods we have discussed is that they can be automated. That is, in the future we may have software which receives input/output assertions as its input, generates the code to satisfy these assertions, and then proves the correctness of the code. Though it is obviously a long way from happening, such automatic program synthesis does not seem to be impossible in principle.

—————————————————————————————— **11.5**

Artificial Intelligence and the Halting Problem

The Relevant Issues of Chapter 2 and 8 discussed applications in the area of computer science known as artificial intelligence (often referred to as AI). This label sometimes conjures up science fiction images of smart machines taking over the world. However, that is an extreme perspective which does not at all reflect the type of work that is actually occurring in this field. Artificial intelligence, in its present state, is really a collection of computer algorithms which attempt to solve certain kinds of problems in a way which parallels human problem-solving capabilities. Among the problems and applications being explored in AI are

☐ Playing games of strategy.

☐ Proving theorems using rules of logic and mathematics.

☐ Processing and understanding natural languages.

☐ Machine learning; that is, the development of programs which improve their performance based upon their past experience.

☐ Computer vision; that is, the development of software to process and understand electronic images received by camera-like sensory devices.

☐ Expert systems; that is, the development of software which is able to reason as an expert would in a limited domain such as medical diagnosis.

The algorithms which are used in AI are marked by two traits. First, they are extremely consumptive of time and space resources, often involving extensive tree searches to find the appropriate path to a problem's solution. Second, they are general-purpose algorithms that often can be reused or easily adapted. For instance, a chess-playing program may be driven by an algorithm which embodies more general rules of game playing. Of course, the specific data structures within such a program will be unique to chess, but the algorithm which manipulates and chooses possibilities from such structures will be general enough to function with structures representing other games also. In this sense, data abstraction is particularly important in AI. We must separate the general-purpose algorithm underlying the program from particular data structures and heuristics (rules of thumb used to guide the search for a path to a problem's solution) used in a given application of the algorithm. It is the general nature of AI algorithms that often distinguishes them from other algorithms. A given AI algorithm may thus be applied to a variety of problems. Perhaps this quality of AI algorithms will make possible dramatic, quantum leaps ahead in the future, thereby enabling the computer to become our problem-solving assistant in ways that are presently difficult to even imagine.

The Halting Problem: Theoretical Limits of Computing Machines

An interesting question posed by the general-purpose algorithms of AI concerns the theoretical limits of computing machines. As AI systems develop in the future, are there problems which, in principle, such systems will not be able to solve? Or, is any problem potentially fair game for such a system? Interestingly, answers to these questions were developed on a theoretical basis in the 1930s before the advent of the first electronic computers in the following decade. Two mathematicians played particularly prominent roles in developing this theoretical basis.

Kurt Gödel, a German-born mathematician, astounded other mathematicians in 1934 by proving what has come to be known as Gödel's Theorem. According to this theorem, in any formal, axiomatic system powerful enough to provide a basis for arithmetic, there are undecidable propositions. That is, there are statements within such a formal system such that neither the statement nor its negation can be proved. This essentially says that formal logical systems sufficiently powerful to allow mathematical reasoning will always contain questions which cannot be answered by reasoning within the system itself. Prior to Gödel's Theorem, many mathematicians believed that axiom systems could ultimately be developed which would allow us to conclusively prove answers to all meaningful questions. Gödel shattered these beliefs by proving them to be impossible; in essence he proved that there were limits to what could be proved by purely logical reasoning.

At the same time Gödel was developing his powerful theorem, the British mathematician Alan Turing was developing a model of hypothetical computing machines knows as Turing machines. Turing machines consist of:

- □ Input and output units.

- □ Memory consisting of an infinite number of cells organized sequentially on a tape. Each cell can contain a symbol from a finite alphabet such as the digits used to represent numbers. Note that the infinite nature of memory on Turing machines provides those theoretical machines with a capability that cannot be realized on any real computer.

- □ A finite collection of states in which the machine could exist at any given time. These states could be viewed as analogous to the registers which exist in the central processing unit of all modern computers.

- □ A control unit capable of checking the contents of any memory cell and potentially altering it depending on the current configuration of the machine's states.

Since speed of computation is not a consideration with Turing machines, the infinite memory of a Turing machine makes it impossible for any real machine to ever exceed the capabilities of a Turing machine. Turing machines thus represent a theoretical limit to the future possibilities of real machines. If we can show there are formal problems which no Turing machine can solve, then we have also shown that *no* real computer will *ever* be able to compute a solution to such a problem.

How is the work of Gödel and Turing related? The argument Gödel used in showing that formal axiom systems powerful enough for arithmetic contain undecidable propositions may easily be adapted to show that there are problems for which a Turing machine cannot compute a solution. In fact, we can even give a specific instance of such a problem. This problem is called the Halting Problem. Informally, we can state the Halting Problem as follows: Can we tell whether or not a given program (algorithm) will terminate (halt) or loop indefinitely when provided with a given set of input data? A more formal statement of the halting problem is

Is there a program (algorithm) which will receive as its input another program and the input for that other program and output a zero if the other program will halt for that input and a one if it will loop indefinitely for that input?

A schematic representation of the input/output for a program capable of solving the Halting Problem is given in Figure 11.16.

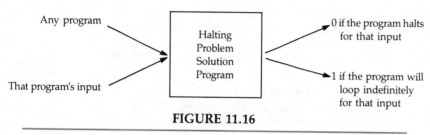

FIGURE 11.16

Input/output for program which solves Halting Problem

For instance, suppose we wanted to know if a given program to determine whether a number is prime would halt if it were fed the number 173. Then we would merely provide this program along with the input 173 to our Halting Problem solution program, and it would output 1 or 0 accordingly.

A valid question regarding such a solution program is how it could receive another program as input. A convenient way of enabling this would be to assign a unique number to each possible input program. How would a program's unique number be determined? Ultimately that program is just a (very) long string of binary 1s and 0s. We could simply view the string of 1s and 0s associated with the program as the unique binary number we assign to the program. This number must be unique since any other program must differ in at least one binary digit position.

Not only can we assign each program a unique number, but we can assign one unique number to the combination of inputs in Figure 11.16. Notice that in this figure, the halting problem solution program may have arbitrarily many inputs, as designated in the following table:

Input	Explanation
i_0	The unique number we have associated with the input program.
i_1	The first input value for the program.
i_2	The second input value for the program.
.	.
.	.
.	.
i_n	The last input value for the program.

Gödel showed in his classic results that if p_k represents the kth prime number, then the number

$$p_0^{i_0} \times p_1^{i_1} \times p_2^{i_2} \ldots \times p_n^{i_n}$$

is a unique single number determined by the input sequence i_0, i_1, i_2, . . . , i_n. This scheme, known as Gödel numbering, means that the schematic in Figure 11.16 may be collapsed to a program having one unique input value which encompasses both the input program and the program's input. Hence, we have a new and simpler representation of the Halting Problem solution program as pictured in Figure 11.17. Note that we need not be concerned with the potentially large value for this input number because our theoretical Turing machine computer knows no bounds for numbers—it cannot overflow.

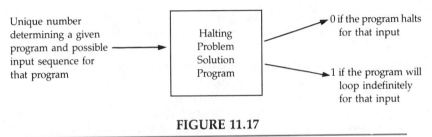

FIGURE 11.17

Halting Problem solution program with only one input

Gödel's argument showing the existence of undecidable propositions in formal axiom systems can then be adapted to show the impossibility of such a program to solve the halting problem. The argument is a classic example of a proof by contradiction. Let us suppose that there actually existed a Halting Problem solution program such as that pictured in Figure 11.17. From this assumption, we will argue towards a contradiction, hence proving that such a program is impossible.

If such a program existed, then we will use it as the front end for constructing a new program. This new program will start with the code for the Halting Problem solution and then take the 0 and 1 produced and act in the following manner:

1. If the Halting Problem solution program outputs 0, our new program will enter an infinite loop.

2. If the Halting Problem solution program outputs a 1, our new program will print "Done".

It is intuitively clear how this appendage to the Halting Problem solution program could be constructed. It will merely consist of an **IF** statement such as

```
IF halting problem solution = 0 THEN
   WHILE 1 = 1 DO BEGIN END  { Loop infinitely }
ELSE
   write ('Done')
```

With this easy addition, we would now have a new program such as that pictured in Figure 11.18.

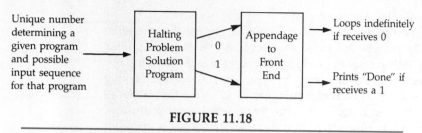

FIGURE 11.18

New program with Halting Problem solver as front end

Now consider the following question: Will this new program loop infinitely upon receiving its own unique identifying number as input? If the new program does not loop infinitely, then the Halting Problem front end will produce a 0 and hence the new program will loop infinitely (a contradiction). On the other hand, if the new program does loop infinitely, then the halting problem front end will produce a 1, and hence the new program will print "Done" and not loop infinitely (another contradiction). Therefore, either way we are faced with a contradiction. We must conclude that the Halting Problem solution program does not exist since its existence would lead to this logical impossibility.

The essence of this proof lies in constructing a program that can then somehow receive itself as input. It is not coincidental that such self-reference should remind us a bit of recursion. Just as we have shown recursion to be a very powerful algorithmic technique (see Chapter 8), we now have seen a similar kind of self-reference lying at the heart of one of the most important results in theoretical computer science. What are the implications of proving the impossibility of an algorithm to solve the Halting Problem? In a broad sense, it tells us that there are questions which even the most powerful logic machines imaginable will be unable to answer. These questions are unanswerable not because they are questions of interpretation. Rather they are questions (like the Halting Problem) that can be formalized within logic itself. Moreover, further adaptations of Gödel's arguments demonstrate that the Halting Problem is not alone among the problems that cannot be algorithmically solved. It can be shown that there is actually an infinite reservoir of such problems. Thus, it is also in principle impossible to even enumerate all of them, declare that all other problems are solvable, and hence be sure that we are pursuing only solvable problems.

With respect to artificial intelligence, the theory regarding unsolvable problems has helped to focus philosophical debate about the future of the field. Science fiction and popular press predicitons of "all-knowing" machines are demonstrably impossible. Artificially intelligent machines will always encounter the limits of unsolvable problems which the theory dictates. The real question is not one of machine intelligence but rather one of human intelligence. Does our intelligence as human beings embody more than the logical, algorithmic capabilities (and limitations) of a Turing machine? This question is perhaps an appropriate one with which to end our computer science text; we leave it to the philosophers and psychologists for future debate.

Key Terms

abstract syntax trees
artificial intelligence (AI)
assembler
assembly code
automatic program synthesis
Backus-Naur grammar
binary buddy system
binary code
boundary tag buddy system
coalesce
compaction
compiler
deadlock
expert systems
Fibonacci buddy system
formal verification
fragmentation problem
Gödel numbering

Gödel's Theorem
Halting Problem
input assertions
lexical analysis
loop invariants
machine language
method of inductive assertions
natural languages
operating system
output assertions
parser generator
parse trees
parsing
semantics
source program
Turing machine
undecidable propositions

Exercises

1. Prepare in short essay form definitions for each of the Key Terms listed at the end of the chapter.
2. Research a topic from any Relevant Issue presented in this book and prepare a written or oral report on it.
3. Using the format described in Section 11.2, attempt to write a Backus-Naur grammatical description for the entire Pascal language (or any other language with which you may be familiar). If you have access to a parser-generator program as described in Section 11.2, learn how to use it to check your grammar for potential inconsistencies.
4. In Section 11.3, we described three memory management schemes which might be used by an operating system: binary buddy, Fibonacci buddy, and boundary tag buddies. Write a program in which random numbers are used to simulate users requesting memory and then returning it. Interface this program with each of the three memory management schemes presented in Section 11.3 and accumulate statistics regarding various measures of space efficiency for each of these three methods.
5. Using the formal algorithm verification techniques presented in Section 11.4, prove the correctness of the following algorithms. Remember to identify input assertions, output assertions, and loop invariants.

a. PROCEDURE Difference (x,y : integer;
                              VAR z : integer);

   { Receives integers x and y. Computes their
     difference x-y and returns it in z. }

   VAR w : integer;

   BEGIN
     z := x;
     w := y;
     WHILE w > 0 DO
       BEGIN
         z := z-1;
         w := w-1
       END
   END;

b. PROCEDURE Cube (x : integer;
                      VAR z : integer);

   { Receives nonnegative integer x. Returns
     the cube of x in z. }

   VAR a,b,c: integer;

   BEGIN
     a := 1;
     b := 0;
     c := x;
     z := 0;
     WHILE c > 0 DO
       BEGIN
         z := z + a + b;
         b := b + 2 * a + 1;
         a := a + 3;
         c := c - 1
       END
   END;

6. In Section 11.5, the following areas of application within artificial intelligence were cited:

□ Game playing.

□ Theorem proving.

□ Natural languages.

□ Machine learning.

□ Computer vision.

□ Expert systems.

Research any one of these areas and prepare a written or oral report on progress which has already been made and on prospects for the future.

7. Autological words are words that describe themselves. Hence, the word *short* is autological because it is a short word, and the word *English* is autological because it is an English word. Heterological words are words that do not describe themselves. Thus, the words *long* and *French* are heterological words. Using these definitions, provide answers to the following questions:

   a. Is the word *heterological* heterological or autological? Justify your answer.

   b. What similarities do you see between the reasoning you used in part a and that used in proving the nonexistence of an algorithm to solve the Halting Problem?

Review of Standard Pascal

It should be emphasized that this appendix is a *review* of Pascal. It is not designed to teach you the basics of programming in Pascal but rather to present some compact "memory joggers" which should help you recall features of Pascal which you once learned but which may have become rusty due to unavoidable nuisances such as summer vacations. The review is organized around short program segments, each of which illustrates a particular Pascal programming structure.

General Program Form

```
PROGRAM DoNothing (input, output);
CONST
  One = 1;

VAR  {Global variables}
  Alpha, Beta, Gamma : real;
  Delta : integer;

{Procedures and functions are located here.}

BEGIN {Main program}
  readln (Alpha, Beta);
  Gamma := Alpha + Beta;
  Delta := One + One;
  writeln (Gamma, Delta)
END.
```

Conditional Statements: IF-THEN, IF-THEN-ELSE, and CASE

```
IF TestScore >= 70 THEN
  BEGIN
    Passing := Passing + 1;
    writeln (Name, 'passed')
  END;


IF TestScore >= 70 THEN
  BEGIN
    Passing := Passing + 1;
    writeln (Name, 'passed')
  END
```

```pascal
ELSE   {Now do something for failing students also}
  BEGIN
    Failing := Failing + 1;
    writeln (Name, 'needs help')
  END;



CASE Grade OF
  'A': GradePoints := 4;
  'B': GradePoints := 3;
  'C': GradePoints := 2;
  'D': GradePoints := 1;
  'F': GradePoints := 0
END;
```

Looping Statements: FOR, WHILE, and REPEAT-UNTIL

```pascal
FOR Number := 1 TO 100 DO
  writeln (Number : 10, Number * Number : 10);



Number := 1;
WHILE Number <= 100 DO
  BEGIN
    writeln (Number : 10, Number *  Number : 10);
    Number := Number + 1
  END;



Number := 1;
REPEAT
    writeln (Number : 10, Number * Number : 10);
    Number := Number + 1
UNTIL Number > 100;
```

Procedures

```pascal
PROCEDURE  ReadAndTotal (Sentinel : real;
                         VAR Sum : real;
                         VAR Count : integer);

  {Read real values until Sentinel is entered.  In Sum,
   return accumulated total of values read.  In Count,
   return number of values which were read. }

  VAR Value : real;

  BEGIN
    Sum := 0;
    Count := 0;
    readln(Value);
```

```
      WHILE Value <> Sentinel DO
        BEGIN
          Sum := Sum + Value;
          Count := Count + 1;
          readln(Value)
        END
      END;
```

Sample Call.

```
ReadAndTotal(-1.0, TotalSales, SalesPeople);
```

Functions

```
FUNCTION Sum(Sentinel : real) : real;

  {Read real values until Sentinel is entered, returning
   the Sum of these values.  A count of the number of values
   cannot be returned since functions can only return one value.}

  VAR  Value, RunningSum : real;

  BEGIN
    RunningSum := 0;
    readln(Value);
    WHILE Value <> Sentinel DO
      BEGIN
        RunningSum := RunningSum + Value;
        readln(Value)
      END;
    Sum := RunningSum
  END;
```

Sample Call.

```
TotalSales := Sum(-1.0);
```

Subrange Types

```
TYPE
 TwentiethCentury = 1900..1999;
```

Enumerated Types

```
TYPE
  Rating = (Excellent, VeryGood, Good, Fair, Poor, Dismal);
```

Array Definition

```
TYPE
  TestScores = ARRAY [1..NumberStudents, 1..NumberTests] OF real;
  StudentAverages = ARRAY [1..NumberStudents] OF real;
  TestAverages = ARRAY [1..NumberTests] OF real;
```

```
VAR
  CompSciScores : TestScores;
  CompSciStudentAve : StudentAverages;
  CompSciTestAve : TestAverages;
```

Array Use

```
{Loops to accumulate average for each student}

FOR s := 1 TO NumberStudents DO
  BEGIN
    CompSciStudentAve[s] := 0;
    FOR t := 1 to NumberTests DO
      CompSciStudentAve[s] := CompSciStudentAve[s] + CompSciScores[s,t];
    CompSciStudentAve[s] := CompSciStudentAve[s]/NumberTests
  END;
```

Record Definition

```
TYPE
  NameString = PACKED ARRAY [1..NameLength] OF char;
  StudentRecord = RECORD
                    Name : NameString;
                    CredTaken : integer;
                    CredEarned : integer;
                    TotalGradePts : integer
                  END;

  StudentList = ARRAY [1..NumberStudents] OF StudentRecord;

VAR Students : StudentList;
```

Record Use

```
{Loop to print all student records}

FOR s := 1 TO NumberStudents DO
  WITH Student[s] DO
    writeln (Name: NameString, CredTaken: 10, CredEarned: 10,
             TotalGradePts: 10);

{An alternative to the WITH statement is to use Pascal's dot notation,
 for example, Student[s].Name, to qualify each field in the record.}
```

File Definition

```
TYPE
  NameString = PACKED ARRAY [1..NameLength] OF char;
  StudentRecord = RECORD
                    Name : NameString;
                    CredTaken : integer;
```

```
                        CredEarned : integer;
                        TotalGradePts : integer
                     END;
   StudentFile = FILE OF StudentRecord;

VAR
  Students : StudentFile;
  TempRec : StudentRecord;
```

Creating a File

```
{The following program segment will create the file Students.  We assume
 the existence of a procedure GetData which reads a record from the standard
 input (usually an interactive terminal) and returns the record in TempRec.
 We also assume that no more data are to be written to the file when GetData
 returns a Sentinel value for the Name field in TempRec.}

rewrite(Students);
GetData(TempRec);
WHILE  TempRec.Name <> Sentinel DO
  BEGIN
    Students^ := TempRec;
    put(Students);
    GetData(TempRec)
  END;
```

Reading Records from a File

```
{The following program segment will read records from the file Students
 and print them (assuming the existence of an appropriate PrintData
 procedure). }

reset(Students);
WHILE not eof(Students) DO
  BEGIN
    TempRec := Students^;
    PrintData(TempRec);
    get(Students)
  END
```

Special Note to Turbo Pascal Users

Turbo Pascal does not provide the standard **put** and **get** procedures. Consequently, in Turbo, the pair of statements

```
Students^ := TempRec;
put(Students);
```

must be replaced by the single statement

```
write(Students, TempRec);
```

Similarly, the pair of statements

```
get(Students);
TempRec := Students^;
```

must be replaced by

```
read(Students, TempRec);
```

Conformant Array Parameters in Pascal

From an abstract perspective, the ability of a programming language to express an algorithm should not be tied to a particular type of data. In this regard, standard Pascal has been justly criticized. To illustrate this, consider the following bubble sort procedure (discussed in Chapter 2).

```
{Global declarations}

CONST MaxIndex = 100;
      StringLength = 40;
TYPE  String = PACKED ARRAY [1..StringLength] OF char;
      SortType = String;
      SortArray = ARRAY [1..MaxIndex] OF SortTypes;

PROCEDURE BubbleSort(n : integer; VAR KeyList : SortArray);

VAR i, j : integer;
    Temp : SortType;

BEGIN
  FOR i := 1 To n-1 DO
    FOR j := 1 TO n-i DO
      IF KeyList[j] > KeyList[j+1] THEN
        BEGIN
        Temp := KeyList[j];
        KeyList[j] := KeyList[j+1];
        KeyList[j+1] := Temp
        END
END;
```

The bubble sort algorithm itself will work with an array of any size. However, the preceding Pascal procedure which implements the bubble sort is limited strictly to arrays of base type SortType and indexed by the subrange 1..MaxIndex. To sort an array of a different base data type or indexed by a different range, you must change the definition of SortType and MaxIndex. For a program in which two arrays of different types must be sorted, the situation is even worse. You must write nearly duplicate code for two separate bubble sorts.

Conformant array parameters are now offered by many versions of Pascal as a partial solution to this awkward situation. In particular, conformant array parameters will allow you to use the same procedure for arrays which do not have the same index range. Conformant array parameters only represent a partial solution because they will not allow you to use the same procedure for arrays of different base data types. Conformant array parameters are declared in the formal parameter list of a procedure by

specifying parameters for the upper and lower limits of the index range of
the array being passed to the procedure. The syntax of such a parameter in
our previous bubble sort would be:

```
PROCEDURE BubbleSort(n : integer;
                        VAR KeyList : ARRAY [Low..High : integer] OF SortType);
```

In this procedure header, SortType is the base data type of the parameter
KeyList; this type cannot change from one call to another. Integer is the
data type of the index range Low..High. You may call this procedure with
any array whose index range is a subrange of integer. Any other ordinal
type could also be used here in place of integer, but you would then be
limited to calling the procedure with arrays whose index range is a subrange of that ordinal type.

Inside the procedure, the logic of the algorithm is expressed using the
conformant parameters Low and High. Thus, our BubbleSort procedure
with conformant array parameters would appear as follows:

```
PROCEDURE BubbleSort (n : integer;
                        VAR KeyList : ARRAY [Low..High : integer] OF SortType);

      {Given array KeyList indexed from Low to High and containing
          n entries, use bubble sort algorithm to return KeyList with these
          n entries arranged in ascending order.}

VAR i ,j : integer;
    Temp : SortType;

BEGIN
  FOR i := TO n-1 DO
    FOR j := Low TO Low+n-(i+1)DO   {Index for comparison expressed
                                       via conformant parameter}
      IF KeyList[j] > KeyList[j+1] THEN        {Must interchange}
        BEGIN
        Temp := KeyList[j];
        KeyList[j] := KeyList[j+1];
        KeyList[j+1] := Temp
        END
END;   {BubbleSort}
```

The Low and High indices for a conformant array parameter do not
appear in an actual call to the procedure. For example, suppose we had
two arrays X and Y declared by

```
VAR
  X : ARRAY [1..100] OF SortType;
  Y : ARRAY [-10..10] OF SortType;
```

Suppose also that we wanted to invoke the BubbleSort procedure on the
first 60 entries in X and all 21 entries in Y. Then the respective calls for X
and Y would appear as

```
BubbleSort(60, X);
```

and

```
BubbleSort(21, Y);
```

A Pascal compiler which allows conformant array parameters will be "smart enough" to automatically provide the values 1 and 100 for Low and High when we call BubbleSort with X and similarly to provide the values -10 and 10 for Low and High when we call it with Y.

Random Access Files in Various Versions of Pascal

The original standard for Pascal developed by Kathleen Jensen and Niklaus Wirth (*Pascal User Manual and Report* (Berlin: Springer-Verlag, 1974)) made no provision for random (direct) access files. From the perspective of learning structured programming concepts, this is not a serious omission. From the perspective of applying data structure concepts in the real world, however, it is a major omission. This is because most programs with a database orientation involve storing large amounts of data in files and then accessing the data by a search strategy which guarantees a quick response time. Without direct access, a tedious sequential search is the only method possible. Hence, what has emerged is that most implementors of Pascal compilers have developed their own procedures for directly accessing records which reside in a disk file.

A general picture which applies in all of these various implementations is given in Figure C.1.

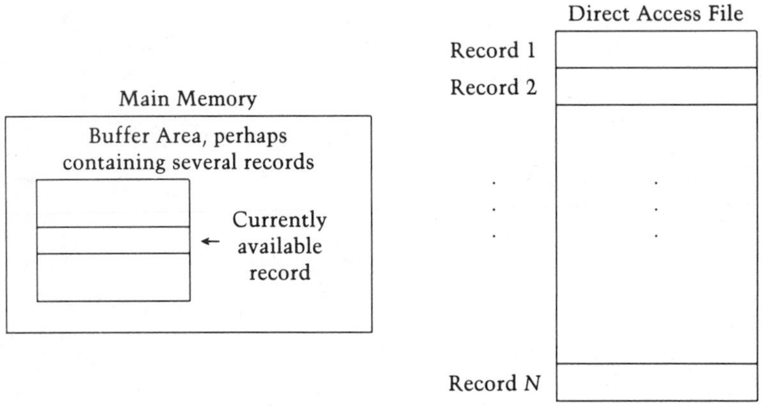

FIGURE C.1

General Random Access File Set-Up

A record from a random access file may be acted upon (for instance, updated) only when it has been fetched as the currently available record in the main memory buffer associated with that file. (Actually, application programmers may think of the currently available record and the file's buffer as coinciding, though this is an oversimplification that can affect the efficiency of the search technique being considered. See Chapter 10 for a discussion of this point.) Hence the problem of programming in Pascal with random access files becomes one of being able to

1. Fetch in the ith record from the file as the currently available record in main memory (where i is an arbitrary positive integer less than or equal to the number of records in the file).

2. Update the currently available record in main memory.

3. Write the currently available record in memory to the ith position in the file

Step 2 may typically be accomplished by using standard Pascal's up-arrow notation for a file variable. (See Chapter 3, Section 3.4 for a discussion of this notation.) For example,

```
f^.IDNumber := 4918;
```

will assign the value 4918 to the IDNumber field of the record currently available in main memory. Note that this assignment is only made in memory; nothing is altered in the file until this record is written out to the appropriate file position.

Thus, it is only steps 1 and 3 which require special nonstandard Pascal procedures. Once such procedures exist, search algorithms which apply to arrays may also be appropriately applied to random access files. Hence, a random access file may be conceptually thought of as a large array which resides on disk.

In the examples which follow, we assume that f is a Pascal file variable associated with records of an appropriate type (other than TEXT). For each implementation of Pascal specified, we describe how to open, fetch, and update records for random access file processing. If you do not see your system specified, the examples should nonetheless provide points of comparison which will help you to understand the local documentation describing similar facilities for your environment.

Oregon Software's (OMSI) Pascal-1 and Pascal-2

☐ To open a file for random access:

```
reset(f,filename specified with '/seek' switch);
```

☐ To fetch ith record as currently available record:

```
seek(f,i);
```

☐ To write currently available record to ith file position:

```
seek(f,i);
    .
    .    (Appropriate updating)
    .
put(f);
```

DEC's VAX-Pascal

☐ To open a file for random access:

```
open(f,access_method := direct, organization := relative);
```

☐ To fetch *i*th record as currently available record:

```
find(f,i);
```

☐ To write currently available record to *i*th position:

```
locate(f,i)
put(f);
```

or

```
update(f);   {if file already positioned at ith record}
```

Turbo Pascal

☐ To open a file for random access:

```
assign(f,filename);
reset(f);
```

(Keep in mind that in Turbo Pascal, records are numbered beginning at 0.)

☐ To fetch *i*th record into TempRec as the currently available record:

```
seek(f,i);
read(f,TempRec);
```

(In Turbo, the record is accessed in a declared record location, such as TempRec, instead of by accessing the buffer directly via f^.)

☐ To write the currently available record in TempRec to *i*th file position:

```
seek(f,i);
write (f, TempRec);
```

Macintosh and Lightspeed Pascal for the Apple Macintosh Family

☐ To open a file for random access:

```
open(f,filename);
```

□ To fetch *i*th record as currently available record:

```
seek(f,i);
```

□ To write currently available record to *i*th file position;

```
seek(f,i);
  .
  .
  .
put(f);
```

Hints and Solutions to Selected Odd Numbered Exercises

In general, solutions are presented for those exercises which do not require development of a lengthy Pascal procedure or function. Your answers to questions requiring such a procedure or function can best be checked by entering them on an actual computer and testing them by the methods described in Chapter 3.

Chapter 1

1. Software engineering is a methodical approach to software development. It is a process which starts with an abstract view which is refined step by step towards the actual software implementation.

3. The system analyst is responsible for translating the needs of the user into specifications for the programmer.

5. For an array:

```
: 1 : 2 : 3 :
: 4 : 5 : 6 :
```

A row-major form is:

```
: 1 : 2 : 3 : 4 : 5 : 6 :
```

while a column-major form is

```
: 1 : 4 : 2 : 5 : 3 : 6 :
```

7. Any application that would call for a list of items or records to be recorded would be appropriate for a general list.

9. All of the memory available for the average computer to store variables is organized in a sequential manner. So, to implement a two-dimensional array, the computer has to use a mapping function (similar to those discussed) to map the array onto its available memory. This need for mapping makes a two-dimensional array less efficient than a one-dimensional array with the same number of cells.

    However, if you are trying to implement a two-dimensional array by using a one-dimensional array, you have to use a mapping function anyway, so there is no disadvantage to using a two-dimensional array in this situation.

11. An abstract record for the library for each book might look like:

```
                    number
    Book record --  title
                    author
                    checkout info -- date due
                                  - name -- first
                                           middle
                                           last
```

Chapter 2

1. a) n b) n log$_2$ n
c) n log$_2$ n

3. a) $n^3 \log_2 n$
b) 4^n
c) 2^n

5. 43 60 60 60 60
40 40 43 43 43
18 18 18 40 40
24 24 24 24 39
39 39 39 39 24
60 43 40 18 18
12 12 12 12 12

7. lo hi mid
18 90 52
18 50 40
46 50 46
46 40 out here...

9. If the data is physically ordered, then it is actually in that order in the computer's memory. If the data is only logically in order, then the physical order of the data is arbitrary, but a series of pointers show the order of the data relative to some key field.

11. In general, algorithms that improve the speed of a program require more memory to implement. On the other hand, an algorithm that requires less memory usually takes more time to execute.

13. A program that manipulates data in main memory is generally faster than a program that manipulates data stored on a disk. This is because the time required to manipulate data in main memory is much less than the time it takes to access the data on a disk.

15. Since a pointer sort works only in main memory, and only pointers are manipulated, and not the data itself, there would be no order of magnitude improvement achieved by breaking the 1000 records down into four groups. Whether broken into groups or not, the sort would have an $O(n^2)$ run-time unless the more powerful methods of Chapter 9 were used. However, since $4 * 250^2$ is less than 1000^2, we would expect the segmented sort to run somewhat faster.

Chapter 3

1. The test data should include tests for the best and worst case situations for the binary algorithm on several different sizes of lists, including lists of extremely small size. The tests should also include cases where the target does not exist, where the target is the first element, and where the target is the last element in the list.

3. The advantage of using fixed length string storage is that no computation is required to find the string. The workspace/index method requires that the needed string be computed from a larger string. However, the fixed length method wastes memory unless all of the strings sizes are known exactly ahead of time because the fixed length must be as long (if not longer) than the longest string stored. On the other hand, the workspace/index method is useful because it only takes up a certain amount of memory, and no more. Storage space is not wasted at the end of each string as is the case with the fixed length method.

5. If the goal would be just to find all non-sparse, or all sparse answers, then the method is practical. However, if the goal is just one record inside the table, the method becomes inefficient. A series of links has to be traversed repeatedly for each inquiry into the table. If the inquiries are deep within the table, then a large number of links has to be traversed for each inquiry, making this implementation impractical.

7. If a sequential search is used on the student list, then the add and delete routines no longer have to reshuffle the student list for each operation. This would save a lot of time when adding or deleting students from the list. However, this would mean that the student list is no longer in physical order, making some reports more difficult to give.

9. A functionally cohesive module in a structure chart is a module that performs one, and only one, logically remote function with a minimal amount of interaction with other modules in the structure chart. This eliminates possible side effects on other modules in the structure chart.

11. The string PHILLIES can be added to the workspace, but only after the available empty space is consolidated. One possible configuration would be:

List

BREWERSINDIANSORIOLESBLUEJAYSANGELSPHILLIES

string	start	length
Brewers	1	7
Indians	8	7
Orioles	15	7
Bluejays	22	8
Angels	30	6
Phillies	36	8

Free space pointer:44

13. The ParkingFee module is not a "robust" module. If neither a 'c' nor a 't' are entered, then it is quite possible that a fatal error could occur. A conditional check should be made, making the user reenter the input if it is not valid.

Chapter 4

1. What might happen when Str2 is assigned to Str1 is that no new copy is made of the string 'COFFEE'. Instead, the pointer for Str2 is directed to the same location as the pointer for Str1. When Str1 changes, it is possible with this implementation that Str2 also changes. So, the output given would be 'TEA' and not the 'COFFEE' that we would expect.

3.

Data	Link
Locke	2
Miller	3
Smith	end of list
Foster	1
Allen	4

Head: 5

5.

Data	Link
Locke	2
Miller	3
Smith	end of list
Foster	1

Head: 4

7.

Position	data	Link
0	*dummy	1
1	James	end of list
2		3
3		4
4		5
5		6
6		7
7		8
8		end of list

Head: 0
Avail: 2

Position	data	Link
0	*dummy	2
1	James	end of list
2	Chilton	1
3		4
4		5
5		6
6		7
7		8
8		end of list

Head: 0
Avail: 3

Position	data	Link
0	*dummy	2
1	James	3
2	Chilton	1
3	Sefton	end of list
4		5
5		6
6		7

Head: 0
Avail: 4

Position	data	Link
7		8
8		end of list

--

Position	data	Link	
0	*dummy	2	
1	James	4	Head: 0
2	Chilton	1	Avail:5
3	Sefton	end of list	
4	Lee	3	
5		6	
6		7	
7		8	
8		end of list	

--

Position	data	Link	
0	*dummy	1	
1	James	4	Head: 0
2		5	Avail:2
3	Sefton	end of list	
4	Lee	3	
5		6	
6		7	
7		8	
8		end of list	

--

Position	data	Link	
0	*dummy	1	
1	James	4	Head: 0
2	Wagner	end of list	Avail:5
3	Sefton	2	
4	Lee	3	
5		6	
6		7	
7		8	
8		end of list	

--

Position	data	Link	
0	*dummy	4	
1		5	Head: 0
2	Wagner	end of list	Avail:0
3	Sefton	2	
4	Lee	3	
5		6	
6		7	
7		8	
8		end of list	

--

Position	data	Link	
0	*dummy	1	
1	Aaron	4	Head: 0
2	Wagner	end of list	Avail:5
3	Sefton	2	
4	Lee	3	
5		6	
6		7	
7		8	
8		end of list	

--

9.

Position	data	flink	blink	
0	*dummy	1	end	head: 0
1	James	end	0	avail:2
2		3	end	
3		4	2	
4		5	3	
5		6	4	
6		7	5	
7		8	6	
8		end	7	

Position	data	flink	blink	
0	*dummy	2	end	head: 0
1	James	end	2	avail:3
2	Chilton	1	0	
3		4	end	
4		5	3	
5		6	4	
6		7	5	
7		8	6	
8		end	7	

Position	data	flink	blink	
0	*dummy	2	end	head: 0
1	James	3	2	avail:4
2	Chilton	1	0	
3	Sefton	end	1	
4		5	end	
5		6	4	
6		7	5	
7		8	6	
8		end	7	

Position	data	flink	blink	
0	*dummy	2	end	head: 0
1	James	4	2	avail:5
2	Chilton	1	0	
3	Sefton	end	4	
4	Lee	3	1	
5		6	end	
6		7	5	
7		8	6	
8		end	7	

Position	data	flink	blink	
0	*dummy	1	end	head: 0
1	James	4	2	avail:2
2		5	end	
3	Sefton	end	4	
4	Lee	3	1	
5		6	2	
6		7	5	
7		8	6	
8		end	7	

Position	data	flink	blink	
0	*dummy	1	end	head: 0
1	James	4	2	avail:5
2	Wagner	end	3	
3	Sefton	2	4	

Position	data	flink	blink	
4	Lee	3	1	
5		6	end	
6		7	5	
7		8	6	
8		end	7	

Position	data	flink	blink	
0	*dummy	4	end	head: 0
1		5	end	avail:1
2	Wagner	end	3	
3	Sefton	2	4	
4	Lee	3	0	
5		6	1	
6		7	5	
7		8	6	
8		end	7	

Position	data	flink	blink	
0	*dummy	1	end	head: 0
1	Aaron	4	0	avail:5
2	Wagner	end	3	
3	Sefton	2	4	
4	Lee	3	1	
5		6	end	
6		7	5	
7		8	6	
8		end	7	

---

11. The pointers used in the pointer sort algorithm were in separate and distinct records from the data, with the logical order imposed only after all the data was inserted.

13. A dummy header will allow easier manipulation of an empty list, when adding to an empty list, and when deleting from a one-element list. The dummy header allows the code to physically work with a non-empty list when logically no list exists.

15. When you are inserting in a list, generally you have to traverse the list until you pass the point where you want to insert the new node. If you have a doubly linked list, this causes no problem because the previous node is readily available. However, with a singly linked list, you have to have a "tag along" pointer which points to the node where you just came from. This complicates matters considerably.

17. Pointers are actually memory locations. These can be stored to the disk, but nothing guarantees that the same memory places will be available the next time you try to use the program. So, instead save the data in order, or impose an array implementation of pointers, and then rebuild the linked list once the program is run again.

19. The statement to advance to the next node in an array implementation would be: p := arr[p].next. This assumes that the array is called arr, and the link field is in a record called next. The statement to advance to the next node in a pointer variable implementation

would be: p := p^.next. This assumes that the normal declaration is made and that the pointer for the next node is in a pointer field called next.

Chapter 5

1.

Front	Rear	Array
1	1	smith
		___
		___
		___
1	2	smith
		jones
		___
		___
1	3	smith
		jones
		greer
		___
		___
2	3	___
		jones
		greer
		___
		___
2	4	___
		jones
		greer
		carson
3	4	___
		___
		greer
		carson
3	5	___
		___
		greer
		carson
		baker
3	1	charles
		___
		greer
		carson
		baker
3	2	charles
		benson
		greer
		carson
		baker
4	2	charles
		benson

```
Front    Rear    Array
                  _____
                  carson
                  baker
4        3        charles
                  benson
                  miller
                  carson
                  baker
```

3. The initial setting for a circular queue should be front = 1 and rear = 5.

5. See table 5-3 for answers.

7. If we allow a user to withdraw a batch job from the schedule, we must be able to search the queue of jobs to find that particular job, and remove it. It is obvious that a linked list implementation would allow for easy removal of jobs. Further, since searching for a particular item is easiest with a doubly linked list, this is the implementation which should probably be used.

9. a) To create a queue the REAR should be equal to the FRONT, and both = 1. To detect an empty queue REAR should be equal to FRONT. A full array is detected when REAR + 1 = ARRAY-SIZE

   b) To create a queue the rear should be equal to the front, and both = 1. To detect an empty queue REAR should be equal to FRONT. To detect a full queue REAR will be one less than FRONT (depending on how the array wraps. Note that this will waste one open space).

   c) In all cases, REAR will have to be a dummy pointer, an extra link.

Chapter 6

1. Infix Notation: A + B * (C–D) / (P – R)
   Postfix Notation: ABCD–PR–/*+
   Prefix Notation: +*/–CD–PRBA

3. The case study would evaluate the function by computing 3^2^3 as 729. It arrives at this answer by computing 3^2 and taking this to the power 3. To correctly evaluate this expression, the order has to be first compute 2^3 and then take 3 to this power. (Here ^ indicates exponentiation.)

5. The stack grows as follows:

```
Return Point   M  N    Weird value
       1       1  3     ?
  __
       1       1  3
       3       1  2     ?
  __
```

```
Return Point    M  N   Weird value
        1        1  3
        3        1  2
        3        1  1       ?
  --
        1        1  3
        3        1  2
        3        1  1
        3        1  0       ?
  --
        1        1  3
        3        1  2
        3        1  1
        3        1  0
        2        0  1       2
  --
        1        1  3
        3        1  2
        3        1  1
        3        1  0       2
  --
        1        1  3
        3        1  2
        3        1  1
        4        0  2       3
  --
        1        1  3
        3        1  2
        3        1  1       3
  --
        1        1  3
        3        1  2
        4        0  3       4
  --
        1        1  3
        3        1  2       4
  --
        1        1  3
        4        0  4       5
  --
        1        1  3       5
```

The output from this program is:

```
1 3
1 2
1 1
1 0
0 1
0 2
0 3
0 4
5
```

7. The postfix expression produced was: PQF−Y/+. So, the stack of
   real values that would develop as this is evaluated for the given
   values is:

   ```
   1st char    10
   2nd char    10 18
   3rd char    10 18 4
   4th char    10 14
   5th char    10 14 2
   6th char    10 7
   7th char    17
   ```

9. The postfix expression PQY/ABD+−+Y** would yield the following stack as it is evaluated for the given values:

   ```
   1st char     1
   2nd char     1 4
   3rd char     1 4 2
   4th char     1 2
   5th char     1 2 4
   6th char     1 2 4 3
   7th char     1 2 4 3 2
   8th char     1 2 4 5
   9th char     1 2 −1
   10th char    1 1
   11th char    1 1 2
   12th char    1 2
   13th char    2
   ```

11. When the infix priority of a given operator is greater than the stack
    priority of another given operator, that means that the operator
    with the lower stack priority has a lesser overall algebraic priority.
    In the normal system which we use, the + and the − have a low
    stack priority when compared with the infix priority of the * or the
    /. Similarly, when the stack priority of a given operator is high, it
    will be performed before other "incoming" operators.

13. Every call to a procedure or function adds another record to the
    stack of program flow, the return point, local variables, and so on.
    Since recursion generally relies upon many procedure or function
    calls, algorithms using recursion tend to use a lot of stack space.
    However, recursive algorithms tend to require less code to imple-
    ment, and so take less storage space to actually hold the program.

15. The Towers of Hanoi algorithm requires $O(2^n)$ moves for n disks.

17. Each of the logical operators mentioned would be assigned an infix
    priority and a stack priority just like all of the other operators.
    However, most of these priorities would be lower. The $\langle,\rangle,\langle=,\rangle=$,
    and $\langle\rangle$ would be assigned values lower than the + and the −. The
    AND, and OR would be below all of the operators. On the other
    hand, the NOT would have a high priority above everything else
    except the parentheses.

Chapter 7

1.

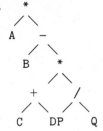

3.

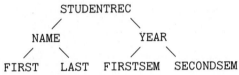

5. The output becomes:

```
A
C
G
I
K
H
J
B
E
D
```

7. For the WRITELN located after all of the recursive calls:

```
T
Y
X
B
G
F
H
N
M
Z
A
```

For the WRITELN located first:

```
A
B
Y
T
X
Z
F
```

```
G
M
N
H
```

For the WRITELN located between the two recursive calls:

```
Y
T
B
X
A
F
G
Z
H
N
M
```

9. a).

	Data	LeftChild	RightChild
1	C	2	–
2	R	–	3
3	G	–	–
4	F	–	–
5	X	–	4
6	Y	–	–
7	B	6	5
8	A	7	1
9		–	–

ROOT 8
AVAIL 9

b).

	Data	LeftChild	RightChild
1	C	2	–
2		–	3
3	G	–	–
4	F	–	–
5	X	9	4
6	Y	–	–
7	B	6	5
8	A	7	1
9	J	–	–

ROOT 8
AVAIL 2

11.

DISTANCE		PATH	INCLUDED
Milwaukee	0	–	Milwaukee
Chicago	9999	1	
New York	9999	1	
Wash DC	9999	1	
Miami	9999	1	
New Orl	9999	1	
Dallas	9999	1	
Okla Cty	9999	1	

DISTANCE		PATH	INCLUDED
Pheonix	1771	1	
Las Veg	9999	1	
Los Ang	9999	1	
San Fran	2257	1	
Seattle	9999	1	
Minneap	9999	1	
Milwaukee	0	–	Milwaukee
Chicago	9999	1	
New York	9999	1	
Wash DC	9999	1	
Miami	9999	1	
New Orl	9999	1	
Dallas	9999	1	
Okla Cty	9999	1	
Pheonix	1771	1	Pheonix
Las Veg	9999	1	
Los Ang	9999	1	
San Fran	2257	1	
Seattle	9999	1	
Minneap	9999	1	
Milwaukee	0	–	Milwaukee
Chicago	9999	1	
New York	9999	1	
Wash DC	9999	1	
Miami	9999	1	
New Orl	9999	1	
Dallas	9999	1	
Okla Cty	9999	1	
Pheonix	1771	1	Pheonix
Las Veg	9999	1	
Los Ang	2671	12	
San Fran	2257	1	San Fran
Seattle	3065	12	
Minneap	9999	1	
Milwaukee	0	–	Milwaukee
Chicago	9999	1	
New York	9999	1	
Wash DC	9999	1	
Miami	9999	1	
New Orl	9999	1	
Dallas	4111	11	
Okla Cty	9999	1	
Pheonix	1771	1	Pheonix
Las Veg	2943	11	
Los Ang	2671	12	Los Ang
San Fran	2257	1	San Fran
Seattle	3065	12	
Minneap	9999	1	
Milwaukee	0	–	Milwaukee
Chicago	9999	1	

```
DISTANCE              PATH      INCLUDED
New York  9999         1
Wash DC   9999         1
Miami     9999         1
New Orl   9999         1
Dallas    4111        11
Okla Cty  9999         1
Pheonix   1771         1        Pheonix
Las Veg   2943        11        Las Veg
Los Ang   2671        12        Los Ang
San Fran  2257         1        San Fran
Seattle   3065        12
Minneap   9999         1
```

and so on. . .

13. Similar to Exercise 11.

15.

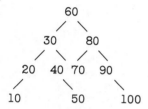

This tree is a well-balanced tree, very full with the least amount of depth possible. Since the depth is the major factor affecting search efficiency for the tree, it has the best possible big-O value.

17. A tree structure is a hierarchical ordering of data.

19. In a linear representation of a tree, each node has to be calculated from its parent. However, in a linked representation, the position is instantly known via a pointer from its parent.

21. The prefix traversal leads to the reverse-Polish notation.

31. The tree would appear as:

```
P
|
Q—A—B—X
|   |   |
|   G   |   K—L
|       H—I—J
|
T—U—V—W
        |
        C—D—E
             |
         M—N—O
```

The record description for this type of tree would be similar to a binary tree, but instead of leftchild and rightchild, there would be sibling and first child.

Chapter 8

1. This function is not recursive because no further calls are made to the functional factorial. This function will not work, because it is not syntactically correct.

3. a)

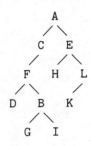

b)

	LeftChild	Data	RightChild	RightThread
1	3	A	5	F
2	7	B	11	F
3	6	C	1	T
4	12	D	6	T
5	8	E	10	F
6	4	F	2	F
7	6	G	2	T
8	1	H	5	T
9	5	K	10	T
10	9	L	12	T
11	2	I	3	T
12	1	HEADER	12	T

5. The output would be:

```
1 16
9 16
9 11
9 10
9
```

9. To thread a tree for postorder traversal, the threads of the right-most nodes would have to point back to the header, but the header would also have to be pointed to by the leftmost nodes. So, when the header was reached by traversing the threads, you would not know if you had really traversed all of the nodes.

17. The references to the left thread would have to be removed if the predecessor thread were not maintained.

Chapter 9

1. The output would be:

```
1 7
60 12 90 30 64 8 6
```

```
1 4
60 12 90 30

1 2
60 12

1 1
60

2 2
60 12

2 2
60 12

and so on...
```

3. The array would change as follows:

```
60 12 90 30 64  8 6
60 12 90 30 64  8 6
60 64 90 30 12  8 6
6  64 60 30 12  8 90
8  30 60 6  12 64 90
12 30  8 6  60 64 90
6  12  8 30 60 64 90
8  6  12 30 60 64 90
6  8  12 30 60 64 90
```

5. The output would be:

```
1 6
1 8 2 7 3 6

1 3
1 8 2

1 2
1 8

1 1
1
and so on...
```

7. The array would be changed as follows:

```
1 8 2 7 3 6
1 8 6 7 3 2
1 8 6 7 3 2
8 7 6 1 3 2
2 7 6 1 3 8
2 3 6 1 7 8
1 3 2 6 7 8
2 1 3 6 7 8
1 2 3 6 7 8
```

9. The sort derives its name from the heap structure that it uses in sorting the data. As the data is sorted, it is constantly rearranged so that it is always in a heap.

11. It is named after its inventor D.L. Shell!

13. The bubble sort is better than the quick sort when the data is already in order.

15. The advantage to using increments of prime value size lies in the fact that the increments will not divide evenly into each other so that all of the segments are distinct.

17. The worst case is $O(n \log_2 n)$, the best case would be the same.

19. The final increment must be one.

21. Where the pivot point is chosen makes no difference at all. The only change would be in how the best and worst case data sets would be organized.

23. The best case data set would have the data already in order. The worst case data set would have the data so that none of it is partially sorted at all. That is, each segment would initially be in descending instead of ascending order.

Chapter 10

1. a.) The KEYS would have the following positions:

```
Rec No.    Key
1          333
2          632
3          1090
4          459
5          379
6          238
7
8
9
10         1982
11         3411
```

b.) With the quadratic method the KEYS would have the positions:

```
Rec No.    Key
1          333
2          632
3          1090
4          238
5          459
6
7
8          379
9
10         1982
11         3411
```

c.) With the chaining method the KEYS and LINKS would be:

Rec. No.	Key	Link	Rec No.	Key	Link
1	333	13	12	3411	14
2	632	0	13	459	0
3	1090	0	14	379	15
4			15	238	0
5			16		
6			17		
7			18		
8			19		
9			20		
10	1982	12	21		
11			22		

3. a.)

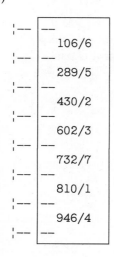

b.)

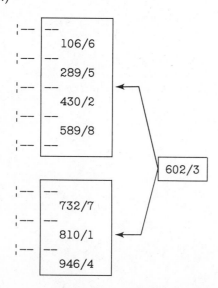

5. As suggested in the text, the double linked list is the best choice for implementing linked lists with hashing. When the order of the list is disturbed during a change of a key field, or a deletion of an item in the list, the linked list must be rebuilt. If a double linked list is not used, the list would have to be traversed to find the predecessor node in the linked list. The double linked list makes rebuilding lists much easier.

9. With hashing techniques, a duplicate record is just another case of the hashing collision with a special twist. The first record which is found is not necessarily the correct record to find. With the linked list collision solution, the problem would not be too great, but with some of the other collision solutions the efficiency might be reduced to a sequential search. With the ISAM technique, no serious problems are encountered. The duplicate keys would be in the same region, so the sequential search would still be small enough to be of no great consequence. With the binary tree, B-tree, and the trie, a collision resolution algorithm would have to be created to deal with duplicate keys.

Index

ALGORITHMS IMPLEMENTED IN PASCAL

Algorithm			Page Reference